COMPLETE PHOTOSHOP CS3 FOR DIGITAL PHOTOGRAPHERS

COMPLETE PHOTOSHOP CS3 FOR DIGITAL PHOTOGRAPHERS

COLIN SMITH

TIM COOPER

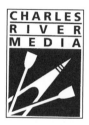

CHARLES RIVER MEDIA

Boston, Massachusetts

Cover Design: Tyler Creative
Cover Image: Colin Smith

CHARLES RIVER MEDIA
25 Thomson Place
Boston, Massachusetts 02210
617-757-7900
617-757-7951 (FAX)
crm.info@thomson.com
www.charlesriver.com

This book is printed on acid-free paper.

Colin Smith and Tim Cooper. *Complete Photoshop CS3 for Digital Photographers.*
ISBN-10: 1-58450-536-2
ISBN-13: 978-1-58450-536-5

Library of Congress Cataloging-in-Publication Data
Smith, Colin, 1966-
  Complete photoshop CS3 for digital photographers / Colin Smith and Tim
Cooper.
     p. cm.
  Includes index.
  ISBN 1-58450-536-2 (pbk. with cd : alk. paper)
  1. Computer graphics. 2. Adobe Photoshop. 3. Photography--Digital
techniques. I. Cooper, Tim. II. Title.
  T385.S62225 2008
  775--dc22
                        2007016838

Printed in the United States of America
07 7 6 5 4 3 2 First Edition

CONTENTS

CHAPTER 6   **LOCAL ENHANCEMENTS: SELECTIONS AND MASKS**   **195**

CHAPTER 7   **SHARPENING AND NOISE REDUCTION**   **227**

CHAPTER 8   **SIZING AND PRINTING YOUR IMAGES**   **249**

CHAPTER 12   COMBINING IMAGES FOR CREATIVE RESULTS   377

APPENDIX   ABOUT THE CD-ROM   435

INTRODUCTION

Recently I spoke to a photographer friend who has been shooting film for many years, after she finished explaining why film is better and that digital is not ready for the professional photographer, treading very carefully, I took a few moments to discuss the advantages of digital. A little time passed and I forgot about our discussion. Suddenly the phone rang, it was her, "I want to invite you to my newest exhibition, by the way, I'm now shooting digital and I love it!" These are the words that photographers are saying all over the world, with the "digital revolution" in full swing.

It is a pleasure to write this book at such a critical and pivotal time in the history of photography. Right now, there is a revolution under way—the explosion of digital photography. Every day people say, "I'm taking the plunge, I'm going digital." In this mass exodus from film to digital, there is one tool right in the center—Adobe® Photoshop® has become the darkroom of the present. Some advantages of this new darkroom are the results are instant, the possibilities have been greatly expanded, and it smells much nicer without all the messy chemicals involved in traditional development! In addition, this new darkroom is more accessible than before; not only professionals have access, but now, it is also within the reach of all photographers.

Adobe has acknowledged this revolution with the release of Photoshop CS, CS2, and now CS3. This new release of the world's most powerful image-editing program is jam packed with new features designed especially with you—the photographer—in mind. Everything is streamlined, from importing your images and organizing them, to new correction tools and better ways of enhancing images, to enhanced 16-bit/HDR support, to overhauled Camera Raw functionality, all new Bridge and much more. No stone is left unturned in this book; we examine all the new features in Photoshop CS3 and the best way you can use them to make your images look better.

I am very excited to be bringing you this third edition of this book. This time around, I have bought my good friend and amazing photographer Tim Cooper on-board. I met Tim while lecturing at Rocky Mountain School of Photograpy several years ago. He was then the director of education and director of the digital program. Tim has a lot to offer since he has been teaching photography for over 15 years. Tim is a real expert in things like shooting, experimenting with color, and printing photos. You will find his input a real boost to this already excellent book (Ok, I'm bi-ased). Tim's experiece especially shines through in the areas of Camera Raw and printing. We have discovered so many new things and better ways of working that we can't wait to share with you. Adobe has continued to gratify us with yet more features for photographers in CS3. As well as a ton of brand new content, we have rearranged portions of the book to provide a real-world logical workflow. We have gone through every word and clarified and improved the content as well as adding all new examples, better images and have also included all the working images on the CD so you, the reader, can follow along with effortless ease. We are very proud of this book that you hold in your hands and we know by the time you have finished it, you will never approach your images the same way again. You will keep this book close by as a constant reference as you work on your precious photos.

INTENDED AUDIENCE

This book is written with two groups of people in mind.

The first group is the mass of photographers who have made the transition from film to digital. The new darkroom is now sitting on your desktop with Photoshop running—there are so many options and dialog boxes, where do you start? This book shows you how to process your images and produce professional results. New challenges abound with digital—this book is your guide to how to overcome these obstacles and how to produce the results you want. Professional-level techniques help you develop an efficient workflow. In many cases, several different methods are presented for each challenge. This allows you to choose the method that works best for your needs and to develop your own workflow.

The second group is amateur photographers and hobbyists. Perhaps you have been using a personal computer for years and are already somewhat familiar with Adobe Photoshop, or you have never even seen Photoshop before. This book reveals the secrets to producing clearer, sharper, and more professional-looking images. Photoshop is a vast program that can perform many tasks. It can be very intimidat-ing, and only the "pros" know the techniques to perform the tasks that you need to bring out the best in your images. The mysteries are revealed in this book, bringing within your reach the results you have always dreamed of.

We also go beyond just cleaning up your images. You learn how to manipulate images digitally and do things that were impossible with film. You learn how to apply special effects and even how to get the best results while printing.

This is not a book for those people who want to learn how to take photographs. Many books on the market can help you choose cameras and shoot better pictures. A few tips are mentioned in Chapter 1, "Getting Started Using Bridge," to make your images more friendly for use in Photoshop. When you have finished clicking the shutter and uploading your images to a computer, you are ready for this book. This book is about Photoshop and what happens to your images after the shutter stops and the mouse begins the clicking.

TOPICS COVERED

Chapter 1, "Getting Started Using Bridge," explores file formats, resolution, ISO and other shooting considerations. The chapter then delves into Adobe Bridge, the asset management program that is included with Photoshop CS3. This is an application in itself and is newly designed to make everyone's life easier. This tool provides a way to organize, label, and view your images in one place. You can attach information to images that can be searched and categorized. To top it off, you will be able to automate many tasks and save many hours of work by letting Photoshop do the hard work for you. You can then present your images on slide shows, the printed page, and over the Internet.

Chapter 2, "From Bridge to Photoshop: The Adobe Raw Converter," begins with a more in-depth look at the photographic file. Here you will learn the advantages of shooting and processing 16-bit Raw images. Photographers shooting JPEGs will be happy to hear that the power and ease of the Raw Converter is now available to them. Chapter 2 enables you to gain a complete understanding of the Raw Converter as well as learning the best methods for processing your images.

Chapter 3, "Cropping and Perspective," walks you through the technical and creative aspect of cropping your images. You will also learn how to correct common photographic problems such as chromatic aberration, exaggerated perspective, lens distortion, lens vignetting, and tilted horizons.

Chapter 4, "Tonal Correction and Enhancement," takes you to the core of the digital darkroom. This is where you learn about histograms and use them as a visual cue as you correct your images. Are the images too dark, too bright, or lacking in contrast? You learn the techniques to tame overexposed images, open up the shadows, and bring back brightness to dull images. You may be surprised at just how much detail Photoshop can bring back to a bad image.

Chapter 5, "Color Correction and Enhancement," takes a look at strategies to bring out the best color in images. We look at color correction, such as removing color casts and warming and cooling the appearance of photos. We can even take faded images and inject new life into them using the methods taught in this chapter.

Chapter 6, "Local Enhancements: Selections and Masks," unveils the secrets of crafting a truly fine photograph. Since the earliest days of the chemical darkroom, the ability to work on specific areas of an image has separated the snapshooter from the artist. This chapter takes the complex subject of masking and presents it in an easy to understand fashion.

Chapter 7, "Sharpening and Noise Reduction," empowers you to present your images like a pro. Although a great improvement over their predecessors, digital cameras come with their own set of problems such as image softness and noise. This chapter will introduce you to these problems and show you how to fix them using tools such as Noise Reduction filters, Smart Sharpen, and the Unsharp Mask.

Chapter 8, "Sizing and Printing Your Images," enables you to create prints that not only match your monitor, but also your vision. This chapter shows you how to resize your photo to retain maximum image quality for both print and web. Tired of having prints that look nothing like what you saw on your monitor? Learn how to make use of printer profiles to ensure that your printer's output matches your monitor.

Chapter 9, "Image Retouching," takes you on a journey as we retouch images. This is where we perform digital cosmetic surgery. We reduce wrinkles; remove redeye, tattoos, freckles, acne, and birthmarks; shrink noses and waistlines; and generally flatter the people we take pictures of.

Chapter 10, "Frame and Color Effects," kicks off some of the more creative content in the book. We look at the best ways to convert color images to grayscale as well as sepia tone effects. We change the depth of field on an image using the advanced features of the exciting new filter, lens blur. We also frame our photos with different kinds of borders and edges.

Chapter 11, "Special Effects," is a lot of fun. We explore special effects such as turning photos into hand-drawn images and paintings. We create trendy effects and fake effects that could only be performed with expensive filters in the past.

Chapters 12, "Combining Images for Creative Results," teaches you how to combine your images in different ways. From producing panoramic images to creating collages and animations, you discover that the journey doesn't have to end with a single photograph. Photoshop has given you the power to do amazing things with your images, and this book puts that power into your hands.

BASICS

1

GETTING STARTED USING BRIDGE

In This Chapter

- Considerations Before Shooting
- Adobe Bridge: Organization and Automation
- Launching Bridge
- Navigating Bridge
- Customizing the Bridge Windows
- Managing Your Workspace
- Rotating Images
- Opening Images with Bridge
- Rating and Labeling Images
- Organizing Contents of Folders
- Using Keywords
- Metadata
- Batch Renaming
- Exporting the Images to a CD-ROM
- Automation
- Web Gallery

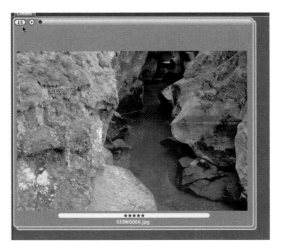

The focus of this book is on the postcapture phase of photography. Plenty of good books available on the art of photography will help you capture wonderful images. This book shows you how to organize, enhance, and repair images; how to do creative things with those images; and how to output them. You should be aware of a few considerations before shooting, however, that affect your output and ability to work with your images. This chapter will introduce you to a few tips and then go on to explain different file formats and the best time to use each.

With Photoshop CS3, we have seen a big jump ahead in Camera Raw. The following chapter has been expanded to include these new features. This chapter will reveal the ability to batch-process multiple Raw (and JPEG!) files quickly and painlessly using CS3's new Bridge application.

CONSIDERATIONS BEFORE SHOOTING

This section will introduce such issues as resolution and image formats. We will look at the kinds of settings recommended to get the best possible images from your camera. This is just a brief introduction; we will get into more detail throughout the book.

Resolution

Resolution is one of the biggest factors in enabling you to output nice, sharp images. The most obvious resolution consideration is that the more pixels in the image, the larger you can print the final image. If the resolution is insufficient, the print will suffer from pixelization. In extreme cases, pixelization looks like LEGO® structures. Photoshop does, however, have some very impressive interpolation technology that enables you to enlarge your images substantially and still have an acceptable quality print. Still, printing a sharp, clean 20 × 24 image from a 4-megapixel capture is a little ambitious.

Another resolution consideration is cropping. If an image is taken with a higher resolution than is needed, you will have plenty of overhead, or reserve pixels, to work with. This overhead is very useful when cropping away precious pixels.

The bottom line is this: If you want flexibility with your images, always shoot with the maximum resolution available on your camera. You can decrease the image resolution, but once it is shot, you can't increase it. After all, why buy a 5-megapixel camera capable of shooting 2560 × 1920 pixels and shoot only at 640 × 480 pixels? Of course, there are always exceptions, such as limited storage space and instances in which images are not needed in a high resolution (when emailing a snapshot or for use on a Web site, for instance). Keep this in mind for now, and we will discuss resolution and resizing in more detail in Chapter 3, "Cropping and Perspective."

File Formats

Cameras offer different types of image formats. The types of file formats used by cameras and the best times to use them are discussed briefly in the following sections.

JPEG

The Joint Photographic Experts Group format (JPEG or JPG) is standard on all cameras. Pronounced "jay-peg," this is the most common type of compression used on photographic images today. There are different levels of compression used; a high amount of compression produces a very small file size, but the image will suffer from artifacts, blurring, and damage to the color. This is usually the kind of result you can expect from the low-quality setting on a camera and is not recommended. The high-quality setting will use a low amount of compression, and the file size will be a little larger but still substantially smaller than an uncompressed image. The quality of the high-quality JPEG is very good. When using compression or compressed format types such as JPEG, you should shoot with the highest quality JPEG setting on the camera and fit an acceptable number of images on your card without too much quality loss. The quality of these JPEGs on newer cameras is surprisingly good, and you would be hard-pressed to notice the effects of compression.

Raw

The second is Raw format, which is offered by higher-quality and more expensive cameras. The Raw format retains the pixel information directly from the camera's charged coupled device (CCD) or complementary metal oxide semiconductor (CMOS) sensor (a digital camera's version of film) and saves it unprocessed by the camera. The image is tagged with the camera's settings, but these settings are not embedded. This enables you to process the images on a computer later and adjust the settings while importing the image (see Chapter 2). Raw files are the digital equivalent of a negative. Photoshop has some sophisticated tools for working with Raw images. Another advantage of shooting in the Raw format is that images can be captured in 16-bit. We examine Raw and 16-bit in the next chapter. If you are lucky enough to possess a camera that supports Raw, this is the best setting to use for most shooting.

TIFF

TIFF was a popular format with older, higher-end digital cameras. It is one of the most common uncompressed file formats used for photographs and graphics on the computer. If you do not have a Raw setting on your camera, TIFF is a good alternative to JPEG. I do recommend using Raw rather than TIFF, if it is available. TIFF images do not suffer from the results of image compression like a JPEG. A disadvantage of using TIFF, however, is very slow captures, with long rendering times on the camera. Because there is a much bigger file to write to the card, this causes a long delay between pictures. In addition, the memory card fills up quickly. Experiment for yourself by shooting some images in TIFF and JPEG; examine them carefully to decide which format works best for you. In reality, you will probably alternate between the two settings. The slow rendering time of TIFF could cause you to lose too many shooting opportunities of live action or fast-paced activities such as sporting events. On the other hand, if you are shooting still objects in a studio, there is no reason not to use TIFF.

Digital Zoom

I never use the digital zoom on my camera—I always use the optical zoom. The digital zoom basically crops and interpolates the image to make it appear closer. This can be performed with better quality in Photoshop later when you are not dealing with camera shake.

Flash/Lighting/Exposure

Lighting configuration and flash versus nonflash shooting is a whole subject in itself. Two good books in the actual photography phase of image capturing are *Complete Digital Photography* by Ben Long (Charles River Media) and *Shooting Digital* by Mikkel Aaland (Sybex). The important thing is using the correct exposure, making sure that there is sufficient lighting, and using the correct shutter speed for the scene you want to shoot. The use of natural light, studio lighting, and reflectors that bounce light to fill the darker areas is very common with photographers. Even a large piece of white sponge board can be used effectively to bounce extra lighting into a scene. When a flash is used, it's a good idea to diffuse it with a gel or tissue paper to avoid overexposing the highlights. Taping some tissue paper over the flash softens the light that comes from the flash and produces more pleasant overall lighting on the subject. Also, if you are using a flash, make sure that you are close enough to the subject for the flash to be effective, and check the manual's specifications for recommended shooting distance for the camera or external flash. An external flash can be used effectively to lighten a shadowed portion of the scene. This is called *fill flash*.

A well-exposed image contains image detail in both the highlights and the shadows. The exceptions are for creative purposes. Most good-quality digital cameras have white balance settings that compensate for different kinds of lighting. Most cameras use icons that represent different lighting situations such as sunlight, overcast, and tungsten and fluorescent lighting. If you are unsure of the correct setting, the Auto setting will produce good results most of the time. Choosing the correct camera settings when you shoot reduces the need for color correction later. Keep in mind that it's easier to repair a slightly underexposed image than an overexposed one.

ISO

Your camera may provide the ability to change the ISO (International Standards Organization) setting. In film, you would choose a different film that is manufactured to capture in lower or brighter lighting conditions. On your digital camera, you only have one chip, so changing the ISO doesn't produce a "real" effect. It's best to stick with the lowest ISO (100) and increase the shutter time or open the aperture wider if possible. Using a higher ISO could introduce a lot of noise to your image.

Take a Lot of Pictures

The more images you take, the better photographer you will become. With digital photography, the expense of developing pictures is eliminated, which can be very liberating. When traveling (especially abroad or to exotic locations), many people suffer from having to pay to develop 10, 20, or more rolls of film. While traveling, the expense of developing can weigh heavily on the decision of whether to shoot an image. Now, however, this is a concern of the past. Your memory cards store images, as can devices such as the Apple® iPod™. At the time of this writing, the iPod can hold as much as 80 gigabytes of data. That's a lot of images. The more images you take, the more you have to choose from. When in doubt, go ahead and click! Do try to steady the camera as much as possible, and use a tripod whenever possible.

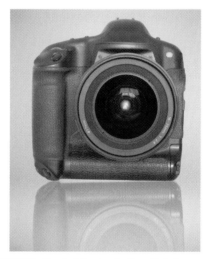

FIGURE 1.1   Tool of the trade, the digital camera.

ADOBE BRIDGE: ORGANIZATION AND AUTOMATION

Although Photoshop CS2 provided a new application called Bridge, CS3 really puts it into overdrive. Adobe Bridge is a stand-alone application, meaning that it can function without Photoshop running. It is, however, included when you purchase Photoshop.

Using the New Bridge

The Bridge is a file and asset management system that spans all the applications in the Adobe Creative Suite. You can work with image files, Illustrator files, multipage PDFs, QuickTime movies, Flash SWFs and FLVs, InDesign documents, and more. Don't worry if Photoshop is the only application you own from the suite because Bridge is still indispensable with Photoshop as a standalone application. The new Bridge still provides ways to organize your images, but viewing and sorting them has become much better. In this chapter, we will explore its plethora of features and time-saving conveniences.

Downloading Your Images into the Bridge

Let's start by downloading some images. Photoshop CS3 has introduced a new Photo Downloader to ease the process of moving your images onto the computer. The Photo Downloader can place them into a folder of your choice, create subfolders, divide your images up by date, rename them, and even make copies and save them elsewhere! Unlike some other programs out there, the Downloader is simply using the Bridge application to download images to a folder (that you choose) on your computer. It is *not* importing them into the program. Your images are still accessible from any other program that can do so. To download your images via the Photo Downloader, follow these easy steps:

1. Plug your camera into your computer or remove the Compact Flash card and plug it into your Compact Flash Card Reader (I prefer the latter for speed and saving your camera's battery).
2. From the File menu, choose Get Photos from Camera. You will be faced with the dialog box in Figure 1.2. Click the Advanced dialog box.

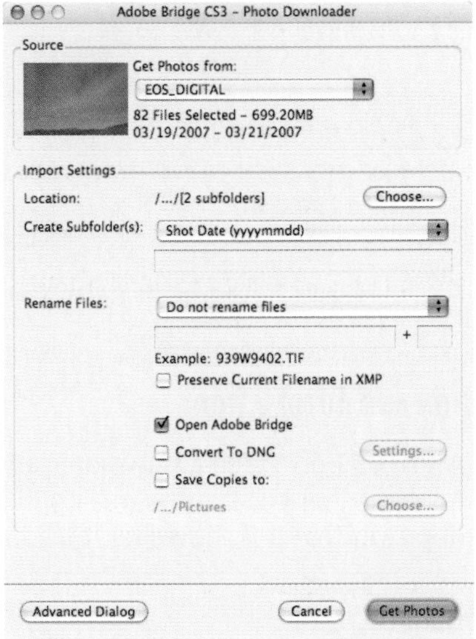

FIGURE 1.2   The Photo Downloader.

3. Figure 1.3 shows the full dialog box. Start at the top and work your way down. If there are any files on the card (or in your camera) that you do not want to download, uncheck the box next to the thumbnail. The Downloader will ignore these images.
4. The Get Photos From menu allows you to choose the location to get your photos. Choose a folder from the location settings to store your photos.

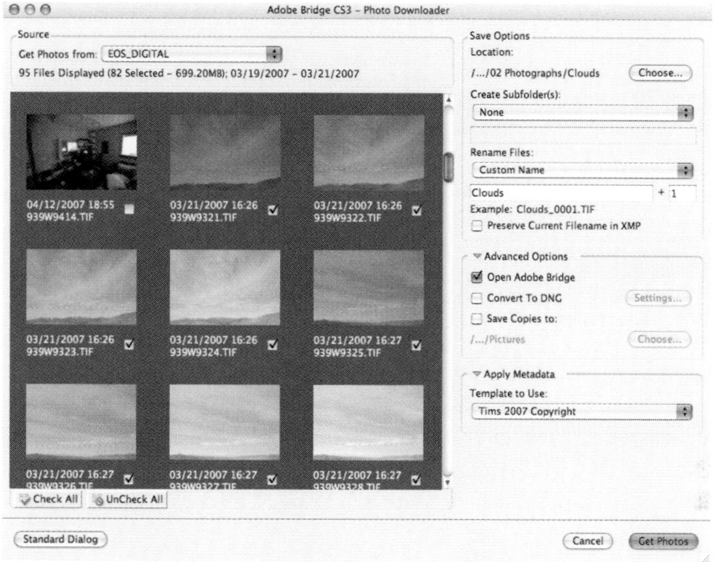

FIGURE 1.3   The Advanced dialog box.

5. In the Create Subfolder setting, decide if you want to leave all of the images in one folder or create subfolders by shot date.
6. Under Rename Files, choose from a custom name or a host of variations on date shot and custom name.
7. In the Advanced Options, you can opt to open Bridge, convert your files to DNG, and even save copies to another location.
8. The Apply Metadata section allows you to apply a template (previously made by you) to all of the images that you are downloading. This feature is worth the price of the upgrade alone! Figure 1.3 shows that I will apply my Copyright Template to the downloaded images.
9. Click Get Photos, and let the download begin.

Building a Custom Metadata Template

It is a good idea to apply your custom metadata template (including copyright) immediately on import. By doing this, your name, phone number, address, email address, and so on are preserved with the rest of the metadata. This step saves you the worry of whether or not you have embedded this information. To create a custom metadata template:

1. Click on any image to select it. Choose File > File Info. You will see the dialog box shown in Figure 1.4.
2. Click on Description, and fill out the boxes as shown in Figure 1.4.
3. Click on IPTC Contact, and fill out the appropriate boxes as shown in Figure 1.5.

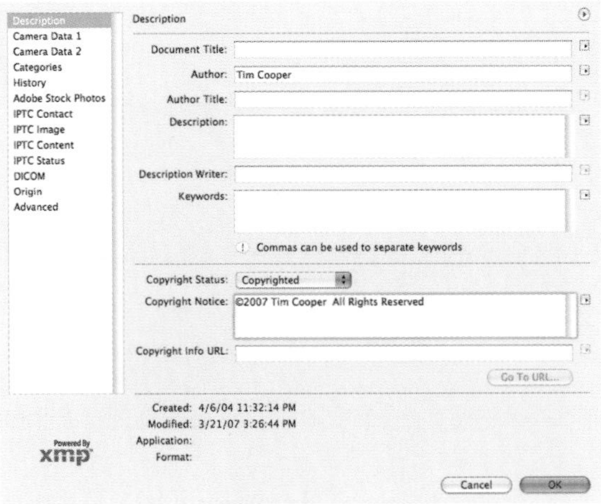

FIGURE 1.4   The Description pane.

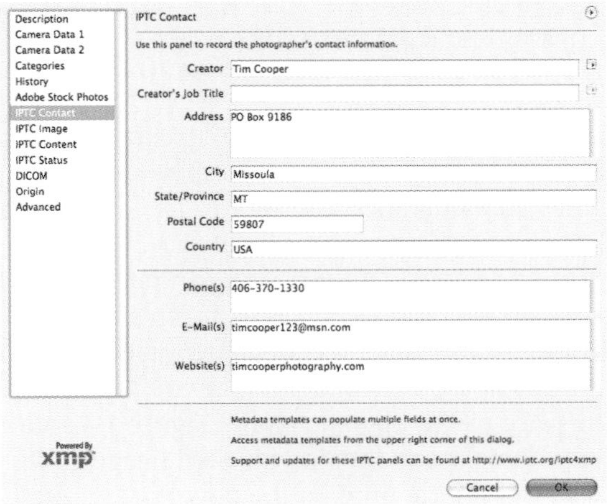

FIGURE 1.5   The IPTC Contact pane.

4. Click on IPTC Status, and type All Rights Reserved in the Rights Usage Terms box. This is a good overall template that will go a long way in informing people that your images are not to be stolen or used in any way. Of course, it can't stop them from doing this, but it will give you some legal recourse. The best way to protect your images is to register them with the U.S. Copyright Office and use technology such as Digimarc, which digitally watermarks your images (*www.digimarc.com*).

To save this as a template, click the right-facing arrow in the upper right of the dialog box, and choose Save Metadata Template. Give it a meaningful name, and click Save. That's it! Your copyright template is ready to be applied to your images upon download.

LAUNCHING BRIDGE

Now that your images are downloaded, it's time to take a peak at them! The Bridge is where most people go to begin working with their pictures. From here, the sky is the limit. Because it is a separate application (although heavily linked to Photoshop), I keep both Photoshop and Bridge shortcuts on my desktop. This way I can launch either program without launching the other. If you only have Photoshop open, and you want to launch Bridge, the easiest way is the Go To Bridge button on the Options bar. This button, as shown in Figure 1.6, resides in the upper center of the Option bar and remains as a permanent feature.

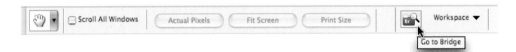

FIGURE 1.6   The Go To Bridge button.

To launch Bridge, click the Go To Bridge button. You can also launch Bridge by using any of the following:

- Choose File > Browse.
- Use the shortcut keys Ctrl+Alt+O (Cmd+Option+O for Mac).
- Choose the Bridge application from the Start menu on the PC or the Applications folder on the Mac.

Bridge is divided into four main regions, as shown in Figure 1.7.

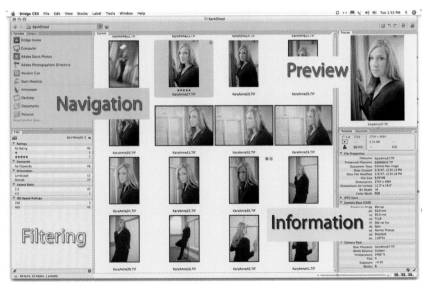

FIGURE 1.7   Adobe Bridge.

Navigation: Locate images and folders on your computer and external drives.
Preview: Preview the images in the folders.
Information: Find all your image and camera information.
Filtering: Quickly sort through your images to find the one you need. By hiding or showing images that meet certain criteria, you can make your job much easier.

NAVIGATING BRIDGE

Bridge functions very much as a visual navigation tool. You will notice that the Folders window looks and acts a lot like the File Explorer in Windows or like the Finder on the Mac. You can navigate to any folder using the Folders window; click on a folder to display its contents. When you are in a folder, its contents will be displayed in the main window as thumbnails, as shown in Figure 1.8.

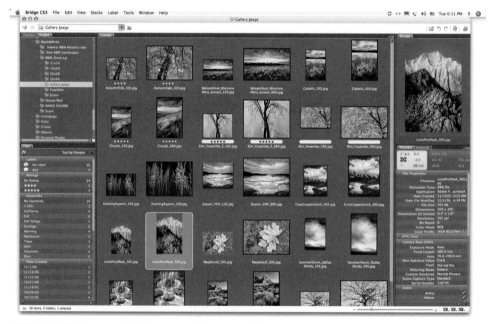

FIGURE 1.8 Clicking on a folder to reveal its contents.

Navigation can also be performed from the drop-down menu in the Bridge menu bar as shown in Figure 1.9. Notice that it displays the full path as well as the Favorites folder and the Recent folder. This is a great time-saver because it saves hunting for your images.

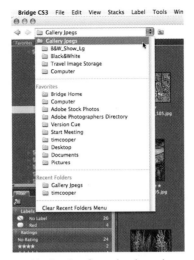

FIGURE 1.9   Navigating from the drop-down menu.

CUSTOMIZING BRIDGE WINDOWS

Customizing Bridge Windows in CS3 is easier than ever.

If you double-click the name on the window pane, such as Filter, Folders, Preview, and Metadata, the pane will collapse or expand. This allows more screen real estate for the things that are important to you. Figure 1.10 shows the Filter window collapsed to provide more space for navigating the Folder pane.

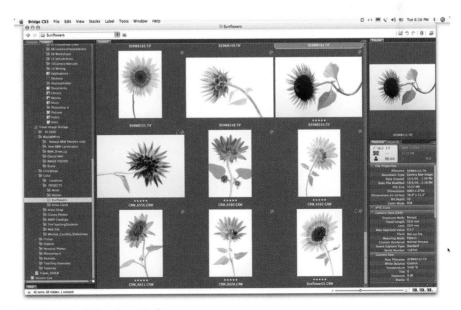

FIGURE 1.10   Collapsing windows.

You can also resize panes by clicking and dragging the middle of the dividers. This is handy for making a bigger preview to see a bit more detail. Figure 1.11 shows the Metadata and Keyword panes collapsed and the middle divider moved. The preview will expand to fill the preview window and will scale to the window size. This is a great configuration for viewing large previews of all the images in a folder.

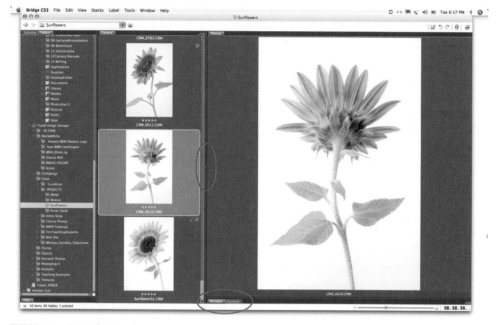

FIGURE 1.11   Drag the windows to resize them.

Another option is to hide all the windows except for the thumbnails. You will see a double-sided arrow in the bottom left of the thumbnail pane. Click this arrow to toggle the expanded view of the thumbnails, as shown in Figure 1.12. Click the button again to return to Normal view.

Different Views

There are many ways to view images inside Bridge, and these can be quickly changed by clicking on the buttons at the bottom right of the window, which are labeled 1, 2, and 3. Or if you are fond of keyboard shortcuts, Ctrl (Cmd for Mac) F1-F6 will show these views as well. (F5 does a voiceover on Mac; try it, it is . . . odd.) The views are listed here:

   Default view: This is the view that we have been looking at so far. Bridge has a dynamic slider that allows you to resize the thumbnails on the fly. Slide the lever, and watch your thumbnail size change. Click the little button to

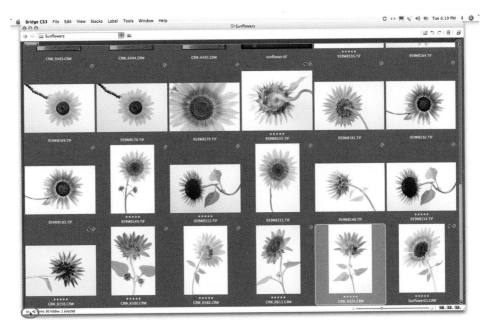

FIGURE 1.12   Expanded thumbnail view.

the left to minimum size or the button on the right to maximum size. Figure 1.13 shows the slider feature in action.

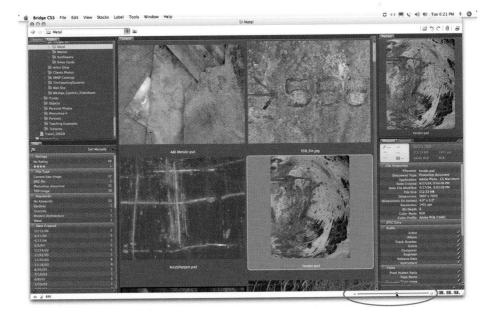

FIGURE 1.13   Changing the thumbnail size.

Light Table view: This is the same view given when you click the double-sided arrow in the bottom left of the thumbnail pane (see Figure 1.14).

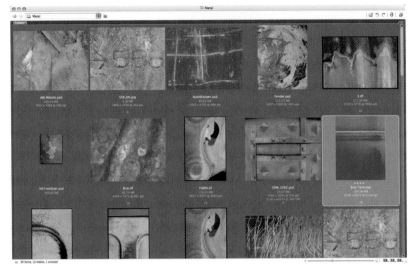

FIGURE 1.14   Light Table view.

File Navigator view: Press Ctrl+F3 (Cmd+F3 for Mac). This view focuses on your Folder and Favorites panes. This is a great view if you are working on locating photographs. You can collapse the Favorites tab from this view so that the whole left side of the Bridge is one long folder tree as shown in Figure 1.15. (The Tab key toggles this option as well.)

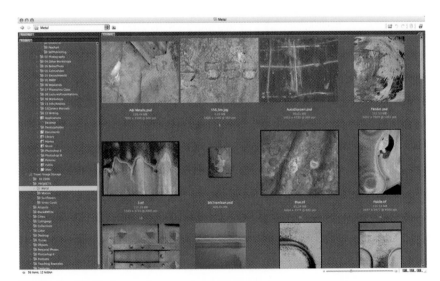

FIGURE 1.15   File Navigator view.

Metadata Focus view: Press Ctrl+F4 (Cmd+F4 for Mac). This is the view to use when looking for information about your files. Clicking once on an image in the Content pane will highlight it. When an image is highlighted, its properties can be viewed in the Metadata pane to the left. Here again I collapse my Favorites pane to make room for more metadata. In this view, the image *GreenMetal* is selected as shown in Figure 1.16. You can see the file information revealed next to the image, including any keywords that you may have applied. To the left in the Metadata pane, you'll see two new areas introduced in CS3: the Camera view and the File view. These boxes sit at the top and give relevant info about the file at a glance. For a more exhaustive collection of info, scroll down.

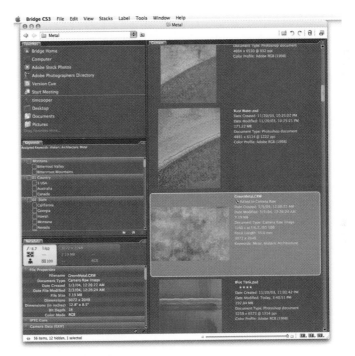

FIGURE 1.16   Metadata Focus.

Horizontal and Vertical Filmstrip view: Click the 2 button, or press Ctrl+F5 (Cmd+F5 for Mac) for the Horizontal Filmstrip, or press Ctrl+F6 (Cmd+F6 for Mac) for the Vertical Filmstrip. These views show the thumbnails as a filmstrip, with larger previews. This is a digital lightbox view, which is very useful for photographers looking through collections, searching for that "perfect" image. The Preview is nice and big, and moving through your images is as easy as moving the slider bar at the bottom. Figure 1.17 shows the Horizontal Filmstrip view.

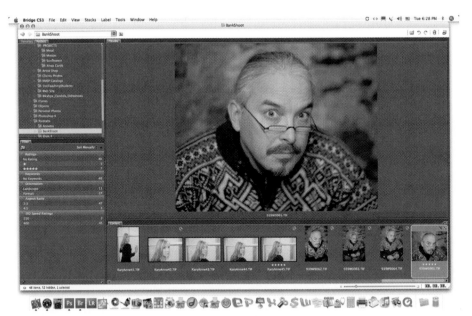

FIGURE 1.17   Horizontal Filmstrip view.

To view two images side by side: Ctrl+click (Cmd+click for Mac) or Shift+click, or drag a region with the mouse on the second thumbnail that you want to view. It will appear in the Preview pane next to your initial image as shown in Figure 1.18.

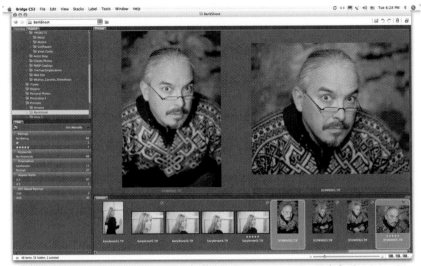

FIGURE 1.18   Viewing more than one image in the Preview pane.

As nice as the view is here, there is only one way to determine if an image is critically sharp: viewing it at actual pixels (100%). In the past, you had to open the image to determine if it was perfectly sharp. CS3 now includes a Loupe tool that lets you make that determination immediately. Simply click on any portion of the image in the Preview pane, and you will see the Loupe tool appear (see Figure 1.19). Move it around the image to view that portion at actual pixels. If you just see squares of color, give it a second to load. You can watch the loading process at the bottom.

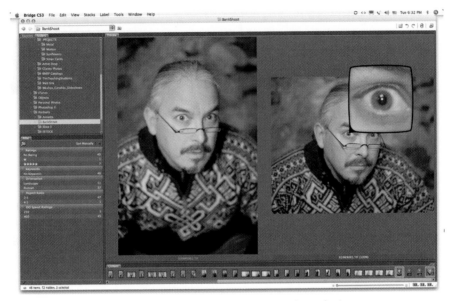

FIGURE 1.19   Click on the image in the Preview pane to activate the Loupe.

Some hints to working with the Loupe tool include the following:

- Move the Loupe by clicking inside the Loupe and dragging it to the desired location. Clicking inside the Loupe makes it disappear. Click on the image again to get it back.
- Click on the second image, and you will now have two Loupes active (see Figure 1.20).

If you want to move multiple Loupes simultaneously, press the Ctrl (Cmd for Mac) key while you are moving one Loupe.
The pointed end of the square shows you what area you are viewing.
Dragging the Loupe too close to an edge may make it change its orientation so that you can get a full view, very cool.
You can change your view inside of the Loupe from 100% to 800% by rolling your mouse scroll wheel or using the keyboard plus (+) or minus (–) sign. Use the 100% for the most accurate view.

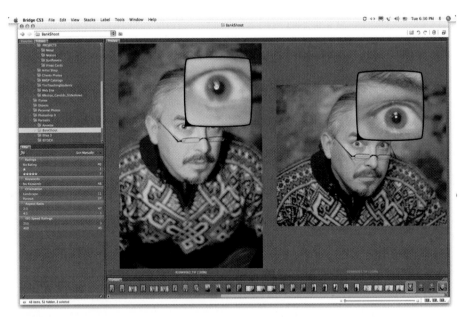

FIGURE 1.20   Two active Loupes.

Slideshow Mode view: This is a great way to view your images very large and
without the distraction of other images. Press Ctrl+L (Cmd+L for Mac) to
launch the slideshow. The image that is highlighted in the folder will be
shown by itself on the screen. To view the next image, press the right arrow
key. In this way, you can view an entire folder of images one at a time with
a large preview. To check for sharpness, click on the image, and it will blow
up to actual pixels (100% magnification). Click and hold to drag the image
around the screen. Press the Escape key to return to the normal Bridge
view. To check out all of the features of the slideshow, press H, and a list of
options will appear.

Those are the views that will interest photographers. The three boxes at the
bottom-right side of Bridge give you access to all of them. These buttons are also
programmable. If you find that you only use the Default, Light Table, and Horizontal Filmstrip views, you can set these boxes as shortcuts to these views. Simply click
on one of the boxes, and choose your desired view from the flyout menu as shown
in Figure 1.21.

You can also save your favorite setup by following these steps:

1. Arrange the size and location of the tabs and view to suit your taste. Do this
   manually or by using the boxes in the lower right.
2. Choose Window > Workspace > Save Workspace.
3. Give your new workspace a name, and click Save. You can also apply keyboard shortcuts for quicker access.

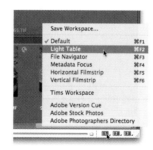

FIGURE 1.21   Saving a preset.

There are other preset views in those menus such as Adobe Version Cue, Adobe Stock Photos, and Adobe Photographers Directory, although these are designed for the professionals in fields such as graphics or advertising.

The New Stacks Feature

Of great use to the photographer, however, is a great new feature offered in CS3 called Stacks. This tool gives you the ability to put your images in stacks, just as if you were working on a light table! This enables you to reduce clutter by grouping similar images into stacks. For example, you may have three different exposures of the same subject. If you have no reason to view them all at the same time, just put the most appropriate one on top and choose to have the others stacked below. Likewise, you may find that you have many variations of the same image or perhaps a group of photos that you plan to merge to HDR or a set of shots for panoramas. The possibilities are endless. Figure 1.22 shows a folder that contains several sequences of images that will later be stitched into panoramas as well as variations on exposure. To clean up this folder, you will create several stacks.

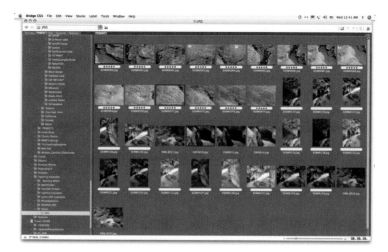

FIGURE 1.22   Folder that can be cleaned up with stacks.

1. To create a new stack, select the images, and press Ctrl+G (Cmd+G for Mac). To choose other images to add to the stack, Ctrl+click (Cmd+click for Mac) on the images, and drag them into the stack.
2. Once they are in a stack, a number will appear in the upper left indicating how many images are in the stack as shown in Figure 1.23. Click on the number to expand the stack. Click on it again to collapse the stack.
3. Change the image on the top of the stack by opening the stack and moving your favorite to the front position. Close the stack and it will be on top.

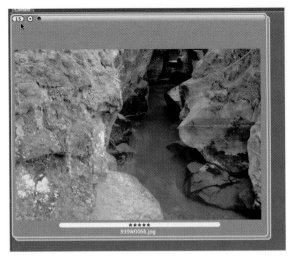

FIGURE 1.23   A stack of images.

4. Figure 1.24 shows the same folder after the images have been organized into stacks. This looks much better.

The following are a few hints for working with the Stacks feature:

- If you already have a stack made, you can add to the stack by dragging an image and dropping it onto the stack.
- Applying a Label or Rating to a stack will apply it to all the images within that stack. This works when it is either expanded or collapsed.
- Double-clicking on a stack when it is collapsed only opens the top image. Double-clicking when it is expanded opens all of the images.
- When you are in collapsed mode, if you have 10 or more images in a stack, you get a small gray bar across the top with a dark circle in the left corner. Click and drag this circle to the right, and the stack plays a little slideshow of the images within the stack (see Figure 1.25).
- You can remove an image from a stack by expanding the stack and right-clicking on that image. Choose Ungroup from Stack from the Stack flyout menu, or simply drag it out of the stack.

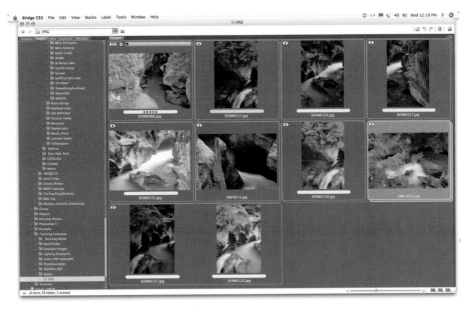

FIGURE 1.24   A folder with several stacks.

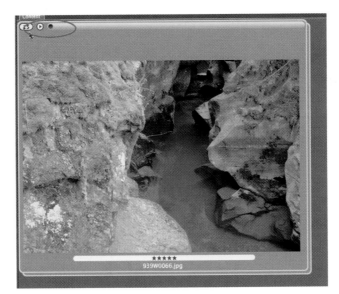

FIGURE 1.25   The Slide Show feature.

- To move a different image to the top of the stack, expand the stack. Click and drag the desired image to the front of the row. Collapse the stack, and the new image will be on top.

MANAGING YOUR WORKSPACE

We have just looked at many ways to customize the way that Bridge looks and works. Depending on what you are doing, you may prefer a different setup. The solution is to come up with several different setups, one for cataloging images, another for light table work, and perhaps another for navigation. Don't feel you have to conform to the preset views offered by Adobe. You can create different views that are more comfortable for your personal workflow.

You can save your customized views and recall them in an instant using the Workspace menu.

To save a workspace:

1. Drag everything around until you are happy with the setup.
2. Choose Window > Workspace > Save Workspace.
3. Choose a name for the new setup, and click OK. In this box, you can also save a keyboard shortcut to call back this view.

To recall a workspace, choose Window > Workspace, and choose your workspace from the drop-down menu. Here you will also see the size factory presets we have already discussed. Your new custom settings are at the bottom of the menu. Figure 1.26 shows the Workspace menu.

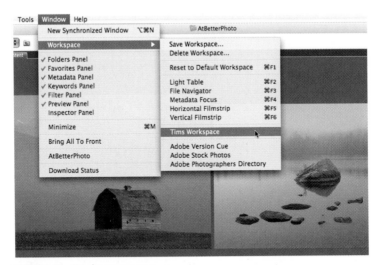

FIGURE 1.26   Workspace menu.

ROTATING IMAGES

When you shoot with the camera held sideways, you create images with a portrait orientation rather than the usual landscape orientation. There is no way for Bridge to know that you rotated the camera, so all the images are displayed in landscape by default. (Many cameras offer autorotation features; if you have used this feature, the images will be shown in their correct orientation, and no rotation will be needed in Bridge.) You could get a sore neck tilting your head all the time to view these images. The obvious solution is to rotate the images in Bridge.

To rotate the images:

1. Click on the thumbnail to select multiple thumbnails, Ctrl+click on each additonal image you want selected (Cmd+click for Mac).
2. Click on the rotation buttons on the menu bar in Bridge, as shown in Figure 1.27.

The image(s) will be rotated 90 degrees.

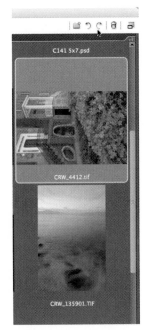

FIGURE 1.27   Rotating images.

OPENING IMAGES WITH BRIDGE

There are several ways to open images in Photoshop from Bridge. To open a file, do one of the following:

- Double-click on the thumbnail or preview.
- Choose File > Open.
- Right-click, and choose Open.

By default, Bridge stays open after you have opened an image. To open an image and minimize Bridge at the same time, hold down the Alt key (Option key for Mac) and double-click a thumbnail.

You are not limited to opening a single image at a time; a series of images can be opened at once. You can browse the thumbnails and select them by holding down the Ctrl key (Cmd key for Mac) and clicking a thumbnail. When you click the thumbnail, it is highlighted and added to the selected thumbnails.

When you have finished selecting all the desired thumbnails, double-click any one of the highlighted thumbnails to open all the selected images as a series of images.

RATING AND LABELING IMAGES

It doesn't take too long to build up a large collection of images with a digital camera. In film days, there was always a cost every time the shutter was pressed. With digital, the price is in your time. So how do you sort and organize all these images? Bridge has two tools to help you: Rating and Labeling.

Rating

Rating is a quick way to label images. You can choose from 1 to 5 stars for each image. Rank them according to quality of shot or relevance to your need. Select the thumbnail, and choose the star rating from the Label menu. Press the Ctrl key and the numbers 1, 2, 3, 4, 5 (Cmd key for Mac), or just click inside the thumbnail. Slide your cursor over the number of stars that you want to assign to the image as shown in Figure 1.28.

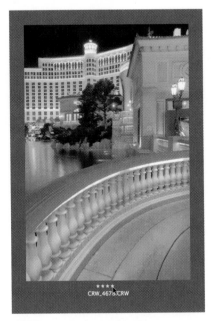

FIGURE 1.28   Rating an image.

Labeling

Another way of tagging images is by using the Labels. Labels are a little different from ratings because you select a phrase that will show as a color rather than a numerical rating. The different names of the Labels are shown in Figure 1.29. To apply a colored label, right-click on the thumbnail, choose a label from the drop-down menu, and then select an item from that list, as shown in Figure 1.30. Ratings and labels can be used in conjunction with each other as you can see in the folder shown in Figure 1.30.

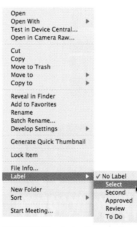

FIGURE 1.29 Labeling an image.

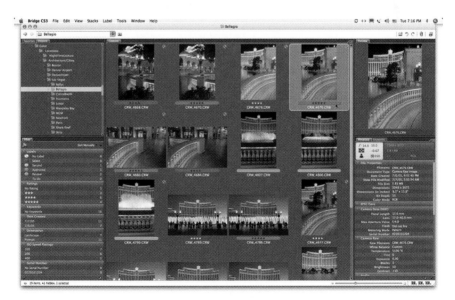

FIGURE 1.30 Images that have been labeled and rated.

The Label name can be changed to whatever is most beneficial to your workflow. While in the Bridge, select the Preferences menu and choose Labels on the left side. Here you can change the words by typing in the box.

After you go through a folder and rate and label all of your images, you can change your view so that the Content pane will only show you certain types of images. You are not deleting them; rather you are just asking the Bridge to make visible only the 5-star images in this folder. Or you may want to view just the images labeled red. To view only those images, look to the all-new Filter pane. This is a great addition to the Bridge. As you add labels, ratings, and keywords to your images, those items will appear in the Filter pane. Clicking on the left side of either the 5 Stars or the Red Label will force the Bridge to show only those images that match that criterion. For example, in Figure 1.31, the folder can be filtered by any of the colored labels or the star ratings of 3, 4, or 5. If any images had been rated as 2 stars, then that rating would appear. In Figure 1.31, the Red Label and the 5 Star Rating have been checked. As you can see, the Bridge is only showing those images that are rated 5 Star and have a Red Label.

There are other useful ways of filtering your images as well. All are very conveniently located right in the Filter pane. Keywords, ISO, Date Created, Orientation, and Serial Number are some of the other options.

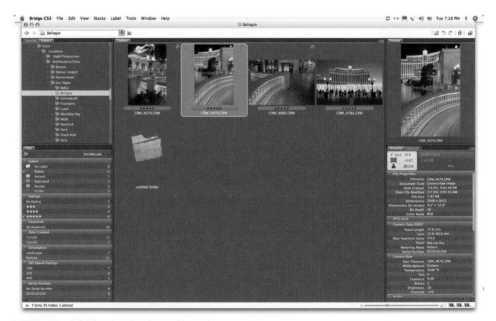

FIGURE 1.31   A folder that has been filtered.

 Multiple images can be flagged all at once by first selecting them and then applying the rating or label.

ORGANIZING CONTENTS OF FOLDERS

Bridge provides a drag-and-drop environment for organizing your images. To move an image to a new folder, simply click and hold the mouse button on a thumbnail. It can then be moved to a folder by dragging to either a folder in the Folders window or to a folder in the Thumbnail window (see Figure 1.32). Release the mouse button to complete the move. To copy an item instead of moving it, hold down the Alt/ Option key while dragging. You will see a small plus sign to indicate that you are copying an image to a new location.

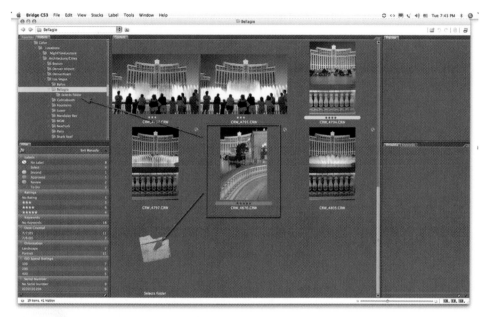

FIGURE 1.32   Moving images to new folders.

Using Favorites

Another time-saving feature in CS3 that has been borrowed from the Web browser world is the Favorites pane. This saves you from repeatedly searching for folders on your computer. Once you mark a folder as a favorite, you can quickly select it from the menu.

To mark a folder as a favorite, first navigate to the folder. Select the folder, right-click on its name in the Folders window, and choose Add to Favorites (see Figure 1.33). The folder (Australia) will now be added to the Favorites list, as shown in Figure 1.34. Alternatively, simply drag and drop the folder from the Content pane or the Folder pane into the Favorites pane.

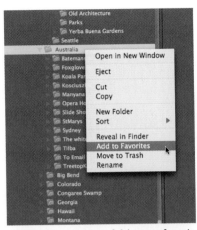

FIGURE 1.33   Setting a folder as a favorite.

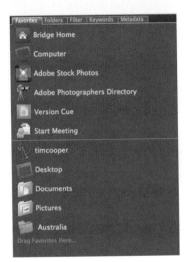

FIGURE 1.34   The folder added to the Favorites list.

To open a folder from the Favorites list, simply click on the folder. The thumbnails will now appear in the Bridge. If you don't want your Favorites folder all cluttered with unused "Favorites," a quick trip to the Bridge Preferences will take care of that. Choose Preferences > General. The Favorite Items will be in the lower right. Uncheck anything that you do not use on a regular basis.

USING KEYWORDS

Keywords can easily be added to images without having to type them each time. These keywords are useful for searching for images later. You can find images from multiple locations and display them together in a single window.

Organizing Keywords

To organize the keywords, follow these steps:

1. Click on the Keywords pane, and you will notice that some keyword sets are already present, such as Events, People, and Places.
2. Keywords are contained in keyword sets. To start creating your own keyword sets, click on the down arrow in the top right of the Keyword pane, and choose New Keyword Set. You can also click the New Keyword icon in the lower right of the pane as shown in Figure 1.35. It will appear at the top of your stack.

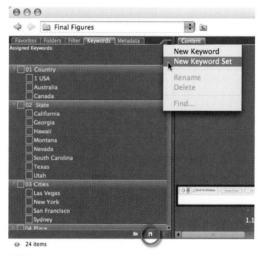

FIGURE 1.35   Keywords pane.

3. To start creating keywords inside the set, either right-click on the set and choose New Keyword, or click on the New Keyword button, and add your new keyword. We have added a new Portrait set and a few keywords in Figure 1.36.

Assigning Keywords

To assign keywords to images, follow these steps:

1. Select the image, and check the box next to the keywords you want to attach to the image.
2. To save time, select multiple images by Ctrl+clicking (Cmd+clicking for Mac) on the thumbnails.

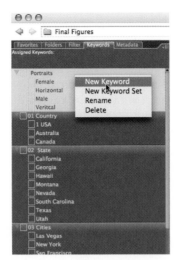

FIGURE 1.36   The Keyword pane with custom keywords added.

Searching the Keywords

You can easily locate these images by performing a search:

1. Choose Edit > Find.
2. In the Look in field, choose the location to search.
3. You can use many criteria to define your search; in Figure 1.37, we have used the keyword Historic Architecture.
4. At the bottom left of the box, you will see the Save As Collection button. This will take the images that are "found" and save them as a collection. This will not duplicate your images. It will just create a shortcut to this particular grouping.
5. Click on Find to begin the search. Figure 1.38 shows the results of the search in the Content Pane.

Working with Collections

A *collection* is a saved search. If you clicked the Save as Collection button in the Find box in the previous section, the location of those images will be saved. Next time you want to view this grouping of images, you easily recall them without having to go through the Find box again.

1. When you click on the Save As Collection button, you will see the Save Collection dialog box, as shown in Figure 1.39.
2. Enter a name for your collection and a folder that you want to store it in. (I created a folder called Collections in my main photographs folder to contain all of these collections.)

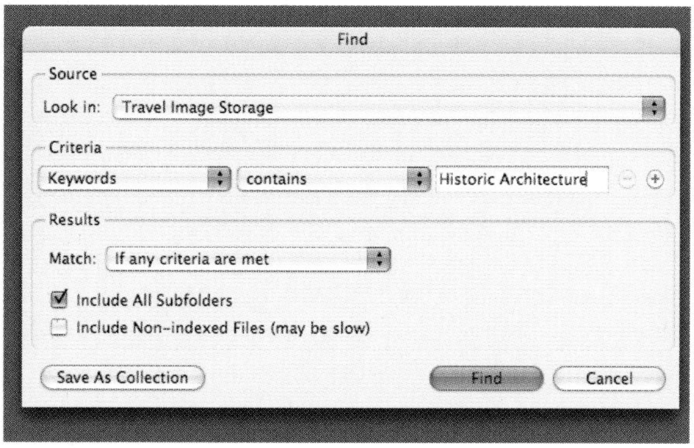

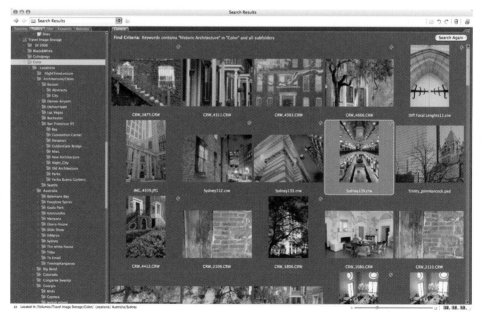

FIGURE 1.37 The Find box.

FIGURE 1.38 The search result.

3. Reopening a collection is basically running the search again. In the Folders pane, navigate to the folder that you saved your collection in. Highlight that folder, and you will see the Collection icon with the name you gave it. Double-clicking this icon invokes the search again, and the images will appear in your Content pane. These collections are dynamic—if an image that matches the

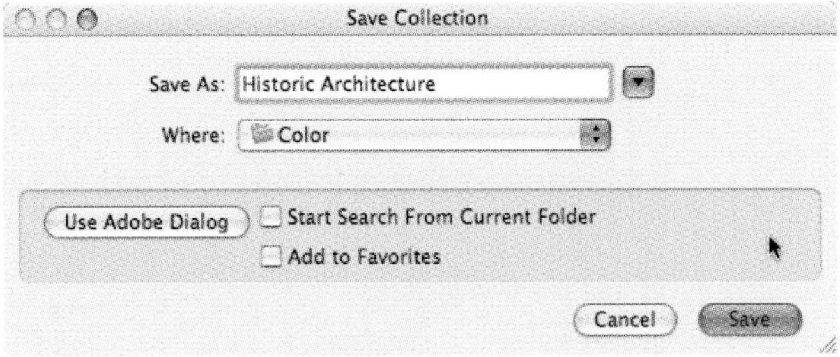

FIGURE 1.39   Choose a name for your collection.

search criteria is added, it will automatically be added to the collection. If you change an image, and it no longer fits the profile, it will automatically be removed from the collection.

METADATA

Photoshop has really boosted the amount of information that you can store with your image. This information is called *metadata*. Photoshop uses the standard of XML developed by Adobe called eXtensible Metadata Platform (XMP). This information is very important when transmitting images electronically and is becoming more important as standards are being set for professionals. This is also very useful for organizing and searching your images. Metadata includes captions, copyright information, keywords, descriptions, credits, and origin. This information will travel with the images saved in PSD, PSB, TIFF, JPEG, EPS, and PDF formats.

Exif

If you shot your image with a digital camera, all the camera information will be stored with the image. This is called the Camera Data or Exif. When you view this information, it will tell you all the camera settings that were used for the picture. Can you imagine how valuable this is? For example, if you have a photo that didn't come out quite right, you can look at the Exif data and see where you went wrong. This will help you learn and avoid the same problems in the future. On the reverse side of the coin, if you have a shot that is just perfect, you can take note of the settings and reproduce them in the future. Can you see how this information is going to help boost the level of photography? A scenario could involve students giving images to their teacher for review. The teacher then critiques the images based on the results and Exif data and offers suggestions for improvement.

Viewing the Data

All the metadata is displayed in the Metadata window when you select a thumbnail. Click on the arrows next to each category to expand or collapse the sublevels and view the information. Figure 1.40 shows this information for a selected thumbnail.

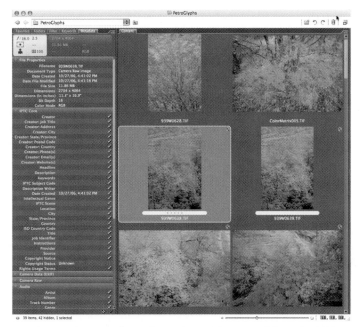

FIGURE 1.40   The metadata information can be viewed from the Bridge.

There are several categories of data:

File Properties: The file information for the image is displayed here.

IPTC Core: This is the standard from the press folks when they started moving their notes along digitally and is used by newspapers and other publishers. They added in standardized fields for general info and also information that is specific to reporters and photographers. Most journalistic groups and on-line stock agencies require IPTC (International Press & Telecommunications Consortium) information for electronic image files.

Camera Data (Exif): All the settings used on the camera at the time of firing.

Adding Information to the Metadata

All this metadata would not be very useful if you couldn't edit and add to the information yourself. All the camera information is saved automatically with the image file, but the rest of the information has to be added manually.

Adding the Information Directly

One way to add various information to an image is to add it directly into the Info field in the Metadata window in Bridge:

1. Click on the Pencil icon to the right of any editable field. (If there is no icon, that field is not editable.)
2. You will see a box appear with a cursor in it. Type in your information. Press the Tab key to advance to the next field.
3. Click the check mark on the bottom right of the window (circled in Figure 1.41) to apply the information to the image. The information will now be saved with the image or as a sidecar file with Raw images. The sidecar is needed because you cannot write to a Raw file. Instead, an extra file is created that travels with the Raw file. Separate the Raw file from the sidecar and this extra information will be lost.

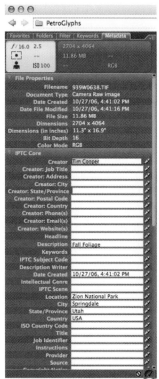

FIGURE 1.41   Committing to the changes in the Metadata pane.

Adding Data Using the File Info Dialog Box

You can also add or edit information using the File Info dialog box as demonstrated earlier in this chapter. This can be accessed by choosing File > File Info from either Bridge or Photoshop itself. You can also access this dialog box by right-clicking on the thumbnail and choosing File Info.

The default category is the Description window. Enter the desired information into these fields as shown in Figure 1.42.

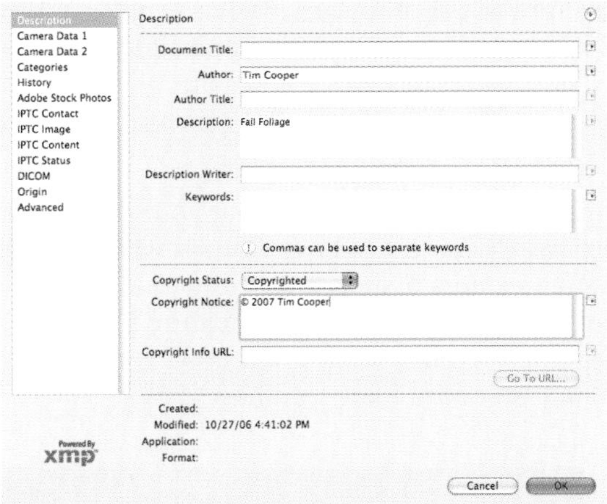

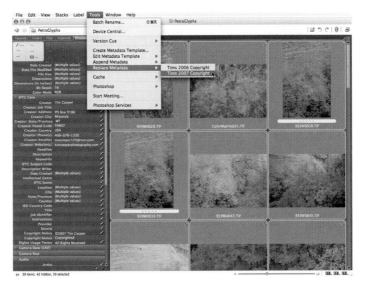

FIGURE 1.42   Using the File Info window.

If you didn't apply this template to the images while downloading, you can apply it now. To apply the template:

1. Highlight a folder in the Folder pane, and choose Edit > Select All. Of course, you could just click on one image at a time, but why bother?
2. Choose Tools > Replace Metadata, and then choose your template as shown in Figure 1.43. The fields will now be filled out with the saved information.

FIGURE 1.43   Choosing your template.

When you apply a template, it will not overwrite any Exif (camera) information. The description, categories, and origin will be replaced by the template's information.

I *highly* recommend that you get into the habit of doing this every time you download a new batch of images if you haven't applied this template during download. This will save you a lot of computer time down the road!

BATCH RENAMING

You have probably noticed by now that your digital camera assigns cryptic names to the images, which doesn't help you much when trying to locate images. For example, the Canon camera assigns an incremental number prefixed by the letters CRW for the Raw images. Nikon uses NEF. Figure 1.44 shows a shining example of these almost meaningless names. The good news is that the Batch Rename feature allows you to rename an entire folder of images.

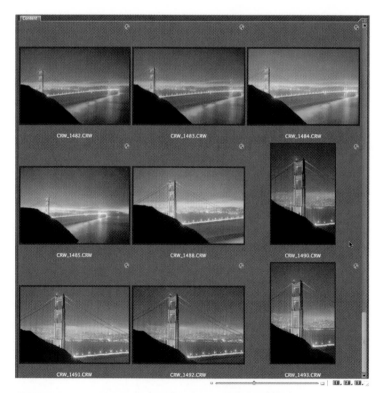

FIGURE 1.44 Digital camera default names applied to files.

1. Choose a folder you want to rename or just highlight a few images if you don't want to rename the whole folder. Perhaps you want to rename smaller groups at a time with meaningful names. In this example, we have chosen a

folder of images of the Golden Gate Bridge. From the menu bar, choose Edit > Select All.

2. Choose Tools > Batch Rename.
3. A dialog box opens like the one in Figure 1.45. You can rename images in the same folder (overwriting the existing image names) or move (or copy) the images to a new folder (useful for organizing images). In this case, we have chosen to use the same folder.

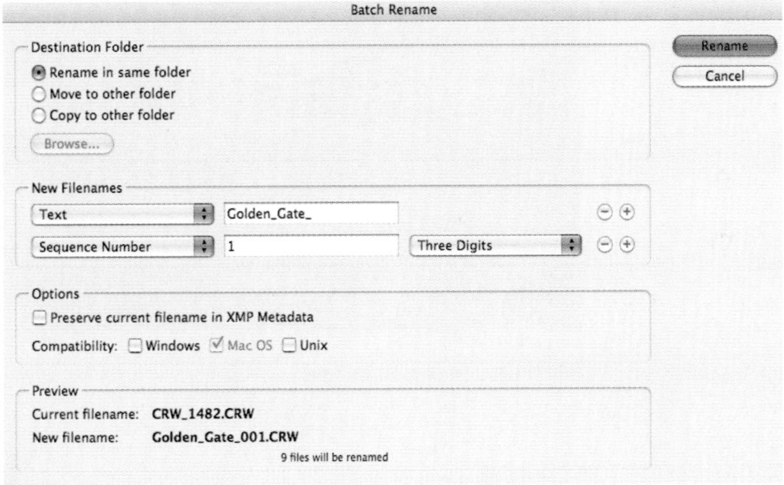

FIGURE 1.45   Batch Rename dialog box.

4. In the Text field, type in the desired filename. (For this example, `Golden_Gate` was used.)
5. The default for the next line is Date Time. Leave this if you want to add in the date. In this example, this field has been changed to Sequence Number. Three Digits is also selected in the next field. If you have a lot of images, consider raising this number.
6. To remove a listing, click the minus sign; to add one, click the plus sign.
7. Check the preview out at the bottom. It shows the current filenames and what they are going to be. In this case, `Golden_gate_001.CRW`, `Golden_gate_002.CRW`, and so on.
8. Enter the starting serial number, in the Sequence Number box and click OK to rename all the images in the folder.

Figure 1.46 shows all the images in the folder sporting their new names—much more interesting than the previous serial numbers.

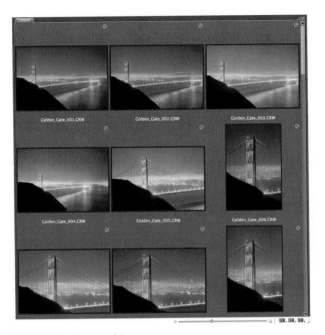

FIGURE 1.46   Renamed images.

EXPORTING THE IMAGES TO A CD-ROM

Why include a section on burning images to a CD-ROM, you may ask? Don't you just copy the images to a CD-ROM and burn it? Yes, you do, but the reason this section is here is to inform you of the image cache. When you make any alterations in Bridge, all the information is saved to a small file called a *cache file*. If you copy the images without the cache to another location, all the Bridge changes will be lost, such as rotation and labels. It's best to keep the cache right in the file with the images. This way, wherever your images go, their cache files can follow. You can set the Bridge to put the cache files into your folder by taking a trip to Bridge Preferences. Under the Advanced tab, check the box next to Automatically Export Caches to Folders When Possible. This will do the trick!

AUTOMATION

Photoshop has an impressive array of automated tasks called *actions* and *scripts*. These features will save you hours of time and will perform difficult and repetitive tasks for you automatically. You simply choose a few parameters and let Photoshop do the rest. In this section, we will discuss a few of these tasks that pertain to photographers.

Traditionally, all the automated tasks were accessed from the File > Automate menu. They are still available from this menu, but they are also available directly from Bridge. These tasks can be accessed in the Tools > Photoshop menu. This makes a lot of sense because you can now perform all these tasks from within Bridge without having to open the images in Photoshop.

 Third parties (or yourself) can create scripts for Photoshop to automate tasks. For information on how to create your own scripts, check out the Scripting Guide PDF in the Scripting Guide folder within the main Photoshop CS3 folder.

Contact Sheet II

A contact sheet is a page with all the thumbnails printed out with their filenames. This is very useful as an overview of your images and invaluable as a catalog tool. For example, you could create contact sheets of all your images and keep them in a binder. Then when you (or a client) need a specific type of image, you could quickly flip through the catalog of thumbnails, rather than browsing through each image. Another use for the contact sheet is to produce a liner for your CD-ROM with all the thumbnails clearly displayed. Let's create a contact sheet, and you will see how easy and useful this feature is.

1. Browse to the folder that contains the images you want to add to the contact sheet.
2. You can create a contact sheet from either an entire folder or just selected images.
3. If you want to use selected images, click on the first thumbnail and then hold down the Ctrl key (Cmd key for Mac). Click on each thumbnail you want added to the selection, and they will be highlighted as you select them.
4. If you want to use the entire folder, choose Edit > Select All.
5. Choose Tools > Photoshop > Contact Sheet II. You will now see the dialog box shown in Figure 1.47.

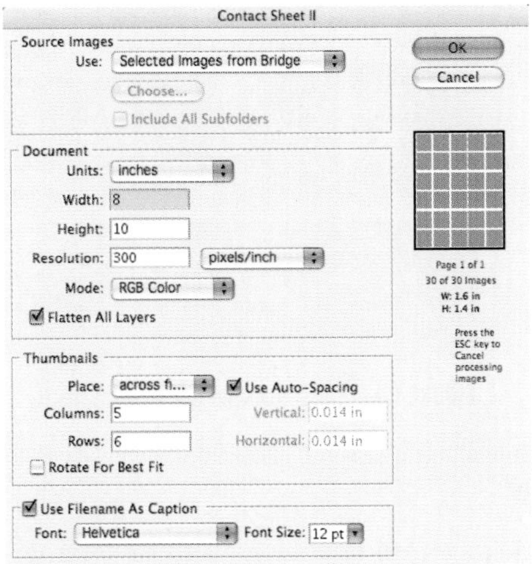

FIGURE 1.47   Setting up the contact sheet.

6. Choose Selected Images from Bridge, as shown in Figure 1.47.
7. Under Document, choose the desired size: 8 × 10 is the default and is the standard size for a photographic contact sheet. If you use this size, you will get a nice border when you print this out on an 8 1/2 × 11 sheet of paper. You can change this to anything you want, including 4.75 × 4.75 for a CD-ROM liner or 4.75 × 9.5 if you want a fold on the label.
8. Select the number of thumbnails you want to appear on each page, and the sizes will be adjusted automatically to fit your criteria.
9. Click OK.

Photoshop will now begin opening the images, resizing them, and arranging them into a new document (contact sheet). If there are too many thumbnails to fit on one page, Photoshop will create multiple pages until all the thumbnails are arranged into contact sheets. Figure 1.48 shows a completed contact sheet.

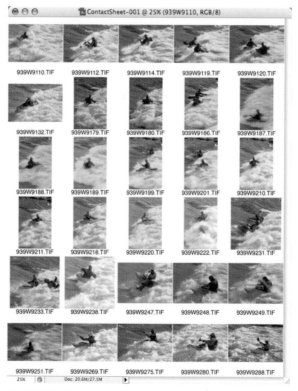

FIGURE 1.48   The finished contact sheet.

Picture Package

The Picture Package tool enables you to save paper and time by squeezing as many copies of an image as possible on a sheet of paper while minimizing wasted space.

This way, you can print out, for example, two 4 × 5 images suitable for framing, with four wallet size prints taking up the rest of the page. Picture Package now supports multiple images in one document.

1. Launch Picture Package in Photoshop by clicking File > Automate > Picture Package or Tools > Photoshop > Picture Package from Bridge.
2. Select the source image either by using a currently selected or open image, or by browsing to the desired image.
3. Choose your page size and layout. There are many different layouts to choose from.
4. If you can't find exactly what you are looking for in the presets, choose the closest, and click Customize. Make any alterations, and then click OK to return to the main dialog box.
5. If you want to add a label to the sheet, choose a label option from the Label section of the dialog box. The Default setting for the resolution is 72 ppi, which is not so good. If you want a higher-quality print for the contact sheet, change the default resolution to 240 or 300. Check the layout preview to make sure everything looks okay, as shown in Figure 1.49.
6. Click OK.

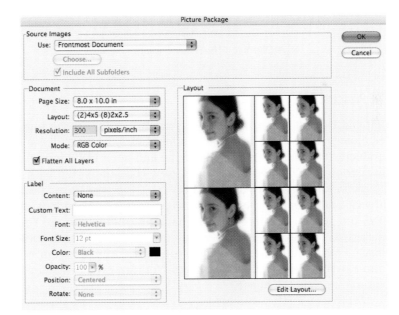

FIGURE 1.49   Picture Package options.

After Photoshop has performed its magic, you will see the results displayed as a new document (see Figure 1.50). You can now print and trim the photos.

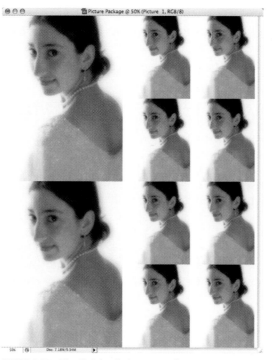

FIGURE 1.50   The finished picture package.

PDF Presentation

Portable Document Format (PDF) is really coming to the forefront of publishing technology, and Adobe has built in a lot of PDF functionality to its Creative Suite of products. Photoshop can natively create and open PDF files. These files can be read by anyone who has the free viewer. New computers ship with the Adobe® Reader (formerly known as the Acrobat® Reader). Otherwise, it can be downloaded for free at *www.adobe.com*. It is beyond the scope of this book to look at all the features of PDF, but several features are invaluable to photographers. You can create a PDF image that compresses very well and enables the viewer to zoom in and out of the image. Perhaps most important, you can set security preferences that prevent people from extracting or printing the images. You can even assign a password that will be required to view the image.

Photoshop has incorporated a very welcome feature that now makes PDF a feasible option for photographers. This feature allows you to create a multipage PDF document, so that you can create your portfolio as a PDF and control the way the viewer sees your images.

1. Select the thumbnails that you want to add to the presentation. Ctrl+click (Cmd+click for Mac) to add to the selection, as shown in Figure 1.51.

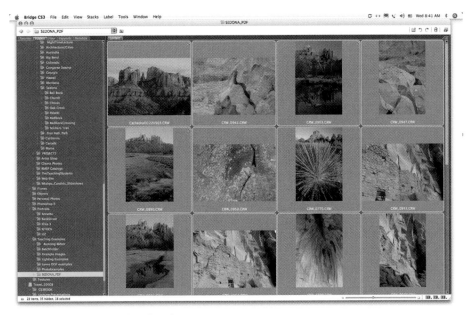

FIGURE 1.51   Selecting thumbnails.

2. Choose Tools > Photoshop > PDF Presentation, and the dialog box shown in Figure 1.52 will open.

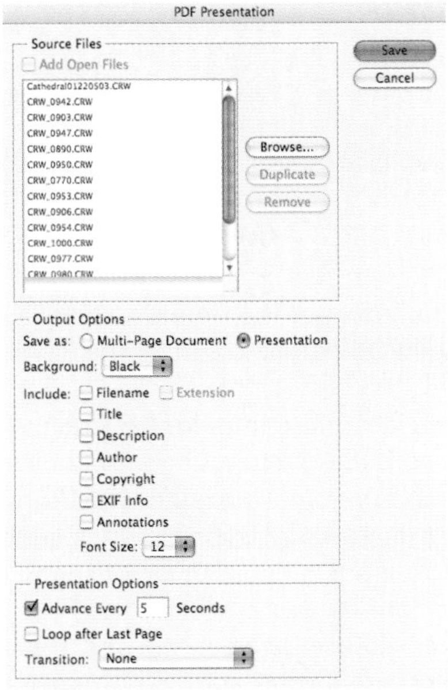

FIGURE 1.52   PDF Presentation dialog box.

3. If you have selected thumbnails, they will appear in the Source Files window; otherwise, click Browse and add the images you want in the presentation.

4. Choose between a multipage document (standard PDF document) or a presentation. The presentation will be a self-running slideshow that will run full screen on any computer equipped with Adobe Reader.

5. If you choose Presentation, choose your options. You can set the delay time between images and decide if the presentation will run once or as an endless loop.

6. Choose a transition effect, which determines how the images will look as they change from image to image. There are quite a few interesting options. Figure 1.53 shows the Random Transition effect being chosen.

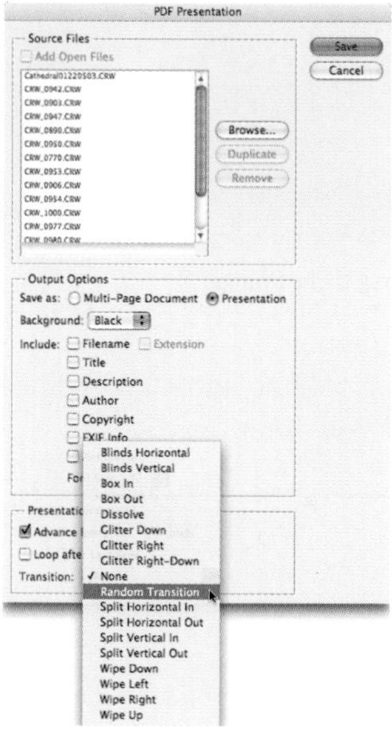

FIGURE 1.53   Choosing transition effects.

7. When you have set the options, click Save. Choose a filename and location where the PDF will be created. The Save Adobe PDF dialog box will now be displayed.

8. Choose the default settings for General (refer to the online help for more information about these settings because they are beyond the scope of this book).

9. Choose Compression from the left column, as shown in Figure 1.54.

10. Choose a downsizing option: 300 is good for high-quality prints, and 72 is good for online viewing but is not suitable for printing. (For online viewing, set 72 in both fields.)

11. You have a choice between Zip and JPEG compression.

12. Zip is a lossless format and will produce the best result, but it will also produce the largest file size. Use this option if you are going to run the presenta-

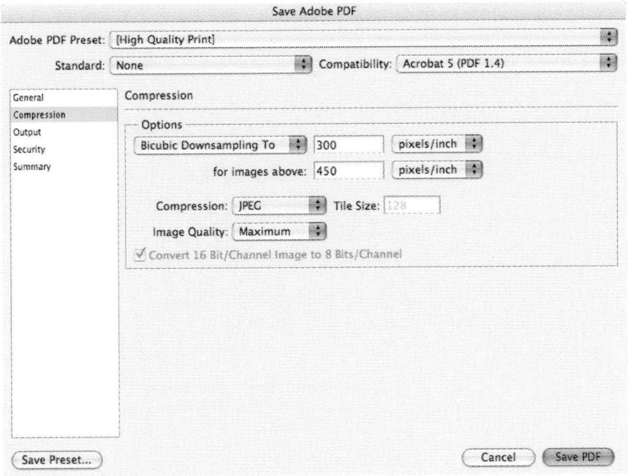

FIGURE 1.54   Choosing PDF options.

tion from a computer's hard disk or CD/DVD. JPEG offers the maximum compression, but at lower settings, it can cause some image degradation. This is the best option for Web use. Choose a quality ranging from Minimum to Maximum. Usually Medium is a good all-purpose setting. You may want to experiment with this until you get a result that suits your needs the best.

13. Choose the Security options. The first field that appears enables you to enter a password to protect the document. The password will be required to open the document. This is great for confidential and sensitive documents. The second field protects the permissions and must be enabled before you can use any of the other security features. Once this is enabled, you can control the other options:

No Printing: Prevents anyone from printing the document. You may also choose the option to allow low-resolution printing.

No Changing the Document: Locks the document and prevents any changes to the document.

No Content Copying or Extraction: Prevents saving copies of the document and locks the images so they cannot be extracted in Photoshop or any other program.

No Adding or Changing Comments and Form Fields: Prevents anyone from changing the comments or editing the forms.

Figure 1.55 shows the PDF Security dialog box with the permissions password set.

The Security settings are awesome for photographers because you could, for example, send the proofs over to a client. The client could then view the images, show them around, and even print low-resolution comps. After you have received payment for the image, you supply a password, and now the client can print and extract the image without limitations. This is just one way you could use this feature—let your imagination be your guide.

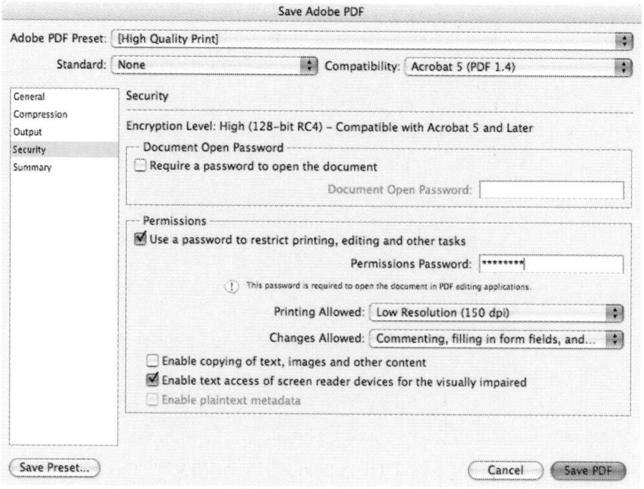

Save Adobe PDF

Adobe PDF Preset: [High Quality Print]

Standard: None   Compatibility: Acrobat 5 (PDF 1.4)

General
Compression
Output
Security
Summary

Security

Encryption Level: High (128–bit RC4) – Compatible with Acrobat 5 and Later

Document Open Password

☐ Require a password to open the document

Document Open Password:

Permissions

☑ Use a password to restrict printing, editing and other tasks

Permissions Password: ********

ⓘ This password is required to open the document in PDF editing applications.

Printing Allowed: Low Resolution (150 dpi)

Changes Allowed: Commenting, filling in form fields, and...

☐ Enable copying of text, images and other content

☑ Enable text access of screen reader devices for the visually impaired

☐ Enable plaintext metadata

Save Preset...   Cancel   Save PDF

FIGURE 1.55   PDF Security options.

14. After you have entered all the settings to your satisfaction, it's time to create the PDF.
15. Click Save PDF to create your PDF.

If you checked the View PDF After Saving box in the General tab, the PDF will launch when it is created. You can now view the slideshow or the multipage document, as shown in Figure 1.56. (The presentation will take up the full screen, and no interface will be visible until you press the Esc key.)

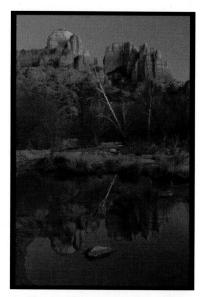

FIGURE 1.56   Viewing the presentation in Adobe Reader.

WEB GALLERY

Ever wanted to put your images up on a Web site but lack the HTML skills? The Web Photo Gallery makes it a snap. Photoshop will create small thumbnails and place them on a page. When you click on the thumbnails, they will launch a larger version of the image. Photoshop resizes all the images and creates all the Web pages necessary for smooth navigation. What is more, the metadata can be used for captions, page titles, and more. You can point the gallery at a folder of images, go get a cup of coffee, and before you return, your Web page is finished and ready for uploading to the Web. Let's see how it works.

1. Navigate to the folder that contains the images you want to place on the Web.
2. Choose Edit > Select All.
3. Choose Tools > Photoshop > Web Photo Gallery.
4. You will now see the dialog box shown in Figure 1.57. Choose a style of page from the Styles list. You can see a graphical preview to the right of the dialog box. You may want to start off creating a Web gallery of just a few images to sample the different styles of Web pages.

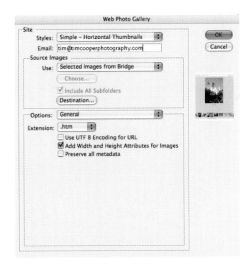

FIGURE 1.57   Web Photo Gallery.

5. Enter your email in the Email field. This will create a link that people can click on to contact you while browsing your page.
6. Choose your source images. Here because we selected all of the images in the folder, we can leave this setting at Selected Images from Bridge.
7. Choose the destination where the gallery will be placed when it's built. In Figure 1.58, we have created a new folder for the gallery, which is a good idea because all the files will be kept together in one place.

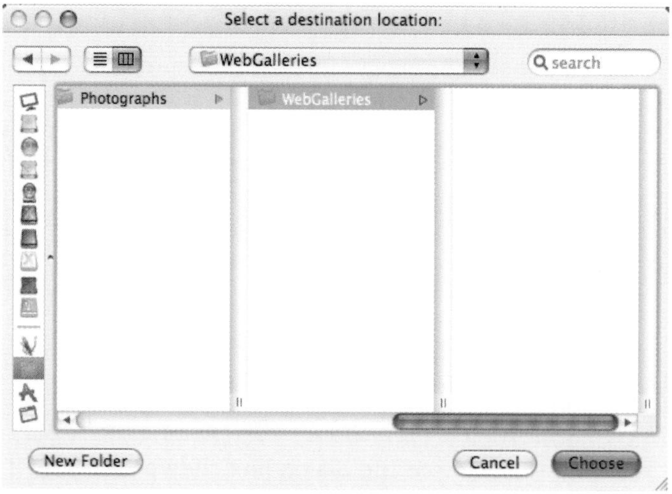

FIGURE 1.58 Choosing a destination folder.

8. To set the options for the destination folder, choose Banner. This title will appear on the top of the Web page.
9. Fill out the Banner options as shown in Figure 1.59.

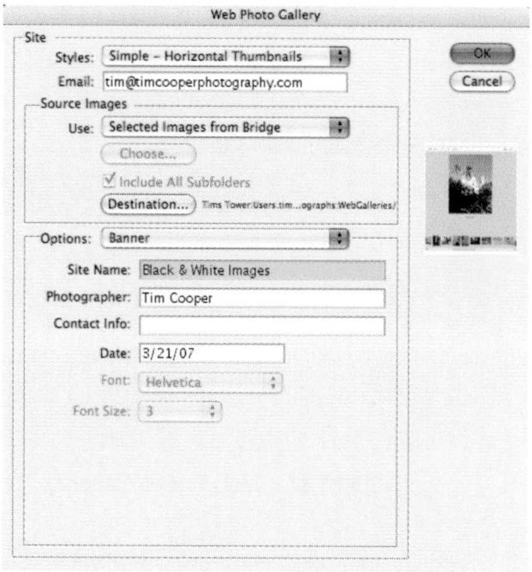

FIGURE 1.59 Choosing the Banner options.

10. Choose Large Images. This is where you decide how large the images will appear on the Web page.
11. Select an image size, or enter your own custom size.

12. Choose a level of image compression. Five is a good setting for a Web page. If you were to put the gallery on a CD-ROM, you would choose a higher setting because download speed is not a concern with a CD-ROM.
13. If you want, you can make two copies of the gallery: one with low-quality JPEG for dial-up connections and another with high-quality JPEG for broadband.
14. Choose the options for Titles as shown in Figure 1.60. This information will be pulled from the metadata.
15. Choose the thumbnail options as shown in Figure 1.61.

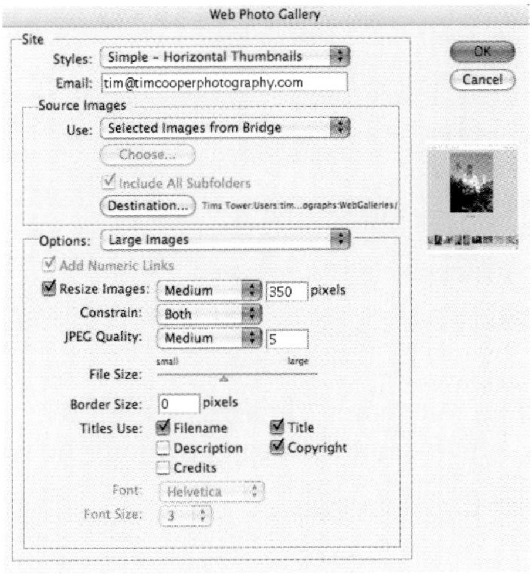

FIGURE 1.60 Choosing the image options.

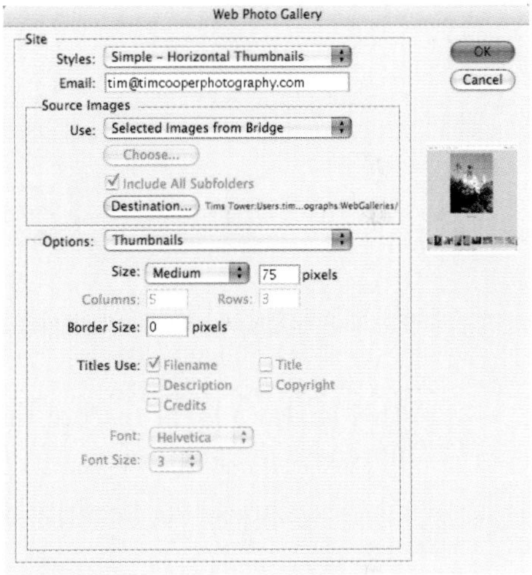

FIGURE 1.61 Setting the thumbnail options.

16. Select a size for the thumbnails. These small images will load quickly and provide a way for visitors to click through to the larger images.
17. Fill out the other options if they are available. If they are grayed out, it means that they are not available for the chosen gallery style.
18. Click OK to run the Web Photo Gallery. You will see some activity as Photoshop goes to work, resizing images and creating HTML pages.

When you are done, the Web page will launch in your default browser as shown in Figure 1.62.

All your files are in the destination folder. Upload the folder to a Web server to display them to the world.

Watermarking Your Images Automatically

While creating your Web galleries, you can choose to have all your images watermarked. This will prevent anyone from using your images without your permission.

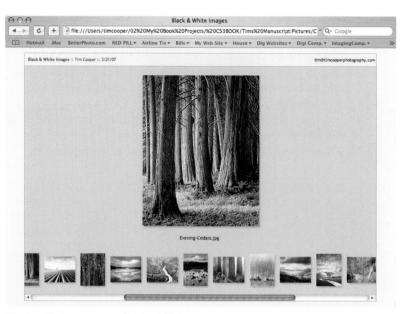

FIGURE 1.62   Viewing the finished Web page.

This is also a great feature for sending out "comp" images; if the client decides to purchase the photo, you can supply a high-resolution copy without the watermark.

1. Choose the Security option as shown in Figure 1.63.

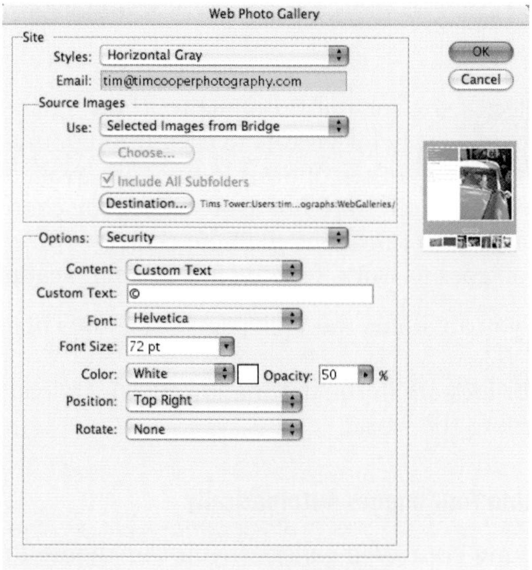

FIGURE 1.63   Choosing the Security options.

2. Choose the Custom Text option.
3. Enter anything you want in the Custom Text field. In this case, we have added the copyright symbol (Alt+0169/Option+G for Mac).
4. Choose a size and color for the watermark. Also choose an Opacity setting as shown in Figure 1.63.
5. Create the Web Gallery just like we did in the previous exercise.

When the Web page is complete, you will see the watermark on all your images, as shown in Figure 1.64.

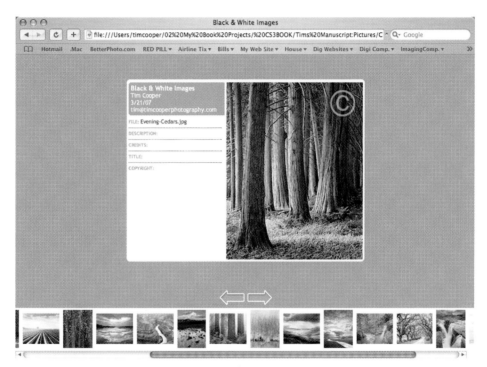

FIGURE1.64   Your images are now watermarked.

ON THE CD

You can find this Web Gallery on the CD-ROM under `Photo_gallery`. Double-click on the `index.htm` file to launch the gallery.

SUMMARY

We covered a lot of ground in this chapter. As you learned, Bridge in Photoshop CS3 can now do a lot more than just organize images. You also learned how to customize the settings to suit your workflow and how to use metadata to tag, organize, and search for your images. You will definitely find these features useful in the future.

We also looked at different tasks that can be automated from within Bridge, including putting your images onto a Web page. PDF security can change the way that photographers share their images, and perhaps now fear of emailing valuable photos will be alleviated. These automated tasks can shave hours off your work schedule.

In the next chapter, you will learn about the new and very powerful Raw Converter that Photoshop CS3 provides.

2

FROM THE BRIDGE TO PHOTOSHOP: THE ADOBE RAW CONVERTER

In This Chapter

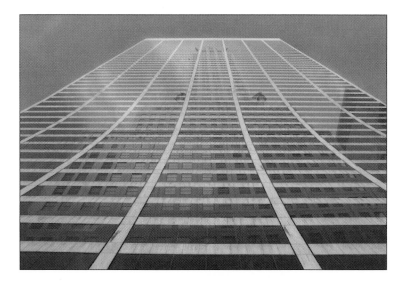

Before we jump into the new and improved Raw Converter, we should spend a little more time looking at the files (photos) that your camera creates. Digital photographers are faced with a seemingly endless array of choices on their cameras. Many of these options are worth exploring to enhance image quality, but a great many only affect shooting convenience. Following are several features that will affect how you work with your file in the Raw Converter. Other choices, such as exposure, metering modes, Auto Focus, and Drive Mode, are critical to the making of fine photographs, but the following represents aspects of the file that are relevant to the processing of the image. Of course, this is just a partial list of features and options, but they are the ones most photographers think about every time they pick up the camera.

- ISO
- File Format
- White Balance
- Picture Styles or Camera Settings

ISO

ISO (International Standards Organization) is a rating that refers to how sensitive the sensor is to light. ISO 100 is considered to be slow, whereas ISO 1600 is considered to be fast. A slow ISO setting means your sensor is not really sensitive to light, so it needs a lot of light to form an image. This means you need either a slower shutter speed such as 1/30 or 1/60, or a larger aperture such as f4 or 5.6. When your sensor is really sensitive (ISO 1600), you can use faster shutter speeds (1/250, 1/500) or smaller apertures (f16, f22) to create the image.

So why not just put it on 1600 all of the time? One word: quality. The higher the ISO, the more likely you are to experience noise in your photographs. Noise is the digital equivalent of film grain just not as pretty. A sensor really only has one sensitivity. If your camera's lowest ISO is 100, then that is your real sensitivity. If 200 is the lowest, than that is your actual sensitivity. To enable a higher ISO or sensitivity to light, the camera must pass more power through the sensor. This extra power creates noise in the resulting file. At best, noise can look like small specks of grain; at worst, it takes on the appearance of an undesirable pattern. As you will see later in the chapter, the Raw Converter can help reduce noise in your photographs, but it will come at a cost.

Depending on your camera model, noise can begin to appear even at ISO as low as 400. To see where you begin to get noise on your camera, simply take the same shot with all of the different ISOs that your camera provides, and examine them in Photoshop at the view setting of Actual Pixels. You will quickly see which ISO setting causes noise.

File Format and Bit Depth

When it comes to choosing a file format for your camera, JPEG and Raw are your primary choices (see Chapter 1 for more information).

Let's review the differences.

- The JPEG format will compress your file so that more images can fit onto a memory card. On most cameras, there are different degrees of compression that deliver various degrees of quality. The highest quality JPEG setting will produce exceptional images due to the fact that there is a minimal amount of compression taking place. The camera is just "saving" the file in this format. It is using the same resolution as the Raw setting, assuring maximum image quality.
- The Raw format on the other hand, applies no compression to your image. It simply takes the data off of your sensor and sends it to the card unprocessed and uncompressed (sort of . . . there is a little compression, but nothing to worry about).
- JPEGs are processed faster in the camera, so you can shoot faster. Raw images take longer to shoot and process.
- JPEGs are immediately ready to use in other applications. Raw images must be "post processed" first.

My recommendation is for photographers to shoot using the Raw format. If, however, you have a camera that does not support this format, the good news is that Adobe has upgraded the Raw Converter in CS3 to accommodate JPEGs as well! This means that JPEGs now have access to the same streamlined image-processing software that Raw images use, The Adobe Raw Converter.

White Balance

With your digital camera, white balance is the equivalent of filtering for different light sources or choosing a designated film to match the light source. For example, if you use a daylight-balanced film (the most common type of film) under tungsten light (a typical light bulb), your image will have a heavy orange cast. This is because tungsten bulbs give off an orange/yellow light. To correct for this, you would buy tungsten film to shoot in this situation. This would produce an image with a neutral color cast. You could also put on a Tungsten Filter to correct for the orange light. This filter would be blue.

In digital cameras (and in the Raw Converter), the white balance setting can do all of this for you. You merely have to change the setting. When you are shooting under tungsten lights, you choose the tungsten setting. If you find yourself shooting under fluorescent lighting, choose the fluorescent setting. It's easy as pie. In the past, it was recommended that when shooting JPEG you should set your white balance on your camera rather than in Photoshop. This is still a good idea. However, now that that you can open any file into the Raw Converter, you may find it easier to set the white balance in the Raw Converter rather than at the time of shooting.

Some common white balance settings found on both digital cameras and as presets in the Adobe Raw Converter are Daylight, Auto, Cloudy, Shade, Tungsten, Flash, Fluorescent, Kelvin and Custom.

Auto white balance will try to balance the scene for you. This works for average types of indoor photography. There are better ways of achieving a good white balance, so reserve the use of this setting for when you are unsure of the light source, for example, when using indoor lighting. Is it tungsten, halogen, or a mix of lighting? If you are unsure, simply set your camera on Auto White Balance Mode. Chances are good that you will end up with very good results.

Daylight will give you good results under . . . well . . . daylight conditions. It will also give proper results during sunsets, sunrises, and night scenes. In any situations where you would use daylight film, this setting will be appropriate.

Flash is designed to give you good color when you are using the on camera flash. It adds in a little yellow/orange to combat the overly blue light of the flash. Consider using the cloudy setting instead of this one, however, to add more warmth.

Cloudy will also add orange/yellow to your picture. Typically, the added orange cast is a little heavier than that of the flash setting. Cloudy days usually produce a significant blue cast.

Open Shade adds even more orange/yellow than cloudy. The light found in open shade is very blue.

Tungsten adds a strong blue cast to overcome the heavy orange coloration of tungsten light sources.

Fluorescent will add a slight magenta color to balance the overall green cast of this light source.

Kelvin is a setting found on higher-end cameras and can drastically change the color balance of your image. The higher end of this setting (8000) will add a lot of warmth, while the lower end (2000) will significantly cool down your image with a lot of blue. The Daylight White Balance setting on a camera is considered neutral. It usually falls within the 5200–5500k range. The Kelvin setting on the camera is mainly designed for people using a handheld color meter. Try experimenting with it to learn more about the color and temperature of light.

Custom is the most accurate of all of the settings. You can use this setting to produce a very exact neutral cast in any lighting situation. Think of the other settings as close but not quite perfect. All light sources are slightly different, and it would be impossible to create a "preset" for all of them. To use this setting, you must first take a picture of a gray or white card in the light source you want to shoot. The camera will then balance the card back to neutral and store this setting. You then choose Custom from your white balance option and it will revert back to the stored setting. Anytime you are under a light source other than daylight, you should use this setting. Look to your camera manual for exact directions on how to use the Custom setting. Manufacturers all vary on how to set your camera up in Custom.

Picture Styles and Camera Settings

Another great feature of the digital camera and the Raw Converter is that it can reproduce the look of many film types! In the Raw Converter, just moving a few sliders can change the feel of your photograph. When working with film cameras, if we wanted to take a portrait, we would choose a film with low saturation and low contrast. This film would have a neutral or warm color cast to it. For general shooting, landscapes or architecture, you could use a film that produced higher contrast and deep color saturation.

With digital cameras, instead of buying different films for each situation, we can simply set the camera to mimic the type of film we want to use. By applying a picture style such as Portrait or Landscape, the camera will change its settings such as saturation and contrast to fit with the image you want to create. With most cameras, you can even go in and adjust these settings yourself. With the Raw Converter, you also have control over the look of your image. Simple sliders allow you to remove or add contrast, brightness, or color saturation.

Let's take a look at the way a digital camera creates an image.

The sensor will capture the image information. At this point, the image data is raw, meaning it has not been changed at all. It then sends this raw information on to the camera's processor. In the processor, it will undergo changes, which are dictated by the way you set your camera. These settings could include File Format, JPEG Compression Setting, Color, Contrast, and Saturation. If you had your camera set to shoot a picture style such as Landscape or Portrait, your camera will also apply the individual settings that these styles represent.

It is in this stage that your camera keeps your file as Raw or changes it to a JPEG. When shooting in JPEG, any settings that you have set on your camera such as contrast or color tone will be permanently applied to the image. The processor will take these settings, apply them to the Raw image information, and then turn this information into a JPEG file.

If you are shooting Raw, these settings get recorded as a set of instructions or directions on how the image should appear when it is opened. They are not permanently applied. These directions can always be changed to suit your needs without any degradation to your file whatsoever. You can always return to the default settings as well. After these settings are applied, the processor sends the information to the compact flash card for storage.

The long and short of the situation is this: If you are shooting in JPEG it is more important to adjust these settings before shooting. When shooting in Raw, these adjustments can be set in the Raw Converter afterwards.

16-Bit Images

So why is it more important to make adjustments in the camera for JPEGs? Bit depth. Bit depth describes the amount of shades or tones a pixel can contain. An 8-bit image contains 256 shades of gray in each channel, whereas Photoshop's 16-bit image contains approximately 32,768 shades in each channel. The reason it's 32,000 and not 65,000 is that technically Photoshop uses only 15-bit color, but for the sake of clarity, we will call it 16-bit from here on. The result of more shades of gray in each channel is smoother gradations in the images, which results in reduced posterization and banding (a harsh, unnatural transition in color) in viewed and, even more noticeably, in printed images.

To take advantage of the denser 16-bit features, the images must be captured in 16-bit color. Taking an 8-bit image in Photoshop and choosing Image > Mode > 16 bits/Channel does not magically convert an 8-bit image to 16-bit. Photoshop cannot add color information that was not captured. Cameras that support the Raw format are capable of shooting images in high bit depth such as 10-, 12-, or 14-bit. Once they arrive in Photoshop, they automatically convert to 16-bit. This conversion does not in any way degrade your image. So, again for simplicity, we can consider that our cameras capture an image in high bit depth. This is important because this high bit depth is excellent for making adjustments and corrections to the images. The extra data helps the image maintain integrity while adjusting it. An 8-bit image can become posterized very quickly, whereas a 16-bit image is much more robust because of the extra image data.

As you learned earlier, all images start out as Raw images. This means they are captured in a high bit depth. If the image is destined to become a JPEG, the camera's on-board processor will apply settings such as contrast and saturation while the image is in this high-bit stage. This is how your camera can produce such high-quality JPEG photographs. The problem occurs when you get the wrong exposure or you need to adjust the contrast in Photoshop or the Raw Converter, after it has become a JPEG. At this point, the image has already been converted down to an 8-bit file. Any drastic changes can produce posterization or rough transitions between tones or color.

Figure 2.1 shows a histogram of an image that is in need of a typical adjustment to increase contrast.

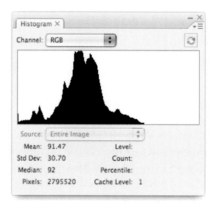

FIGURE 2.1   A typical histogram.

Figure 2.2a shows an 8-bit histogram after the adjustment, and Figure 2.2b shows the 16-bit histogram after the adjustment. Notice the gaps in the 8-bit histogram? These gaps indicate that there is no image data available. The result would be posterization or a very harsh transition of color gradient in the image. Histograms and image correction are covered in more detail in Chapter 4, "Tonal Corection and Enhancement."

The disadvantage of a 16-bit image is file size. A 16-bit image's file size is double that of an 8-bit image. After you begin to modify the image and add layers, the file size can grow very quickly. If you have a fast computer with a lot of RAM and plenty of storage, you may decide to keep the images in 16-bit. If you are working with limited computing resources, a good practice is to perform the image corrections, such

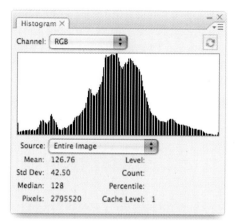 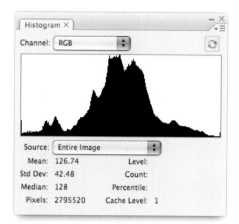

FIGURE 2.2A   The adjustment with 8-bit reveals gapping.

FIGURE 2.2B   The adjustment with 16-bit exhibits no gapping.

as tonal adjustments and color correction, in the Raw Converter and then when you open the image into Photoshop, convert to 8-bit. Directions for this will be covered later in this chapter.

USING CAMERA RAW

As mentioned earlier in the chapter, the Raw file format is a digital equivalent of a negative. All the Raw image data from the camera's sensor is saved, and none of the settings are embedded. When you modify and save a raw image, you never actually alter the image; instead, an eXtensible Metadata Platform (XMP) sidecar is generated. This small XMP file talks to the Raw image and contains metadata that holds information such as white balance, exposure, sharpness, and other details that we will now cover. When opening a Raw image from Bridge, a dialog box appears. Here, you can set the processing options to ensure that the best possible image is opened into Photoshop. Photoshop CS3 now extends the quick and easy processing of the Raw Converter to JPEGs as well. This is an awesome upgrade for photographers who like to shoot in this format. The Raw Converter is so well designed that it drastically decreases the time it takes to perform simple adjustments to your image. One word of caution, however, is to remember that by the time a JPEG reaches Photoshop or the Raw Converter, it is in 8-bit format. This means any adjustments you make will occur to the 8-bit image. So you are still at risk of creating a file with posterization. On the other hand, 16-bit Raw images will be processed by the Raw Converter in their native high-bit depth.

It's worth noting that Adobe has introduced a new format called digital negative (DNG), which is an attempt to standardize Raw file formats and thus preserve the format for the future. In 20 years, some proprietary formats may not be supported. Camera Raw allows you to convert your Raw files to the DNG format.

The latest version of Adobe Camera Raw 4.0 will truly offer some photographers the option of one-stop shopping. For many folks, a trip to Camera Raw will complete their entire editing workflow. For others, the time spent in Photoshop proper may be greatly decreased. Let's take a look at it!

Camera Raw is divided into three main regions, as shown in Figure 2.3.

Preview: This is the area in which you will be able to view your image.

Processing: This area lets you tweak the look of your image via the sliders as well as crop, straighten, and retouch.

Output/Workflow: The output area controls what will happen to your image when it opens into Photoshop or is saved as another type of file.

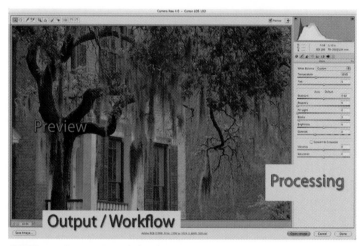

FIGURE 2.3   Camera Raw dialog box.

This new Camera Raw dialog box will seem familiar to those who have worked in Photoshop CS2. The major difference is in the addition of several new image-processing tabs. All of the functionality of previous features remains intact.

There are several ways that you can open your images into Camera Raw:

- From Bridge, double-click on any Raw file. This will automatically launch the Raw Converter and open your image.
- Choose File > Open from Photoshop, and navigate to your Raw file.
- Right-click on your Raw file within Bridge, and choose Open.
- If you want to open a JPEG, TIFF, or PSD into the Raw Converter, right-click and choose Open in Camera Raw.

The Basic Tab

Adobe has done a great job in laying out the processing section of the Raw Converter. We will begin our image processing with the Basic tab as shown in Figure 2.4. The Raw dialog box opens to this tab by default.

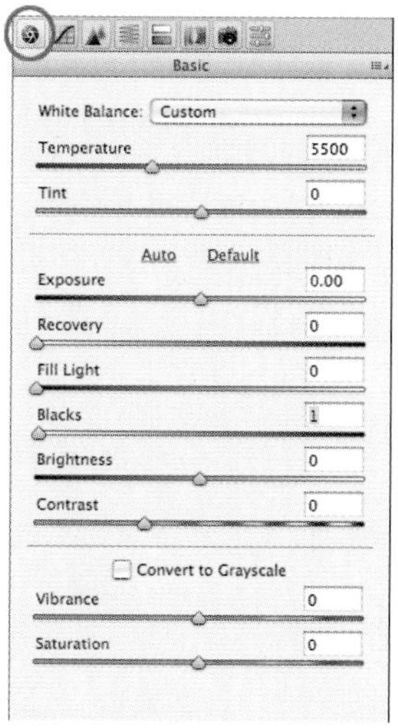

FIGURE 2.4   The Basic tab of the Camera Raw dialog box.

White Balance

The first step is to adjust the overall color of the image. Photography is the art of capturing reflected light. Each type of light has a different color temperature (measured
in Kelvin). If you didn't set your camera to the prevailing light source while shooting, or you chose the wrong White Balance setting, here is your chance to change it.
Figure 2.5 shows an image shot with Daylight White Balance set on the camera.

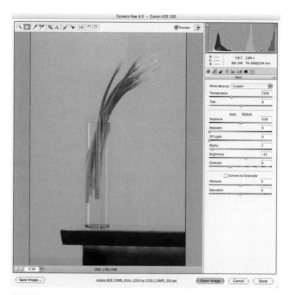

FIGURE 2.5   Original image.

1. Choose the White Balance option that most closely resembles the shooting conditions, such as cloudy, shade, incandescent light, and so on. If this setting looks like the color balance on your camera, it is no accident. That is exactly what you are doing. This setting adjusts the image for different lighting conditions and removes the color casts that may be present. In the example in Figure 2.6, the image was shot under some sort of unknown light source, so the Auto Setting is the best option for this particular image.

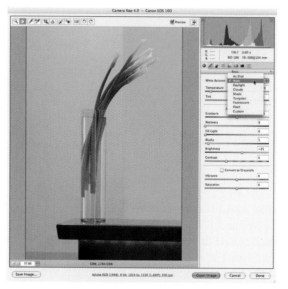

FIGURE 2.6   Choosing White Balance options.

The White Balance settings change the color temperature and tint. It's a good idea to choose the setting that looks best and then make small changes manually.

2. Use the Temperature slider to fine-tune the color settings. If the slider is moved to the left, the image becomes cooler with more blue; if the slider is moved to the right, it becomes warmer with more yellow. Photographers will often use a slightly warm light for portraits because it's more flattering for skin tones.
3. Adjust the Tint slider if you would like to adjust the color tint of the image. Move it left for more green or right for more magenta.
4. In Figure 2.7, the Temperature slider was tweaked further to remove more yellow, and the Tint slider was moved to add more magenta.

Adjusting Image Tone

The next task to be performed in the Camera Raw dialog box is to adjust the image's tonal values. Before getting into adjusting the tonal values, however, a review of image tonalities is in order. The histogram can be broken up into segments to simplify

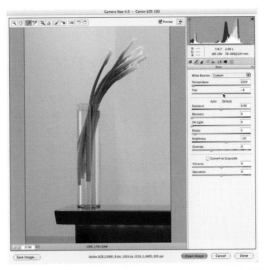

FIGURE 2.7   Fine-tuning the Temperature and Tint sliders.

the description of tonalities within an image (see Figure 2.8). We call these regions the shadows, three-quarter tones, midtones, quarter tones, and highlights. The shadow region of the histogram represents the darkest of the tonalities. The three-quarter tones represent the values that are dark but not as dark as the shadows. The midtones are just what you think they are—the middle brightness values. The quarter tones represent lighter tones such as pastel colors. The highlight region covers the brightest pixels in the image.

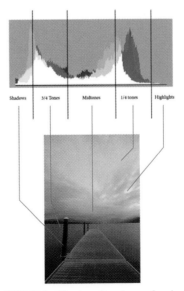

FIGURE 2.8   The tonal regions of a photograph.

When you are finished correcting the color balance, the next step is to look at the overall brightness and contrast of the image. We want to brighten the image and optimize the contrast without losing any pixel data. When we lose data, we call it *clipping* an image. Clipping occurs when some of the highlights or shadows are lost by overcorrecting the exposure or shadows (forcing to pure white or black). You can see the image information displayed as a histogram in the top right of the dialog box (see Chapter 4 for more information on histograms). The goal is to remove the empty areas to the left and right and have the histogram displayed in the window without losing any of the ends (clipping). The two settings that really concern us at this point are the exposure and shadows.

The Exposure Slider

Use this slider to adjust the luminosity of the image. Moving the slider to the right makes the image appear as if it had been given more exposure at the time of capture. Moving it to the left provides less exposure. To use this slider, hold down the Alt key (Option for Mac), and slide the Exposure slider. Holding down the Alt/Option key shows image clipping. You want to move the slider right on the threshold where clipping just begins, as shown in Figure 2.9. The spots that are revealed are the very brightest points of the image.

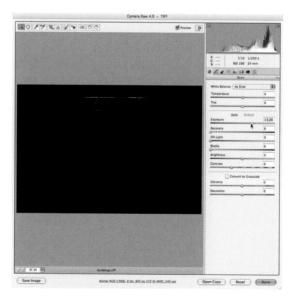

FIGURE 2.9   Setting the highlights.

The Blacks Slider

This slider is the same thing as the Shadows slider in CS2. It will make the shadows darker while having less influence on the midtones and highlight values. Now do exactly the same thing with the Blacks slider that you did with the Exposure slider. You should see the darkest points of the image displayed as colored speckles, as shown in Figure 2.10.

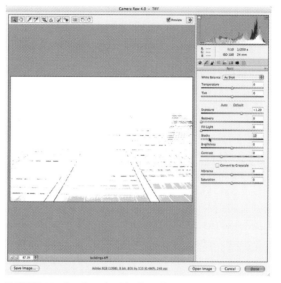

FIGURE 2.10   Setting the Blacks values.

As you can see from the before and after in Figures 2.11a and 2.11b, the luminosity of the image is now adjusted. The highlights and shadows are now correct, and the image has much more contrast.

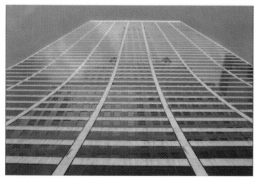

FIGURE 2.11A   Original image.

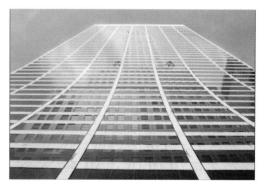

FIGURE 2.11B   After adjusting the Exposure and Blacks.

An alternative method to holding down the Alt/Option key is to click the arrows above the histogram as shown in Figure 2.12. This will cause the clipping in the shadows to be revealed as blue and the highlights as red on the preview.

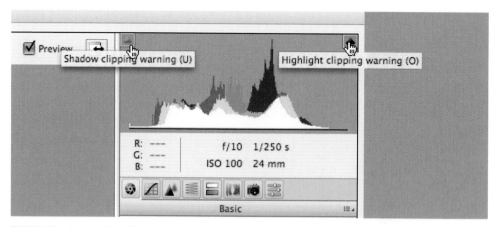

FIGURE 2.12   Setting the clipping warnings.

If you hold down the Alt key (Option key for Mac), the Open and Cancel buttons will change to Open Copy and Reset. Open Copy will open the image in Photoshop without saving the settings to the Raw files metadata, and Reset will restore all the sliders to the initial value when you first opened the image in the Camera Raw window. This is like the panic button when you have really messed things up and need to start again.

The Exposure and Blacks sliders are typically the first place you go after adjusting the color, but what about the other sliders? The Contrast and Brightness sliders are the next two adjustments that you would make to an average image.

Contrast Slider

This adjustment increases or decreases the contrast above the shadows and below the highlights. Think of it as increasing the contrast in the midtones section of the photograph. If pushed too far, the shadows and highlights of the image will begin to clip.

The Brightness Slider

This slider works mainly on the midtones of an image. Pushing the slider to the right will brighten up the midtones, while pushing it to the left will darken them. Used sparingly, the brightness adjustment will not have a heavy effect on the shadows and highlights.

The Recovery Slider

This slider is one of several new additions to the Basic tab. The Recovery slider attempts to bring back detail in the highlight areas. It is well placed after the Exposure slider. There may be times when setting the Exposure slider to produce an overall good look will blow out the highlights in certain areas. That's where the Recovery slider comes in. Moving the slider to the right will bring detail back in the brightest areas. Do not depend on this new feature to save your images from gross overexposure. It will not reveal detail in images that are badly blown out, but you will be surprised at what this new feature can accomplish! Figure 2.13 shows an image whose highlights look beyond retrieval. By raising the Recovery slider, I was able to bring back detail in the washed out fountains (see Figure 2.14).

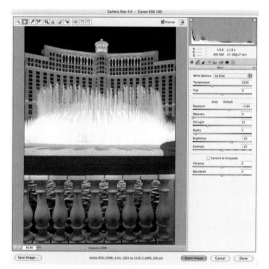

FIGURE 2.13   Original image.

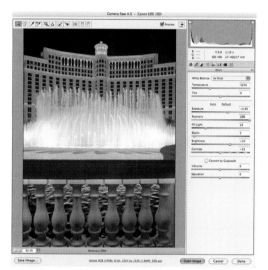

FIGURE 2.14   After increasing the Recovery adjustment.

Fill Light Slider

The Fill Light slider is another new addition to the Basic tab. The Fill Light slider will lighten the three-quarter tones while only subtly affecting the shadows and midtones. This is important because when a photo loses its darkest tone, it starts to look washed out. By moving the slider to the right, the three-quarter tones of your image will become brighter. Be careful with this adjustment, however. A heavy hand here will produce strange edges where the dark tones meet lighter tones. You are better to leave this a little below the desired value and work on further brightening with curves.

Saturation Slider

Moving this adjustment slider to the right increases the overall saturation of the image. A little goes a long way with this slider. Compared to the new Vibrance slider, this tool becomes a very blunt instrument. Oversaturation is a sure sign that your image was digitally manipulated, so easy does it.

Vibrance Slider

The **Vibrance slider** is another welcome addition. This tool applies a nonlinear increase in saturation so pixels that are less saturated are more affected. It also has a built-in skin tone protector to prevent a face from becoming overly red, which is very cool. Care should be taken, however, with both the Vibrance slider and the Saturation slider. A much more surgical approach to color can be applied within the new HSL feature (more to come on this later in the chapter).

The Curves Tab

The second processing tab in line is the Curves tab. For those photographers who break into a nervous sweat upon hearing the word Curves, you can thank the team at Adobe. They have made this box much more intuitive with their introduction of the "Parametric" curve. Upon entering this tab, you now have the choice of working with Parametric and/or Point curves. The Parametric Curve box opens by default (see Figure 2.15), but you can simply click on the Point tab to work with the traditional curve (see Figure 2.16). A full explanation of Curves is supplied in Chapter 4.

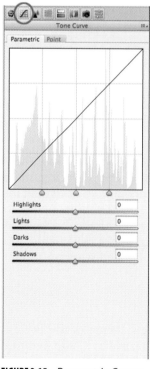

FIGURE 2.15 Parametric Curves tab.

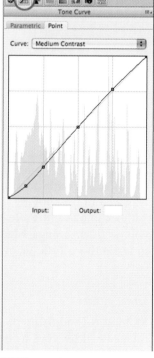

FIGURE 2.16 Point Curves tab.

The first thing you will notice in the Parametric Curves box is the addition of sliders at the bottom and the middle of the box. The middle sliders are a great way to visualize where the effect of the lower sliders will occur. In Figure 2.17, the areas that will be affected by the corresponding sliders are color-coded. The Shadow slider affects the region of your image in blue, the Darks slider affects the green area, the Lights affects the red area, and the Highlight slider affects the yellow area. (*Note:* This is not how the Parametric box appears, just my illustration for your edification.)

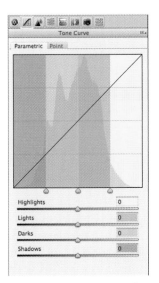

FIGURE 2.17   Parametric curve showing where the sliders will have their effect.

Another feature in the Parametric Curves box is the ability to choke down or widen the individual regions that will be affected by the sliders. In Figure 2.18, I have clicked on the region sliders and moved them out. Now my Shadow and Highlights regions are smaller, and my Lights and Darks regions have expanded. You can also move the Midtone Region slider to alter the division of Lights and Darks. The new Parametric Curves box is worth experimenting with even if you have always been afraid of curves in the past.

The Details Tab

The tab to the right is the Detail tab. This is where sharpening and noise reduction can be performed (see Figure 2.19).

It is usually best to perform most sharpening in Photoshop after all the other corrections are complete. I leave my sharpening set to the default value that Camera Raw assigns.

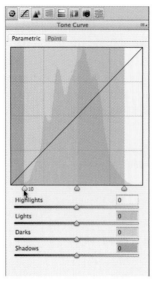

FIGURE 2.18 Moving the regions.

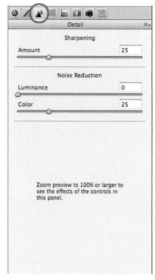

FIGURE 2.19 The Details tab.

Use the Luminance Smoothing slider to minimize noise that may have appeared from using a high ISO. Look at the darker portions of the image to spot the grain. Always zoom to 100% when working on grain and sharpening images so that you can see the true result of the adjustments. Use the Color Noise Reduction to combat any colored specks that may have appeared from long exposures; the most common are blue spots in a night scene.

HSL/Grayscale Tab

Hold on to your hats, the HSL/Grayscale tab hides one of the most useful photographic innovations since the introduction of the Raw file! This tab as shown in Figure 2.20 allows you complete control over the color in your photographs.

It is also an extremely effective method of creating grayscale images from color files. This box breaks up the three color components of Hue, Saturation, and Luminance into individual tabs. You can then adjust the Reds, Oranges, Yellows, Greens, Aquas, Blues, Purples, and Magentas within each tab. Here is a look at what the three components actually control:

Hue: The name of the color, such as red, blue, or orange. This name describes where the color sits on the color wheel. We do know, however, that there is a wide range of colors that we could call red. For example, you may have red that is similar to that of pepper. By using the Hue tab and choosing the Red slider, you could make that red appear more blue or more orange.

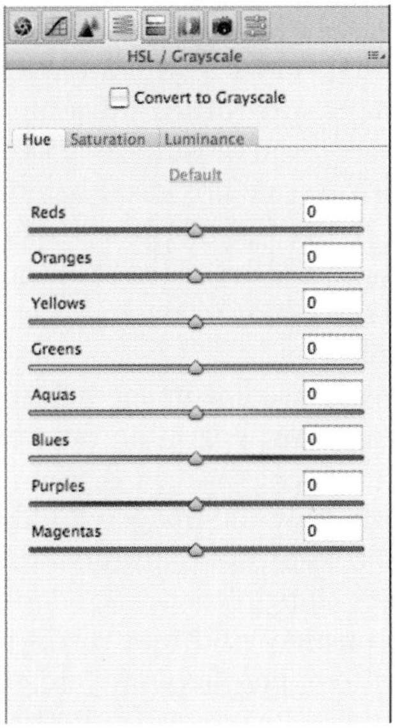

FIGURE 2.20   The HSL/Grayscale tab.

Saturation: The intensity of the color. Reducing the saturation will bring a color closer to gray. Increasing the saturation will make the color appear more vivid.

Luminance: The brightness of the color. This effect is often confused with saturation. When darkening a color, it may appear to become more saturated. Lightening the same color may appear to make it less saturated. The truth is you are really just changing the brightness. A moment or two of comparison between these two sliders will reveal their subtle differences in character.

Creating a Grayscale Image

The HSL tab is used to create grayscale images. As you can imagine, the HSL tab puts a lot of power into the photographer's hand. Nowhere is that more evident, however, than when changing a color image to grayscale. Creating great grayscale images has never been easier. A good grayscale image will have a pleasing range of tones from pure black to pure white, with good separation through the midtone gray values. There are exceptions to this rule, of course, such as high-key or low-key images. In general, though, this is a good formula for success. The biggest issue with black-and-white photography has always been the separation of tones. This problem existed in film as it does with digital images. Our eyes have the benefit of separating tones by color. So we note the color contrast between a red value and green value even though they may be the same exact brightness level. When converting to black and white, the brightness value has always been the main consideration. Until now.

The HSL/Grayscale box is revolutionary in its capability to individually alter the brightness of individual colors within an image. This translates to brighter or darker grays in the final image. Any future grayscale image should always begin with a visit to the Basic tab, to set the Exposure, Blacks, Contrast, and Brightness sliders. Very rarely will the HSL/Grayscale box itself be enough to create great black and whites. You may also need to set the black-and-white points as well as the local contrast through the Basic tab to finish the job. You can start with the HSL/Grayscale tab and then move to the Basic tab or vice versa. Let's begin with the HSL/Grayscale tab in the following examples.

Figure 2.21 shows the color image before any changes have been made. Notice that there is sufficient color separation but very little brightness separation between the color values.

Figure 2.22 shows how the image would look if you simply clicked in the Convert to Grayscale box. Photoshop automatically sets the color sliders by examining the brightness of the colors in the image and trying to replicate them in a grayscale image. Sometimes you may find that this is just what the doctor ordered. In other cases, you may want to experiment and create your own values. Look closely at this image and the original color image in Figure 2.21 to note the correlation between brightness of color and the resulting gray value.

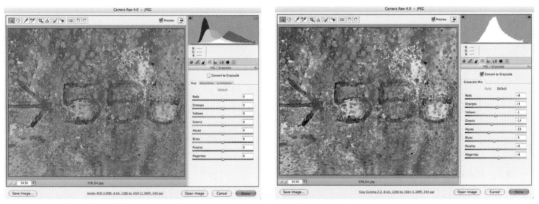

FIGURE 2.21   The original image in color.   **FIGURE 2.22**   Auto settings.

Once you decide to manually set your own values, the sky is the limit! In the original color image, you can see that there is an abundance of red and orange metal. The small dots of blue/purple add a nice counterpoint. The goal in this image is to separate these colors as best as possible so that they translate into different tones of gray in the final grayscale. In Figure 2.22, the Red, Orange, and Yellow sliders have been moved to the right, which has the effect of darkening down those colors. Aquas, Blues, Purples, and Magentas have been lightened (see Figure 2.23).

The opposite approach has been taken with Figure 2.24. The red family has been lightened and the blue family darkened. This set of values is strikingly different from the previous photo.

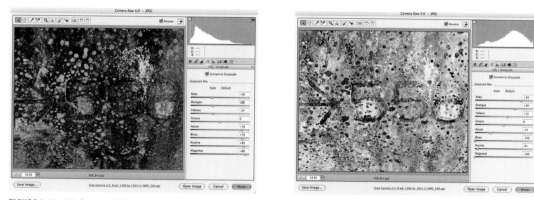

FIGURE 2.23   Lightened blues.   **FIGURE 2.24**   Lightened reds.

In Figures 2.23 and 2.24, the contrast has been increased and the black-and-white points have been set to get the final image. This is always an important consideration in creating the finished look of a fine black-and-white print. Do not solely depend on the grayscale portion of the Raw convert to create a finished black-and-white photograph.

These sliders are very much image dependant. Raising or lowering the values can work wonderfully on one image while nearly destroying another. Always check that your adjustments are not creating posterization, which is a very possible result with this tool!

Split Toning Tab

Following the HSL/Grayscale tab is the Split Toning tab (see Figure 2.25). Split toning is a favorite technique among many photographers who use black-and-white darkrooms. It was a way that you could get different color tones in different areas of your image. A typical split toning technique was to have the shadows show a cool blue color, while the midtones and highlights were pushed toward a warmer brown or yellow tone. This combination had the advantage of adding the color contrast of cool/warm in addition to the tonal contrast of dark and light. Recreating this technique in Camera Raw is easier, faster, more efficient, and much less hazardous to your health. The really cool thing is that you can also try this technique on color images. There is no reason that the photo has to be a traditional black-and-white image to enjoy the benefits of split toning.

The Split Toning box is broken up into three segments. Highlights, Balance, and Shadows. The Hue sliders in the Highlights and Shadows sections allow you to choose the Hue (color) that you want applied to the region. It can be hard to choose a color without first increasing the saturation. This will intensify the hue making it easier to visualize the final color. Move your Saturation slider up to 50, and then move your Hue slider until the desired color is produced. Return to the Saturation slider, and reduce or increase the value until the proper intensity of color is created. Do this for both the Shadows and Highlights regions.

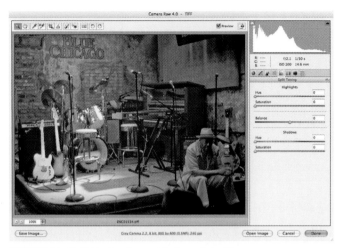

FIGURE 2.25 Split Toning box with the original image.

When these steps are complete, you can adjust the Balance slider to introduce more of the highlight color into the shadows or vice versa. Moving this slider to the right will begin to push the highlight color down into the darker midtones and eventually the shadows themselves. Move the slider to the left, and the shadow color will start to replace the highlight color in the lighter midtones and eventually the highlights.

Incidentally, moving the Balance slider all the way to the left or the right is an easy way to reproduce the look of warm or cool tone black-and-white printing papers. Remember to go easy on the saturation when trying this technique. Figure 2.26 shows an image that has been split-toned.

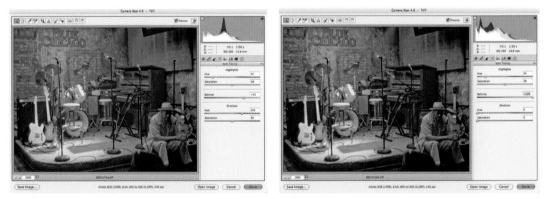

FIGURE 2.26 Split-toned image.   **FIGURE 2.27** Warm-toned image.

Lens Corrections Tab

The options in the Lens Corrections tab allow for compensation of the chromatic aberration and lens-vignetting amount.

Chromatic Aberration: If you zoom into an image very closely (200–400%), chromatic aberration can sometimes be seen. This effect causes a slight, colored halo around the edges. In Figure 2.28, you can see where red appears to halo the outside edges of the green leaves.

Figure 2.29 shows the same image after reducing the Fix Red/Cyan Fringe slider. When you see a red fringe, move the Fix Red/Cyan Fringe slider toward Red. If you see a yellow fringe, move the Fix Blue/Yellow Fringe slider toward Yellow. Moving the sliders will actually shift the color channels in Photoshop to compensate.

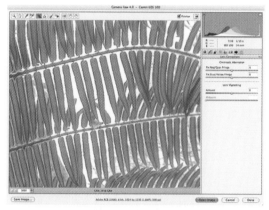

FIGURE 2.28   Aberration on the edge pixels.

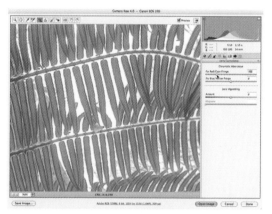

FIGURE 2.29   Aberration corrected.

Lens Vignetting: Sometimes a lens does not distribute light evenly across the image. Because of the curvature of a lens, the edges of the image sometimes appear darker than the center. This is called a *lens vignette*. By adjusting the Lens Vignetting Amount and Lens Vignetting Midpoint sliders, you can compensate and enjoy an even distribution of light across the image. This is also a useful setting for creating a special effect and introducing vignetting around the image on purpose.

Calibrate Tab

This tab adjusts the hue and saturation of each color channel separately; use this only if you are an advanced user. You can make adjustments to compensate for bad coloring in your camera and save the settings. Another option is to use the Calibrate tab for special effects such as making green grass look more green, or changing the blue in the ocean. With the introduction of the HSL/Grayscale tab, you might rarely visit the Calibrate tab.

Preset Tabs

The Preset tab is a place to find your saved settings. Often it will save time to create and save settings such as Chromatic Aberration or Lens Vignetting. To save individual tab settings:

- Open an image made with a particular focal length lens.
- Fix the chromatic aberration.
- From the small diagonal arrow in the top right of the tab, choose Save Settings. You will see the Save Settings box in Figure 2.30.

Uncheck all of the settings that you don't want to save. In Figure 2.31, all are unchecked but the Chromatic Aberration setting. Click Save.

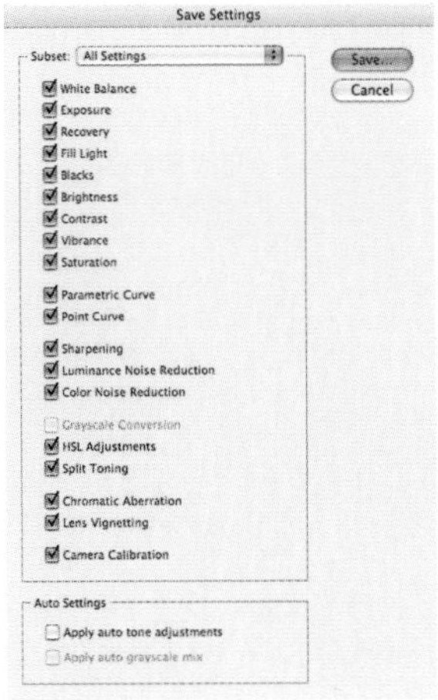

FIGURE 2.30 The Save Settings box.

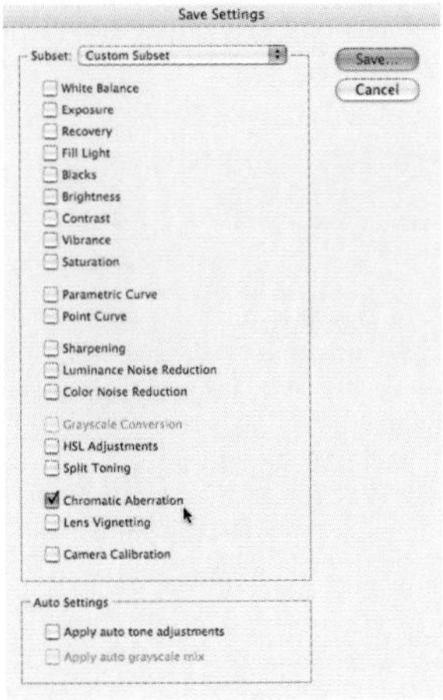

FIGURE 2.31 Checking only the Chromatic Aberration setting.

1. The next box that appears will give you a chance to name your saved setting. Give it a name that describes what it does. In Figure 2.32, I have called my setting 20 mm Chromatic Aberration. Now anytime that I shoot with a 20 mm lens, I can quickly apply this saved setting. Click Save. You can see a list of my saved settings in Figure 2.33.

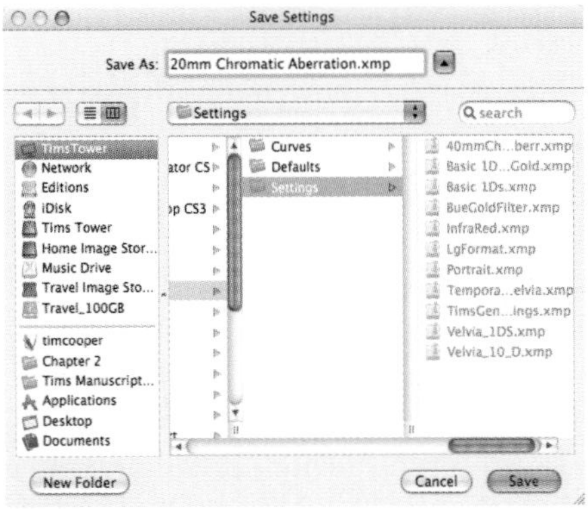

FIGURE 2.32 Naming the setting.

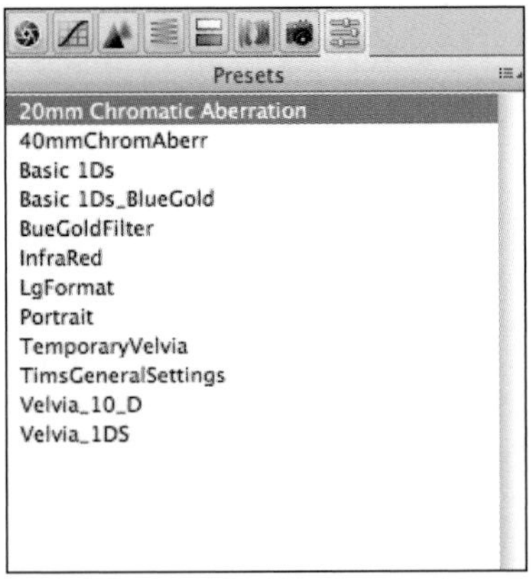

FIGURE 2.33 The Presets tab with saved settings.

The best thing about presets is the way in which you can apply them. Once a setting is saved, you don't even have to open the Raw Converter to apply them! Say for example I have just downloaded 50 images from a recent shoot. Of the 50, 30 of the images were made with my 20 mm lens. I would highlight all 30 images made with this lens in Bridge. Next, I would right-click on any of the highlighted images, and choose Develop Settings from the resulting flyout menu. Here I will see all of my saved settings! I would choose the 20 mm Chromatic Aberration Setting (see Figure 2.34). That portion of the Raw conversion will automatically be applied to all of the highlighted images.

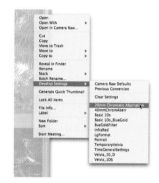

FIGURE 2.34   Applying a preset from Bridge.

CROPPING AND STRAIGHTENING IMAGES

A great addition to Photoshop CS2 was the ability to straighten and crop images inside Camera Raw. This applies nondestructive cropping and straightening, which means that the settings can be discarded at any time, even after you have restarted your computer.

TUTORIAL 2.1	STRAIGHTENING AN IMAGE

It's a simple process to straighten a crooked image.

ON THE CD

1. Open the image `ch_2_Straighten.tif` included in the `Chapter 2` folder on the CD-ROM as a reference.
2. Choose the Straighten tool as shown in Figure 2.35.
3. Click and drag along the line that you want to become the new horizon.
4. Release the mouse, and a box will appear showing the new image bounds as shown in Figure 2.36. When this image is opened in Photoshop, it will be cropped to these bounds.
5. To redraw the line, grab the Straighten tool and redraw. To clear the crop box, click and hold on the Crop tool, and choose Clear Crop.

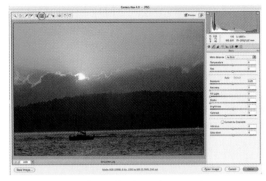

FIGURE 2.35   Applying the Straighten tool.

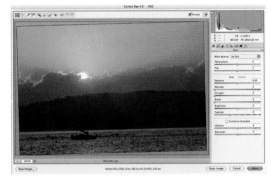

FIGURE 2.36   Straightened image in Camera Raw.

ON THE CD

TUTORIAL 2.2   CROPPING

Cropping will work similarly to straightening. ch_2_Crop.jpg is included in the Chapter 2 folder on the CD-ROM as a reference. Open it from Bridge by right-clicking and choosing Open in Camera Raw.

1. Choose the Crop tool from the top of the Raw dialog box.
2. Click and drag around the area that you would like to keep in the image as shown in Figure 2.37.

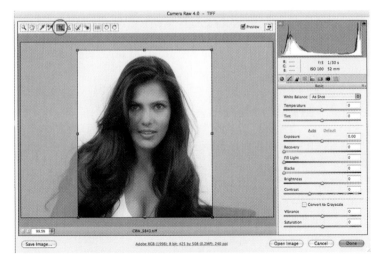

FIGURE 2.37   Cropping an image in Camera Raw.

3. Select the bounding boxes to make any adjustments.
4. When the image is opened in Photoshop, it will be cropped. The crop will not be permanent in the Raw image and can be removed or adjusted at any

time in the future. If you do not like your crop, right-click inside the box and choose Clear Crop from the drop-down contextual menu.

5. Click and hold on the Crop tool to reveal a drop-down menu of crop presets. These presets are conveniently set to common print proportions such as 2 × 3 (4 × 6), 5 × 7, and 4 × 5 (8 × 10). To enable a preset crop, click on the desired proportion from the drop-down list and drag a crop on your image. Once the crop is drawn out, you can reposition it at any time by clicking inside the box and moving the crop. Drag the corner handles to resize the box while retaining the preset proportions.

TUTORIAL 2.3   CLEANING UP DUST

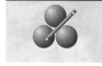

Photoshop CS3 introduces the ability to clean up your images in the Raw Converter. This new addition may allow the complete processing of an image within the Camera Raw box. For some images, you may not even need to go into Photoshop! Let's see how it works.

1. The image `ch_2_CleanUp.crw` is in the `Chapter 2` folder on the CD-ROM. Open it from Bridge by right-clicking and choosing Open in Camera Raw.
2. From the lower-left Zoom Level box, choose 100%.
3. Click on the Retouch tool as shown in Figure 2.38.

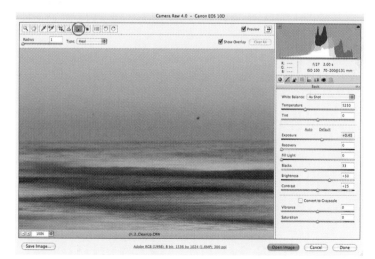

FIGURE 2.38   The Retouch tool.

4. Click in the middle of a dust spot, and draw outwards until the circle is a little larger than the spot itself (see Figure 2.39). The Healing brush will automatically find an appropriate area from which to sample from and heal your target area. The newly sampled area will show up as a second circle as shown in

Figure 2.40. If you are unhappy with the location of this circle, click inside the circle, and drag it to a new location. The sample will automatically update.

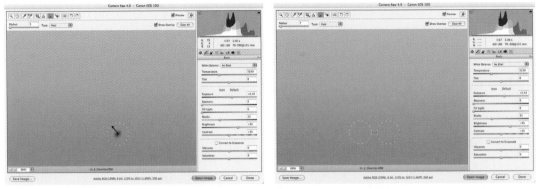

FIGURE 2.39 Drawing out the healing circle.   **FIGURE 2.40** The original area and the sampled area.

5. Find another spot to clean up, and click on it. The circle will remain the same size. If you need to change it, go up to the Option bar, and raise or lower your radius to suit your needs. As you continue cleaning up spots in your image, the overlay (circles) will stay in position to let you know where you have been working (see Figure 2.41).

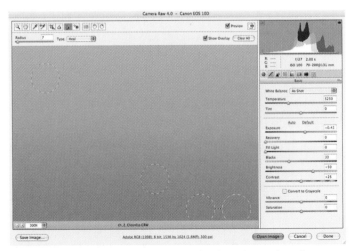

FIGURE 2.41 The circles show the areas that have been cloned.

6. To undo a spot, press Ctrl+Z (Cmd+Z for Mac). To undo multiple spots, press Ctrl+Alt+Z (Cmd+Option+Z). To undo all of the spots, click the Clear All button.

7. Clicking Done in the Raw Converter will save the changes to the image. When you reopen the image, however, the healing circles will not be visible. Click on the Retouch tool to make them visible.

8. When you need to make an exact duplicate of an area, change the Type box from Heal to Clone.

TUTORIAL 2.4   **RED EYE REMOVAL**

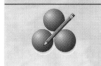

The folks at Adobe have also added in a Red Eye Removal tool in the latest version of Camera Raw. Its operation is similar to that of the Retouch tool.

ON THE CD

1. The image ch_2_RedEye.jpg is in the Chapter 2 folder on the CD-ROM. Open it from Bridge by right-clicking and choosing Open in Camera Raw.

2. Choose the Red Eye tool from the toolbar at the top of the Raw Converter as shown in Figure 2.42.

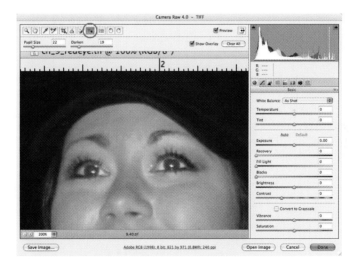

FIGURE 2.42   The Red Eye Removal tool.

3. Click outside the eye, and draw a box around it, as shown in Figure 2.43. When you release the mouse, the box will automatically constrict to just the around the pupil and fix the red eye (see Figure 2.44).

4. If the entire area of red is not fixed, you can adjust the Pupil Size slider to reduce more of the red.

5. If the pupil is not as dark as you would like, increase the Darken slider.

6. Repeat for the other eye.

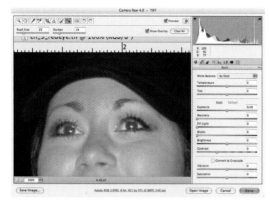 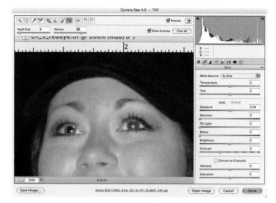

FIGURE 2.43   Drawing around the area to fix.   **FIGURE 2.44**   The Red Eye removed.

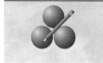

TUTORIAL 2.5   WHITE BALANCE TOOL

This was probably my favorite addition to the Raw Converter in CS2. This makes getting the correct color balance in an image a snap!

1. Open an image that has some area that should be neutral white, black, or gray in the image. A gray or white card will do nicely. Whenever I am in a scene where I think the color of the light is off, I throw my gray card in the scene for one exposure so I can make use of this tool.
2. Click on the White Balance tool as shown in Figure 2.45.

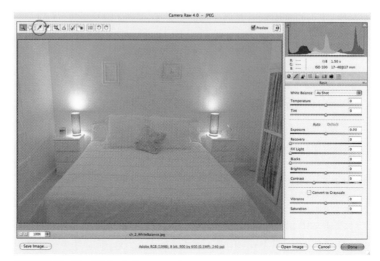

FIGURE 2.45   The White Balance tool.

3. Click on the neutral white, black, or gray in your image. That's it! The Raw Converter completely balances that tone (see Figure 2.46).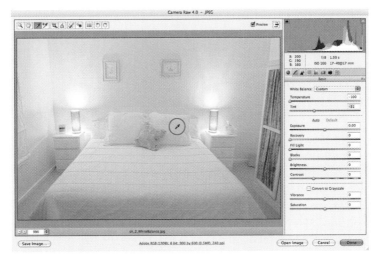

FIGURE 2.46   The corrected image.

Output from Camera Raw

Once you are finished with all your image processing in Camera Raw, it's time to decide what to do next. You have several choices. All of your options for output are in the Output/Workflow section of the Camera Raw box. This section is outlined in red in Figure 2.47.

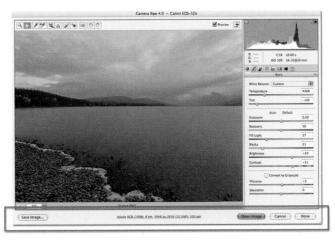

FIGURE 2.47   The Output/Workflow section of Camera Raw.

To access the Color Space, Bit Depth, Size and Resolution, click on the blue underlined link at the bottom center of the box. The dialog box in Figure 2.48 will appear.

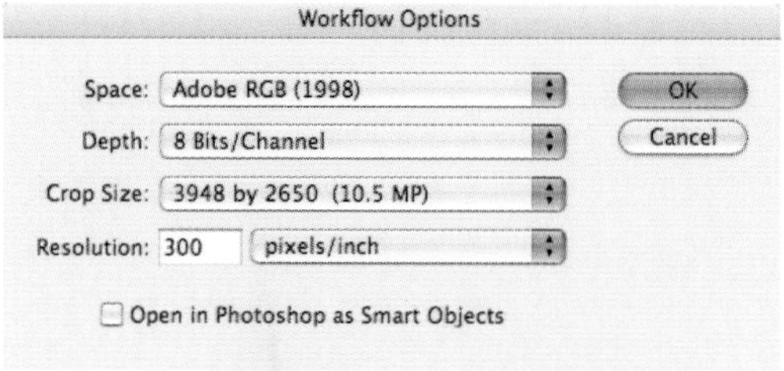

FIGURE 2.48 The Workflow Options dialog box.

Generally, it's a good idea to use Adobe RGB as the colorspace because this will produce predictable colors when we decide to print later.

Choose either 8-bit or 16-bit channels. If further image correction will be done in Photoshop, 16-bit is a good option to use. If the corrections will be minor, 8-bit is fine.

The Crop Size menu allows you to change the size of the image; however, I usually leave this at the default setting. Chapter 8 goes into depth on how to enlarge and shrink images.

The Resolution box is a convenience item. It has no bearing on the quality of the image. Leave this set at 300 ppi unless you have an Epson printer, in which case, you can change this to 360 ppi.

Finally, choose one of four options to process the image.

Save: Choosing this option allows you to save a duplicate of the working image in either the regular formats or create a new Raw file in the DNG format as shown in Figure 2.49.

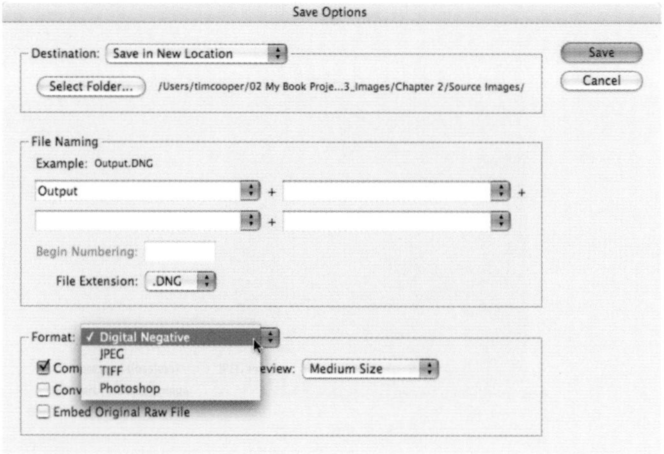

FIGURE 2.49 Saving a DNG file.

Open: This launches the image into Photoshop with your adjustments and settings applied.

Cancel: This option closes the Camera Raw window and discards any adjustments.

Done: This closes the Camera Raw dialog box and writes the settings to the Raw file's sidecar XMP file. (These settings will remain with the image the next time it's opened.)

WORKING WITH MULTIPLE RAW IMAGES

A huge time saver for the Raw photographer is the opportunity to work with multiple images simultaneously. You can now view multiple Raw images in the Raw dialog box and share various settings across images. This allows you to process multiple images very quickly.

1. Choose several images from Bridge. To select multiple images, hold down the Alt/Option key, and click on the desired Raw thumbnails. To remove a thumbnail from the selection, click on it again while still holding down the Alt/Option key.
2. Either double-click on one of the selected thumbnails, or right-click and choose Open in Camera Raw.
3. You will now see the Camera Raw dialog box with a filmstrip on the left containing all the selected Raw files. Figure 2.50 shows multiple Raw files. To view any of the files, click on the thumbnail, and it will appear in the main Raw window.

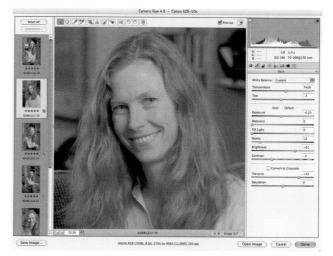

FIGURE 2.50   Opening multiple images in Camera Raw.

4. Make the desired adjustments to the image. When only one file is selected, the changes you make occur to that file only. Here I will choose the file with

the gray card in it to adjust the color with the White Balance tool (see Figure 2.51).

5. To apply your changes to all of the files, choose Select All at the top left of the Raw dialog box. All the images are now selected, as shown in Figure 2.52.

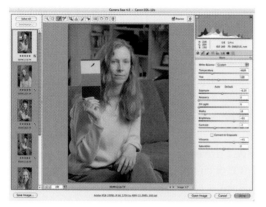

FIGURE 2.51 Correcting color with the White Balance tool.

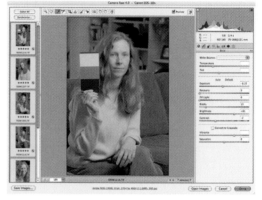

FIGURE 2.52 Multiple images selected in Camera Raw.

6. Click the Synchronize button.

7. The Synchronize dialog box opens. Either accept the defaults to copy all the settings of the current image to all the images in the filmstrip, or choose individual parameters. You can save time and choose subsets from the drop-down menu. Figure 2.53 shows the Synchronize dialog box.

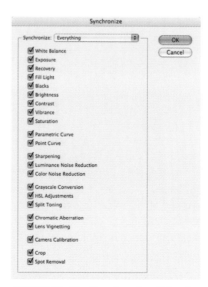

FIGURE 2.53 The Synchronize dialog box.

8. All the settings have been transferred over to the other Raw files as shown in Figure 2.54. You can either click Done to save the settings and not open any images, or choose the images you want to launch in Photoshop, and then choose Open. Note: You may want to do a little fine-tuning of each image in Camera Raw before saving or opening.

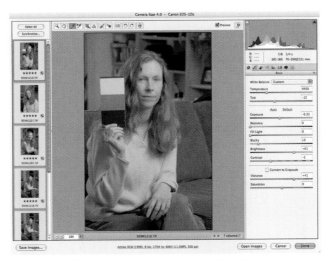

FIGURE 2.54   Sharing the settings across multiple images.

Batch Processing in Bridge

You can also process multiple images without having to open them up in the Raw Converter. Someday you may have hundreds of images all from the same shoot that you need to batch process.

1. Open one of the images into Camera Raw.
2. Adjust the file to suit your needs.
3. Click the Done Button.
4. When you return to Bridge, select all of the images to which you want to apply those settings.
5. Once they are all selected, right-click on any of one of the images, and choose Develop Settings > Previous Conversion. You can watch as the Bridge updates all of your files to the new settings.
6. After your files are updated, you will notice that Bridge displays a small icon next to any modified Raw files. This icon tells you that you are not looking at the default settings but, rather, a modified file.

A great thing about this method is that it can be performed from Bridge—you don't even have to launch Photoshop. This is a good method to speed up your work-flow and save time by getting a good starting point on each image. If you're doing a studio shoot, the settings will work pretty well for all the pictures under the same lighting configuration. If you change the position of the lights or model, you may have to modify the settings for the new configuration.

Remember that these settings are only applied to the sidecar XMP file by default (or database, depending on how you have set Camera Raw Preferences in Bridge). At any time, you can right-click on the thumbnail and choose Clear Camera Raw Settings. This will reset the image to the settings on the camera at the time you captured the image.

 A less glitzy feature that has been added into these tabs is the ability to reset just the sliders within an individual box. Double-clicking on the slider itself after making an adjustment will return it to its default position. This is a great alternative to resetting the whole image.

SUMMARY

You learned about the advantages of shooting in the Raw format and how to produce better-looking images from your initial captures. Keep in mind a couple of disadvantages of Raw. The biggest is that you still have to process the images on your computer before they can be used. The other big drawback is that it's not quite as easy to share the images with someone else until you have processed them. Once you get comfortable with the process, you will find that the extra effort is well worth the advantages of working in Raw. If your camera does not support Raw, the Raw Converter will now work with JPEGs and TIFFs as well. If after reading this chapter you are a little confused with some of the terminology or principles, don't worry. These principles are explained in much more detail in the following chapters.

II

ENHANCEMENT

CROPPING AND PERSPECTIVE

In This Chapter

- Lens Correction Filter
- Creative Cropping
- Cropping for Perception
- Straightening
- Increasing the Canvas size
- The lens Correction Filter

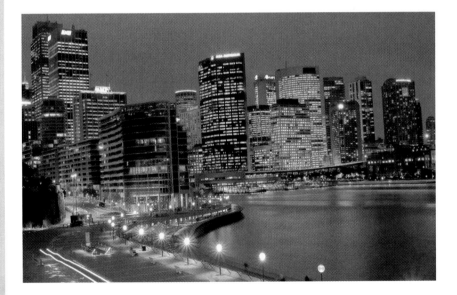

Cropping an image is one of those steps that can be performed at any point in your workflow. While some photographers choose to crop right away, others may wait until the printing stage to crop an image. There are advantages and disadvantages to both methods. This chapter will cover when and how to use the Crop tool, in addition to teaching you how to crop your images for maximum impact. We will wrap up this chapter with a powerful tool called the Lens Correction Filter. This tool, introduced in the previous version of Photoshop, can be a photographer's best friend. You will see how easy it is to now fix warped, distorted, and otherwise out-of-perspective images.

Why Crop?

Generally, there are two reasons for cropping an image. The first reason is to enhance the look of the image. This could mean cropping out unwanted sections or objects in your photograph or simply cropping in more tightly to heighten the impact of the main subject. The second reason to crop is to match the proportions of your photograph to a particular size requirement, such as printing paper or mat board.

In the case of enhancing the look of the image, try cropping right away. This not only makes your file size smaller and easier to work with, but it also allows you to make creative judgments based on the elements that remain in your image. Your eye will not be influenced by extraneous subject matter. If, however, the final print proportion is more important to you, you should consider waiting until the printing stage to crop. Take a portrait for example. You may be asked to make a 4" × 6", a 5" × 7", and an 8" × 10" print of this image. Each one of those will need to be cropped to different proportions. In this case, cropping is better left to later to accommodate all possibilities.

Creative Cropping

Let's take a look at ways to enhance the impact of your image by using the Crop tool.

Changing Composition and Emphasis

When you crop an image, essentially you are taking out digital scissors and cutting away the unwanted parts of an image until you are left with the perfect composition. This is a great way to draw attention to a certain part of an image and create a mood. It also works well for zooming in on a photograph. It is always better to crop within Photoshop than to resort to using a camera's digital zoom. For example, the picture in Figure 3.1 shows an image taken in South Carolina using a 200 mm lens, the longest we had. A longer lens would have made the photograph seem a touch more intimate as well as cropping out some unwanted elements on the bottom right. The cropped image in Figure 3.2 shows more of an emphasis on the canoe and tree canopy and less on the distracting foreground elements in the river.

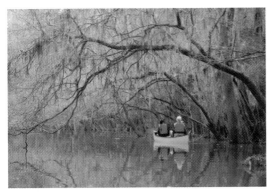

FIGURE 3.1   The uncropped image: the canoe is too small and other elements creep into the frame.

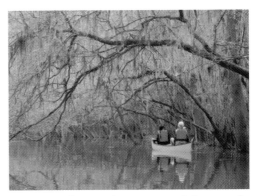

FIGURE 3.2   The same image cropped: the canoe is now emphasized.

To crop an image:

1. Choose the Crop tool from the toolbar.
2. Click, hold, and drag diagonally across the image to produce a square/rectangle shape made up of marching ants. This box defines the part of the photo that will remain after the crop.
3. After you draw out your crop, you have a few options that you can set from the top menu bar, starting with Cropped Area, Delete, or Hide options (see Figure 3.3).

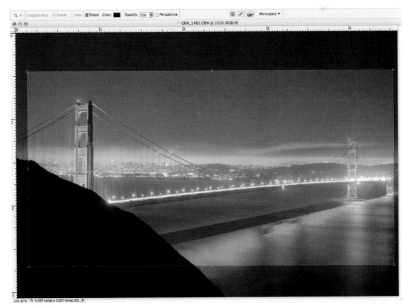

FIGURE 3.3   The Crop tool options.

a. If you choose Delete, your image will be cropped, and all the "trimmed fat" will be tossed away. This is the most common option. This is a permanent step, however, so be sure to work on a copy of your original.

b. If you choose Hide, the image will be cropped, but no image information will be lost. The image will still be there, and only the canvas will be reduced. You can get back the detail again by increasing the canvas size. (This is the best option if you are "comping" a layout and may want to change things later.)

4. The Shield options are next and are also shown in Figure 3.3.

a. By default, the Shield option is checked, the Color is black, and the Opacity is 75%. The Shield darkens the part of the image that will be removed when you apply the crop. Having the shield on makes it easier to judge composition.

b. Click once on the Color box to choose your shield color.

c. The Opacity slider determines how transparent the shield will be. Adjust this to suit your tastes.

5. When you are happy with your composition and settings, apply the crop by clicking the check mark on the right side of the toolbar, by pressing the Enter key (Return key for Mac), or by double-clicking anywhere inside the cropping area.

Cropping Out Unwanted Detail

Pictures of people often beg to be cropped. This is especially true if you are putting your images online and want to keep them as small as possible or when you have limited space in a print piece. You see a lot of pictures that have unneeded detail and extreme headroom, as in Figure 3.4, that take up valuable space and force the faces to be so small that you cannot recognize the people. If you are smiling right now, you have probably faced this same frustration. Let's emphasize the facial expression, which will communicate more through your work than needless background elements will.

Of course, there are times for a more creative shot with lots of interesting background detail, but this is not one of those times. Don't be afraid to be bold and ruthless. There is no law that says that you cannot crop the subject as we did in Figure 3.5. Notice how it draws us more into the picture and gives a better sense of expression; the viewer is more involved and not just a casual observer.

Cropping for Perception

In the old movie westerns, the prop builders built the doors smaller to make the men appear large and intimidating. In contrast, the doorways the women used were made larger so the women would appear daintier. This is all about perception.

Another reason to crop an image is to change the perception. A classic example is the tall building. Figure 3.6 shows a typical snapshot of a tall building. By trimming out the sides and making the canvas narrower, we are putting more emphasis on the vertical aspect of the image. We are adding emphasis to the fact that the building is

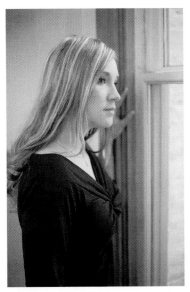

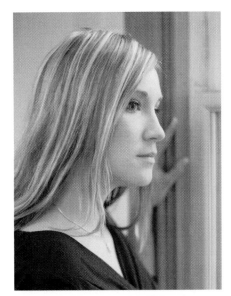

FIGURE 3.4   The image uncropped—
nice picture, but a bit distant.

FIGURE 3.5   Cropped for emphasis, the
picture draws the viewer into the picture.

tall and exaggerating that aspect of the picture. Notice that the picture looks more
natural in Figure 3.7.

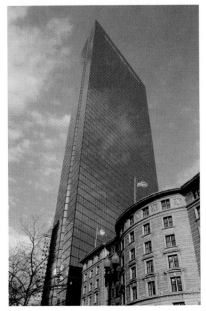

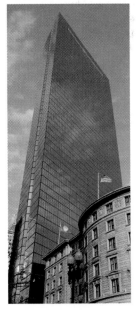

FIGURE 3.6   A tall building in a typical
snapshot.

FIGURE 3.7   The same building with an emphasis
on the vertical aspect, just by cropping the image.

Practical Cropping

In addition to creative cropping purposes, there are also some practical reasons to crop images and some really useful things you can do with the Crop tool.

 When you have many active layers in your image, the file size begins to get very large and causes your computer to slow down. Even if parts of an image are off the screen, they still count toward image size. By selecting your entire image and cropping, you can sometimes greatly reduce the file size.

Straightening

Often, a handheld photo wasn't taken quite straight and is a bit tilted. This can also happen when scanning. Put a super-smooth picture onto a super-smooth glass plate and add a bit of warmth from the bulb to create a dry environment, and you have a recipe for a super-slippery top. Trying to keep the image perfectly straight while carefully closing the lid will qualify you to perform in a circus. Remember that you will lose some image around the edges when cropping, so you should always be as careful as possible when shooting and scanning.

Having said that, you will be well familiar with a crooked picture such as that in Figure 3.8.

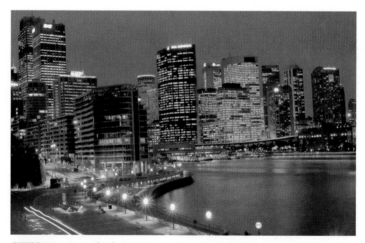

FIGURE 3.8   A crooked picture.

Let's straighten things up a bit:

1. Draw a rough marquee with the Crop tool. Grab the resizing handles, and fill most of the image area with the bounding box.
2. Move the mouse outside the box at a corner. You will notice that the pointer has turned into a curved arrow, which indicates that you are about to rotate the image. Begin to rotate the selection until it is at the desired angle.

Move the selection edge until it lines up with a vertical edge that can be used as a visual guide as we did with the edge of the building in Figure 3.9.

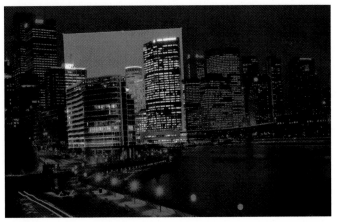

FIGURE 3.9   Use vertical objects as guides and rotate the crop selection.

3. After you have everything lined up, click and drag the side handle and stretch the crop selection to the edge of the image as shown in Figure 3.10. Make sure the selection border doesn't run off the image.

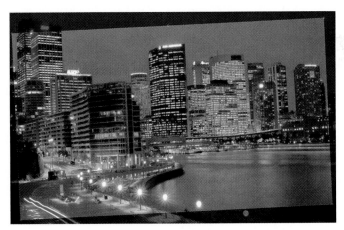

FIGURE 3.10   The crop ready to be applied.

4. Now that everything is ready to go, apply the selection by double-clicking with the mouse anywhere within the selection area.

You will now have a nicely straightened image, as shown in Figure 3.11.

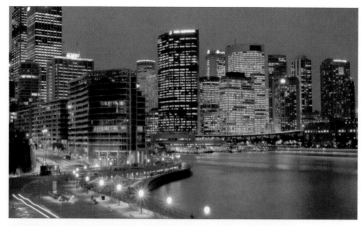

FIGURE 3.11   The straightened image.

There is also another way to straighten images that is a bit quicker:

1. Choose the Measure tool from the Tool Palette (it's hiding under the Eye-dropper).
2. Click and drag along one of the sides of the image. You are selecting your desired horizon in this step.
3. Choose Image > Rotate Canvas > Arbitrary.
4. The Rotate Canvas box will open with the correct angle and proper rotation already revealed.
5. Click OK, and your image will be straightened.

Auto Cropping (Crop and Straighten Photos)

To save time while scanning multiple images, several images are placed on the scanner surface at once and then scanned together (see Figure 3.12). When you want to use these images later, you have to copy each image to a new document, straighten, and crop them individually. All this can become very time consuming—remembering my magazine days, I say *very* time consuming, not to mention tedious and boring!

If you have been a "scanner monkey," we have some exciting news for you. Photoshop CS3 is equipped with a one-click Crop and Straighten Photos command. The software looks at an image similar to Figure 3.12 and can detect the white space around the photos. It approximates the picture edges, straightens them, lifts them off the document, and places each picture into its own document. Sounds like science fiction? Try it; it really works.

It's as simple as opening a picture and clicking File > Automate > Crop and Straighten Photos, as seen in Figure 3.13.

Now just sit back and relax, or go grab a cup of coffee. In a few moments, your images will all be processed automatically, as shown in Figure 3.14. You have to get excited about this feature because it's so easy and saves so much time. What's more, the original is left intact.

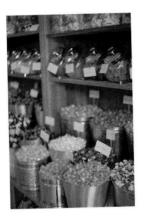

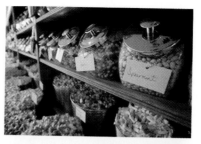

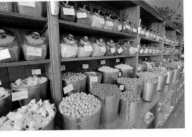

Batch...
PDF Presentation...
Create Droplet...

Crop and Straighten Photos

Contact Sheet II...

Picture Package...

Conditional Mode Change...
Fit Image...
Merge to HDR...
Photomerge...

FIGURE 3.13   Launching the Crop and Straighten Photos feature.

FIGURE 3.12   Multiple images scanned at once.

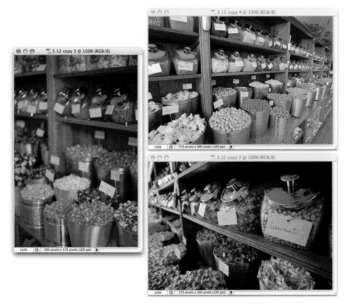

FIGURE 3.14   The images all processed automatically.

Increasing the Canvas Size with the Crop Tool

Let's explore one of the weirdest but very useful features of the Crop tool. Have you ever heard of a Crop tool that makes the image bigger? The Crop tool in Photoshop will crop to whatever it has selected and that includes off the canvas!

1. Open an image and apply the Crop tool to fill the entire document.
2. Zoom out a bit so that you can see some of the canvas area around the image.
3. Drag the Crop tool past the image and onto the canvas, as seen in Figure 3.15.

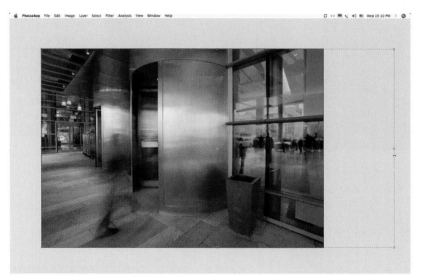

FIGURE 3.15   Dragging the Crop tool into the canvas.

4. Apply the crop, and the canvas is extended to fit the crop size. This is just the thing we need to add a bit of space and make a ticket out of our picture. We added just a bit of text to the final image to show an example of how you can use this effect in the real world (see Figure 3.16).

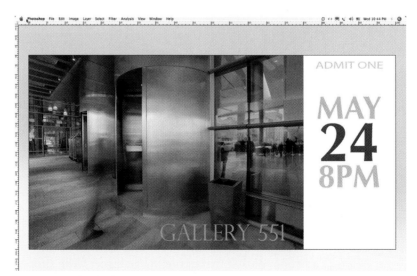

FIGURE 3.16   The final cropped image.

Perspective

Perspective is quite literally the way we see things. When an object moves away from us, it appears to shrink in size. We all know that the size does not really change—it just appears that way. For instance, look at a long fence: as it winds off into the distance, the posts appear to grow smaller and to come closer together. When you look up at a tall building, you notice perspective as the top seems to get narrower. Perspective is essential to making an image appear realistic.

Removing Perspective

The problem is that the camera lens and the angle of the camera can exaggerate perspective, causing areas of the subject to look out of proportion. There are a couple of easy ways to fix this problem in Photoshop.

ON THE CD

1. Open the Doorway image from the CD-ROM, as shown in Figure 3.17.

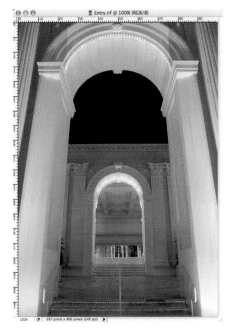

FIGURE 3.17   The image with an exaggerated perspective.

2. Notice that the image seems to be smaller at the top than on the bottom because the image was shot from a low angle, and a fairly wide-angle lens was used to compose the original shot. If speed is more important than accuracy, the following method is the right choice.
3. Choose the Crop tool, and check the Perspective button on the top toolbar, as shown in Figure 3.18. This option enables you to transform the corners freely.

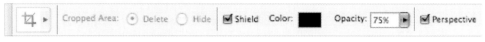

FIGURE 3.18 The Perspective button.

4. Drag the corners toward the center to compensate for the perspective. Figure 3.19 shows the perspective crop in place. Don't overdo it; you will want to leave some perspective or the image will look like the top is larger than the bottom. Remember that perspective is natural.
5. Apply the transformation (Crop) and the image changes to the shape of the cropped area. Notice in Figure 3.20 that the picture still looks natural, but the perspective is more realistic.

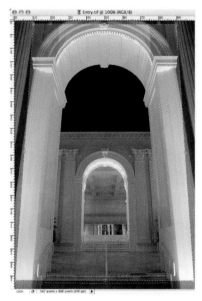

FIGURE 3.19 The Perspective Crop option in use.

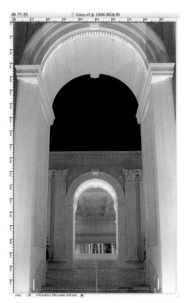

FIGURE 3.20 The final corrected image.

You also can straighten and creatively crop the image at the same time.

LENS CORRECTION FILTER

Using the Crop tool to correct perspective is a quick way to get the job done. If you need a higher level of accuracy however, the Lens Correction Filter is the best tool for the job. By using this tool, all manner of distortion can now be removed. There are also two not-so-obvious features in this tool. If you read Chapter 2, you saw how you can fix Chromatic Aberration and Lens Vignette in Camera Raw (See Chapter 2 for more information on Chromatic Aberration and Lens Vignette.) Perhaps you asked yourself the question, "What if my image isn't in Raw Converter?" Keep in mind that with Photoshop CS3, all images, whether Raw or JPEG, can now be opened into the Raw converter. Now all of the same easy adjustments that the Raw converter affords are available to any type of photographic file, including TIFF and PSDs!

The Lens Correction filter can fix the following:

Distortion: Lens distortion that appears with very wide or long lenses.
Straightening: Tilting a crooked image.
Chromatic Aberration: Colored fringe around an object in a photo.
Lens Vignette: Where the edges of an image are darker or brighter than the center.
Perspective: Exaggerated effect of an object appearing smaller as it gets further away; also called keystoning in photography.

Let's repair an image that suffers from perspective problems. We used a wide-angle lens (24 mm) for this shot of a church. Because of the wide-angle lens and the fact that the photographer is looking up, the perspective is exaggerated. Notice how the top of the church seems to be leaning in. Our goal is to remove some of the perspective effect. We don't want to completely remove it, or the image will look unnatural.

ON THE CD

The image LeaningChurch (see Figure 3.21) is provided on the CD-ROM for your reference.

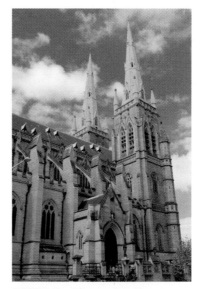

FIGURE 3.21   The starting image.

1. Choose Filter > Distort > Lens Correction. You will now see the Lens Correction dialog box.

2. Adjust the Vertical Perspective slider to compensate for the way the towers are leaning in, as shown in Figure 3.22. Look at the grid to line things up. Remember to keep a little perspective. You can show or hide the grid by checking the Show Grid box at the bottom of the page.

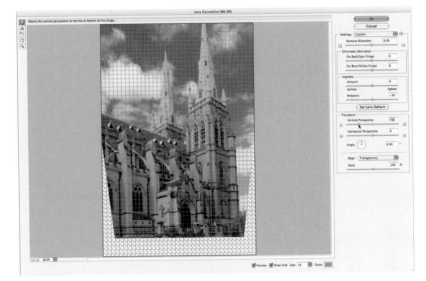

FIGURE 3.22 Fixing the vertical perspective.

3. Adjust the Horizontal Perspective slider as shown in Figure 3.23. This helps compensate for the horizontal perspective.

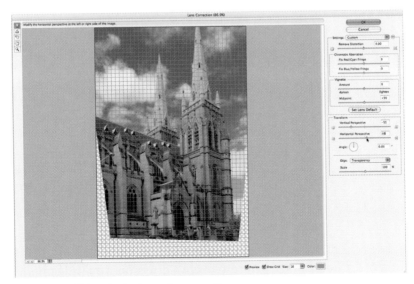

FIGURE 3.23 Fixing the horizontal perspective.

The forced perspective has now been fixed but not without a cost. Notice that there is a gap in some of the corners and that the top of the tower has been cutoff. For this reason, it is a good idea to give an image a little more space during the initial composition when you know you will be using this filter. To rid the image of the blank canvas (the gray and white checkerboard), first apply the filter and then crop the image as you usually would.

Another way is to increase the size of the image in the filter until it fills the window. This is a good option if you are working on an image that needs to remain the original size. Drag the Scale slider as shown in Figure 3.24.

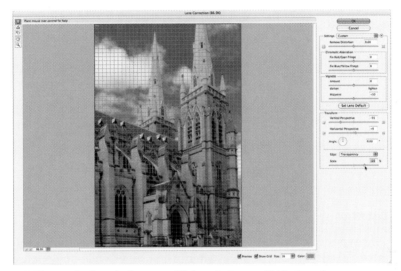

FIGURE 3.24   Scaling the image to fill the window and hide the edges.

Another way to deal with the edge is to choose Edge Extension from the Edge drop-down menu as shown in Figure 3.25. This is only a good option when the edges are a solid color or continuous pattern. This will stretch the edge pixels to fill the canvas. Figure 3.26 shows the final image after fixing horizontal and vertical perspective and using the Scale slider to fill the canvas.

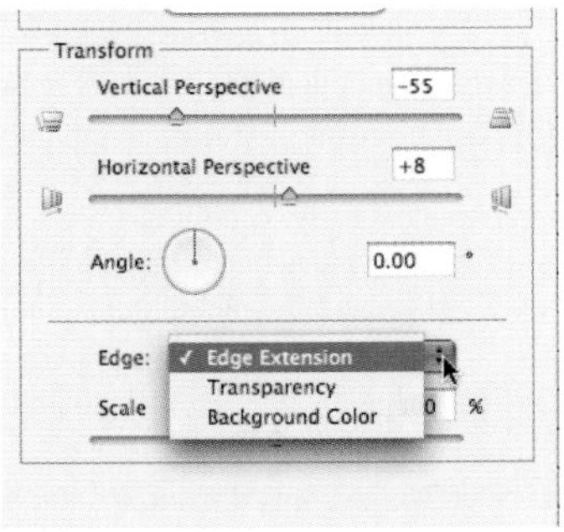

FIGURE 3.25   The Edge Extension option.

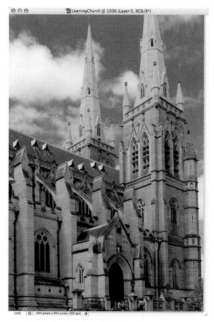

FIGURE 3.26   The final image.

Distortion

Two types of common image distortion are associated with wide and long lenses. Barrel distortion can be seen when using super wide-angle lenses, and pincushion distortion can appear when using telephoto lenses. The Lens Correction Filter in Photoshop easily fixes both of these problems.

ON THE CD

1. Open BarrelDistortion.jpg from the CD-ROM (see Figure 3.27) or use one of your own images.

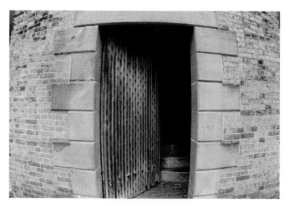

FIGURE 3.27   The original image showing barrel distortion.

2. Open the image in Lens Correction Filter > Distort > Lens Correction.
3. Adjust the distortion in one of two ways.
   a. Move the Remove Distortion slider to the right.
   b. Click the top left icon (shown in Figure 3.28), and then click and drag in the image. You will notice as you drag through the image that it bloats (fatter) and pinches (thinner).

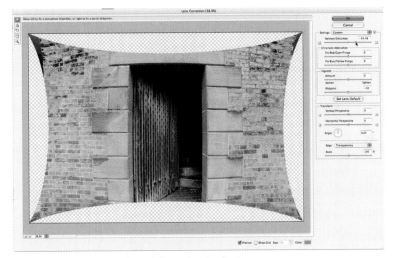

FIGURE 3.28   Fixing the barrel distortion in the image.

4. In this same manner, you can fix an image that suffers from pincushion distortion. In Figure 3.29 a familiar church was photographed using a longer lens. The stairs at the bottom show a slight amount of bowing inward toward the center of the photograph. By moving the Remove Distortion slider to the left, you will begin to "bloat" the image, which will remove the pincushion distortion as seen in Figure 3.30.

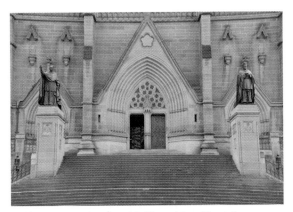

FIGURE 3.29   An image with Pincushion Distortion.

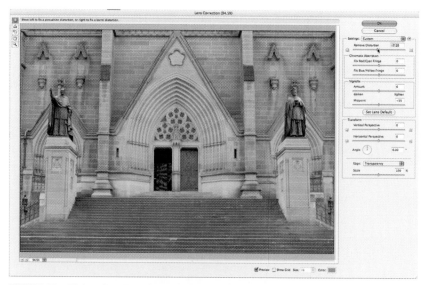

FIGURE 3.30   Fixing the pincushion distortion in the image.

Straightening an Image

Fixing a crooked horizon or building in the Lens Correction Filter is quite simple. It works in the same manner as the Straightening tool in the Camera Raw converter. Simply click on the Straighten icon in the upper-left toolbar, and draw out a line along whatever element within the photograph that you wish to have straight. Figure 3.31 shows a photograph taken at the beach. The horizon line of the ocean is visibly askew.

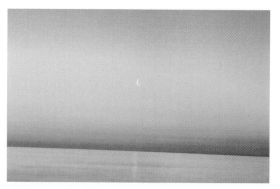

FIGURE 3.31   An image with a tilted horizon.

To straighten the horizon, open the Lens Correction Filter:

1. Click on the Straighten tool (second down from the top).

2. Locate an element in your image that should be straight. In this case, it is the ocean horizon.

3. Click on one end of the element and draw a line along it. When you release your click, you will see the image automatically straighten out (see Figure 3.32). If the image still seems a little off, simply redraw your line. You can continue drawing until you get it right. Look to the grid to assist you in your final assessment.

4. Use the Scale slider to enlarge (crop) your image and remove the blank canvas. Figure 3.33 shows the final image after straightening and scaling to crop your image.

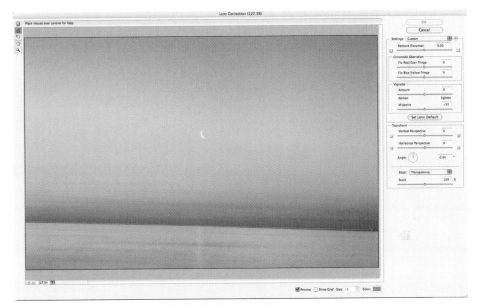

FIGURE 3.32   Drawing the line with the Straighten tool.

FIGURE 3.33   The image after fixing the tilting ocean.

Adding Perspective

Correcting images is the main goal of the Lens Correction Filter, but that doesn't mean you can't use it to enhance the look of an image! The Lens Correction Filter is equally adept at adding or removing perspective. This is really useful when you want to add the perception of more distance, and you can even make it appear as if the viewer has changed viewing positions. In this example, it will look like we have moved closer to the subject and used a wide-angle lens. Figure 3.34 shows the original image with no perspective.

1. Open `AddPerspective.jpg` from the CD-ROM, or use one of your own images.
2. Open the image in Lens Correction Filter > Distort > Lens Correction.
3. Adjust the barrel distortion by moving the slider to the left.
4. Adjust the vertical perspective by moving the slider to the left (see Figure 3.35).
5. When satisfied with the adjustments, click OK and crop the image.

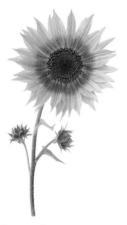

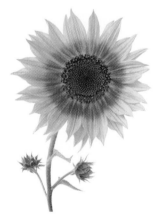

FIGURE 3.34   The original image.

FIGURE 3.35   The image after adding in vertical perspective and barrel distortion.

When working with the Lens Correction Filter, the toolbar shown in Figure 3.36 and the options shown in Figure 3.37 can really make using this filter quite a bit easier. Following are a few hints on working with the Lens Correction Filter:

- When you hover your mouse over a tool, a description of its use and directions appear in the pane above and to the right.
- Click on the Size box at the bottom of the panel to change the size of your grid.
- If you want to move the grid around so that it lines up with certain vertical or horizontal aspects of your image, click on the Move Grid tool, and simply drag your grid around.
- Double-click on the Color box at the bottom to choose a new color for the grid.
- When checked, the Preview box shows the image as it will appear with your current settings. Unchecking this box shows you the before version.

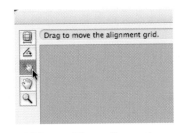

FIGURE 3.36   The toolbar at the upper left of the Lens Correction Filter pane.

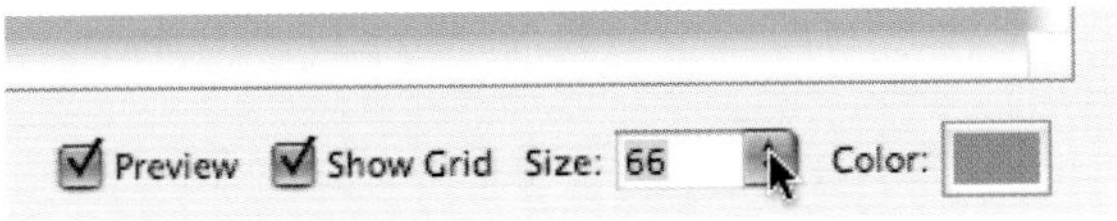

FIGURE 3.37   The options at the lower center of the Lens Correction Filter pane.

- Double-clicking on the Magnifying Glass icon shows you the image at Actual Pixels, and double-clicking on the Hand tool fits the image onscreen.

SUMMARY

This wraps up this chapter on cropping. You learned a lot about the Crop tool and its many functions. You discovered that the Crop tool has a number of hidden uses and is a lot more than just a way to trim images. We also covered one of my favorite tools: the Lens Correction Filter. Used for both correcting and enhancing perspective, this tool will save you a lot of time when trying to correct your images. Remember, though, Photoshop is about more than just correcting. Don't forget to play and be creative!

TONAL CORRECTION AND ENHANCEMENT

In This Chapter

- Tonal Correction and Enhancement
- The Anatomy of a Color Picture
- Histograms
- Brightness/Contrast
- Shadow/Highlight
- Levels
- Exposure
- Auto Settings
- Getting Good Results from the Auto Settings
- Curves

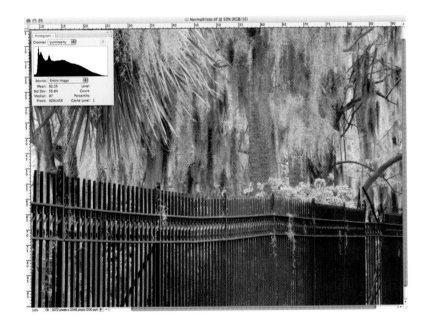

In this chapter, we will discuss the tools to correct and enhance the overall brightness, contrast, and image tone in photographs. We will get to all the nitty gritty of adjusting and correcting images soon. First, there is something important that needs to be pointed out. One of the greatest things about using Photoshop is the ability to work on a photograph without being stuck with the final result. This is called *nondestructive editing*. Today you may feel that image needs more contrast, but when you revisit the image tomorrow, you may change your mind and decide to reduce the amount of contrast. This measure of control is achieved through the use of adjustment layers. *Adjustment layers* are wonderful because the settings are never set in stone. Adjustments to an image can be made in one of two ways. The first way is to access them through the Image > Adjustments menu. The second way is to access them through the Layers > New Adjustment Layers menu. Adjustment layers provide mostly the same adjustments and functionality as the Image > Adjust method, but you make the changes to a special adjustment layer, which can be changed at any time. This difference produces several advantages:

- The original image is left untouched, thus preserving it. You aren't changing any pixels, just the adjustments on the adjustment layer.
- Adjustment layers add nothing to the file size. (Unless you paint on a mask.)
- You can use multiple adjustments of the same filter for precise results.
- Adjustments can be combined with Layer Blending modes.
- If you change your mind later, it is easy to make modifications. Even after you have closed and reopened the file, the adjustments remain editable.
- If you don't like the results, you can delete the adjustment layers, and your original image is unaffected.

As you can see in Figure 4.1a, you can make multiple adjustments on a single image. You can even have multiple instances of the same type of adjustment. For example, you could have three level adjustments, five curves, and two color balances in the same image.

Figure 4.1b shows the anatomy of an adjustment layer. It is made up of both an adjustment and a mask. Clicking the eyeball on and off will turn the adjustment

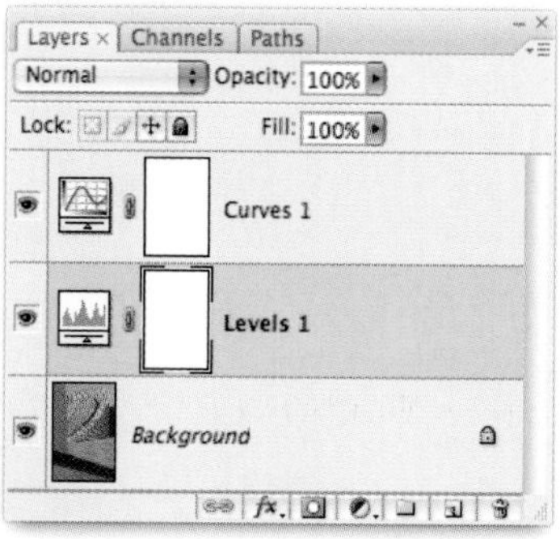

FIGURE 4.1A   Two adjustment layers in the Layers Palette.

layer on and off. If the eyeball is off when printing, the effect of that layer will not print. Double-clicking on the Adjustment icon will reopen that particular adjustment for further tweaking. The mask is automatically created with the adjustment layer. This will be of great value when you want to apply adjustments to small areas rather than the whole image. Selections, masks, and local corrections will be covered in depth in Chapter 6, "Local Enhancements: Selections and Masks."

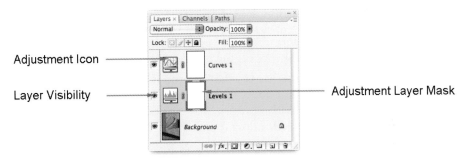

Adjustment Icon

Layer Visibility

Adjustment Layer Mask

FIGURE 4.1B Anatomy of an adjustment layer.

Using Adjustment Layers

Creating new adjustment layers is easy:

1. Choose Layer > New Adjustment Layer, or click on the Adjustment Layer icon (half black/half white circle) in the bottom of the Layers Palette, as shown in Figure 4.1c.

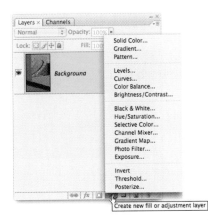

FIGURE 4.1C Creating a new adjustment layer.

2. The Adjustments dialog box opens.
3. Make your adjustments.
4. Click OK.

Adjustment layers are saved with the file, so even after you close an image, you can always reopen it and make further adjustments at any time. Again, to change the settings in an adjustment layer, double-click on its icon in the Layers Palette, and the dialog box will open.

TONAL CORRECTION AND ENHANCEMENT

We live in the real world, and no matter how hard we try, all of our shots are not perfect. Sometimes unexpected results creep into our images, or we see ways they could be improved.

This chapter deals with understanding what is going on behind the scenes with your image and fixing images that are too dark, too light, or lacking contrast. You might have a great shot but want to emphasize the detail in a different section of the image. This chapter will show you how to bring out the hidden detail in almost any image. You will also learn how to adjust good pictures and make them even better.

THE ANATOMY OF A COLOR PICTURE

Originally, there was just black-and-white photography. Then a revolution called color appeared on the scene. It seems so long ago now, as we shoot high-resolution digital photos and think nothing of it. There are two basic parts to a color photograph:

- The grayscale tones (black and white) called luminosity
- The color information

Figure 4.2 shows a color photo broken apart. On the left, you see the color information in the picture, and in the middle, you see the luminosity image—combine the two, and you get a color image.

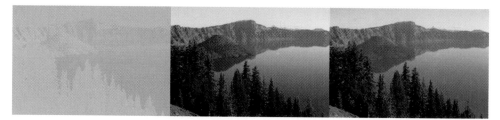

FIGURE 4.2   The color information and grayscale information make a color image.

It's hard to believe that the faded, flat color information refers to the colors used to create the vibrant blues in the lake seen in the photo. But it's true, and you can see for yourself by opening the layered image `color-tone.psd` from the `Chapter 4` folder on the CD-ROM and dragging the color over the grayscale, as shown in Figure 4.3.

This shows the importance of the tones in the grayscale portion of the image. You can see that all the contrast and details come from the grayscale portion of the

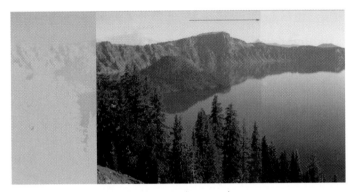

FIGURE 4.3   Combining the color and grayscale.

image and that the color offers none of this detail at all. We will be dealing with the color portion in Chapter 5, "Color Correction and Enhancement," but in this chapter, we will be enhancing the luminosity or grayscale information to improve the appearance of our pictures.

HISTOGRAMS

Histograms are the little mountain-shaped graphs that represent the tonal properties in an image. Tonal properties are the 256 levels of grayscale that give the image its contrast and sharpness. Because 16-bit images contain over 65,000 levels of gray, we will use 8-bit photos for this section for simplicity (the theory is identical for 16-bit). Some digital cameras have histograms in their displays. Histograms are not new or unique to imaging. Scientists have used histogram charts since 1891 for various purposes.

Figure 4.4 shows the histogram you are probably most familiar with. This view is from the Levels Adjustment dialog box which can be reached from the menu by selecting Layer > New Adjustment Layer > Levels.

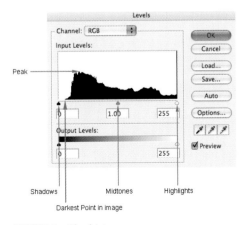

FIGURE 4.4   The histogram.

The following list describes the three regions of the histogram.

Highlights: Whites (255 or 100% brightness).
Midtones: Grays.
Shadows: Blacks (0 brightness).

The histogram is broken into 256 levels of brightness. A setting of 0 means no light at all is present and will be reflected as black. A setting of 255 indicates that this is the highest level of light and will be shown as white. This 256-level scale is used throughout Photoshop. It stops at 255 and not 256 because the counting begins at 0 and not 1.

The histogram shows a visual graph of the image. The shadows are on the left, and the highlights on the right. The horizontal measurement is in brightness from 0–255. The gray bar underneath (below Output Levels) indicates what part of the grayscale you are looking at, as seen at the bottom of Figure 4.4.

The mountain shape represents image data. The top of the mountain is the peak. The peaks show the way pixels are dispersed in the image. Where pixels are present, the peak will be higher. If there are no pixels at a particular level of gray of the image, then a gap will appear in the histogram, indicating no data in that tonal range.

Where the "mountain" part of the graph begins and ends (from right to left) indicates where the pixels lie. In Figure 4.4, you can see a gap at the left of the histogram (marked as the darkest point in the image). This means no image data is in that area. This translates to the image lacking any pure blacks.

Also notice that the highlights are climbing on the right. This is called *clipping*. Clipping is when some of the detail gets cut off on an image because its tones lie outside of the camera's recordable range, for example, blacker than black or whiter than white (these are rendered as black or white without detail). In this case, some highlight detail is being clipped off the image. An image where the flash is too bright and everyone's face is burned out with white is an example of clipping in the highlights.

Figure 4.5a and Figure 4.5b show how tones in a photograph play out on the histogram. In this example, the shadows are number 1, the midtones are number 2, and the highlights are number 3.

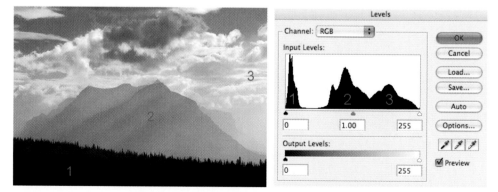

FIGURE 4.5A/B   The three regions of the histogram.

In a nutshell, the graph in a well-balanced image will be low on the two ends. The well-balanced histogram will be just touching the left and right edges. There is no such thing as a perfect graph in the middle of the histogram, as all images will show a different graph. A solid shape is more desirable than a broken shape, where gaps may appear. Gaps are shown by white vertical lines running through the histogram and reaching the bottom. *Gapping* indicates abrupt transitions in color tones, known as *posterization* or, in extreme cases, *banding*. Figures 4.6a and 4.6b show a typical image and its corresponding histogram.

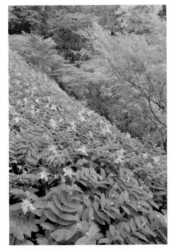

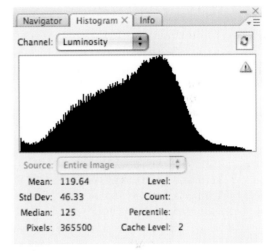

FIGURE 4.6A/B   A well-balanced image with image data throughout.

We will now explore some different histograms. Notice the images in Figures 4.7 to 4.12. These images are exaggerated for the sake of illustration. Studying these images will help you understand how a histogram maps out an image.

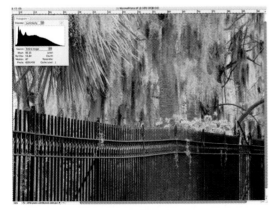

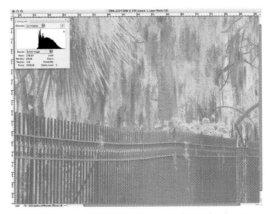

FIGURE 4.7   A well-balanced image.

FIGURE 4.8   A washed out image, lacking shadows.

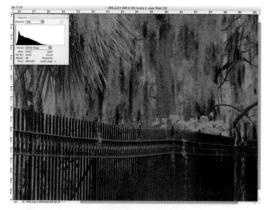

FIGURE 4.9 A dark image, lacking highlights.

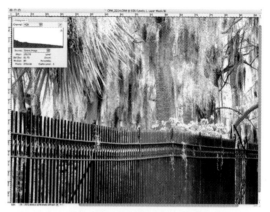

FIGURE 4.10 Too much contrast (image beginning to posterize); notice the presence of gaps in the histogram.

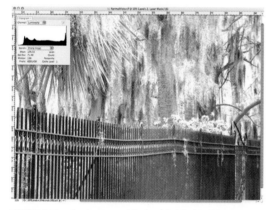

FIGURE 4.11 An image with the highlights blown out. Notice the clipping on the right of the histogram.

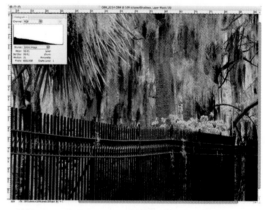

FIGURE 4.12 An image with blocked up shadows. Notice the clipping on the left of the histogram.

The Histogram Palette

In Photoshop CS3, a feature called the *Histogram Palette* allows you to keep a histogram displayed on the desktop at all times so you can see what effect the adjustments are having on images.

To display the Histogram Palette, select Window > Histogram.

Palette Options

You can view the Histogram Palette in several ways. To access the options, click on the down arrow at the top right of the palette, and choose your desired options from the drop-down menu. Figure 4.13 shows the drop-down menu.

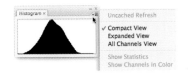

FIGURE 4.13   Compact view with drop-down menu.

The Compact view nests with all the other palettes in Photoshop and stays out of your way while you are working. This offers a visual view of your image with minimum information.

The Expanded view is larger and offers more options than the Compact view and is ideal for most situations. The All Channels view shows you a separate histogram for each channel in the image (see Figure 4.14). If you choose Show Channels in Color, each histogram will be displayed in the host channel's color.

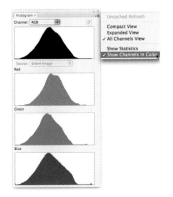

FIGURE 4.14   The Histogram Palette in All Channels view.

Reading the Histogram's Statistics

If you choose the Show Statistics option from the drop-down menu, you will see eight sets of figures in the Histogram Palette, as seen in Figure 4.15.

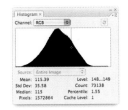

FIGURE 4.15   Sampling the stats.

The four figures on the left show the overall statistics of the image. You may be familiar with some of the terms because they are math terms.

Mean: Remember that there are 256 levels of gray in an image. This shows the average brightness from 0–255 (not 256, because we begin counting from 0 and not 1). An all-black image would show as 0, and an all-white image would show as 255.

Std Dev: Standard Deviation, which measures how the pixel ranges are dispersed in the image.

Median: Often defined as the vertical line that divides the histogram of a frequency distribution into two parts having equal area. We can call it the middle point of the image's grayscale value.

Pixels: The number of pixels present in the image.

The stats on the right-hand side are a bit easier to understand. These are the stats you get by sampling the histogram.

Level: This displays the grayscale level you are currently sampling, from 0–255. It can also show a range if you are sampling more than one level at a time.

Count: The number of actual pixels that fall into the selected range.

Percentile: The percentage of pixels in the selected range compared with the entire image.

Cache Level: How recently your histogram has been refreshed. A cache level of 1 means that your histogram is current. (More on this subject later in this chapter.)

To sample the histogram, click inside the window with the mouse, and you will see a line, as shown previously in Figure 4.15. This line is the brightness range you are currently sampling, from 0–255. You can also sample a range of tones by clicking and dragging with the mouse as shown in Figure 4.16.

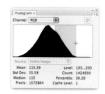

FIGURE 4.16   Viewing stats on a range of tones.

Photoshop will cache (pronounced *cash*) the histogram display in memory. This means that Photoshop remembers the latest settings in memory rather than displaying them in real time. The reason for this is speed. If the histogram wasn't cached, performance could be affected and slow down your computer. On a larger image, more caching will take place, whereas a small image may not be cached at all.

You will need to keep an eye on the Cache Level. When you see a little triangular warning icon in the histogram, this indicates that the view is cached and not current. To update, simply click on the warning icon or the Refresh button if you are in Expanded view, as seen in Figure 4.17.

When you are in the Adjustment Composite and adjusting your image, you will see the histogram change to reflect your adjustments. The original histogram graph will be ghosted (Figure 4.18), so you can compare the adjustments to the original before committing to an adjustment. When you apply your changes, the ghosted histogram will vanish.

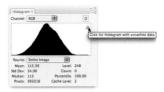

FIGURE 4.17   Refreshing the cache.

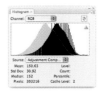

FIGURE 4.18   Original setting is ghosted.

A Word of Warning

In my band days, we were always told that musicians make the best sound people, not the actual sound engineers. Why is that? Because the sound engineers might rely on their readings and instruments too much and forget that music is about actual sound and not just readings and recorded levels. Musicians rely on their ears for the best sound possible and then check the readings to make sure everything is functioning correctly and make a few tweaks if needed. It is the same in the area of imaging; don't be so glued to the histogram that you make all your decisions based on your readings. Use these tools to help; they are incredibly useful, but still you should trust your eye. After all, others will be viewing the images with their eyes and not through histograms.

Enough of all the histogram theory—let's jump in and enhance some images now!

We will be looking at four tools for adjusting the image tones in order of the simplest to the most complex and accurate: Brightness/Contrast, Shadow/Highlight, Levels, and Curves.

BRIGHTNESS/CONTRAST

This is the simplest of the four tools that you can use to adjust the tones of images. Brightness/Contrast is really quick and easy to use. In CS3, this tool has received a welcome makeover. The Brightness/Contrast command now allows you to brighten, darken, and increase and reduce contrast within your images in a much more intelligent way. The previous Brightness/Contrast tool simply shifted all of the pixels up or down when adjusting brightness, which often resulted in a loss of image detail. This is no longer a worry as the new tool applies a proportionate adjustment to the image. Although this command is greatly improved, it is still not as precise as Levels or Curves.

1. Select Layer > New Adjustment Layer > Brightness/Contrast. Figure 4.19 shows the image with the dialog box.

2. Drag the Brightness slider to the left to darken or to the right to brighten. Figure 4.20 shows the brightened image. You will notice that the image is brightened, but it is lacking contrast. That is because the shadows have also been lightened. This loss of contrast is the reason for the second setting in the dialog box.

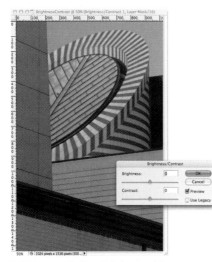

FIGURE 4.19 Before Brightness/Contrast.

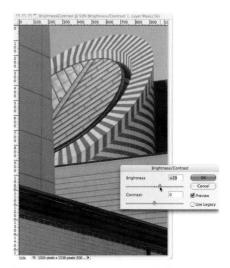

FIGURE 4.20 Brightening up the image.

3. Adjust the contrast to compensate for the brightening.

In Figure 4.21, you can see the image now has much more snap than it did in Figure 4.20. The only drawback to Brightness/Contrast Adjustment is that you cannot control specific areas to work on. The upside is that is easy to use and a great general fix.

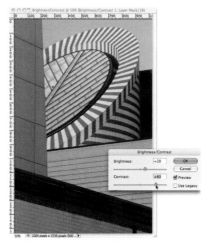

FIGURE 4.21 Increasing the contrast.

SHADOW/HIGHLIGHT

This adjustment has been designed to lighten the shadows and darken the highlights. This allows you to bring back detail that has been somewhat obscured by too much or too little exposure. For example, in a picture that suffers from too much exposure, there is an area that is almost all white, and most of the detail has been lost in this bright area. You can now pinpoint just that tonal area and bring back highlight detail without affecting the rest of the image. The opposite is also true for an image that is too dark and loses all the detail in the shadows. Be aware that there must be *some* image detail captured in the photograph, or there is nothing to bring out.

When you make the changes, you can adjust the range of shadows/highlights you want to modify. For example, you can adjust all the shadows or just the very darkest shadows. Think of this tool as the graphic equalizer for image tone. (If you have a sound background, it's more like a parametric EQ.) A great thing about this tool is that you can target the shadows and brighten them without changing the rest of the image. A great example is when you have taken a picture of a person against a brighter background, and the subject ends up very dark. Using the Shadow/ Highlight filter, you can lighten up the person without changing the background.

The Shadow/Highlight Adjustment does not come as an adjustment layer. If you want the flexibility of an adjustment layer, use it as a Smart Filter. This leaves you free to reinterpret your changes at a later date.

1. Open your file from Photoshop as a Smart Object by choosing File > Open as Smart Object.
2. Select Image > Adjustments > Shadow/Highlight.
3. Click on the Show More Options box, and the dialog box opens to show all the options.

You will see three regions of adjustments: Shadows, Highlights, and Adjustments. The main areas to consider right now are Shadows and Highlights. Each has three sliders as shown in Figure 4.22.

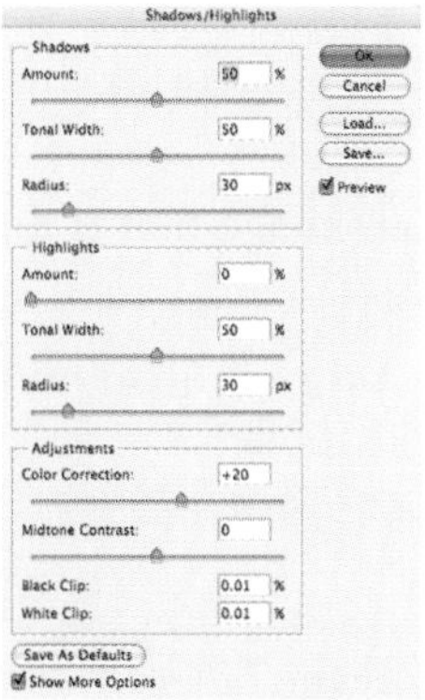

FIGURE 4.22   The Shadow/Highlight Dialog box.

Amount: This determines the strength of the adjustment: 0 has no effect, and 100 has full effect. Adjust this slider to suit your desired results, like the volume knob on your radio.

Tonal Width: This sets the range of tones to be adjusted. A lower setting will affect just the darkest shadows and brightest highlights. A higher setting will affect more of the image, including midtones. Experiment with this slider to encompass just the depth of shadow/highlight you want to adjust.

Radius: This tool does its magic by trying to determine individual objects in the image. By adjusting the radius, you set the distance on the image that Photoshop will affect. The filter averages adjustments based on the target tones compared with the brightness of surrounding pixels. The radius determines how many surrounding pixels will be considered for the adjustment. A lower setting will keep the adjustments more localized, and a larger setting will spread out the contrast more evenly. You really want to keep your eye on this setting to avoid unsightly halos in your image. Halos could be described as the mixing zone where the filter is not completely on or completely off. It generally will show as a slightly lighter area surrounding a darker area. Typically, raising your radius will make the deepest blacks stay darker, which is a desired effect. You want to open up your shadows with this filter but still maintain some deep black in your image to keep it looking realistic. Changing your Black Clip point in the Adjustment section will also help you with this.

The third area has four controls:

Color Correction: Adjusts the saturation of colors.

Midtone Contrast: Allows the contrast of the midtones to be reduced or increased.

Black Clip and **White Clip:** These two settings allow you to stop the filter from affecting the deepest black pixels and brightest white pixels. Adjusting these settings can help you keep the radius lower, thereby avoiding unsightly halos. By default, they are both set to .01. We usually raise the Black Clip to 1 and start raising it from there. Remember, the higher this number, the deeper the blackest black will be. The White Clip works in the same way. By raising this number, you will be forcing the filter to ignore the brightest white pixels. Raising this number will keep the brightest white pixels white.

Figure 4.23 shows an image that is too dark in the foreground, and the detail is lost.

1. Select Image > Adjust > Shadow/Highlight. You can see that the dialog box is open in Simple mode.
2. Click on the Show More Options box, and the dialog box opens to show all the options.
3. Beginning with the shadows, adjust the Tonal Width slider by sliding until you have selected only the range of shadows you want to affect. (Slide the Amount setting up to exaggerate the adjustment so that you can see the range better.)

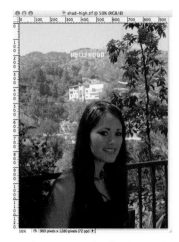

FIGURE 4.23   The image in the foreground is too dark.

4. Adjust the Amount slider until you have brightened up the shadows sufficiently.
5. Do some fine-tuning with the radius until you are happy with the shadow contrast.

Repeat each step for the highlights. If the image appears oversaturated or undersaturated, make some adjustments with the Color Correction setting. If the midtones look like they need some help with contrast (turning gray because of the radius setting), adjust the Midtone Contrast setting.

You now have a corrected image (see Figure 4.24). The woman has been brightened, but the Hollywood sign has been unaffected (unlike with Brightness/Contrast). If you need to make changes in the midtones, consider using Shadow/Highlight first and then using Levels or Curves for more control over the midtones.

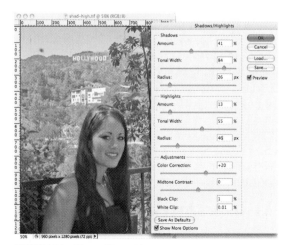

FIGURE 4.24   The adjusted image.

LEVELS

Now that you have learned about histograms, let's use them to make some adjustments. The most hands-on place for using histograms is the Levels Palette. The Levels Palette is really an adjustable histogram. You will notice that there are three triangles under the histogram:

Black Point Input Slider (Shadows): The left triangle is the Black Point Input slider, which sets the black point of the image. Sliding this to the right darkens the shadows. All pixels to the left of the slider will be turned black.

White Point Input Slider (Highlights): The right triangle is the White Point Input slider, which sets the white point. By moving this slider to the left, you will lighten the highlights. The pixels will be turned pure white above this slider, and no pixels will be displayed to the right of it. They will be clipped (turned pure white).

Midtones: The center slider controls the midtones. When you slide this to the left, the grays will brighten, and when you slide it to the right, they will darken.

For more on Levels, refer to Chapter 5, where we set the white, black, and gray points.

Quick Corrections with Levels

Hang on to your hats—this section is going to move very quickly. We are going to fix the most common problems with images: underexposure and overexposure.

Fixing Underexposure

The image in Figure 4.25 looks too dark because it is underexposed. When the image was taken, there was very little light present. Click Layer > New Adjustment Layer > Levels. In the Levels Palette, you will notice that there is no pixel information in the highlight area.

Click and drag the White Point Input slider to the left until you just touch the pixel area, as shown in Figure 4.26. You will notice that the image brightens up. If you see no change, click the Preview check box.

The image is looking much better, but it is still a bit dark in the midtones. Slide the middle slider to the left to brighten up the midtones, as shown in Figure 4.27. Notice how much better the image looks after just two slides of the Levels controls.

Fixing an Image That Is Too Bright

In Figure 4.28, you will notice that the image seems washed out, as if we are looking through mist. Actually, we were looking through some clouds when this picture was taken. The result is a hazy-looking image. It doesn't have enough contrast. We can strengthen the image by bringing back some of the shadows.

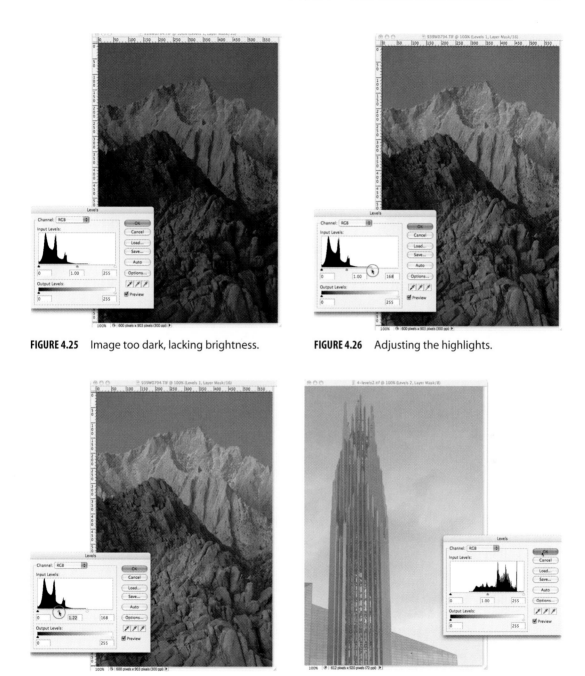

FIGURE 4.25   Image too dark, lacking brightness.

FIGURE 4.26   Adjusting the highlights.

FIGURE 4.27   Adjusting the midtones.

FIGURE 4.28   Image lacking shadows.

1. Open a Levels adjustment layer.
2. Drag the Black Point Input slider just into the "mountain" to the right, as shown in Figure 4.29.

Notice that all the haze has disappeared, and the image is much stronger.

3. In the histogram, you can see that the image is also missing some highlight detail.
4. Slide the White Point Input slider to the left a bit, as in Figure 4.30.

See how much better the image now looks.

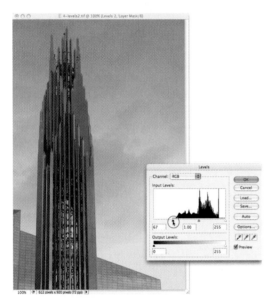
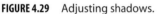

FIGURE 4.29   Adjusting shadows.

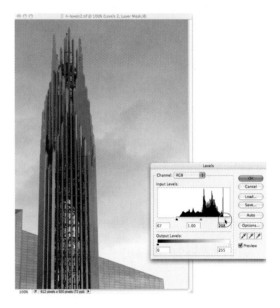

FIGURE 4.30   Adjusting the highlights.

EXPOSURE

There is yet another way to fix the exposure on your image. It is the aptly name adjustment called Exposure. Introduced in the previous version of Photoshop, its primary purpose is to make tonal adjustments to 32-bit (HDR) images (covered in Chapter 12, "Combining Images for Creative Results"). It is also very useful in correcting 8- and 16-bit images. This adjustment works a little like the Brightness/Contrast slider with a difference. Exposure is a great tool for brightening or darkening images while maintaining complete control over the contrast of the image. The sliders in the Exposure box are somewhat cryptic, but the following explanations are simple:

Exposure: Brightens the highlights.
Offset: Darkens the midtones and shadows.
Gamma: Adjusts the overall brightness.

These three sliders really enhance your ability to make precise adjustments to your images.

Figure 4.31 shows an image (`4-exposure.jpg` on the CD-ROM) that is underexposed in the foreground. The sky has a nice moody look though.

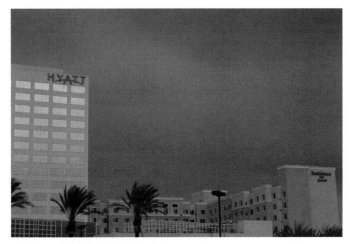

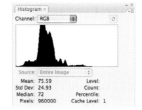

FIGURE 4.31   Original image.

Now look at Figure 4.32, and notice how the sky retains the nice moody look while the foreground is significantly lightened. This was achieved by an increase in Exposure to lighten the foreground and an increase in Gamma Correction to darken down the overall brightness.

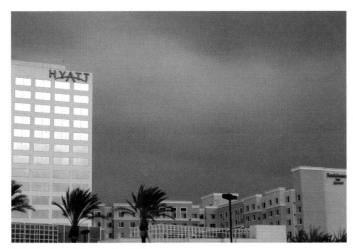

FIGURE 4.33   The Exposure Dialog box.

FIGURE 4.32   Adjusted with Exposure.

AUTO SETTINGS

When you open the Levels box, you will see the Auto button. This can be configured to be the Auto Levels, Auto Color, or Auto Contrast control.

Click the Options button, and you will see a dialog box with three options:

Enhance Monochromatic Contrast—Auto Contrast: Sets the overall darkest point as black and the overall lightest point as white.

Enhance Per Channel Contrast—Auto Levels: Similar to Auto Contrast, except this adjustment happens in each channel. This can sometimes introduce a color cast.

Find Dark and Light Colors—Auto Color: Attempts to color correct an image by using the average of the darkest and lightest pixels

Often, this produces good results. We started with the image from Figure 4.28, created a Levels adjustment layer and then clicked the Auto button. The result is in Figures 4.34a and 4.34b. The result isn't quite as good as doing it yourself, but it makes a improvement very quickly. Auto Levels analyzes the image and sets the darkest point in each channel as black and the lightest point as white.

Another way to access the Auto settings is by clicking Image > Adjustments > Auto.

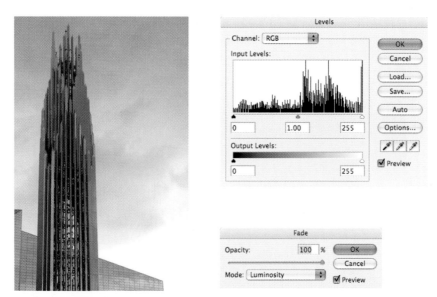

FIGURE 4.34 Changing the blending mode to Luminosity in the Fade command.

GETTING GOOD RESULTS FROM THE AUTO SETTINGS

These two auto settings get very good results if you perform a little trick.

Auto Levels does a great job with the contrast but can mess the color up. The trick then is to apply the filter without changing the color:

1. Apply Auto Levels.
2. Immediately choose Edit > Fade.
3. Change the Blending mode to Luminosity as shown in Figure 4.34c. The color is now restored and only the Luminosity of the image is affected.

The opposite is true for Auto Color:

4. Apply Auto Color.
5. Choose Edit > Fade.
6. In the dialog box, change to Color blending mode, so that only the color is affected.

CURVES

Of all the correction tools available, Curves gives you the most precise adjustments possible. With Curves, you can target any tone in the image and increase or reduce it. You have exact control over your entire image. Figure 4.35 shows the same image before and after Curves. Look at the overall difference, and notice how the details in the rocks and trees show clearly in the improved image. Notice the natural skin tones and the detail in the face. Curves give you the ability to turn snapshots into photographs. By the end of this section, you will be making corrections like this using the Curves feature.

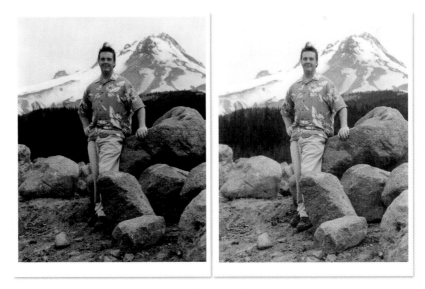

FIGURE 4.35   Image adjusted using only Curves.

Understanding Curves

The drawback to the Curves features is that there is a bit of a learning curve (forgive the pun). Stick with us here and don't just flip through to the next chapter. When you learn how to use Curves, it will change the way you use Photoshop and make you the king of image correction. Once you master Curves, you will rarely use any of the other correction tools in Photoshop. Hard to believe? Take a walk through the world of Curves and judge for yourself.

Open the Curves dialog box by selecting Layer > New Adjustment Layer > Curves. Figure 4.36 shows a stripped down view of the Curves Palette leaving only the Output and Input sections.

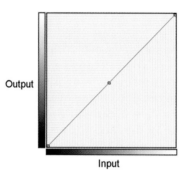

FIGURE 4.36   Input and output tones.

For now let's focus on three things:

Input: The horizontal grayscale gradient on the bottom.
Output: The vertical grayscale gradient on the left.
Curve: The red line.

The input tones are the starting values of the image and will never change. These are the tones seen in the original image.

Figure 4.37 shows the luminosity from an image. We have selected one tone of 5% brightness, one of 50% brightness, and one of 90% brightness. Follow the red lines from the image to the curve to see where the image value falls on the curve. The blue line shows you the relationship between the curve and the input horizontal gradient.

In Figure 4.38a, follow the red arrows and you will see that the tone intersects with the diagonal line. The diagonal line is the curve. Now follow the intersecting line to the left (see Figure 4.38b), and you will see the vertical gradient. Notice that the shade of gray is exactly the same. The vertical gray represents the output or what shade the tone will become. This is what that tone will look like after adjustment.

The relationship from the input gray to the output gray is called *mapping*. The curve will determine where the points intersect.

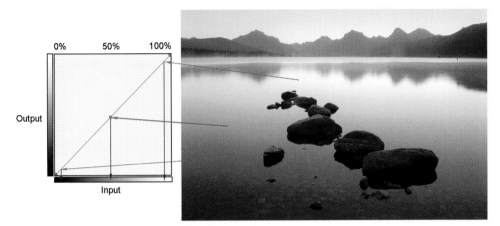

FIGURE 4.37   Luminosity and values on the graph.

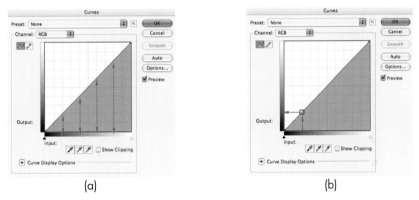

(a)   (b)

FIGURE 4.38   (a) The gray scale relationship to the curve. (b) Mapping the input to the output of the curve.

If you adjust the curve, the mapping will change. Notice in Figure 4.39 that the shape of the curve is changed. We started with the same input gray as in Figure 4.38 but dragged the point up the graph. Now follow the red arrow. The input is still the same, but the output value (tone) has changed.

What has changed? The vertical intersect point is now higher. Follow it to the left, and see where it is now on the output bar. The shade of gray is lighter than it was. We have just lightened the darker tones in the image. Notice that the curve doesn't just change the point that we moved, but it also affects the other points on the curve. Follow them and see how the output tones have changed.

In a nutshell, the bar across the bottom determines what shade of gray you are working on in the image. Black is to the left, and white is to the right. If you move the curve up, it lightens the image; and if you move the point down, it darkens the

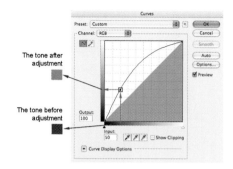

The tone after adjustment

The tone before adjustment

FIGURE 4.39 Adjusting the curve changes the mapping.

image. You cannot move it up from white because there is nothing brighter. You cannot move the curve down from black because there is nothing darker.

To determine the change, follow the graph up from the input level, see where it intersects with the curve, and follow it to the left to see what your output will be.

Using Curves

Now that you have an understanding of how the Curves feature works in theory, we can take a look at the Curves dialog box. CS3 introduces some welcome features to the old Curves box, which will be covered at the end of this chapter. First, we will look at the mechanics of curves and how to use the controls; then we will adjust some images and finish this section with a few tips on using the Curves feature and a closer inspection of its new features.

Creating Curves

By default, every curve begins with the same diagonal line. This indicates that the curve is in a neutral state, no changes have been made, and the input and outputs are the same as seen in Figure 4.40.

To make changes to the curve, click on the curve with your mouse, and an adjustment point will appear (see Figure 4.41). Drag the point up to brighten the tone or down to darken the tone. You can add as many as 14 points on a curve. This will bring you to 16 points in total, because black and white points are always shown. To remove any points, just drag them out of the Curves window. All points displayed as solid are selected, and those displayed as hollow are unselected. Only selected points can be moved on the curve. To select more than one point at a time, hold down the Shift key. To pinpoint a specific tone from the image, Cmd+click (Ctrl+click for PC) on the desired tone in the image. This will put a point on the curve at exactly that tone. Click OK to apply your adjustment.

The Pencil tool also can be used to draw a freehand curve (see Figure 4.42). This would have more uses in a special effects situation because it is not accurate enough for adjusting images precisely.

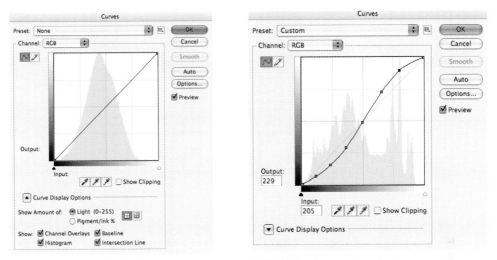

FIGURE 4.40 Curves dialog box.

FIGURE 4.41 Curves with adjustment points.

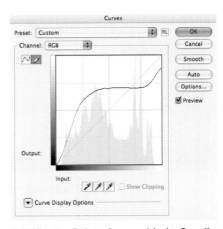

FIGURE 4.42 Points drawn with the Pencil tool.

Different Types of Curves

An infinite number of curves can be created for images. However, there are some typical shapes that achieve certain results. These curves range from image correction to special effects. CS3 introduces some useful preset curves for you to work with. Spending some time experimenting with these presets will teach you a lot about how the Curves box works. To apply a preset curve, click the double blue arrow next to the preset box and choose a curve as shown in Figure 4.43. You can fine-tune your curve further after you load a preset by moving the present points or creating more of your own. Curves will work with color images, but in this case, let's display them in grayscale so that you can see the effect on the image tones. Figures 4.44a to 4.44l show different types of curves.

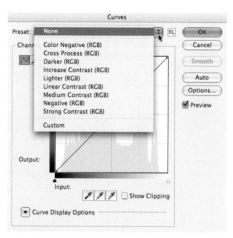

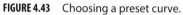

FIGURE 4.43 Choosing a preset curve.

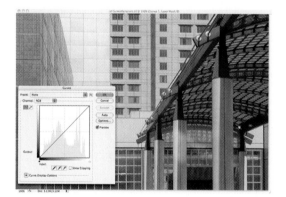

FIGURE 4.44A Original.

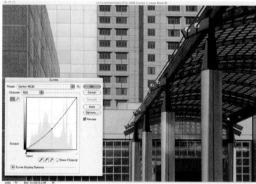

FIGURE 4.44B Darker preset darkens the midtones.

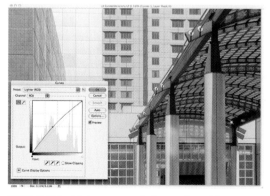

FIGURE 4.44C Lighter preset lightens the midtones.

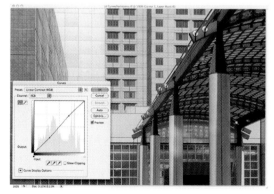

FIGURE 4.44D Linear Contrast preset adds a slight amount of contrast to midtones.

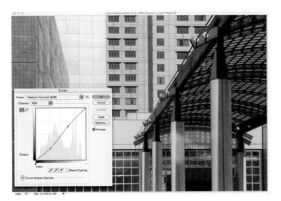

FIGURE 4.44E   Medium Contrast preset adds more contrast in midtones than Linear Contrast preset.

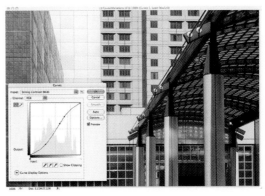

FIGURE 4.44F   Strong Contrast preset applies a heavy increase in midtones.

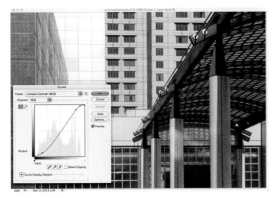

FIGURE 4.44G   Increase Contrast preset is the strongest of the Contrast presets. A significant lightening of the light tones and darkening of the dark tones results.

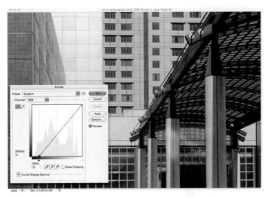

FIGURE 4.44H   Clipping the shadows. Note the relationship of the shadow point and the histogram.

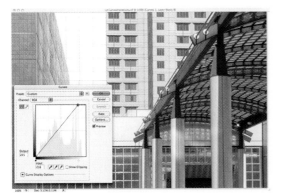

FIGURE 4.44I   Clipping the highlights. Note the relationship of the highlight point and the histogram.

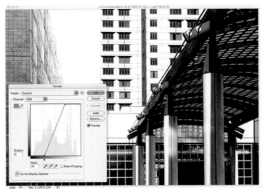

FIGURE 4.44J   Posterizing the image through severe contrast increase. Highlights and shadows are clipped.

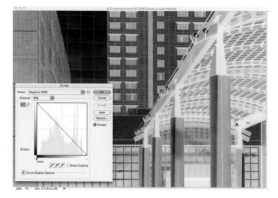 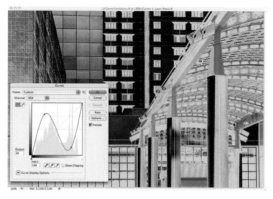

FIGURE 4.44K   The Negative preset inverts the image.   **FIGURE 4.44L**   Solarizing the image.

Correcting Images with Curves

We are now going to correct two images with the most common tonal problems. The first image is hazy and lacks contrast. The second image is so dark that you would think it was beyond repair. It's time to unleash the magic of the Curves feature.

Adding Contrast with Curves

The image in Figure 4.45 is very faded and hazy. It was shot from the top of the Sears Tower on a hazy day with a Sony DSC-717 F. You have probably seen many pictures with this problem. This is how to fix it.

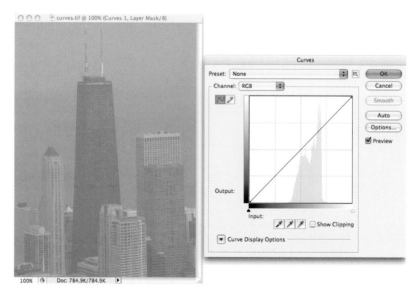

FIGURE 4.45   The image before adjusting the curves.

1. Open the Curves box by selecting Layer > New Adjustment Layer > Curves.
2. The image lacks contrast, so the first move is to create an S curve. At the 3/4 brightness point, drag the curve up to brighten the highlights (see Figure 4.46).

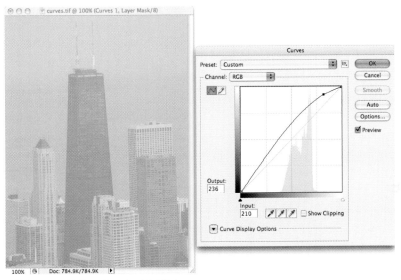

FIGURE 4.46   Lightening the highlights.

3. Drag the shadows down to deepen them. Notice in Figure 4.47 that the image has more overall contrast now.

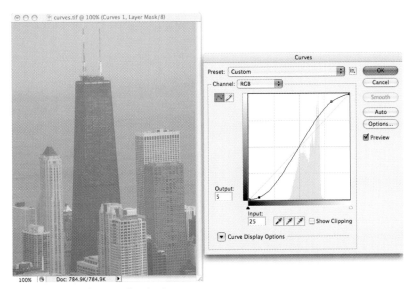

FIGURE 4.47   Darkening the shadows.

4. When you move the mouse into the image area, it turns into a Sampler tool. Click and drag the tool over the image, and you will see a circle on the curve. This indicates which image tone you are sampling.
5. Sample a tone in the image you want to emphasize by clicking on the desired tone. In this case, it's the John Hancock Building.
6. Press the Ctrl key (Cmd key for Mac) and click your mouse with the Eyedropper; an adjustment point will be added to the curve (see Figure 4.48).

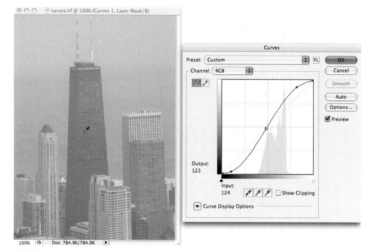

FIGURE 4.48   Sampling a midpoint.

7. Although the contrast has been increased, the image is now a touch too bright. Drag down on the curve at the newly selected point as shown in Figure 4.49. This darkens the image at the chosen tone, lowering the overall brightness of the midtones.

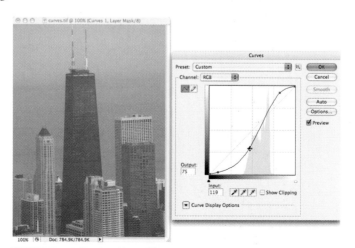

FIGURE 4.49   Adjusting the midpoint.

At this point, we could be satisfied with the adjustment; it is a lot better than it was. Just for fun though, let's brighten up the sky a bit.

1. Ctrl+click (Cmd+click for Mac) on a brighter part of the sky with the Eyedropper tool to add the sky's tone to the curve (see Figure 4.50).

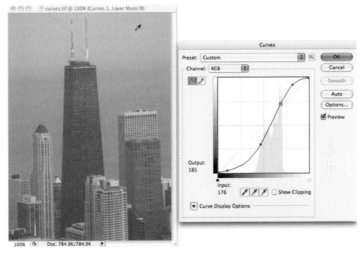

FIGURE 4.50 Sampling a highlight.

2. Drag the point up to brighten the sky. Notice that the curve is very steep between the two brightest points (see Figure 4.51). Be gentle with the curve. Try not to bend it too much. If a curve becomes too steep or even drops, this can cause colorizing problems such as solarizing and inverted colors.

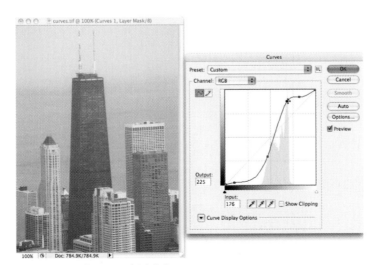

FIGURE 4.51 Adjusting a highlight.

As a tweak, we smoothed off the curve in the highlights. This has caused a little clipping in the white, but it is quite acceptable in this case. Notice the difference between the image before and after (see Figure 4.52). It's amazing what the Curves feature can do.

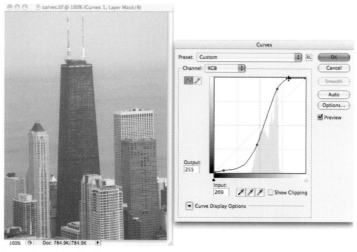

FIGURE 4.52   Final adjustments.

Brightening an Image with Curves

The camera often captures more detail than you realize. You just need to know how to bring it out. Figure 4.53 shows very little image detail. For this reason some folks might think it is beyond saving. Not so. Half of a minute in the Curves box is all it will take to fix this image.

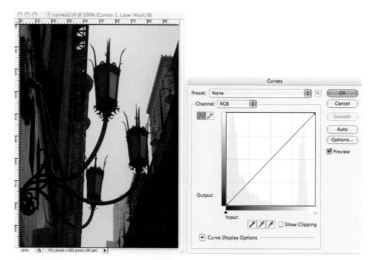

FIGURE 4.53   The beginning image.

1. Open the Curves dialog box.
2. Lighten the shadows until you can see some detail come into the image (see Figure 4.54). Moving the shadow point up from the bottom will turn your deepest blacks to mud. This is not a desired effect, but we will tweak this later. The goal right now is to see some image detail so that we can work with it.

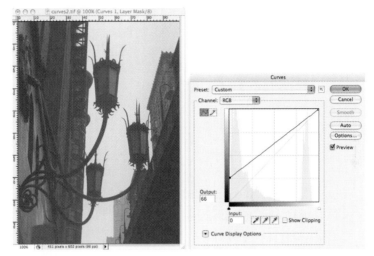

FIGURE 4.54   Adjusting the shadows.

3. Lighten the highlights until the lightest point of the image is where you want it to be (see Figure 4.55). These are some extreme adjustments, but this is an extreme image.

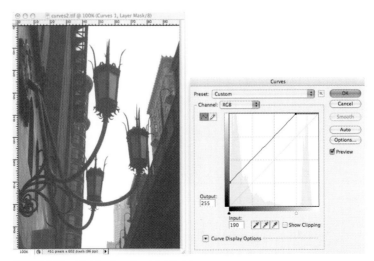

FIGURE 4.55   Lightening the highlights.

4. Move your mouse into the image and sample a midtone in the area where you want to bring out the detail (see Figure 4.56).

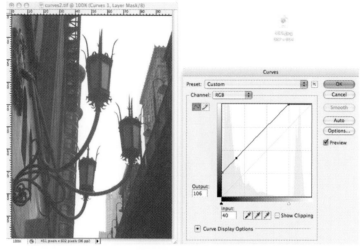

FIGURE 4.56 Sampling the midtones.

5. Move the curve up at this midtone. Notice how the image has brightened up in the mids now (see Figure 4.57).

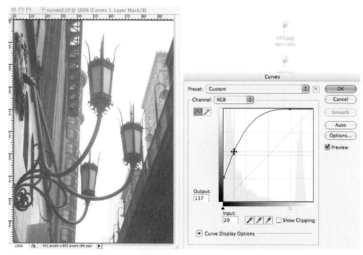

FIGURE 4.57 Adjusting the midtones.

6. In step 2, we brightened the shadows so that we could see some detail to work with. Let's darken the shadows now because they look too bright.
7. Drag down on the darkest point just a little bit (see Figure 4.58).

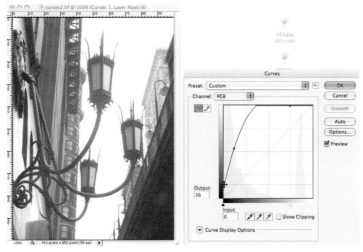

FIGURE 4.58   Darkening the shadows.

8. Finally, we make a little adjustment in the higher midtones to make the highlights and midtones a bit softer (see Figure 4.59).

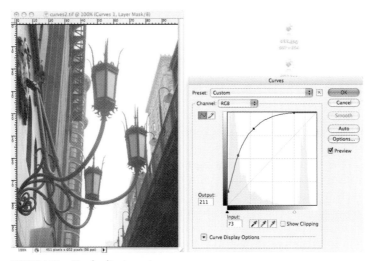

FIGURE 4.59   Final adjustments.

There you have it. We have brought out detail and color from an almost blacked-out image. Can you see the power of curves and why it is worthwhile to learn this feature?

Some New Features

As mentioned earlier in this chapter, some new features have been added to the Curves box that make it easier for the photographer to both visualize the tones and adjust the curve. If you have worked in Curves before, you will have already noticed the addition of the histogram behind the curve. The second thing you may have noticed is the Curve Display Options button. When clicked, this button reveals several options for modifying the way the Curves box will be displayed. See Figure 4.60 for a look at the options.

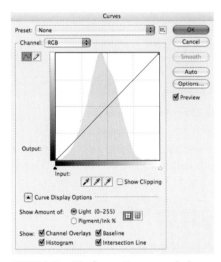

FIGURE 4.60   Display options revealed.

Fortunately for us, Adobe has done a good job of designing the default settings for this box. When you first reveal the options, you will notice that all of the boxes are checked.

The histogram provides a great visual and makes it easier to understand the correlation between the Levels and Curves commands. It is now possible to bypass the Levels box entirely, as all of the features are now represented in Curves! In Figure 4.61, you will see that you are starting with a flat image. You can increase the overall contrast of the image by moving the Shadow point to the right and the Highlight point to the left as shown in Figure 4.62. Moving these points is the exact equivalent to moving the White Point and Black Point (Shadow and Highlight) sliders in the Levels box. Simply push them over until you reach the image information as shown by the histogram.

Figure 4.62 also highlights the new Intersection Line feature of Curves. We added a red vertical line over the intersection line to make it easier to see. Now as you move the points on the curve, you can look to the intersection line—both vertical and horizontal—to help visualize where the tones will be mapped to. You can see that we were able to precisely position the highlight point by watching the intersection line as it moved along the histogram.

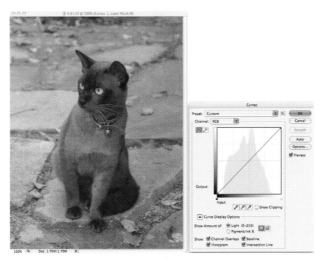

FIGURE 4.61   Opening the Curves box with a flat image.

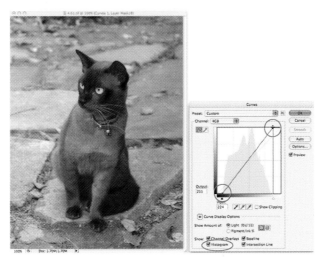

FIGURE 4.62   Increasing the overall contrast by setting the Shadow and Highlight points by the histogram.

With the Baseline box checked, we get a reference for where the curve was when we started. Figure 4.63 shows the Baseline in red. With the Channel Overlays box checked, we can see the individual curves that may have been altered in the color channels. For changing the contrast and brightness of an image, the RGB channel is the only channel that needs adjusting, but for advanced color correction, you can individually alter each channel from within the Curves box. Figure 4.64 demonstrates how to access the color channels as well as showing the effect of checking the Channel Overlays box.

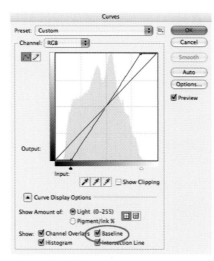

FIGURE 4.63   Baseline highlighted in red.

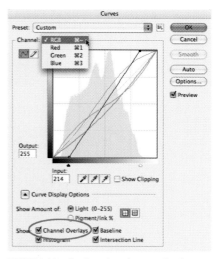

FIGURE 4.64   Seeing the changes in the color channels via the Channel Overlay.

The Show Clipping box is unchecked by default for good reason. When this is checked, you cannot see your image! This box allows you to easily assess any clipping that may occur in the shadows and the highlights. Check the Show Clipping box and you will see your image turn entirely white. Now as you move your Shadow slider, color will begin to appear. When any of that color turns to black, it is the indication that these pixels are starting to clip. Back off from the adjustment until the black disappears. Figure 4.65 shows that the first pixels to clip will be around the cat's ear. Begin to move the highlight point on the curve, and the image will turn black. The first signs of clipping will be those pixels that turn white. Figure 4.66 shows that the

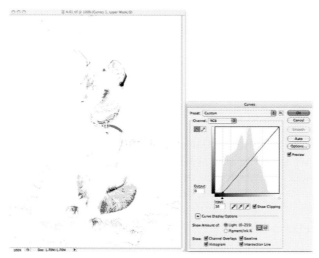

FIGURE 4.65   A slight clipping of the shadows.

first highlight pixels to clip will be around the cat's collar and bell. Figure 4.67 shows the final adjustment.

Holding down the Alt/Option key does the same thing as the Show Clipping box and is usually a quicker option.

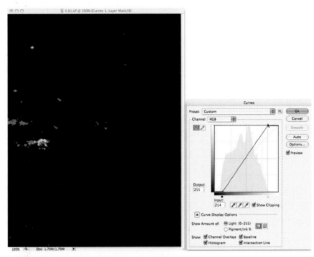

FIGURE 4.66   A slight clipping of the highlights.

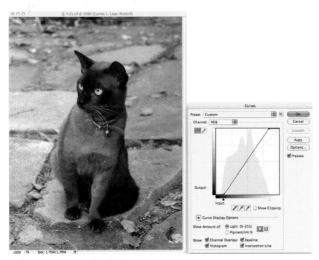

FIGURE 4.67   The final adjustment.

Tips for Using Curves

Here are a few tips to make you more productive with the Curves feature:

- Click back and forth between the icons that look like small windows in the Curves box to change the grid. You can also press the Alt key (Option key for Mac) and click in the Curves window for the same effect.
- Hold down the Shift key, and click on adjustment points to select more than one point at a time.
- Press the arrow keys on your keyboard to move the selected points.
- Avoid falling curves, which means that tones have become inverted at that point.
- Press Ctrl+Tab (Cmd+Tab for Mac) to move through adjustment points on the curve.
- Press Ctrl+click on the image (Cmd+click for Mac) to add an adjustment point to the curve.

SUMMARY

In this chapter, you learned a lot about the tonal qualities of your images. You learned how to strengthen the details of, brighten, and add contrast to your images. You will not have to despair again if your images don't look quite right out of the camera. You can import them to Photoshop and transform them into masterpieces.

5

COLOR CORRECTION AND ENHANCEMENT

In This Chapter

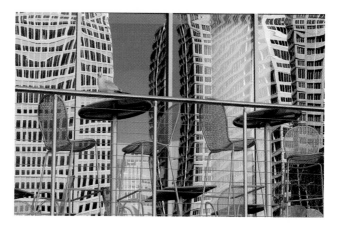

In the previous chapter, we mainly looked at luminosity. *Luminosity* refers to the brightness values of an image. Photographers such as Ansel Adams knew how to work with luminosity for maximum impact. The second part of a digital photograph is the color. Color is used to create moods and add a lot to an image. Think of color as the thin layer of skin-deep beauty in your color photograph. Color can be very fragile but if handled with care can produce wonderful results. Nothing is worse than a color image where the color is off, particularly with skin tones or food. In this chapter, you will learn how to correctly adjust and repair color so that you can deliver vibrant and correct color images.

In the world of computers, there are two ways to understand color. One type of color is called additive, and the other is called subtractive. We are not going to get bogged down in a lot of theory right now, but we will go through a very brief overview to help you understand how color is generated on your computer.

ADDITIVE COLOR

In additive color, all the colors add together to make white. This type of color is based on light. This is the way that the natural eye perceives color. For example, when you view a lemon, you see yellow. All the colors of the spectrum are targeted at the lemon from the sun or other light source. The lemon absorbs all the light except for the part that looks yellow, and the light is then reflected to the viewer's eye and perceived as yellow. A rainbow displays this principle perfectly. When the light hits the raindrops at the correct angle, it splits the spectrum of light, and you can see red, orange, yellow, green, blue, indigo, and violet; all the colors added together make white light. Because of the way this light works, you can imagine that different types of artificial light are not as pure as the sun's rays, and this produces what is called a color cast in your image. A *color cast* is when an image has an unnatural color tint. We can fix this color cast easily in Photoshop, as you will learn in this chapter.

Your computer's monitor also uses additive color. There are three different colors, red, green, and blue (RGB). The monitor mixes these three primary colors (monitor primaries, or RGB primaries) and creates all the colors that you view on the screen.

SUBTRACTIVE COLOR

Subtractive color is so named because an absence of color will produce white (or more correctly, transparency). Subtractive color is not based on light but is based on ink and resembles mixing color as you did with your first paint set. The three main primaries used in subtractive color are cyan (light blue), magenta (pinkish purple), and yellow. Because these colors cannot produce a really dense black, black usually is added in the world of printing. This is where you get CMYK color: C = cyan, M = magenta, Y = yellow, and K = black (called K and not B so it's not confused with blue). Subtractive colors are the colors you will deal with when printing. Even though our home inkjet printers are made up of CMYK inks, you do not have to work in the CMYK colorspace unless you are printing to a commercial printing press. The inkjet printer works by receiving RGB images and changing them into CMYK.

COLOR CORRECTION TOOLS

In the previous chapter, we looked at tonal correction, and we worked on the grayscale portion of images. In this chapter, we are going to look at the color portion of the images. All photography is the art of capturing light, and different types of light affect images in different ways. For example, the sun's quality is a warm/neutral-colored light, but moonlight transmits a bluish cast and is much cooler. Shooting indoors under artificial light tends to give images a yellow cast, whereas fluorescent light adds some green to the image. Some of the best lighting conditions (for portraits especially) are outside with an overcast sky. The clouds nicely defuse the harshness of the sun's rays without taking too much brightness away.

Digital cameras are equipped with a white balance setting that helps you compensate for different lighting conditions. Although most are not needed anymore with digital photography, you can also use different filters to help with the color. Even after all that, sometimes the color is still a bit off in the photo. This is not a problem with Photoshop. There are several ways to restore natural color, and you may even want to use these techniques to alter the color for something more creative, such as to warm the skin tones of a model. If you have the option to shoot in the Raw format, most of your color correction troubles will no longer apply because you can change the setting in the Raw tools provided with Photoshop (Chapter 2, "From Bridge to Photoshop: The Adobe Raw Converter").

For images that are not in Raw (and we all have plenty of them), the following techniques will take the pain out of color correction.

Color Calibration

Before making color adjustments to your images, it's imperative to calibrate your monitor. By calibrating your monitor, you are adjusting it to industry standards. This will give you a faithful reference to go by. The goal is to get the color on your screen to be as close as possible to the devices you and others will use to view and output the images. You can achieve accurate results by using two things: screen calibration and color profiles.

Screen Calibration

To get accurate color on your screen, you will need some kind of measuring device. Monico OPTIX-XR, Pantone Huey, and the ColorVision™ Spyder2 Suite are examples of tools that work well for less than $150. Each of these solutions are bundles of software and hardware. Just about every color calibration system these days will work with both CRT and LCD screens. You will place one of these measuring devices (hardware) on your screen (they either dangle in front or sit with suction cups) and then launch the included software. The devices measure the colors on your screen and then build a color profile that is saved on your computer. This color profile ensures that your colors are accurate and that they look very similar to what someone else will see using a calibrated monitor.

It's fairly simple to calibrate and profile your display using the mentioned tools. Some things to keep in mind:

- Make the room lighting as close as possible to your working conditions before running the calibration.
- Warm up your monitor first, as the brightness and color will shift as the equipment warms up. Most manufacturers recommend at least a half hour of warmup time.
- Recalibrate the screen on a regular basis—every two weeks should be more than sufficient.
- Be careful not to make any adjustments such as brightness or contrast to your screen. If you change any of these settings, you will need to recalibrate.
- Some calibrating systems will ask you to set the Gamma. The Gamma of a PC is 2.2, and the Gamma of an Apple is 1.8.
- Another option you may come across while running the software is white point. You can think of the white point as a very slight color cast to your monitor. Most photographers will use either 5500 or 6500 as their white point. If you use 5500, your monitor will be slightly warmer. Setting it at 6500 will give your monitor a cooler cast. If your monitor is cooler (6500) then you will generally fix your images to be a little warmer. This is the setting that we choose.

Color Profile

The calibration process creates a profile for your monitor. By default, this profile will load up automatically when you start your computer. Your images should also contain a color profile, so that the settings will be translated correctly. A quick trip to the Color Settings box will enable you to manage your color with success. Choose Edit > Color Settings, and set your working RGB to Adobe RGB (1998).

When you open an image and get a warning that says Profile Mismatch, it's telling you that the image you are opening has a different color profile than the settings on your screen. You have two options: Convert the image to your working color profile, or keep it as is.

If the image is coming from a calibrated system, then the color is set to that system's profile. If you will be returning the image to the source it came from (for example, another person) you should keep the embedded profile.

If you plan to work on the image and print the image on your printer, then you should convert it, and then make minor color adjustments, if necessary, to match your screen settings.

If the image has no profile attached, it's a good idea to attach a profile so that you will get consistent color. To assign a color profile to an image, choose Edit > Assign Profile. The most common profile for photography is Adobe RGB (1998). You will find it under the Profile drop-down menu.

If you are shooting your images in Raw, setting the *Space* to Adobe RGB before converting will keep things running smooth. You can do this by clicking on the underlined link in the center bottom of the Raw converter. This will bring you to the Workflow Options box. Space will be the first drop-down menu.

Check Chapter 8, "Sizing and Printing Your Images," for instructions on printing with accurate colors.

Adjusting Color in Your Images

After you have fixed the contrast and the brightness in your image, you may find that there is now an obvious color cast. There are countless ways to fix a colorcast in Photoshop. To cover them all would take up this entire book. Let's focus on a couple of simple methods and then explore some of the more accurate methods. We will end this chapter with a look at how to enhance your color rather than fix it.

Adjusting Color in Camera Raw

Adjusting your image in the Camera Raw converter is one of the easiest ways to correct a color cast. Now that the Converter will work with any type of file, photographers who shoot in JPEG can enjoy all the benefits of this powerful tool. To open any type of file into the Raw Converter, right-click on the image while in the bridge, and choose Open in Camera Raw. See Chapter 2 for more information on adjusting Camera Raw images. For images that are already in Photoshop, here are several ways that you can correct and enhance their color.

Auto Color

This is a hit-or-miss filter. It's great when you are in a hurry or you have only a few seconds to get an image cleaned up a bit. There are limited settings for this adjustment filter, so it is very unpredictable. Auto Color will attempt to balance the color and does a pretty good job a lot of the time. We tend to use this on images that have a heavy color cast. If nothing else, it is a good starting point.

Figure 5.1 shows an image with a green color cast caused by fluorescent lighting. To apply Auto Color, select Image > Adjustments > Auto Color.

In this case, Auto Color did a decent job of removing the green color cast. Notice the color restored on the right wall (see Figure 5.2). There is a bit of a purple color cast on the white areas of the sign, but the image is a huge improvement over the original. A good thing to do directly after applying Auto Color is to choose Edit > Fade Auto Color and switch the blending mode to Color. This will restore the original luminosity of the image. Note that this not an adjustment layer! There are ways around that, however. Click on your background layer to ensure that it is the active layer. Go up to Layer > Duplicate Layer to create a duplicate layer of your background and provide a place for you to perform the Auto Color command.

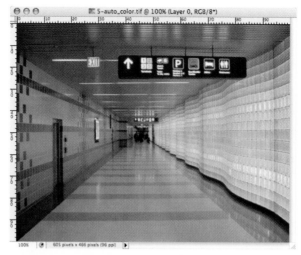

FIGURE 5.1   Image with a green cast.

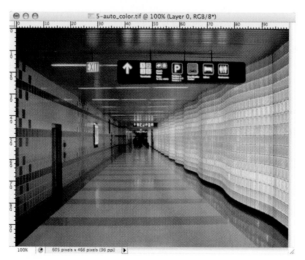

FIGURE 5.2   The image after using Auto Color.

Color Balance

Color Balance is a very useful tool for making color corrections. This tool allows you to target the shadows, midtones, or highlights and then change the balance of color in the image.

Six main colors (the two sets of primary colors) are used in this tool:

- Monitor primaries (additive color) are red, green, and blue.
- Print primaries (subtractive color) are cyan, magenta, and yellow.

In the Color Balance tool, these colors are arranged into three sets of opposites using the primary colors:

- Cyan and red
- Magenta and green
- Yellow and blue

You can target a range of either Shadows, Highlights, or Midtones and then shift the balance of any of the colors. Pushing the slider toward Red removes a cyan cast, pushing the slider toward Magenta removes green, and moving the slider toward Yellow removes a blue cast.

TUTORIAL 5.1   ADJUSTING THE COLOR CAST

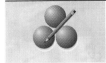

On the CD-ROM, open the file Ch 5-CB.jpg.

Figure 5.3 shows an image that suffers from a bad blue color cast.

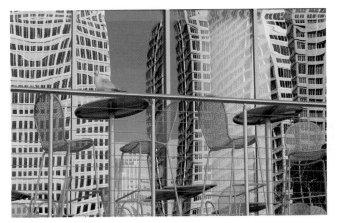

FIGURE 5.3   The original image with a blue color cast.

1. Choose the Color Balance adjustment layer by clicking on the white and black circle at the bottom of the Layers Palette and choosing Color Balance.
2. Keep the Preserve Luminosity box checked. This prevents the tonal qualities of the image from changing.
3. The Color Balance box will open with the Midtones option checked.
4. Slide the balance to more Red and less Cyan (see Figure 5.4a). Also, move away from Blue and toward Yellow. Be careful not to overdo it. Figure 5.4b shows the image after the midtone adjustments.
5. Choose the Highlights option.

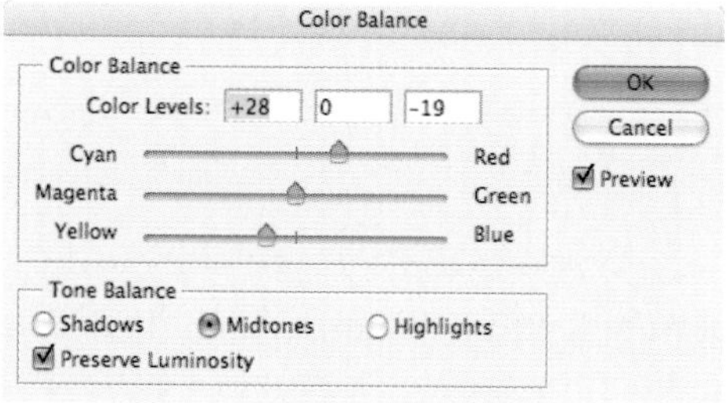

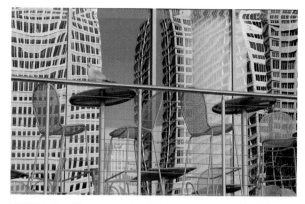

FIGURE 5.4A   Adjusting the midtones.

FIGURE 5.4B   The image after the midtone adjustments.

6. Increase the Red and Yellow settings, as shown in Figure 5.5.
7. Repeat these steps for the shadows as well.

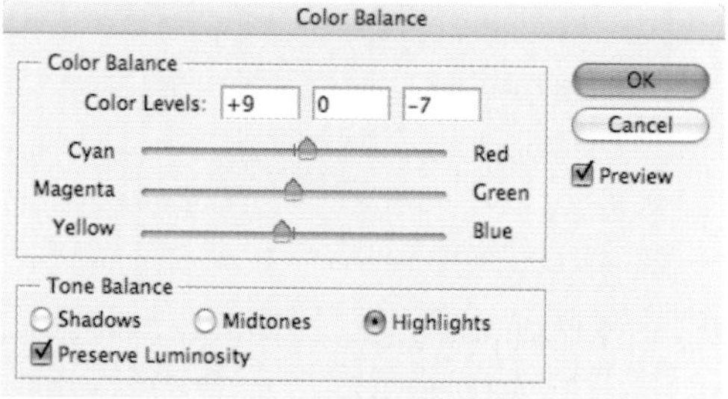

FIGURE 5.5   Adjusting the highlights.

Figure 5.6 shows the image after the adjustments. The picture looks much more natural now. Can you see how we neutralized the blue color cast by shifting the balance of color?

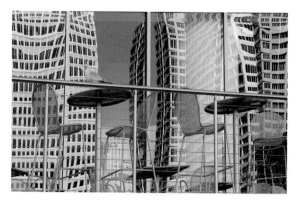

FIGURE 5.6   The final image after shadow, highlight, and midtone adjustments.

Color Correction Using Variations

The Variations tool works just like the Color Balance tool but with a more visual interface. This is one of the most commonly used tools to fix color shifting in an image because of the great results and ease of use.

Figure 5.7 shows an image that is suffering from a pretty bad yellow color cast. There should be some yellowing of the paper to show the signs of age, but the plate should be more neutral colored.

1. Choose Image > Adjustments > Variations. You will see five main areas when you open the Variations dialog box (see Figure 5.8). Once again, if you wish this command was an adjustment layer, choose Layer > Duplicate Layer to apply the Variations to a duplicate of your background image.

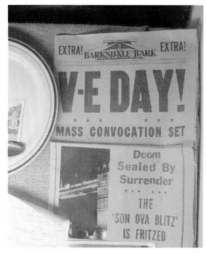

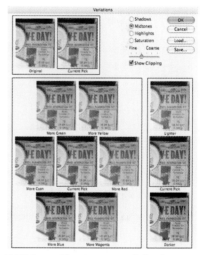

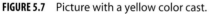

FIGURE 5.7   Picture with a yellow color cast.   **FIGURE 5.8**   The Variations dialog box.

- The top left shows the original image and a preview of the image after the current adjustment.
- The next area to the right allows you to choose a tonal range or the saturation of color.
- Directly under the tonal range, you will see a sensitivity slider that changes the intensity of the adjustment from less (fine) to more (coarse).
- The main area shows previews of the image with color shifting in different directions and the current pick in the center.
- The area to the right is where you can lighten or darken the image.

2. Target the midtones (default).
3. As you slide the intensity slider, you can see how it affects the thumbnails. As you choose the coarser settings, the color differences are more radical (see Figure 5.9).

To adjust the image, click on the thumbnail that is closest to the result you are looking for. The current pick will be updated to the colors of the thumbnail you clicked, as shown in Figure 5.10. Notice that all the thumbnails have changed to offer variations of the newly selected color.

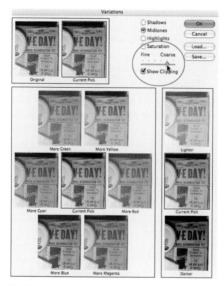

FIGURE 5.9   Changing the intensity.

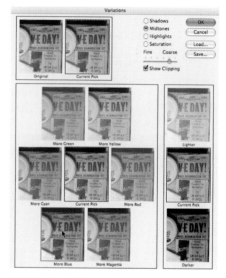

FIGURE 5.10   Making an adjustment.

The color is now close but not quite there, as shown in Figure 5.11.

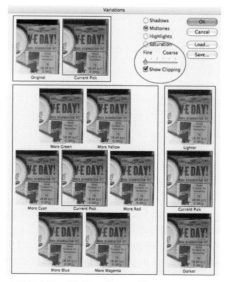

FIGURE 5.11   Making finer adjustments.

1. Lower the intensity to make the adjustment more subtle.
2. Choose more blue.
3. Click on the lighter thumbnail to brighten the image.

If you have Show Clipping turned on, the area will be highlighted in a bright color on some thumbnails, as shown in Figure 5.12. This indicates where the color cannot be faithfully reproduced if the highlighted variation is chosen (outside the color gamut). This is usually a good indication to turn down the sensitivity to a finer setting.

Figure 5.13 shows the image after the color correction has been applied with the Variations feature.

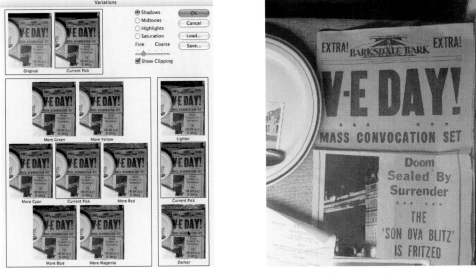

FIGURE 5.12   Clipping indicated.   **FIGURE 5.13**   The image after adjusting.

To reset the colors in Variations, click on the thumbnail at the top left labeled Original. All the settings will be reverted. It's a good thing to click this button whenever launching Variations because the previously used settings are always retained in memory.

TUTORIAL 5.2   USING THE PHOTO FILTER

Another simple tool to correct or enhance color is the Photo Filter. This tool allows you to create a preset color cast (filter) across the entire image. Some of the choices are filters that film photographers will remember using on a regular basis. The warming and cooling filters make up the first section of the presets. In this tutorial, we will use the Photo Filter to fix an image that was shot under tungsten light (see Figure 5.14).

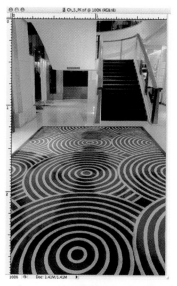

FIGURE 5.14 An image shot under tungsten lights causing it to have an orange/yellow cast.

On the CD-ROM, open the file Ch 5-PF.jpg.

1. Choose the Photo Filter adjustment layer by clicking on the white and black circle at the bottom of the Layers Palette and choosing Photo Filter.
2. By default, the Filter button will be checked, which allows you to choose a filter from the drop-down menu. Choose the Cooling Filter (82) as shown in Figure 5.15. The color square has changed to show you the new filter color.

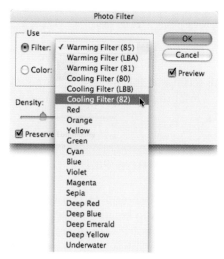

FIGURE 5.15 Choosing the Cooling Filter.

3. The image should look immediately better, but you can adjust the intensity of the filter to suit your taste. In this image, we increased the density to 52 to give a neutral look to the scene as shown in Figure 5.16.

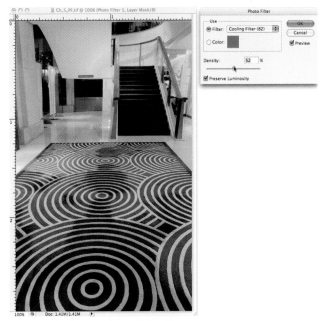

FIGURE 5.16   Adjusting the intensity of the Cooling Filter.

4. The Preserve Luminosity check box should be checked by default. If it is not, check it now. This will help keep the Brightness and Contrast from being affected by the color changes that you are applying. Click OK to finish your adjustment.

5. You can also fine-tune this adjustment. Reopen the Photo Filter adjustment layer by double-clicking its icon in the Layers Palette.

6. Seems that our previous adjustment left a little magenta in our white walls. Let's clean that up by customizing the color that we use as our filter. Start by raising the Density to 100%. This will initially make the color too strong, but we will fix that in the next step. Now, double-click the color square to open the Select Filter Color box (see Figure 5.17).

7. Inside of the Select Filter Color box, we want to desaturate our color somewhat and slightly alter its hue. Do this by clicking on the circle within the color and moving it to the left. You can watch the numbers in the "S" box lower as you move this circle (see Figure 5.18). You are desaturating the color as you move to the left. Choose a number between 50 and 70.

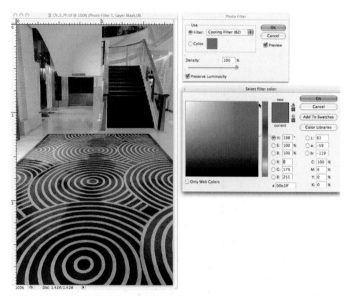

FIGURE 5.17   Double-clicking the color square opens the Select Filter Color box.

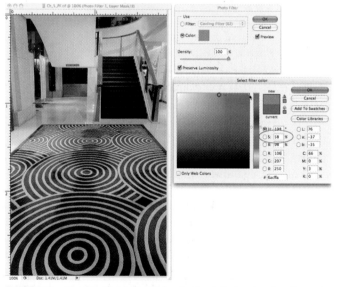

FIGURE 5.18   Moving the color picker to the left desaturates the color.

8. You can now move the Hue Slider up and down to dial in the exact hue that will make the scene more neutral. Here, we have chosen a value of 209 as seen in the "H" box in Figure 5.19. Click OK in the Select Filter Color box, and then click OK again in the Photo Filter box to complete your fine-tuning.

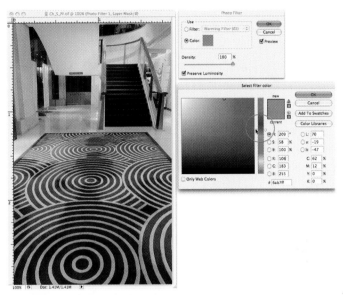

FIGURE 5.19   Moving the Hue slider to fine-tune the filter color.

HUE/SATURATION

The Hue/Saturation adjustment is a very powerful tool that you will find yourself using often once you are familiar with it. Although it can be used to change the color cast of an image, the roughness of the Hue slider does not have the fine-tuning abilities of the other tools that we have covered. It is, however, a great tool to enhance the color of an image. The Hue/Saturation box works on the three different components of color: Hue, Saturation, and Brightness (or Lightness).

Hue: The name of the color—Red. Use this when you want to alter the actual color from Red to Blue, for example. Subtle changes can also be made.

Saturation: The intensity of the color or more correctly the balance of color to luminosity. At a high saturation, the color is very bright and vibrant. At a low saturation, the color turns to gray.

Brightness: Describes the brightness or darkness of the color. Use this slider to correct the brightness after a hue and saturation adjustment lightens or darkens your color. I would avoid using the brightness slider in this dialog box. The exposure adjustment will brighten the image but yield more accurate results.

To study the components of color, open the Color Picker box by double-clicking on either the Foreground or Background color chips in the lower part of the toolbar (see Figure 5.20).

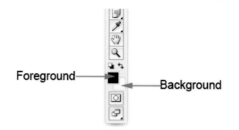

FIGURE 5.20   The Foreground/Background color chips.

In the Color Picker, move the arrows on either side of the color ramp (they both move simultaneously when one is chosen) to select a hue. Notice the number in the H box will change as you move the slider. This value is called the Hue angle. The Hue value and the Hue slider bar are circled in blue in Figure 5.21.

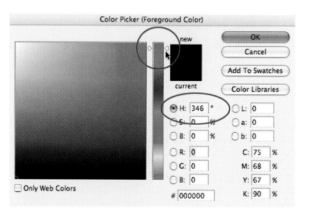

FIGURE 5.21   Changing the hue of a color.

Click inside the color field as you did in the previous tutorial, and you can change the brightness of the chosen hue. By clicking your cursor below, you are darkening the color (see Figure 5.22). The upper center of the box shows you the Current and New colors. Current is what you started with when opening the box, and New is what your color will become after you click OK. Once again, look to the S and B boxes. The numbers inside will change to reflect your new Saturation and Brightness.

In Figure 5.23, we explore the different percentages of a solid color red. Notice how the color becomes less intense as the color is desaturated.

When first working with the Hue/Saturation box, it is not uncommon to overdo the saturation settings. This is always a tell-tale sign of an image being digitally manipulated. Use a soft hand here, and let subtlety by your mantra. Another mistake is to use only the Master slider in this box. This will change the Hue, Saturation, or Lightness of *all* colors in your image. In Figure 5.24, we have a scene that can

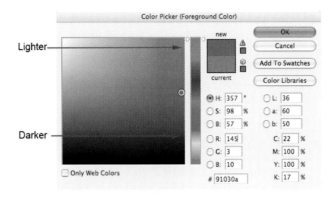

FIGURE 5.22   Darkening the color.

Saturation

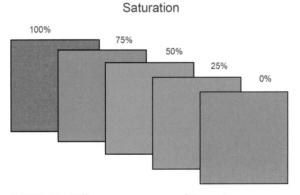

FIGURE 5.23   Different percentages of Saturation.

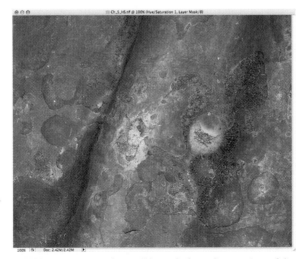

FIGURE 5.24   Image that will benefit from fine-tuning of the color.

benefit from fine-tuning in the Hue/Saturation box. We could try to make the image more appealing by increasing the overall saturation, but this would only make all the colors more intense. By choosing individual colors within the box, we can separate the colors from one another by applying different degrees of Hue, Saturation, and Brightness to each color.

ON THE CD

On the CD-ROM, open the file Ch_5_HS.jpg.

1. Choose the Hue/Saturation adjustment layer by clicking on the white and black circle at the bottom of the Layers Palette and choosing Hue/Saturation.
2. At the top of the box, you will find the Edit drop-down box. Choose Yellow from the list as seen in Figure 5.25. Increase the Saturation. Only the Yellows are becoming more saturated! The blues are left alone.

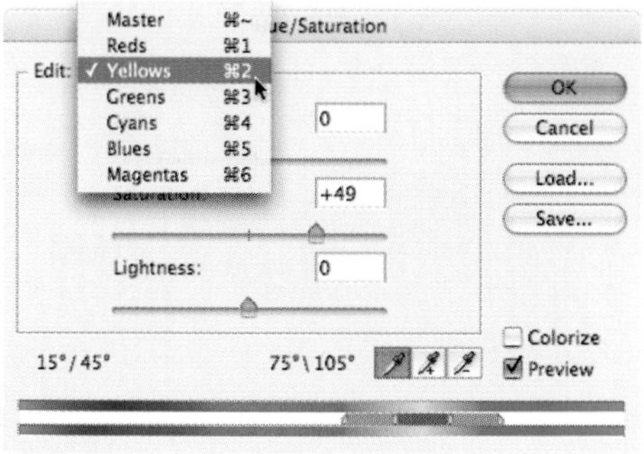

FIGURE 5.25 Increasing the yellow saturation.

3. Choose Red from the Edit menu, and increase the saturation here as well. For this example, we chose a setting of +26. Once again, we are getting a boost to the reds without affecting the blues.
4. Now choose Blue from the Edit menu. Here we want to alter the color to get a better contrast between it and the yellows and reds. Start by lowering the lightness a little. Next, desaturate the color somewhat. Finally, alter the hue by moving the slider to the right. Figure 5.26 shows the settings for each

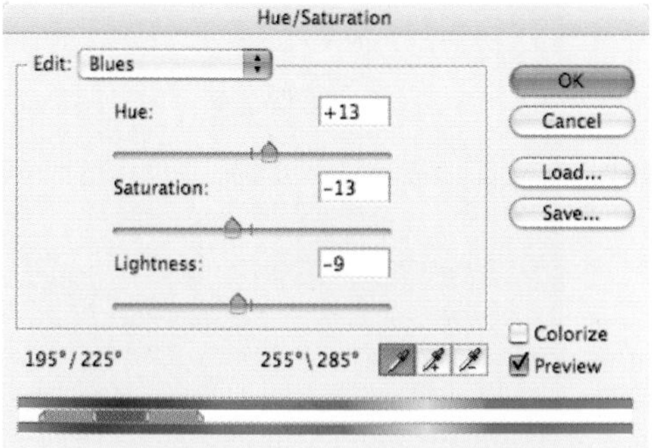

FIGURE 5.26 Changing the blue hue and decreasing its saturation.

edit. The color blue now has much more complexity to it. There is more separation between the main colors as well as more separation within the blue itself. Figure 5.27 shows the before and after.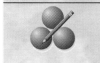

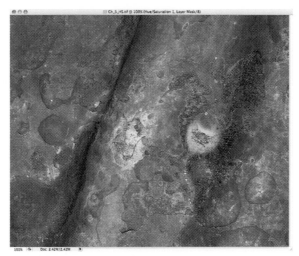

FIGURE 5.27   After fine-tuning the hue and saturation.

ADVANCED COLOR CORRECTION

We are going to look at a few color adjustment techniques that go beyond the simple click-and-slide techniques. These are professional-level techniques that will help you fix almost any image. You will be surprised by the power of Photoshop and also your capability to correct color by the end of this chapter.

Match Color

Another useful color correction feature in Photoshop is Match Color. With this filter, you can copy the color information from one photo to another. This is a great way to fix studio shots that are inconsistent and remove color casts. This tool also opens up some amazing creative opportunities.

TUTORIAL 5.3   **REMOVING A COLOR CAST WITH MATCH COLOR**

We are going to use Match Color to take the warmth from one picture and apply it to another later in this chapter. For now, we are going to use the Match Color option to painlessly remove a color cast from an image.

Begin with an image that has a color cast. Figure 5.28 has an orange color cast from the artificial lighting. You must be in RGB mode for this filter to work properly. If you find that you are working with a CMYK or grayscale image (this technique is fun to try with black-and-white images), go up to Image > Mode and change the image to RGB.

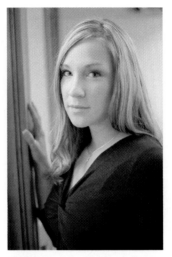

FIGURE 5.28   An orange color cast.

1. Open ch_5_Match.jpg from the Chapter 5 folder on the CD-ROM, or use your own image.
2. From the menu, select Image > Adjustments > Match Color. (There is no adjustment layer available for this adjustment.)
3. You will see the dialog box shown in Figure 5.29. Check the Preview box to make sure it is on.

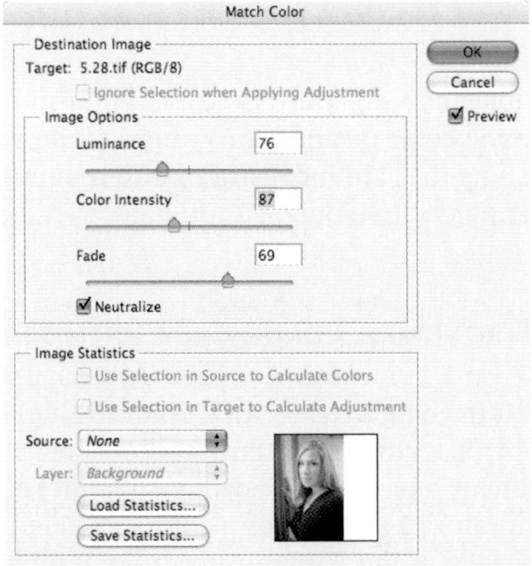

FIGURE 5.29   Adjusting the Match Color settings.

4. Click on the Neutralize box. The overall color temperature of the image should change.
5. Adjust the Fade slider until the image's color looks correct.
6. Adjust the Luminance setting to darken or lighten the image.
7. If you need to adjust the saturation of color, move the Color Intensity slider (this is unnecessary most of the time).
8. Click OK, and you are done.

Figure 5.30 shows the image after correction. This is a pretty quick and painless way to remove a color cast, and it works well on most images. If you just want to adjust a portion of the image or a particular color, make a selection around the area first and then follow the previous steps.

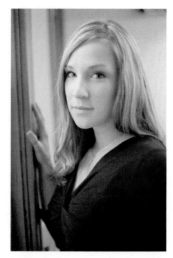

FIGURE 5.30   Image after color correction.

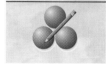

TUTORIAL 5.4   **ADDING LIFE TO AN IMAGE WITH MATCH COLOR**

Match Color also enables you to take the color palette of one image and apply it to another image. In this example, we are going to take an image that was shot after the sun went down, which gave the image a strong blue cast. We will take another image that was shot at sunset and bring the warm colors over to the blue image.

We will begin with a landscape that has a strong blue hue to it, (see Figure 5.31). You can use an image of your own that is on the cool side or use ch_5_match1.jpg from the Chapter 5 folder on the CD-ROM.

ON THE CD

1. Open an image that has a much warmer feel to it (ch_5_Match2.jpg from the CD-ROM). The image in Figure 5.32 shows a much more interesting color in the sky.

ON THE CD

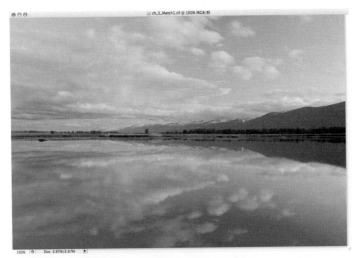

FIGURE 5.31   After the sun sets, the light is very blue.

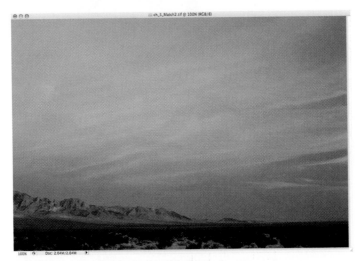

FIGURE 5.32   Better color in the clouds.

2. Click on the image in Figure 5.31, which is the cool landscape.
3. Choose Image > Adjustments > Match Color.
4. Choose the warmer picture under the Source drop-down menu as seen in Figure 5.33.
5. Turn on Preview. At first, you may find the color change too much.
6. Adjust the Fade slider until you are happy with the colorizing.
7. Increase the Luminance setting to brighten the image and increase Color Intensity to adjust the depth of the color, as shown in Figure 5.34.
8. Click OK to apply the changes.

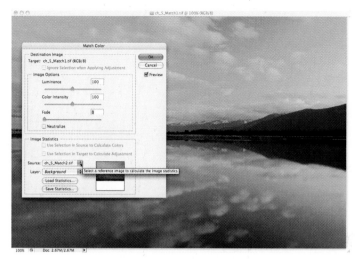

FIGURE 5.33   Initial setting adds a lot of the color.

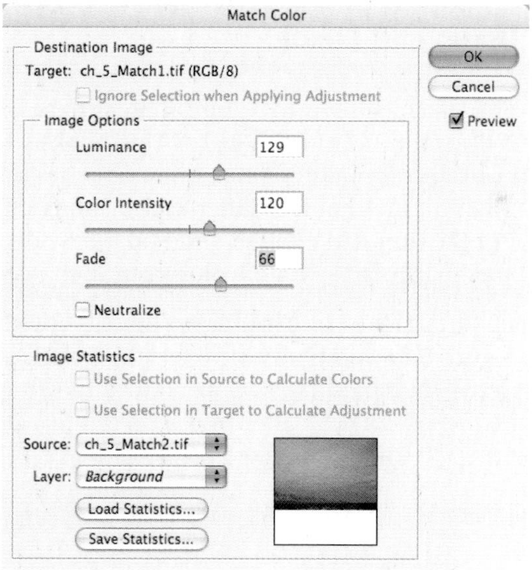

FIGURE 5.34   Adjusting the settings in the Match Color box.

Notice in Figure 5.35 how the Match Color tool was able to move the clouds to a pink color while keeping some of the blue in the sky and water. This is an amazing tool that can make short work of enhancing your images.

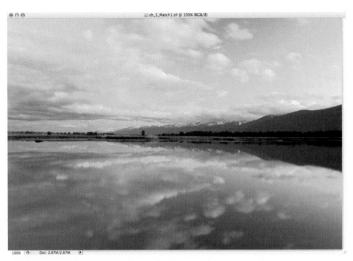

FIGURE 5.35   The image after color correction.

| **TUTORIAL 5.5** | **FIXING AN IMAGE WITH WASHED OUT/SHIFTED COLOR BY USING LAB COLOR** |

The image shown in Figure 5.36 suffers from a reddish color shift and lacks saturation in the color. This book is for digital photographers, but even digital photographers may have to scan an old image or two from time to time that has suffered the fading effect of age. In the case of this image, a lot of the film had expired and had a new date stamped on the box. Needless to say, the images lack a lot of color saturation because of bad film.

ON THE CD

1. Open Ch_5_LAB_before.psd from the CD-ROM, which is the original image in Figure 5.36, with a color cast and lacking any luster. In the real world, there will be times that you are forced to use such an image.

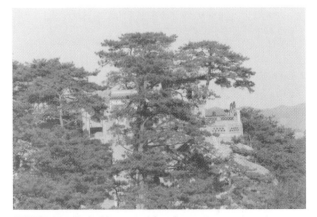

FIGURE 5.36   Faded image with color cast.

2. Choose the Hue/Saturation adjustment layer, or from the menu, select Image > Adjustments > Hue/Saturation.
3. Slide the Hue slider to compensate for the color shift.
4. Boost the saturation to restore some color to the image, as shown in Figure 5.37.

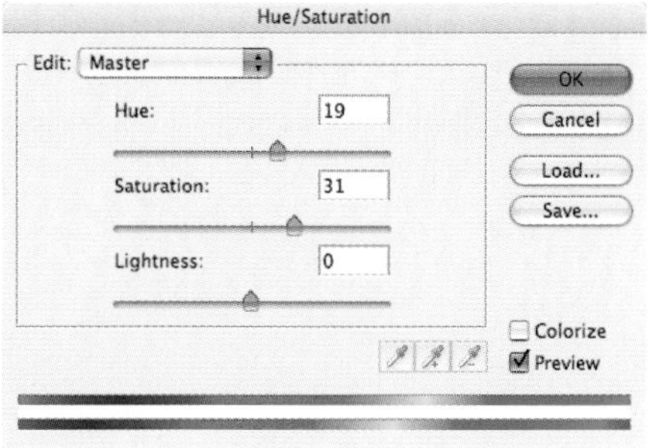

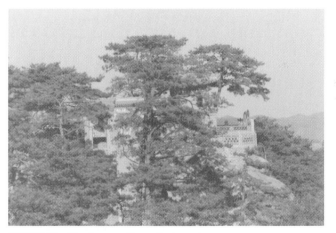

FIGURE 5.37   Hue/Saturation adjustment.

The image in Figure 5.38 is still not perfect, but it is a lot better than it was; the trees are showing some green now.

FIGURE 5.38   The image after adjustment.

Advanced Color Correction with Lab Color

We are now going to branch off into new territory by switching to Lab Color. Lab Color will split the image into three channels:

L (Lightness) Channel: Contains all the grayscale information in the image.
A Channel: Contains the magenta and green color information.
B Channel: Contains the yellow and cyan color information.

TUTORIAL 5.6   SPLITTING AN IMAGE INTO CHANNELS

To split an image into channels:

1. With `Ch_5_LAB_before.tif` still open, go up to the Layer menu and choose Flatten Layer from the bottom of the list.
2. Choose Image > Mode > Lab Color.
3. Open the Channels Palette, as shown in Figure 5.39.
4. Click on the Lightness channel to activate it, as shown in Figure 5.40.

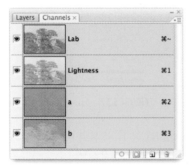

FIGURE 5.39   The Channels Palette in Lab mode.

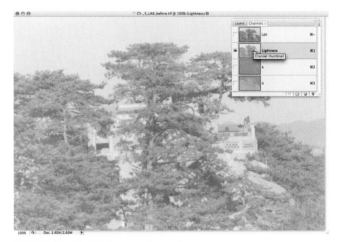

FIGURE 5.40   The Lightness channel.

5. Adjust the contrast on just this channel by adjusting the levels. Select Image > Adjustments > Levels. This will affect only the luminance (grayscale information) and will not shift the colors. Figure 5.41 shows the levels being adjusted. Here we have brought the shadow slider to the right to darken the shadows. (The Lightness channel is also the channel where all sharpening would take place.)

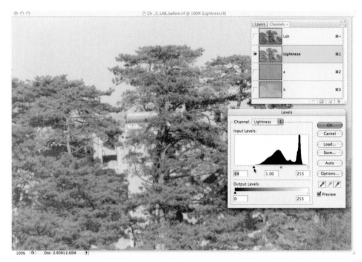

FIGURE 5.41   Adjusting the levels on the Lightness channel.

6. Click on the A channel to select it.
7. Turn on the Visibility icon next to the top (Lab) composite channel; the A channel should now be highlighted with all the channels visible (all eyeballs on), as shown in Figure 5.42.

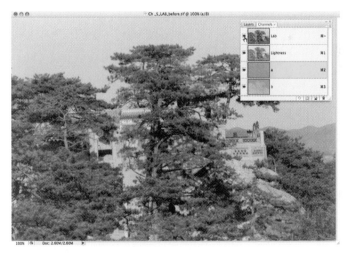

FIGURE 5.42   Image after adjustment.

8. Select Image > Adjustments > Levels.

You will now see the Levels slider, and you can adjust the color shift by sliding the middle slider. If you slide it to the left, magenta increases, and if you slide it to the right, green increases. Move the slider to the right a little, and notice how the green in the trees begins to really pop, as shown in Figure 5.43.

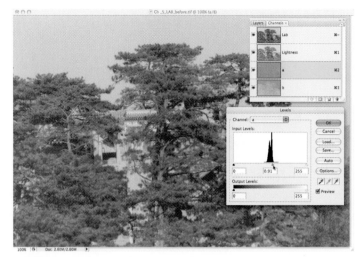

FIGURE 5.43   Increasing the green in the image.

9. Choose the B channel.
10. Open the Levels dialog box again.
11. The B channel contains yellow and cyan; move to the left for yellow and to the right for cyan (blue).
12. Move the slider a little bit to the right as shown in Figure 5.44 to bring some more blue to the sky.

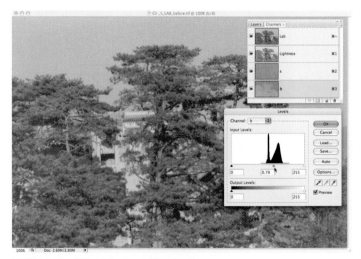

FIGURE 5.44   Adjusting the yellow/cyan.

You can see how much color has been restored in this image using the channels in Lab mode. See Figures 5.45a (the original image) and 5.45b (after the final corrections). When you are happy with the result, return to RGB mode (Image > Mode > RGB).

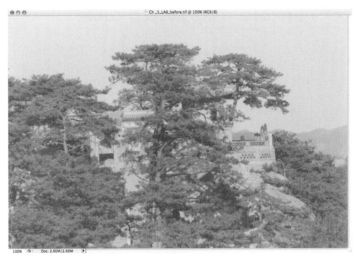

FIGURE 5.45A   The image before adjustment.

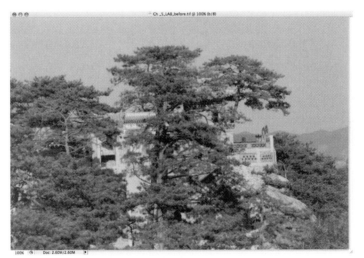

FIGURE 5.45B   The image after adjustment.

ADVANCED COLOR CORRECTION WITH LEVELS

This technique is a contrast/tone and color correction technique all in one. Once you run through this technique, you will see how just about any image can be improved, and you will use this technique many times over. For several years, this was just about the only correction technique we used.

TUTORIAL 5.7   USING LEVELS TO CORRECT COLOR

Open Ch_5_HongKong.jpg from the CD-ROM. Figure 5.46 shows an image from the amazing city of Hong Kong. As you can see, the image lacks a bit of contrast and also has a bit of a color cast to it. It's really not that bad (or is it?); it just looks a bit dirty. You will see a huge difference soon.

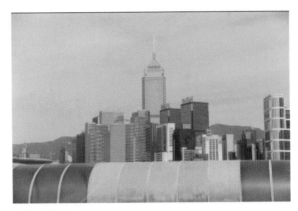

FIGURE 5.46   The image before adjustment.

1. Choose a Levels adjustment layer from the Layers Palette. Now set the black points and white points in the Levels settings.
2. In the Levels dialog box, double-click the Set Black Point tool as shown in Figure 5.47.

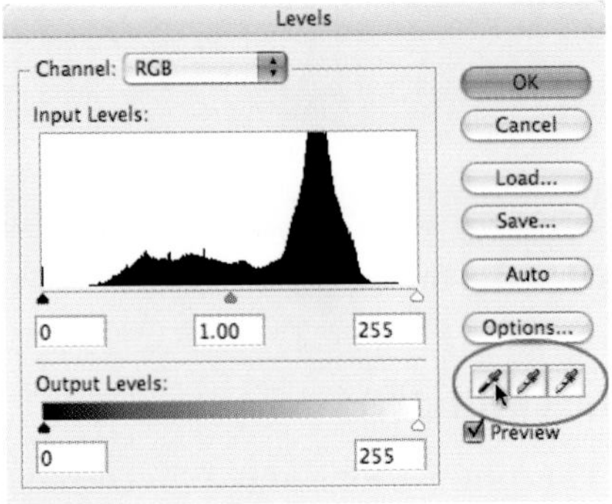

FIGURE 5.47   Setting the black point.

3. You will see the Color Picker box; set everything to solid black and then change the setting under B to 5, as shown in Figure 5.48. (This sets the black point to an *almost* pure black.)

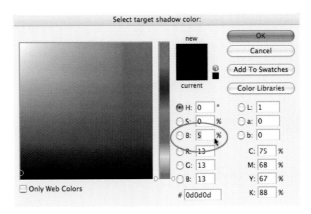

FIGURE 5.48   Black point target.

4. Click OK.
5. Double-click the Set White Point tool, which is the white eyedropper.
6. In the Color Picker, set for pure white, and then enter 95 into the B setting as shown in Figure 5.49. The white point is now set to 95% white.

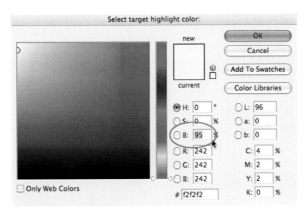

FIGURE 5.49   Setting the white point.

You are now ready to perform the image correction by clicking the Set Black Point tool in the darkest part of the image and the Set White Point tool in the lightest part of the image.

1. Locate the darkest part of the image. Hold down the Alt key (Option key for Mac), and move the shadow slider to the right. The image should turn white as you move the slider, and you will see some areas begin to show through. This is the black point threshold, as shown in Figure 5.50. The areas that start to show are the darkest areas of the image.

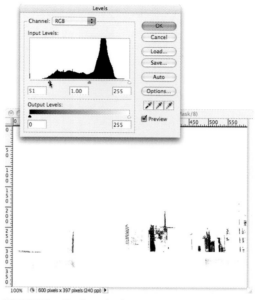

FIGURE 5.50 Finding shadows.

2. Take note of where the dark portion of the image is on the threshold, and return the slider to the far left.
3. Choose the Set Black Point tool, and click on the darkest portion of the image in the main image window, as shown in Figure 5.51. The image will be shifted, and the area you clicked on will now be set to the black that you selected in step 4 of the previous task.

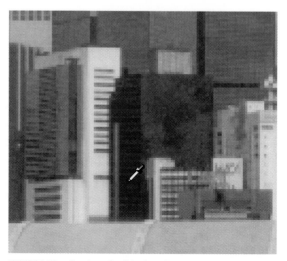

FIGURE 5.51 Setting the black point.

4. Hold down the Alt key (Option key for Mac), and move the right slider to the left to reveal the whitest point of the image. The image will begin as black, and the highlight areas will show through, as shown in Figure 5.52.

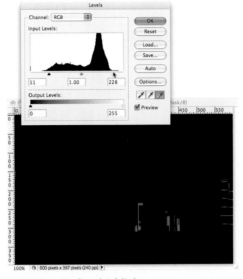

FIGURE 5.52   Finding highlights.

5. Choose the Set White Point eyedropper tool from the Levels Palette.
6. Click on the whitest area of the image as shown in Figure 5.53; the lightness of the image will be adjusted to match.

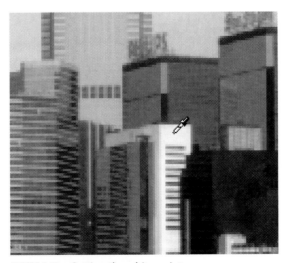

FIGURE 5.53   Setting the white point.

7. The tonal qualities of the image look much better now, and the color cast is reduced a bit. Now you can totally remove the color cast.
8. Choose the Set Gray Point eyedropper from the Levels dialog box. When you click on the image with this tool, it chooses the selected area as the gray point of the image and balances all the color to match.
9. Click on a portion of the image that should be a neutral gray, such as the small tower on the left in Figure 5.54.

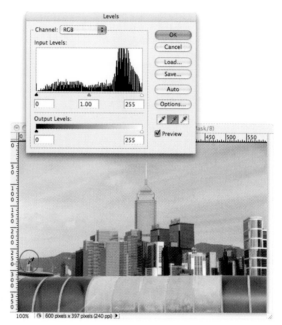

FIGURE 5.54 Setting the gray point.

10. The colors will shift; if you are not happy, keep experimenting by clicking the Set Gray Point tool in different parts of the image.
11. When you are happy with the result, click OK to apply the levels to the image.

You have now learned how to use the Levels tool correctly. It may seem like a lot to do, but with some practice, you can perform this entire correction in under a minute.

Figure 5.55 shows the image before the adjustment was made; Figure 5.56 shows the final corrected image, which is a vast improvement from the original.

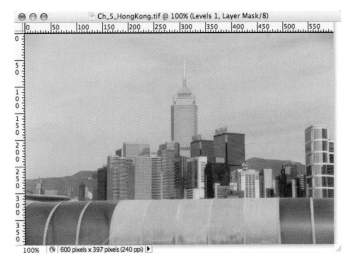

FIGURE 5.55   The image before adjustment.

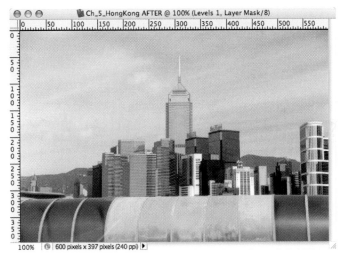

FIGURE 5.56   The image after adjustment.

ADVANCED COLOR CORRECTION WITH CURVES

We covered Curves in the previous chapter as a powerful tool for making tonal corrections and effects. Curves can also be used for color correction. Curves can be considered an advanced color correction method because it is possible to really mess up your images using Curves on color, if you don't know what you are doing. Some people avoid using Curves for color correction because it seems so random and difficult. Others do almost all color correction with Curves because of the control and power available. We'll discuss the benefits by showing you how to use Curves for color correction using a fairly simple method. If you have not yet read the section on Curves in the previous chapter, please do so before proceeding.

TUTORIAL 5.8	**USING CURVES TO ADJUST COLOR**

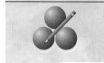

ON THE CD

Figure 5.57 shows an image that has a warm color cast. Open ch_5_Color_ Curves.jpg from the CD-ROM or use your own image.

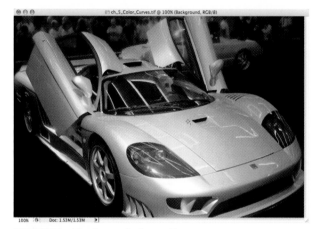

FIGURE 5.57   The image before adjustment.

1. Choose a new Curves adjustment layer. We now want to sample the color in an area that is showing the excess color. (A good place to begin when dealing with people is to sample the skin tones. Accurate skin tones are very important for natural-looking photos.)
2. Hold down Ctrl+Shift (Cmd+Shift for Mac), and move your cursor over the image (it changes to an Eyedropper tool). Click on the region that you want to sample, as shown in Figure 5.58. This adds an adjustment point to the color channels; you will see nothing in the Composite channel (RGB).

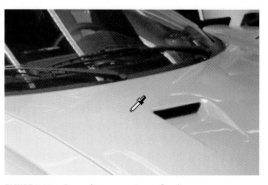

FIGURE 5.58   Sampling a region of color.

3. In the Channels drop-down menu, choose Red, as shown in Figure 5.59. You should now see the adjustment point at the top of the curve.

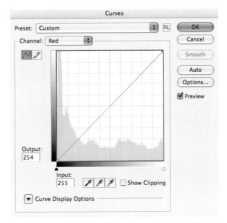

FIGURE 5.59   A point on the curve in the Red channel.

4. Move the point up to increase red or down to decrease it. In this case, we want to reduce red, so drag the point down and watch the image until the red cast disappears. (If you see no change in the image as you move the curve, make sure that Preview is turned on.) The movements usually need to be very subtle. Here moving the point down creates some red in the darker portions of the image. To combat this effect, put a point down on the lower end of the curve and lift it back up to the center line, as shown in Figure 5.60.

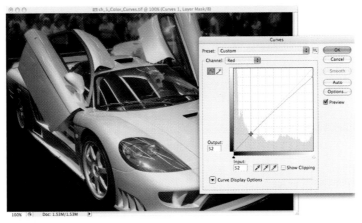

FIGURE 5.60   Adjusting red.

5. Repeat for the Blue channel as shown in Figure 5.61. Judging by the amount of yellow remaining in the image, blue is the next channel that needs the most adjusting.

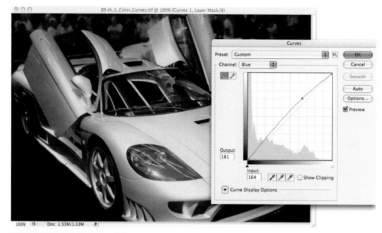

FIGURE 5.61   Adjusting blue.

6. Choose the Green channel and make adjustments as shown in Figure 5.62.

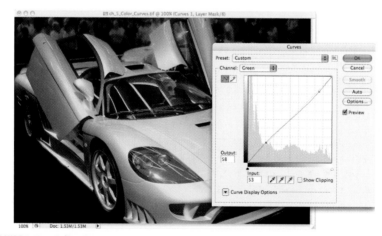

FIGURE 5.62   Adjusting green. You may want to add an additional point on the curve to fine-tune the color correction. Here we have lowered the point in the highlight region and raised the point in the shadow region to bring it back to where it started.

7. Click OK to apply the adjustment layer.
8. The last thing to do is change the Blending Mode of the layer to Color. When adjusting color in Curves or Levels, there can be a noticeable increase or decrease in contrast or brightness. This is not always objectionable. If it is, however, changing the blending mode will keep the curves from affecting the luminosity (brightness/contrast). Figure 5.63 shows how to adjust the blending mode or an adjustment layer.

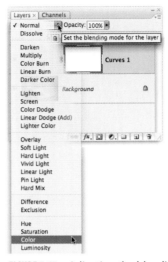

FIGURE 5.63   Adjusting the blending mode of the Curves adjustment layer from Normal to Color.

Figure 5.64 shows the image after the color adjustments with Curves. Notice that the color cast is neutralized, and other subtle coloring is now evident and much more pleasing. If you want to target different tones in the image, create a new Curves adjustment layer and repeat these steps, except for targeting a different color sample.

Reusing the Settings

When working in the adjustment tool dialog boxes, you will see two buttons: Save and Load. Use these options to save the settings so that they can be reapplied to other images that were shot under similar lighting. In the new Curves box, those settings are located under a new button as shown in Figure 5.65. Although Adobe has changed the names to Save Preset and Load Preset, they function in the same manner. Use the Save Preset option to save a setting as a file to your computer. Here is a suggested workflow:

1. Open the image.
2. Make the adjustment, but don't close the dialog box yet.
3. Choose the Save button (or Save Preset).
4. Choose a folder, and save the setting.
5. Click OK to apply.
6. Save and close the image.

Loading the settings:

7. Open an image.
8. Choose the adjustment.
9. Click the Load button (or Load Preset).
10. Locate the setting, and click OK to apply it.

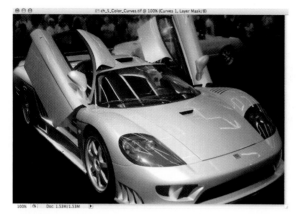

FIGURE 5.64   The image after adjustment.

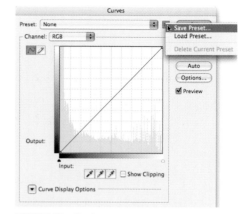

FIGURE 5.65   Saving a curve as a preset.

The image will now have the settings applied to it.

You can also use these settings with actions to batch process multiple images and save time.

SUMMARY

In this chapter, we looked at various color correction techniques that will help you adjust your images to natural-looking colors. We began with some very simple techniques and got more in-depth as the chapter progressed. These techniques will help you salvage all variety of unhealthy images and make them look great.

LOCAL ENHANCEMENTS: SELECTIONS AND MASKS

In This Chapter

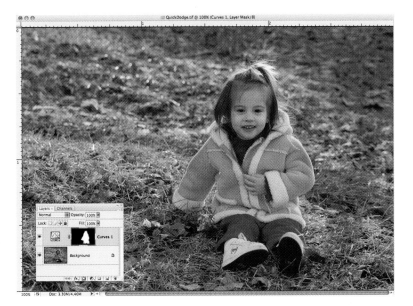

The ability to tweak color, contrast, and brightness within only select areas of an image is one of the greatest advantages to working in Photoshop. In the traditional darkroom, we called it burning and dodging. Burning darkens down a tone, and dodging lightens up a tone. We would use everything from complex chemical solutions, to cardboard, coat hangers, and masking tape to get the job done. Photoshop, on the other hand, allows us to be far more precise without having to break a sweat. In this chapter, we will explore several ways in which you can easily correct or enhance the look of a photograph by making small (or large) changes to specific, local areas of the image.

Figure 6.1 shows an example of what can be easily accomplished with a little "burning and dodging."

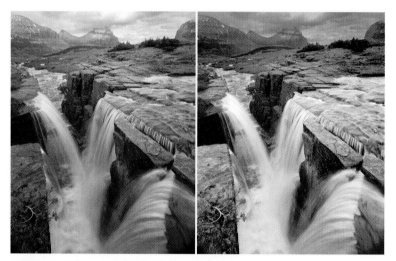

FIGURE 6.1   Before and after burning and dodging.

Adjustment Layer Mask

In Chapter 4, we discussed the advantages of working with adjustment layers rather than applying the edits directly to your background image. Another advantage of an adjustment layer is that it comes with a layer mask. This enables you to apply an adjustment to an image selectively. The layer mask is the box you see to the right of the Adjustment Layer icon. By default, the layer mask is white. This means that the effect is showing full strength.

To select the mask, click on it with the mouse. If you were to paint on the image with a black brush now, you would paint away the effect. If you were to paint with white, you would paint back the effect. Figure 6.2 shows the Layers Palette with multiple adjustment layers and their masks. Figure 6.2 also shows the enlarged thumbnail size. For larger and easier to view thumbnails, choose Palette options from the flyout menu at the top right of the Layers Palette.

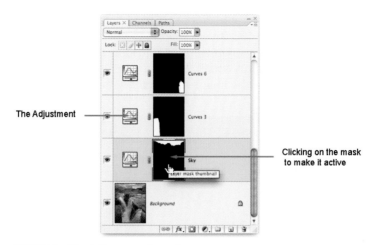

The Adjustment

Clicking on the mask
to make it active

FIGURE 6.2   The Adjustment Layer box.

Simple Local Adjustments

Many times, you will want to touch up just a small part of an image but leave every-thing else as it is. Here is a quick method for achieving those results.

In this example of my niece (see Figure 6.3), the exposure is good on the over-all shot, but I should have used a fill flash to throw a little more light onto her face. No problem. We will use an adjustment layer and paint onto the mask to achieve the effect.

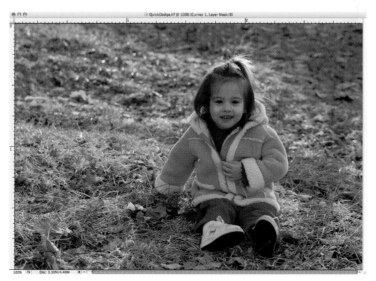

FIGURE 6.3   Original image.

1. Create a Curves adjustment layer by clicking on the adjustment layer icon at the bottom of the Layers Palette.
2. Sample the tone you want to adjust; in this case, it's her face.
3. Brighten up your curve, as shown in Figure 6.4. Her face is now brightened, but the rest of the image has been brightened, too.

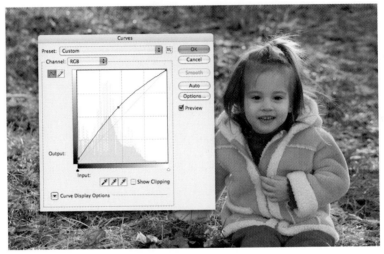

FIGURE 6.4   Brightening up the target portion of the image.

4. Choose the Paintbrush as shown in Figure 6.5a.
5. Set the hardness of the brush to 0. This will give the brush a nice soft edge. Circled in red in Figure 6.5b is the button that accesses the Brush dialog box.
6. Set the foreground color to Black as shown in Figure 6.5c.

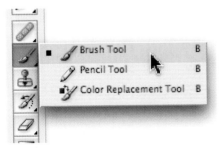

FIGURE 6.5A   Choosing the paintbrush and picking your foreground color.

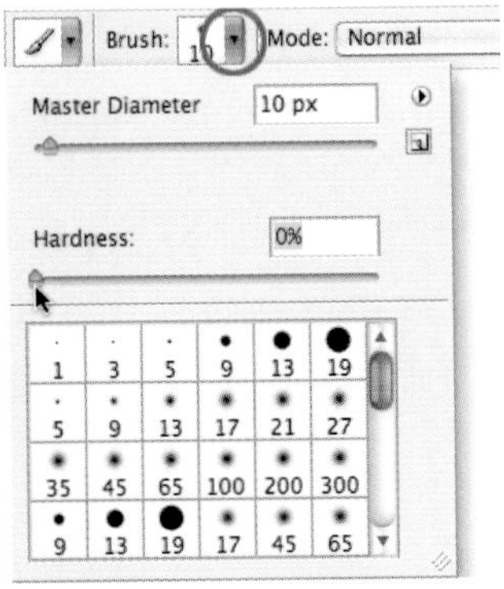

FIGURE 6.5B   Setting the hardness of the brush.

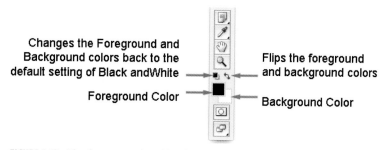

Changes the Foreground and
Background colors back to the
default setting of Black andWhite

Flips the foreground
and background colors

Foreground Color

Background Color

FIGURE 6.5C   The foreground and background color squares.

7. Click on the adjustment layer's mask.
8. Paint the parts of the image that you want excluded from the adjustment (see Figure 6.6). Notice that as you paint, the original image shows through, and you are painting away the adjustment. Here I have painted in all of the surrounding grass, which has become too bright after the adjustment.
9. Paint away all the unwanted adjustment with black.

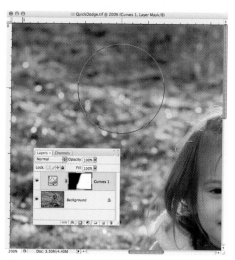

FIGURE 6.6   Painting away the adjustment from the unwanted areas.

In Figure 6.7, you can see that the adjustment layer has only affected her face and her body; the rest of the image has been painted with black on the mask with no effect. Instant fill flash! To speed things along, if you have an image where you have to paint more black than white, you can invert your mask first by following these steps:

1. Follow the preceding steps 1 through 3 to create an adjustment layer with a mask.
2. Click once on the mask, and from the menu, choose Image > Adjustments > Invert. This will turn your mask from White to Black.

3. Choose your paintbrush, and set the foreground color to White. Now you can paint in the adjustment on the face and the body.

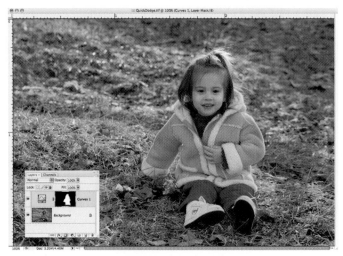

FIGURE 6.7   Selectively adjusted image.

The main idea here is that when you create an adjustment layer, the adjustment applies to the entire image. This is because the mask is white. When the mask becomes black, that adjustment does not apply. This method of working locally on your image is not only easy but also very flexible. If you paint "outside the lines," you can just flip the foreground and background colors and paint in the opposite color to cover your mistake. If you spend a fair amount of time working on masks, you may want to remember the "X" keyboard shortcut. Pressing the X key will exchange your foreground and background colors.

Selections

Creating a selection is another way to localize an adjustment. Selections tell Photoshop to "work in this area only." The cool thing about creating selections is that they automatically get turned into a mask when you create an adjustment layer. This can save time painting on the mask. Start with a fast and simple selection and most of the painting will be done for you. In this next example, we will use a selection to start the process of darkening an overly bright sky as shown in Figure 6.8.

ON THE CD

| TUTORIAL 6.1 | DARKENING A BRIGHT SKY WITH A SIMPLE SELECTION |

Open ch_6_DarkenSky.jpg from the CD-ROM. Figure 6.8 shows that in this image, the sky is just too bright. Darkening it down will greatly enhance the mood of this image.

1. Choose the Lasso tool from the toolbar.
2. Drag the Lasso tool to draw a circle inside the sky as shown in Figure 6.9. When you return to where you started, release your mouse. Try to stay inside the area that you want to affect. Do not try to be exact with your lines by drawing right around the edge. Quick and easy is the way to go. You will fine-tune the edge later.

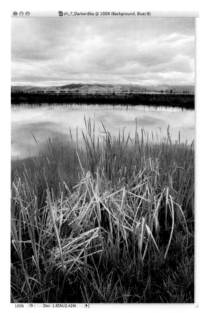

FIGURE 6.8   Original image with bright sky.

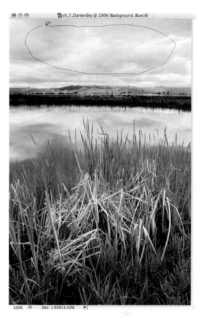

FIGURE 6.9   Drawing a selection.

3. After you have completed your circle, you will see the marching ants. This is the selection.
4. Create a Curves adjustment layer. Notice that your selection has disappeared, and it has automatically turned into a mask. Figure 6.10 illustrates that by creating an adjustment layer the selection turns into a mask. The area you selected is white, and the rest of the image is black.
5. Adjust the curve as shown in Figure 6.11. Creating the selection first gives you the added bonus of being able to see what effect the curves adjustment is having in relation to the area that is not being effected.
6. Now simply choose the Paintbrush from the toolbar, choose a nice soft brush (0% hardness), make sure that white is your foreground color, and paint in the effect of the curve. Once again, where the mask is black, the effect of the adjustment layer does not come through. Where you paint it with white, it does show through.

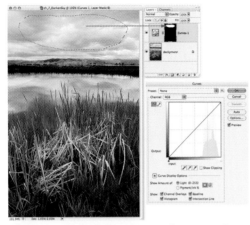

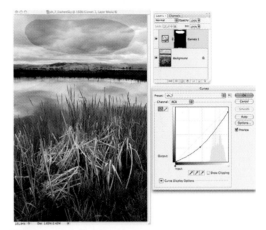

FIGURE 6.10   The selection is turned into a mask when a new adjustment layer is created.

FIGURE 6.11   Adjusting the curve.

Figure 6.12 shows the much improved image after the darkening down of the sky. It does, however, look a little fake. The water in the foreground is now lighter than the sky, which is an uncommon occurrence. Let's darken down the water somewhat. In this case, you can still paint on the mask you just used. Masks are great because you can always go back and repaint over them if you make any kind of mistake or if you want to fine-tune the mask.

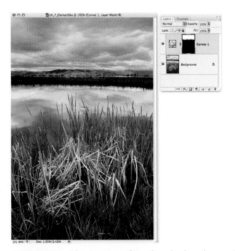

FIGURE 6.12   The image after the sky has been darkened.

7. Click once on the mask to ensure that the mask is active and not your background layer. If you do not have the Paintbrush tool active, go click on it in the toolbar and again choose White and a Soft Edge. This time, instead of painting in all white as you did in the previous example, paint in a shade of

gray. If White lets 100% of the adjustment through and Black 0%, then you can safely assume that a 50% gray will let 50% of the darkening adjustment through. In this case, if you painted with White letting all of the adjustment through, the effect would be too heavy. The water would be too dark.

8. To turn your foreground color gray instead of white or black, double-click on the foreground color chip. This will launch the Color Picker as shown in Figure 6.13. Inside the Color Picker, type 50 in the "B" box, which is shown circled in red (B stands for brightness). This will make the new foreground color 50% gray. Notice that you get a preview of the color in the top of the box where it says New, and you can see the white circle in the left of the box indicating that you are halfway up the Color Picker box between white and black.

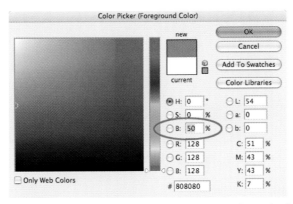

FIGURE 6.13   Choosing a middle gray from the Color Picker box.

9. Paint in the water in the middle of the picture with your new gray brush. Your mask should look something like Figure 6.14.

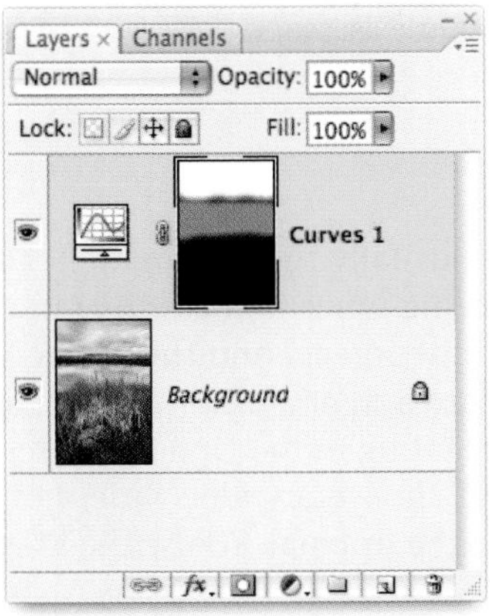

FIGURE 6.14   The mask with gray painted over the water.

Figure 6.15 shows the before and after image. It is amazing what a little localized adjustment can do for an image. 🎨

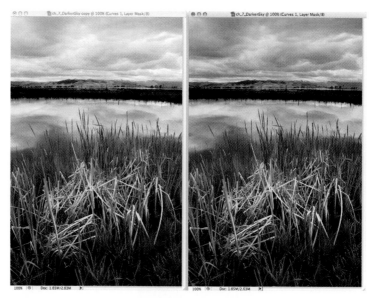

FIGURE 6.15 The image before and after the localized corrections.

A PHOTOGRAPHER'S SELECTION TOOLS

Creating a simple selection with the Lasso tool and then painting on the resulting mask will serve well in countless situations. Sometimes, however, you will be faced with images that need local adjustments within very intricate spaces. In these cases, it may be nearly impossible to paint a mask that will serve your purpose. Figure 6.16 shows an image where we need to make a mask to lighten the foreground. Painting around the trees would be tricky, so we'll use a simple tool called the Magic Wand to create a very precise selection.

The Magic Wand

The Magic Wand is usually the photographer's first favorite selection tool. It creates a selection by choosing tones that are the same or near to the tone that you click on. Click anywhere in the image, and the Magic Wand will choose that pixel and then go through the photo and add other pixels that are similar to it! Presto.

The Tolerance Setting in the Option bar restricts the Magic Wand's range of tone. A higher value will choose a wider variety of tones, and a lesser value will choose only tones closer to the original. To use the Magic Wand tool, simply select it from the toolbar, and click in the area of the image that contains the color you want selected. The Wand does the rest.

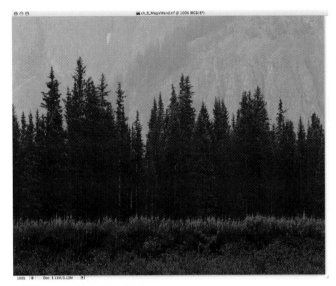

FIGURE 6.16 The original image.

The Anti-Aliased box is checked by default. This setting will smooth out the jagged edge of a selection line. Keep it checked.

When the Contiguous Box is unchecked, the Magic Wand will search the entire image looking for similar pixels to include in the selection.

When the Contiguous Box is checked, it will only select pixels that are both similar in color and adjacent to the original pixel chosen. Both options are useful depending on the type of selection and photograph you are working on.

TUTORIAL 6.2   USING THE MAGIC WAND

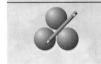

ON THE CD

Open ch_6_MagicWand.jpg on the CD-ROM as shown in Figure 6.16.

1. Click on the Magic Wand tool. (See Figure 6.17 for its location on the toolbar.)
2. The Tolerance should be set at 32 and the Contiguous box checked on the option bar. Uncheck the Contiguous box for this example. Your option bar should look like the one in Figure 6.18.
3. In this image, we want to select the whole foreground of trees, flowers, and grass. With the Magic Wand, click in the tops of the trees. Be sure that you are clicking in the tree and not the lighter background. Your selection should look something like Figure 6.19. We didn't get the whole area in one click so we are going to have to add to the selection.

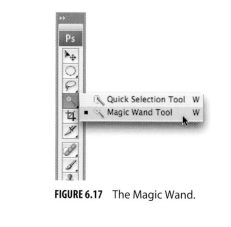

FIGURE 6.17 The Magic Wand.

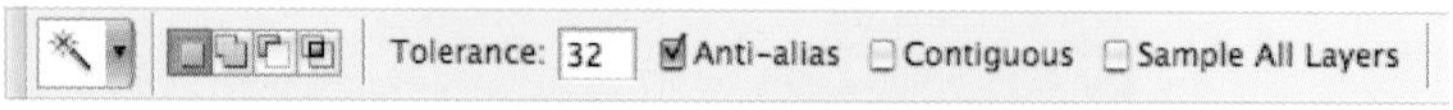

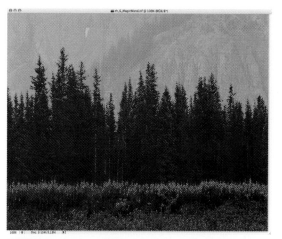

FIGURE 6.18 The option bar when the Magic Wand is chosen.

FIGURE 6.19 Image with most of the trees selected.

4. Click the Add to Selection button in the left of the Option bar (see Figure 6.20). Pressing the Shift key will also cause your selection tool to use the Add To mode. Now click in the parts of the image that should be selected. The Magic Wand will automatically include these as parts of your selection.

5. Depending on the tones in the image, you could spend a while clicking around to include all of the pixels. The thing to remember is that the edge is the most important part of the selection. In Figure 6.21, you can see that I stopped when my edge between the trees and the background looked good. It will be easier to take care of those stray, unselected pixels later.

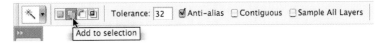

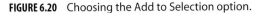

FIGURE 6.20   Choosing the Add to Selection option.

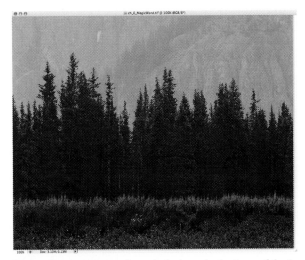

FIGURE 6.21   Some stray unselected pixels at the bottom of the image.

6. Create a Curves adjustment layer to brighten up the trees and foreground (see Figure 6.22). Things should look a lot better already.

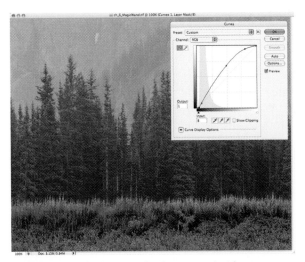

FIGURE 6.22   Lightening up the foreground with curves.

7. We now want to take care of those extra pixels that didn't get selected. Press the Alt key (Option key for Mac) while you click once on your mask in the Layers Palette on the adjustment layer. This will reveal the mask in black and white on your image.

8. Choose the Paintbrush, and pick White as your foreground color. Paint in any of the black areas that should be white in the foreground as shown in Figure 6.23. This is a much faster way to deal with those stray pixels. When finished, press the Alt key (Option key for Mac), and click on the mask again. Your image will return.

Figure 6.24 shows the final image. If you need a fast selection of an intricate area, the Magic Wand tool can work wonders. Can you imagine trying to paint along the edges of all of those trees?

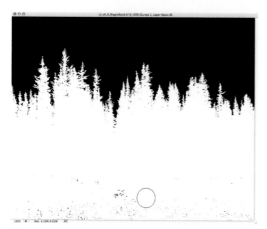 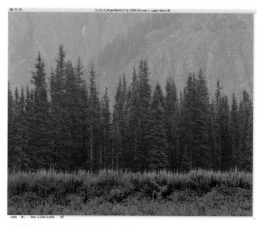

FIGURE 6.23 The mask made visible.   **FIGURE 6.24** The finished image.

Quick Selection Tool

This is a great new selection tool added to CS3. The Quick Selection tool is similar to the Magic Wand in that it creates complex selections . . . kind of quickly. Like the Magic Wand, it relies on adding and subtracting to the selection to create the intricate final mask. It is found under the same tool as the Magic Wand. In this next example, you will use the Quick Selection tool to select just the flower so that you can brighten it without affecting the background.

ON THE CD

TUTORIAL 6.3   USING THE QUICK SELECTION TOOL

Open `ch_6_QuickSelect.jpg` on the CD-ROM as shown in Figure 6.25.

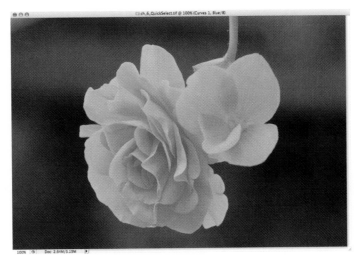

FIGURE 6.25   The original image.

1. Activate the Quick Selection tool by clicking and holding on the Magic Wand tool to reveal it in the flyout menu (see Figure 6.26). From the Brush box in the Option bar, set the size of the brush to about 45.

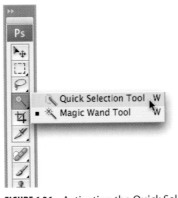

FIGURE 6.26   Activating the Quick Selection tool.

2. Start from one end, and click and drag the tool across the flower as shown in Figure 6.27

3. As you can see, the whole flower was not selected. Like with the Magic Wand, however, you can add to the selection. As soon as you are finished with your first drag, the brush automatically turns into the + Quick Selection tool. There is no reason to change anything on the Option bar. To add to the selection, simply paint around the inside of the flower. If your next stroke doesn't get it all, give it another paint stroke in an unselected area. If

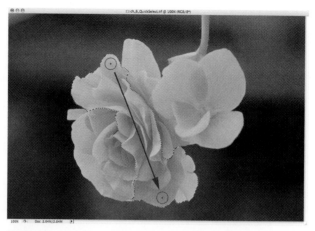

FIGURE 6.27   Painting with the Quick Selection tool.

you need to get into smaller areas, you can change the size of the brush in the Option bar or press the bracket keys [ ]. Left bracket ([ ) makes the brush smaller, and the right bracket ( ]) key makes it bigger. You can get this whole flower selected in just a few strokes of the Quick Selection tool (see Figure 6.28). If you over-select (and you will), use the Alt/Option key, and click in the over-selected areas to remove them from the selection, or choose the Subtract from Selection button in the Option bar.

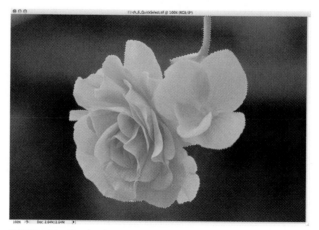

FIGURE 6.28   Final selection.

4. Now create a Curves adjustment layer to lighten the flower. Figure 6.29 shows the final image with the lightened flower. If you find your selection edge is not quite how you want it, keep reading. We will show you ways to fine-tune your edges with the Edge Refinement tool later in this chapter.

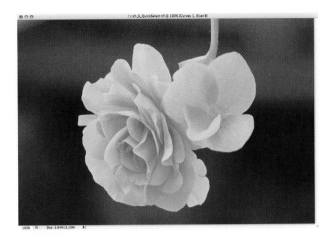

FIGURE 6.29   Final image after applying curves.

Selections with the Color Range Command

The Color Range command is a very powerful tool that allows ample amounts of fine tuning. Its operation is similar to that of the Magic Wand except that it chooses its pixels by color rather than density. It also has the ability to only half select pixels. When the Magic Wand or Quick Selection tool makes a selection, the pixels are either selected or not. On or off. The edit you apply, then, say a change in color, is either applied or it isn't.

The Color Range command can apply the edit in different doses according to the amount that each pixel has been selected. Some pixels will be 100% selected, others 0%, and others could be 20%, 30%, or 60% selected. When a pixel is only 30% selected, it will have only 30% of the edit applied to it. This is what is happening when you apply a feather to a selection. The edges are not fully selected.

The Color Range tool is also great for making quick and effective density selections. Many times, we just want to select a density range, like the shadows or highlights, and be able to apply a simple adjustment to the pixels with this density.

TUTORIAL 6.4	**USING THE COLOR RANGE SELECTION COMMAND**

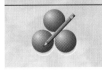

ON THE CD

Open `ch_6_SelectColorRange.jpg` from the CD-ROM as shown in Figure 6.30.

In this example, we will lighten the walkway and ceiling to draw the viewer back into the photograph. Using the Color Range command will make selecting this area very easy.

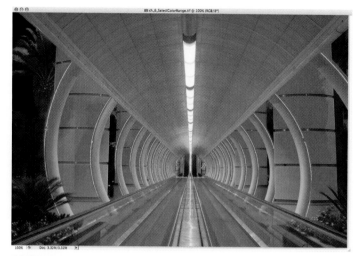

FIGURE 6.30 Original image.

1. Begin by choosing Select > Color Range. You will see the Color Range command box similar to the one in Figure 6.31.

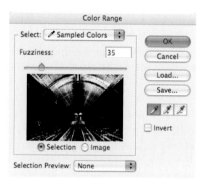

FIGURE 6.31 The Color Range command box.

2. Move your cursor over the main image window, and you will notice that it becomes the eyedropper tool. Click in the ceiling to sample the color green. Use caution when clicking in the window because you do not want to pick up the reddish-green color, just the green. After you click, the black-and-white box in the Color Range box will change to reflect your new selection as shown in Figure 6.32. The white is showing you what is selected, and the black is showing you what is not selected.
3. You need to do some more sampling to select the entire green area of the walkway and ceiling. To add to the selection, click the + eyedropper in the Color Range box, and continue to sample the color green in the main image

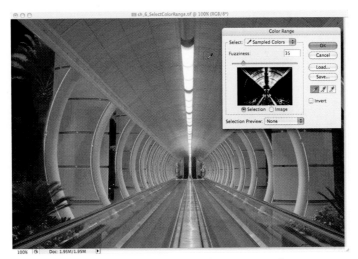

FIGURE 6.32   Sampling a color with the Color Range eyedropper.

window. You can also click and drag across the image to increase the selection. If you start picking up other unwanted colors, the – eyedropper will remove color from your selection. To further refine your selection, you can use the Fuzziness slider. Moving this slider to the left will subtract similar colors from the selection. Moving it to the right will add in similar colors to the selection. This is similar to using the Tolerance setting on the Magic Wand.

4. You should end up with a selection preview similar to that in Figure 6.33. Click OK. This preview will translate into a selection like that shown in Figure 6.34.

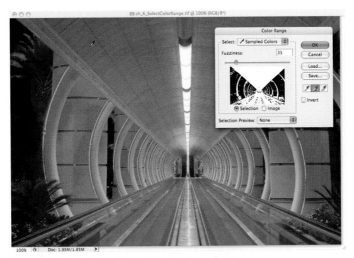

FIGURE 6.33   The box after adding to the selection.

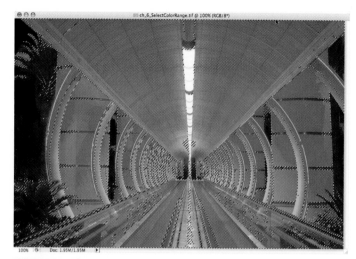

FIGURE 6.34 The resulting selection.

5. Create a Curves adjustment layer to lighten the selected area. If you lighten up the image enough, you will begin to see some areas of posterization where the green meets the red. Figure 6.35 shows the posterized areas circled in blue. The transition between the colors is just too abrupt because the mask is too sharp. This is a common occurrence when using the selection tools. You will almost always need to blur the selection edge. Blurring the edge is similar to painting with a soft edged brush as you did earlier in this chapter. One way to accomplish this is by using the Quick Mask option under the Refine Edge command. More on this in a moment. Another way is to blur the adjustment layer mask.

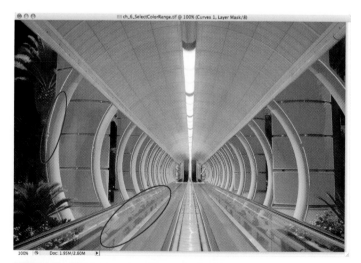

FIGURE 6.35 The image showing posterization.

6. Click on the mask once to ensure that it is active.
7. From the Filter menu, choose Blur > Gaussian Blur.
8. Lower the radius to 0.1 and unclick the mouse. At this point, you have no blur at all. While watching the main image window, slowly move the radius slider back to the right in small increments. Be sure to move it a little and then unclick. This gives the filter time to render. Move it up again. You are looking for the point where the harsh transition between the colors disappears. Figure 6.36 shows a smoother transition between the colors after applying the Gaussian blur to the mask.

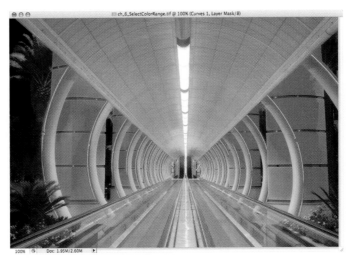

FIGURE 6.36   The final image.

As you can see, the Magic Wand, Quick Selection tool, and Color Range command can be used to create very complex selections. These selections would take a very long time to replicate if you were hand painting on a mask. So when do you choose to use a selection tool versus painting on a mask? Which selection tool do you choose? Here are some guidelines.

1. Determine what it is that you want to do to an area. Darken it? Lighten it? Change its color?
2. Decide whether or not the adjustment can be accomplished without the use of a selection or mask. For example, changing the color of something may be as simple as using the Hue/Saturation box and picking that color from the drop-down box (see Chapter 5). Lightening up the shadows could possibly be accomplished with the Shadow/Highlight tool.
3. If you try these tools and you find that you will need to work locally instead of globally, it is time to decide on a masking technique.

4. Complex selection or hand painting a mask? This will depend on your subject, the surrounding areas, and the edges in between. If the subject and its surrounding area are very different then perhaps your adjustment will not affect the surrounding area, so painting on the mask will be fine. If your subject and surrounding area are similar, and the surrounding area will be adversely affected by the adjustment, you may need to create a more accurate selection of the area.

5. After you have determined that you need to create a complex selection, the next trick is decide which tool to use. Use the Magic Wand if the areas are better separated by brightness. Use the Color Range command if the areas are better separated by color, and use the Quick Selection tool if they are similar in both brightness and color.

Refining Selections

The marching ants that represent selections have been around forever. That doesn't mean that they are the best tool for the job, just what we have had up to this point. With the addition of the Refine Edge tool, Photoshop CS3 now offers a much better way to view selections. In addition, the tool gives you a chance to modify selections as well. Very rarely do you create a perfect selection on the first go around. But that's okay because this new tool gives you ample opportunities to fine-tune the selection before you turn it into a mask.

When you have any selection tool active, such as the Magic Wand or Quick Selection tool, and a selection active (the marching ants are visible on your screen), you will have access to the Refine Edge command. This command will allow you to modify or refine the edges of your selection. When you are ready to further work with selections, click on the Refine Edge button found on the menu bar. You will see the box shown in Figure 6.37.

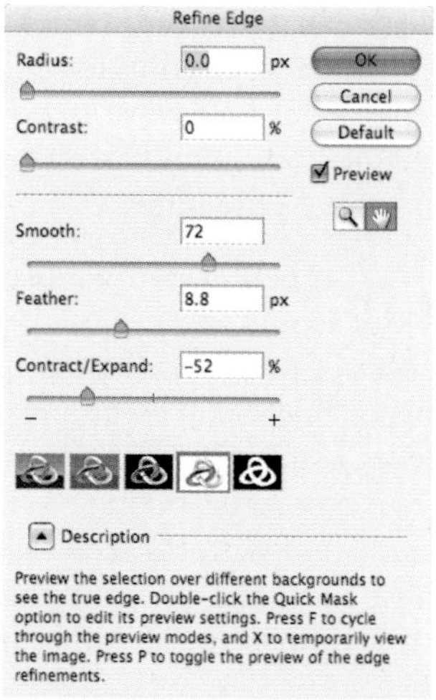

FIGURE 6.37 The Refine Edge box.

The advantage of working with your selections in this box is that you are able to see its true edge. With just the marching ants, it is often difficult to tell how well you have selected an area. The Refine Edge box gives you many ways to preview a selection. The row of icons in the lower section of the box describes how we can view the area of the image that is selected. By placing your cursor over the icon, you receive a description of the view in the lower dialog box. The first icon is the least useful. It is the standard view. It still works with the marching ants, so it is hard to envision. One of the most useful is the On White option, which is the fourth from the left. This works well in general and for darker objects. You also may find the On Black useful for lighter objects. Figures 6.38a–c show a few of the options.

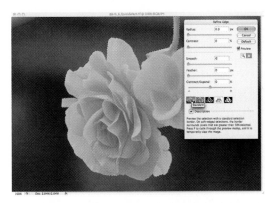

FIGURE 6.38A   Standard view.

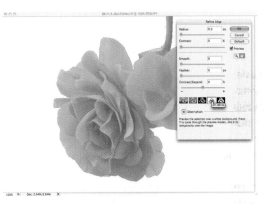

FIGURE 6.38B   Preview with White background.

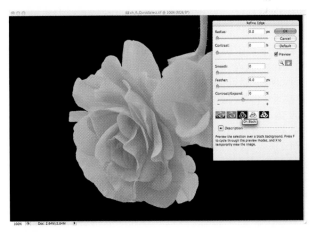

FIGURE 6.38C   Preview with Black background.

Let's take a look at the options in the Refine Edge dialog box. Switching the Preview mode will help you see how the edges are being affected by the different options within the tool.

The first option is **Radius**. By increasing this slider, you are increasing the area around the original edge that will be affected by the settings. Figures 6.39a and 6.39b show the before and after selection in Mask mode. Notice how in Figure 6.39b the increased radius allows the edge to get bigger and how it becomes softer. This will be the effect if this is the only slider that you use. If you go on to further refinement in the bottom of the box, this "radius amount" is defining the region in which the other options will operate.

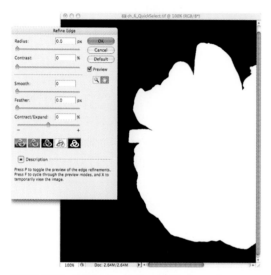

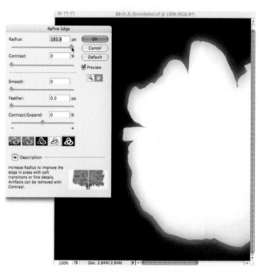

FIGURE 6.39A   Original selection in Mask mode.

FIGURE 6.39B   Selection after the radius has been increased.

The second option is **Contrast**. This slider's main goal is to remove any fuzzy artifacts that may have become apparent when the Radius was enlarged. In this example, we do not have any fuzzy artifacts to work with. Radius and Contrast work together to tighten the selection or make it more detailed, but don't turn up radius too much because that's the job of Feather. Another way to think of the Radius is that it is used to create a soft enough edge for the Contrast to have something to work with.

The **Smooth** slider does just what you think it may do. It smoothes out the rough edges of a selection. Figure 6.40a shows the view On White before the Smooth slider is increased. Figure 6.40b shows the edge after smoothing.

The **Feather** slider is similar to the Radius slider in that it "blurs" the edge of the selection. It differs in that it exerts no control over the region that is being worked on by the other sliders; it is chiefly used for blurring the edge. Use this tool to blend your adjustment from inside the selection to outside the selection. In this view, we are seeing the Mask mode again. Remember that what is white is selected and what is black is not selected. If it is a shade of gray, it is partially selected. This means that only some of the adjustment will come through. Figure 6.41a and Figure 6.41b show the before and after.

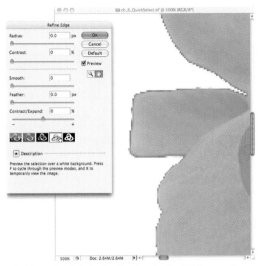

FIGURE 6.40A Original selection in On White mode.

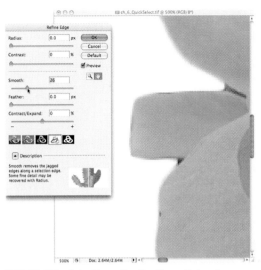

FIGURE 6.40B Selection after the Smooth has been increased.

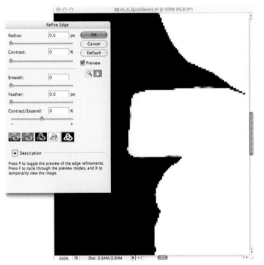

FIGURE 6.41A Original selection in Mask mode.

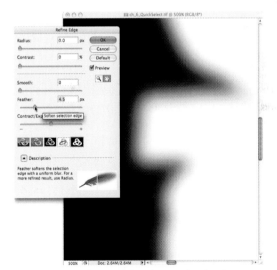

FIGURE 6.41B Selection after the Feather has been increased.

The **Contract/Expand** slider will make your current selection edge grow outward (expand) or inward (contract). If your edge is hard, it will stay hard but just grow inward or outward. If it is soft, it retains its soft nature and contracts or expands. Figure 6.42a and Figure 6.42b show before and after expansion. Notice that to get any noticeable amount of expansion, the Radius slider needed to be increased. Just increasing the Expand amount was not enough for it to be visible. Increasing the Radius increased the region or the area around the edge that will be affected by the expand slider (or any of the other sliders as well). This slider comes in handy for removing halos.

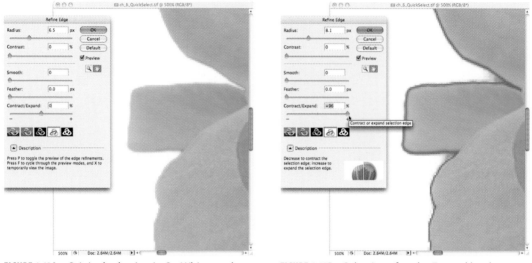

FIGURE 6.42A Original selection in On White mode.   **FIGURE 6.42B** Selection after the Expand has been increased.

Click OK inside the Refine Edge box to commit to the changes that you made. You will be returned to your image with the new selection still active. Remember that you may not see any visible change to the marching ants. Don't worry, though, when you create an adjustment layer, the resulting Mask will look just like the preview!

Refining Masks

Although modifying the edges of the selection with the new Refine Edge tool is quite a leap forward, sometimes you will just need to revert back to the old method of doing these tricks, that is, working on the mask itself. The problem with working on the selection occurs when you are masking out an adjustment layer. The adjustment layer, of course, will produce a change in the image. This change may or may not be obvious at the edges of the selection. With just modifying the selection before the adjustment is made, we have no idea how each side of the selection edge will look. If you create a good selection first, then create the adjustment layer and turn it into a mask, and *then* modify your mask, you will have a real-time visual of the blending.

Figures 6.43a and 6.43b show an image where the sky is masked to reduce its contrast and to darken it down some. With the sky darker, it brings more attention to the foreground rocks.

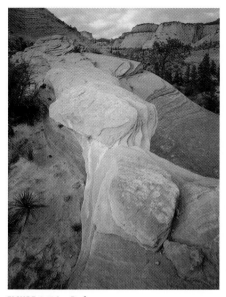

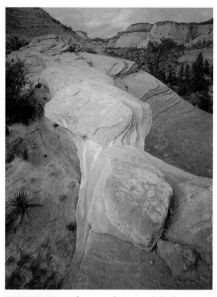

FIGURE 6.43A   Before.

FIGURE 6.43B   After masking and darkening the sky.

When working with a mask, it is always a good idea to click on your mask once (the mask itself, not the adjustment layer) to ensure that you are actually on the right layer and on the mask itself. This will get you into a good habit that will be beneficial to you when you begin to work with multiple images in one document. Figure 6.44 demonstrates how to ensure that the mask is active by clicking on it once. Double-clicking on the mask will bring up the Layer Mask Display options box. We'll explain more on this shortly. If you accidentally double click and get this box, just click OK. No harm done.

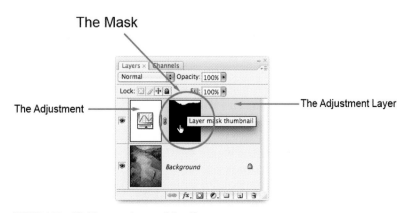

FIGURE 6.44   Clicking on the mask itself.

Once you click on your mask, you are able to modify it in any way that you would a grayscale image. This means you can lighten, darken, increase contrast, blur, sharpen, or apply any other number of filters to it. At the moment, however, we can't really see the mask. This doesn't mean we can't affect it; we just can't see what we are doing. There will be many times when you want to affect the mask without looking at it. One example would be that you have created an adjustment layer with a mask, and the new adjustment is adversely affecting the surrounding areas. By *working* on the mask but *looking* at your image, you can watch how your edits are affecting the mask. Of course, there are those times that you will want to look at the mask directly. There are two ways you can view a mask:

Press the Alt key (Option for Mac), and click on the mask itself. This will overlay the mask in black and white on your image. Figure 6.45 shows the Normal view of the image. Figure 6.46 shows the Mask view. To return to Normal view, just press the Alt key (Option for Mac), and click on the mask again.

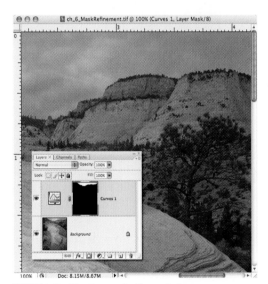

FIGURE 6.45 The image in Normal view.

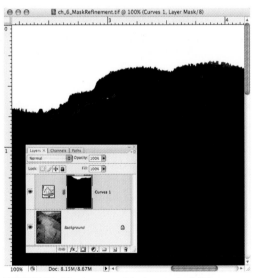

FIGURE 6.46 The image with the mask visible.

Press the backslash key on your keyboard. The backslash key is just to the right of the bracket [ ] keys. This will show the mask as a semitransparent red overlay on your image as show in Figure 6.47. The color and the opacity of this overlay can be changed to suit your needs. Double-click on the mask to bring up the Layer Mask Display Options box (see Figure 6.48). Click OK in this box when you have made the desired changes. The mask overlay will display these new settings until your return to this box to change them. Pressing the backslash key again will return your image to Normal view.

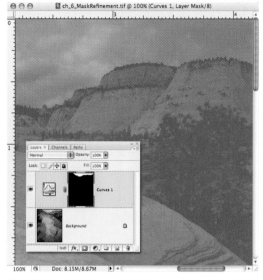

FIGURE 6.47   The image with the mask overlay visible.

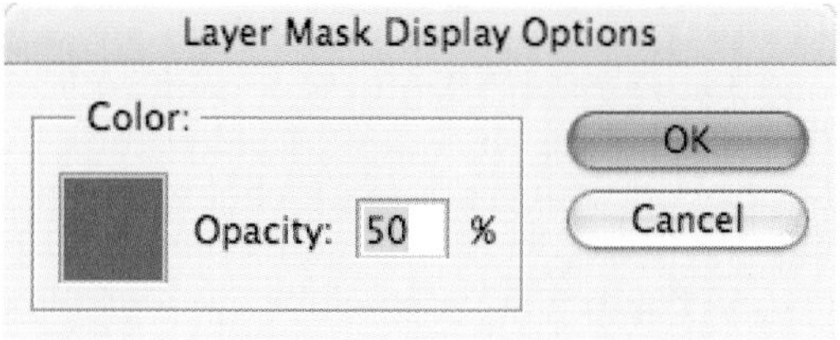

FIGURE 6.48   The Layer Mask Display Options box.

It is beneficial to have both of these options, as neither will work 100% of the time. Sometimes, you may need to see through to your image, while other times it will be easier to work in the black-and-white mode. Now that we can see our mask, let's explore what we can do with it.

1. You can shrink and enlarge your mask by choosing either Filter > Other > Minimum or Filter > Other > Maximum. The Minimum filter will shrink the mask, and the Maximum filter will enlarge it. Figure 6.49 shows the mask being enlarged with the use of the Maximum Filter. Increase the Radius slider within this box to gain the effect. Clicking in your image will reveal that portion of the mask in the Preview window inside the box.

2. You can ease the transition from black to white by blurring your image. Go to Filter > Blur > Gaussian Blur. This is one of those techniques where you should really be looking at your image rather than the mask. Figure 6.50 shows the technique with the mask displayed so we can better see its effect. Raising the radius slider increases the blur.

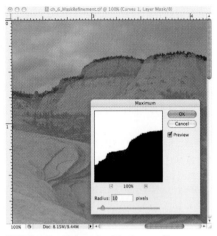

FIGURE 6.49   Using the Maximum filter to enlarge the mask.

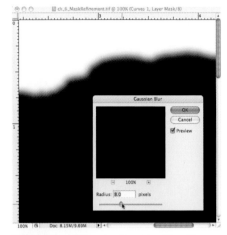

FIGURE 6.50   Using the Gaussian Blur filter to soften the edge of the mask.

3. On occasion, you can create a mask that has shades of gray as well as white and black (see Figure 6.51). This is not uncommon when using Select > Color Range. In cases like these, you may want to subtly alter the tones in the mask. You can adjust a mask with any adjustment (Curves, Levels, and so on) that work on brightness or contrast. Color adjustments will be grayed out when you are on a mask. To alter the contrast of a mask (remember to click once on your mask first), choose Image > Adjustments > Curves. You could also use Levels. The adjustment will be reflected on your mask as shown in Figure 6.52. Remember, White allows your adjustment to be visi-

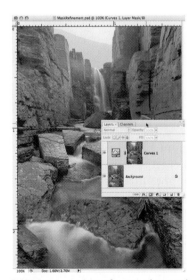

FIGURE 6.51   A view of a complex mask with shades of gray as well as white and black.

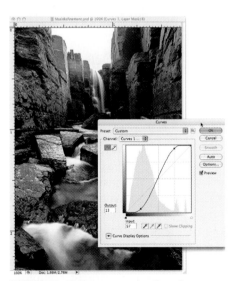

FIGURE 6.52   Using curves to adjust the contrast of a mask.

ble, and Black restricts it. So as you increase the contrast of a mask like this you are simultaneously letting more and less of the adjustment through in different areas of the image.

4. You can also combine the selections with masks. Let's say that on the previous image (see Figure 6.51), you wanted to blur a section of the mask rather than the entire thing. With your mask active, draw a selection of the area that you want to affect. In this example, we will blur the edges of the sky and top of the canyon.

5. Draw a rough selection with the Lasso tool as shown in Figure 6.53. Next, click the Refine Edge button. You need to blur the selection to ensure a good blur on the mask as shown in Figure 6.54.

6. To blur the mask, select Filter > Blur > Gaussian Blur, and adjust the radius to suit your needs. Remember to go to Select > Deselect when you are finished! Figure 6.55 shows the result of selective blurring of the mask.

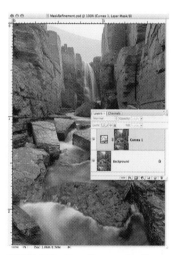

FIGURE 6.53 Creating a selection on a mask.

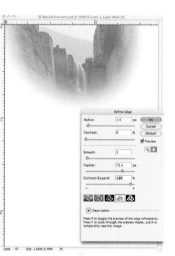

FIGURE 6.54 Blurring the selection using the Refine Edge command.

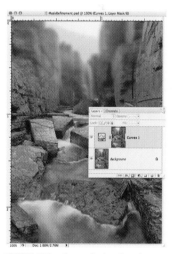

FIGURE 6.55 A mask that has been selectively blurred.

SUMMARY

In this chapter, you delved into the world of localized adjustments. The subtle (or not so subtle) changes in color, brightness, or contrast can transform an average image into a work of art. Remember to first imagine how you want your image to look, and then decide on which tool will best accomplish that. Also bear in mind that some adjustments have enough built-in control that selections and masks are unnecessary. Other times, you'll want to be very precise and just apply the change to a specific area. With a little practice, these techniques will become second nature!

CHAPTER

7

SHARPENING AND NOISE REDUCTION

In This Chapter

- TUTORIAL 7.1 Sharpening an Image Using Unsharp Mask
- TUTORIAL 7.2 Using Smart Sharpen
- TUTORIAL 7.3 Nondestructive Sharpening Using High Pass Filter
- Noise Reduction
- TUTORIAL 7.4 Using Channels for Noise Reduction
- Noise Reduction Filter

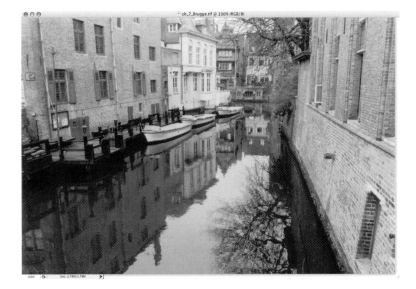

Whether it is improper focus, an unsteady hand, movement, or scanning, many things can introduce blurring to your photos. There is nothing quite like a nice crisp, sharp image, and Photoshop has the tools to help achieve that result without it looking fake. Sharpening is a task that you will perform many times throughout your career, and this chapter will introduce you to several useful techniques.

Unsharp Mask

The most common method for sharpening images goes by the most unusual name: *Unsharp Mask*. What this oddly named filter does is detect the sharp changes in tone in the image, and then it says, "This must be an edge." The Unsharp Mask then brightens one side of the edge and darkens the other side to make it look more pronounced, and the result is a sharper image with more edge definition. We have control over three attributes of the filter:

Amount: This is how pronounced the effect will be by adjusting the contrast. The lighter pixels on one side of the edge will be brightened, and the darker pixels on the other side of the edge will be darkened as you increase the amount.

Radius: The width of the brightening and darkening effect added to the image. The brightening and darkening effect will increase outward from the original edge as you increase the radius. If you turn this all the way up, you will see a "halo" around the edges.

Threshold: Determines what Unsharp Mask interprets as edges by adjusting the sensitivity of edge detection.

TUTORIAL 7.1	**SHARPENING AN IMAGE USING UNSHARP MASK**

Open ch_7_OperaHouse.jpg from the CD-ROM. Figure 7.1 shows the image, which could use a little bit of sharpening.

ON THE CD

1. Choose Filter > Sharpen > Unsharp Mask. You will see the Unsharp Mask dialog box, as shown in Figure 7.2.
2. Click anywhere in the image to sample that region. This new region will appear in the preview in the dialog box.
3. Use the + and – buttons to zoom in or out of the image. The default is 100% view. The preview is best viewed at either 100% for 8" × 12" images or smaller. A 50% view provides better results for images larger than 8" × 12".
4. Make sure Preview is checked so that you can see the result on the image.
5. First, adjust Amount according to the image and how much sharpening you want to apply. Usually 100 is a pretty good starting place.
6. Adjust Radius to get a good result without making the effect look artificial and filtered. Between 0.5 and 2.0 usually works well.

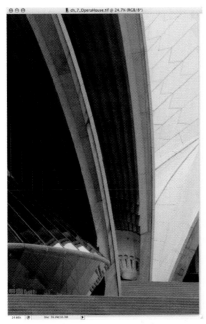

FIGURE 7.1   Image in need of sharpening.

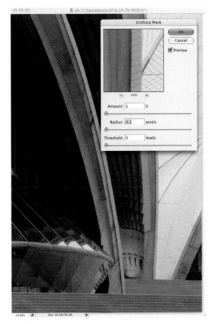

FIGURE 7.2   The Unsharp Mask dialog box.

7. You may need to go back and forth between Amount and Radius a few times to get a good balance. Remember that you should sharpen a bit higher for buildings than you would for people; sharpening people is not flattering because it can bring out flaws in their skin.

8. Finally, set Threshold. In this case, keep it at 0, which tells Photoshop that everything is an edge and to sharpen all edges. If you were sharpening a person's face, you might use Threshold to ignore certain things such as the face's texture. The higher the threshold, the more contrast must be present to be affected.

9. When you are happy with your settings, such as in Figure 7.3, click OK to apply the effect.

Fading the Sharpness (Optional)

Immediately after applying a filter, you can use the Fade option to adjust the intensity of the effect. This option is available only when the previous command was a filter. It is not available after you have done anything else to the image, even changing the visibility of a layer or channel.

To apply this effect:

1. Choose Edit > Fade *name of last filter*.

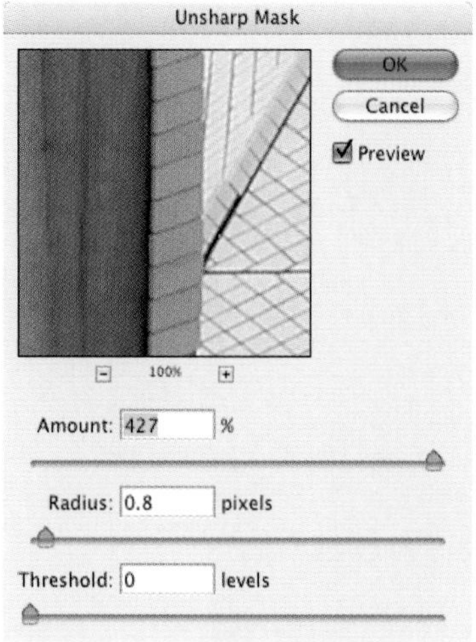

FIGURE 7.3 Setting the options in the Unsharp Mask dialog box.

2. Adjust the opacity if needed; keeping it at 100% retains all sharpness, and moving it toward 0% reduces the sharpening effect. Next set the blending mode to Luminosity. This will ensure that the sharpening effect does not introduce any color artifacts. Figure 7.4 shows the Fade box (to open, choose Edit > Fade) with the blending Mode set to Luminosity.

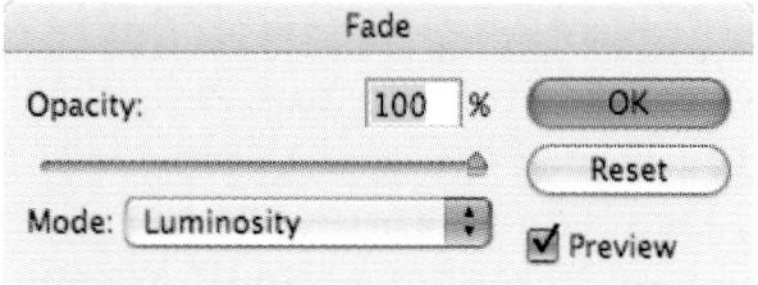

FIGURE 7.4 Changing the blending Mode to Luminosity.

Figure 7.5 shows the image after sharpening.

It's best to avoid overdoing sharpening because it can make an image look too harsh and artificial. Most corrections should be done with subtlety.

Here is a method for setting the sliders that we have found to be fairly foolproof with almost all types of images. Begin by prepping the box before actually starting to sharpen:

1. Open the Unsharp Mask box, and set the Amount to 500, the Radius all the way to the left at 0.1, and the Threshold to 3.

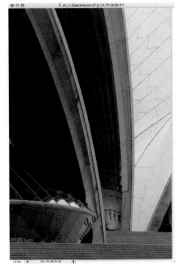

FIGURE 7.5   The sharpened image.

2. Move the Radius slider up one click at a time (one tenth) until the image starts to look over-sharpened. You will notice it first in the sharpest edges. It's easiest to highlight the number in the Radius box and press the up arrow key to move this in small increments.
3. Move the Amount slider to below 100%.
4. Your box is now prepped. Give your eyes a break by looking around the room for a minute or so to readjust them to what real sharpness looks like.
5. Now to sharpen the image, slowly increase the Amount slider until the image looks properly sharp. Remember that at 500, it was too sharp, so it will be somewhere less than that.

Sharpening Using Lab Mode

In previous chapters, we moved into the realms of Lab mode as a way of correcting images. Lab mode is also great for sharpening images because you can apply the sharpening to just the Grayscale channel. This has two advantages:

- It prevents any color shifting because the color information is untouched.
- It minimizes the introduction of noise to the image. Sometimes there is a lot of noise or grain in the color of a photo, particularly in the blue regions. If we were to sharpen the blue, it would also accentuate the grain and noise.

ON THE CD

Open the image ch_7_Brugge.jpg from the CD-ROM or use one of your own images. Figure 7.6 shows the image before sharpening.

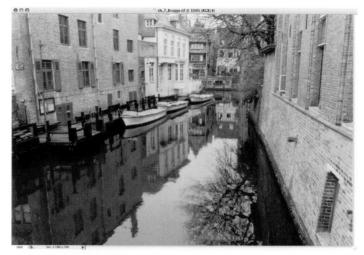

FIGURE 7.6   Image before sharpening.

1. Convert to Lab mode by choosing Image > Mode > Lab Color.
2. Choose the Channels Palette, and click on the Lightness channel, as shown
   in Figure 7.7.

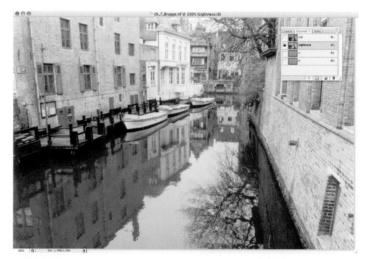

FIGURE 7.7   Choosing the Lightness channel in Lab mode.

3. Apply the Unsharp Mask in the usual way by selecting Filter > Sharpen >
   Unsharp Mask.
4. Choose the best settings for your image as shown in Figure 7.8.
5. Click OK to apply the sharpening effect.
6. Click on the Top channel to display all the channels and preview the image
   in color again.

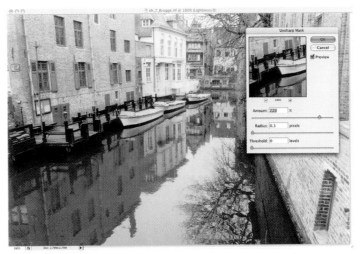

FIGURE 7.8   Applying the Unsharp Mask.

Figure 7.9 shows the image after sharpening to the Lightness channel. This is a great way to apply sharpening. When you are finished, you can convert the image back to RGB mode.

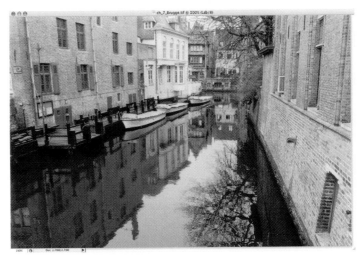

FIGURE 7.9   The sharpened image.

Smart Sharpen

One of the biggest complaints concerning sharpening is that it introduces noise. When you sharpen an image, you also sharpen the grain. With the Smart Sharpen Filter, however, you can now sharpen an image without sharpening the grain.

If you examine a digital photograph, you will notice that most of the noise is present in the shadows and halos in the highlights. This new filter allows you to sharpen the midtones only and isolate the highlights and shadows. By isolating the midtones, we will avoid sharpening the noise.

Figure 7.10 demonstrates an Unsharp Mask on the image. Notice how much noise has been introduced as the image is sharpened. (Note that Unsharp Mask will not add noise to all images, only those that already contain excessive grain such as high ISO images or low-light conditions.)

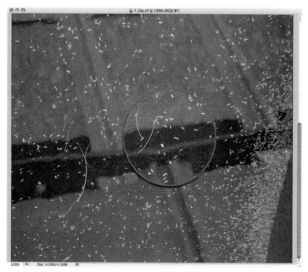

FIGURE 7.10   Unsharp Mask introduces noise.

TUTORIAL 7.2   USING SMART SHARPEN

Let's use the Smart Sharpen to work on this image. Open `ch_7_Smart.tif` from the CD-ROM.

ON THE CD

1. Choose Filter > Sharpen > Smart Sharpen.
2. Make your sharpening adjustments without worrying about noise at this point (see Figure 7.11). Amount controls the strength of the effect, and Radius controls the width of the effect. Use either the Gaussian or Lens type of sharpening. Motion is useful for an image that has a streaky blur.
3. Turn on the Advanced button and click Shadow.
4. Only two sliders really concern you:
   Fade Amount: This is the strength of sharpening in the shadows. Slide to the right to lesson the sharpening in the shadows.
   Tonal Width: This determines how dark the shadows are. Slide to the right to include some midtones.

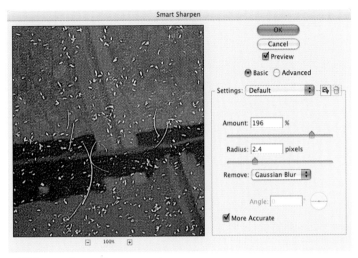

FIGURE 7.11   Smart Sharpen settings.

5. Continue adjusting the Fade and Tonal Width sliders until you have the maximum sharpening and minimum noise in the shadows as shown in Figure 7.12.

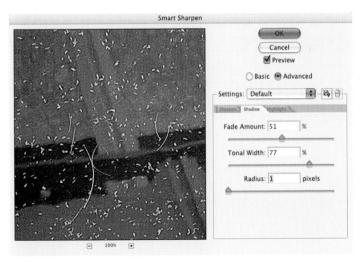

FIGURE 7.12   Fading the shadows.

6. Click on the Highlight tab (see Figure 7.13).
7. This slider works the same way as Shadow. Make adjustments to the Radius if needed; you can usually leave it alone. (This filter is based on the same technology as Shadow/Highlight.)

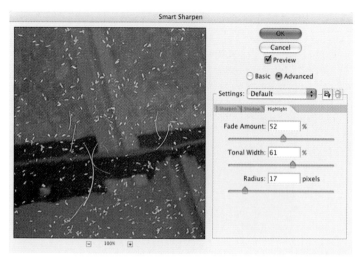

FIGURE 7.13   Fading the highlights.

8. Return to the Sharpen tab, and make some tweaks if you desire. Click OK to apply the filter.

Figures 7.14 and 7.15 show the before and after effects of sharpening. Notice in Figure 7.15 that the image has been sharpened but almost no noise has been introduced. This is a good sharpening effect because it's not obvious that the image has been sharpened.

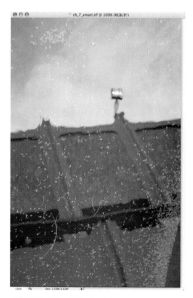

FIGURE 7.14   Original image.

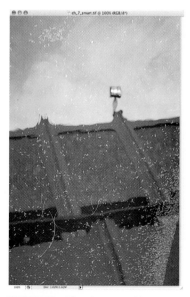

FIGURE 7.15   The sharpened image.

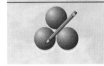

TUTORIAL 7.3   **NONDESTRUCTIVE SHARPENING USING HIGH PASS FILTER**

This technique, sometimes called High Pass Sharpening, sharpens the image very well and is not destructive. It is called nondestructive because it does not affect the original image. Instead, it works through a layer that we will call a sharpening layer. We use High Pass Sharpening to keep the sharpening effect to a minimum in smooth areas such as skin tones or blue skies.

Open `ch_7_HighPass.jpg` from the CD-ROM. Figure 7.16 shows the image before sharpening.

ON THE CD

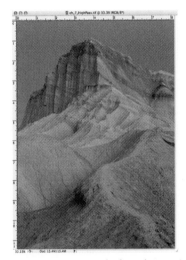

FIGURE 7.16   Image before sharpening.

1.   Duplicate the Background layer by dragging the layer thumbnail to the New Layer icon in the Layers Palette.
2. Change the blending mode of the new layer to Overlay as shown in Figure 7.17a (this will be the sharpening layer). Don't be alarmed when your image changes a bit because that will be remedied shortly.
3. Choose Filter > Other > High Pass (see Figure 7.17b).
4. Turn on Preview, if it isn't on already.
5. Lower the Radius setting to 0.1. Your preview should turn gray. Raise the Radius until you start to see the lines in the image begin to appear. This setting, or a little higher, should be just what you want. A lower setting will give you less sharpening, and a higher setting will give you more. The lines you are seeing in the preview box are the ones that will be sharpened.
6. Click OK to apply the effect to the image.

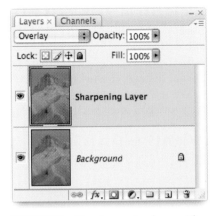

FIGURE 7.17A   The sharpening layer with its blending mode set to Overlay.

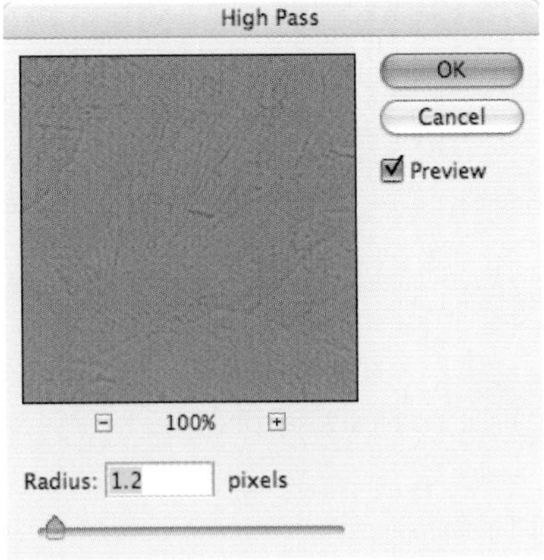

FIGURE 7.17B   Adjusting the High Pass Filter.

Your image is now sharpened as shown in Figure 7.18. If you ever want to reduce the sharpening effect, just lower the opacity of the layer. If you want to remove the sharpening effect altogether, just delete the sharpening layer.

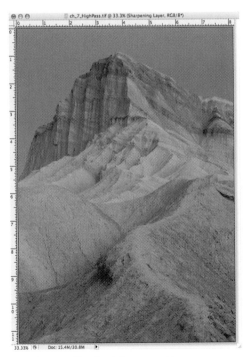

FIGURE 7.18   The final sharpened image.

Noise Reduction

With film, we had to deal with grain, and with digital cameras, we have to deal with noise. There are two types of noise:

> **Luminosity Noise:** Monochromatic noise—there are no colored speckles, just grain.
> **Color Noise:** Colored speckles, usually blue or red dots.

Usually noise is introduced when the lighting is low, or the ISO is turned up on the camera. Whenever you can, use a lower ISO, shoot with a slower shutter speed, and open up the aperture. The techniques you are about to learn are the same for reducing both noise and film grain.

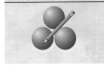

| **TUTORIAL 7.4** | **USING CHANNELS FOR NOISE REDUCTION** |

When reducing noise, it's a good idea to look at the individual channels. Sometimes most of the noise is present in one channel. It makes sense to correct the offending channel rather than blur the entire image. That way, you can reduce the noise without affecting too much of the image. In digital photography, it's common for most of the noise to be present in the Blue channel.

ON THE CD

Open an image that contains noise, such as shown in Figure 7.19. This file titled `ch_7_Chan_noise.jpg` can be found on the CD-ROM in the `Chapter 7` folder.

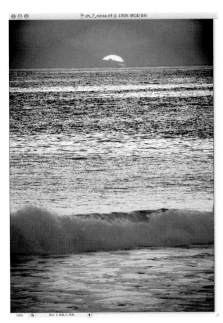

FIGURE 7.19   The beginning image.

1. Choose the Channel Palette. Open it from Window > Channels if it is not already open.
2. Click on the Red channel thumbnail to view the Red channel by itself, as shown in Figure 7.20.
3. View the Green and the Blue channels. Notice that most of the noise is in the Red and Blue channels.
4. With the Blue channel selected, choose Filter > Smart Blur, and play with the settings as shown in Figure 7.21.

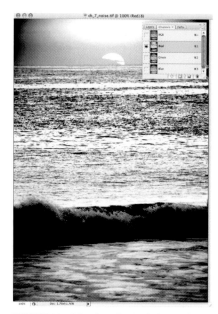

FIGURE 7.20   Viewing the Red channel.

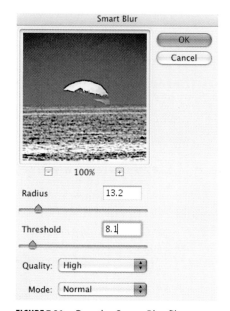

FIGURE 7.21   Run the Smart Blur filter on the noisy channel.

5. Click OK to apply. If you need to, apply Smart Blur to another channel.
6. Choose the RGB thumbnail from the Channels Palette to return to the normal color view.

Figure 7.22 shows the image with the noise reduced. On a particularly bad image, you may need to blur more than one channel. If that is the case, just repeat the steps for the other channels. This is not a perfect solution to noise, but it's better than blurring the whole image. This method does work very well for an image that is excessively noisy in a single channel.

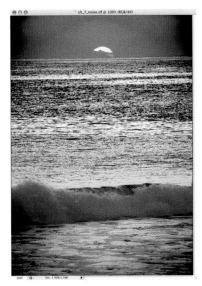

FIGURE 7.22   The final image.

Reducing Luminosity Noise with Smart Blur

ON THE CD

Open an image that has some noise or grain, as shown in Figure 7.23. (ch7_
Noise.jpg on the CD-ROM.)

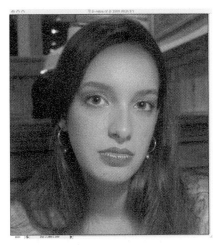

FIGURE 7.23   The image with some noise present.

1. Choose Filter > Blur > Smart Blur (you can also use the Median Filter if you
   prefer to use this to soften the detail).
2. Choose High Quality.
3. Adjust Radius and Threshold until the noise is gone but as much detail as
   possible remains in the image as shown in Figure 7.24.

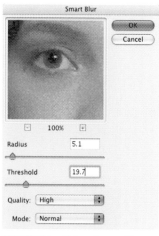

FIGURE 7.24   Using Smart Blur.

4. Click OK to apply. Your image will have all the noise removed as shown in Figure 7.25. The only problem is that, depending on the severity of the noise problem, the image could be too blurred and appear as if it is hand painted or lacking in detail. We can rectify this in the next three steps.

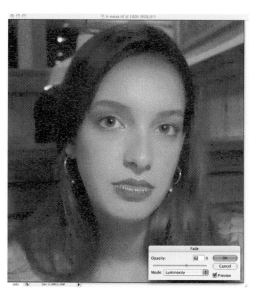

FIGURE 7.25   Blurred image.

5. Choose Edit > Fade Smart Blur. If this command is not available, undo the blur, reapply it, and then choose Fade.

6. Change to Luminosity mode.
7. Adjust the opacity until you reach a good balance of blur and detail, as shown in Figure 7.26.

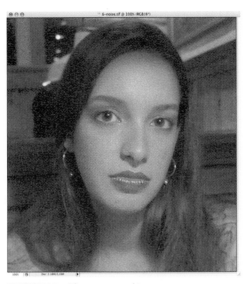

FIGURE 7.26   The corrected image.

Notice that there is still some color noise present in this image. The grain has been reduced, but colored specs are still noticeable. We will use Lab mode to reduce this type of colored noise.

Color Noise Reduction Using Lab Mode

Once again, we come to Lab mode. This is the best method of color noise reduction that preserves as much of the original detail as possible.

With our image still open (`ch_7_Noise.jpg`):

1. Choose Image > Mode and select Lab Color. This will separate the color channels from the luminosity (grayscale).
2. Choose the *a* channel from the Channels Palette.
3. You can see in Figure 7.27 that a lot of noise is present in this channel. The good thing about Lab mode is that the color channels are separate from the grayscale, and you can blur the color channels without affecting the sharpness of the image too much.
4. Choose Filter > Noise > Median. The result should look like Figure 7.28.
5. Select the *b* channel as shown in Figure 7.29.
6. Choose Filter > Noise > Median. The result should resemble Figure 7.30.
7. Choose the Lab Composite channel at the top of the Channels Palette to return to the regular color view.

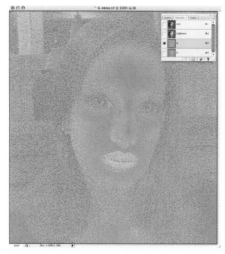

FIGURE 7.27   Examining the *a* channel.

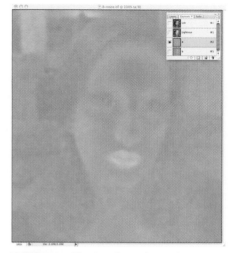

FIGURE 7.28   Blurring the *a* channel.

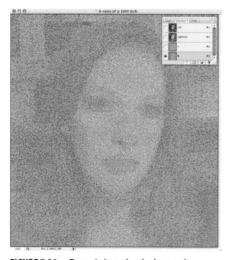

FIGURE 7.29   Examining the *b* channel.

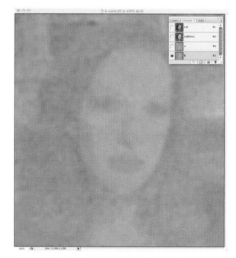

FIGURE 7.30   Blurring the *b* channel.

Examining the image now (see Figure 7.31), the color noise has been removed, and the image has retained its sharpness and detail. To use the image, convert it back to RGB. Note that this example is exaggerated for educational purposes. In a real-world situation, we would try to begin with a better image. Compare the finished result with the starting image.

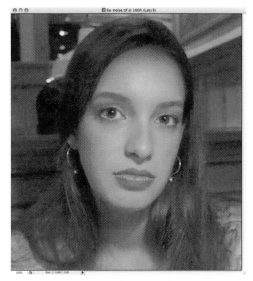

FIGURE 7.31   Image with noise reduced.

NOISE REDUCTION FILTER

Now that you understand all that is going on with noise reduction, we can tell you that there were an easy way to do all this thanks to a new filter in Photoshop CS2. Why learn all this then? Why not start with the filter? Because now you will truly understand what is happening, and you have the ability to work on the channels manually for complete control. You should choose the best method depending on the type of noise. Noise is one of the most difficult things to work with in image correction, and the larger the arsenal of tools you have in your belt, the more success you will have in your imaging career.

ON THE CD

Open ch_7_Reduce_noise.jpg from the CD-ROM as shown in Figure 7.32.

1. Choose Filter > Noise > Reduce Noise.
2. Make the adjustments to the image in Figure 7.33.

Strength: The amount of blurring applied to the image to reduce Luminosity noise.
Preserve Details: A threshold slider.
Reduce Color Noise: Removes color noise also known as chromatic noise.
Sharpen Details: Sharpens the image.
Remove JPEG Artifact: Repairs the blocky damage of image compression in the JPEG format.

3. Click on the advanced Tab.
4. Under the Per Channel tab, choose the Blue Channel from the Channel drop-down list. (We are now blurring each channel as we did in the previous tutorial. (See Figure 7.34.)

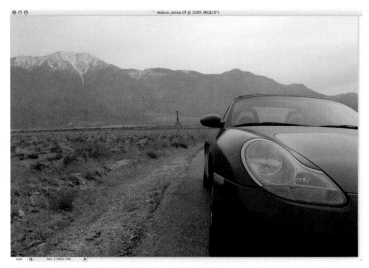

FIGURE 7.32   Image with noise.

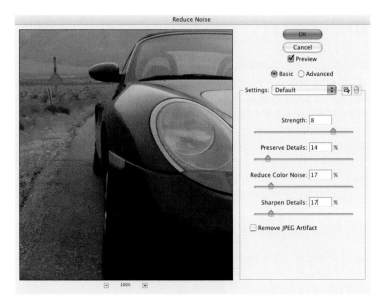

FIGURE 7.33   Reduce Noise dialog box.

5. Adjust the strength setting to set the amount of blur.
6. Now slide out the secret weapon, the Preserve Details slider. This sets the threshold, and you will keep it all the way to the left to blur everything or move to the right to preserve the areas of detail and just blur areas of flat color. As with most filters, this is a balancing act.

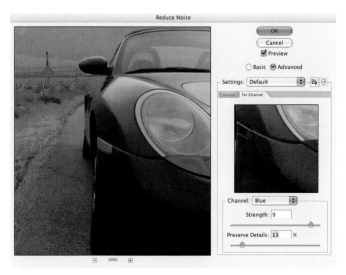

FIGURE 7.34   Reducing noise in each channel.

7. Repeat for each channel, reducing as much noise as possible and yet retaining the detail.
8. Click on the overall tab, and see if you need to fine-tune any of the settings.
9. Click OK to apply.
10. You now have the image with the noise significantly reduced. This is perhaps one of our favorite (practical) new features introduced in the previous version of Photoshop (see Figure 7.35).

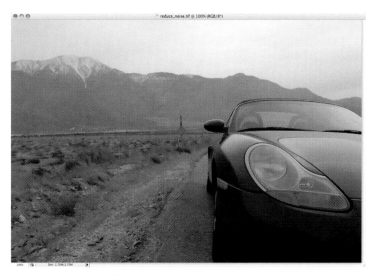

FIGURE 7.35   Image with noise reduced.

SUMMARY

In this chapter, you learned about sharpening and noise reduction. These two techniques can seem to fight against one another, but in a correct balance, they can happily coexist in the same image. The techniques you learned in this chapter will help you to increase the sharpness of your images with a minimum of distracting noise. Bear in mind that these techniques will assist in enhancing your images, but they are not substitutes for good photography. For instance, correctly focusing the camera, holding it steady, and using adequate lighting and correct exposure will minimize the need for sharpening and noise reduction.

SIZING AND PRINTING YOUR IMAGES

In This Chapter

- Resizing Things
- Printing Proportions
- Printing Your Photographs

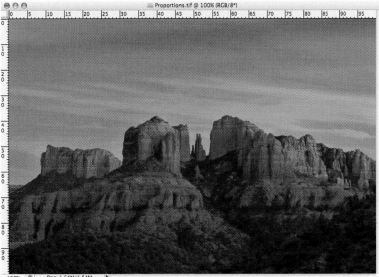

Resizing Things

We are going to jump into a little light theory before we start having all the fun of printing your images. If you are not comfortable with resolution and resizing algorithms, this small section will help you. If you are already familiar with the concept, you should still skim through this material in case you missed some of the new upgrades since Photoshop CS.

Resolution

Whatever the reason for resizing your images, there are a few things that you should know. The first thing you should understand is resolution. Resolution is how many pixels there are in an image. We measure resolution in pixels per inch (ppi), which is the measure of the number of pixels displayed in an image. A digital image is composed of samples that your screen displays in pixels. Adobe Photoshop uses ppi for image resolution, but you may hear it called dots per inch (dpi) as well. Dpi, however, is the measure of the resolution of a printer. It properly refers to the dots of ink or toner used by an image setter, laser printer, or other printing device to print your text and graphics. In general, the more dots, the better and sharper the image. Dpi is printer resolution. When we refer to resolution, we will be referring to ppi.

There are three main target resolutions for Photoshop files:

Offset printing: The best resolution for the professional offset press printing world is generally 300 ppi (half the target linescreen).

Inkjet printers: Use 360 ppi for Epson printers and 300 ppi for Canon, HP, and Lightjet printers. Lightjet (or similar technology) printers are the machines primarily used by photo labs and online photofinishers.

Online: The standard resolution for Web and multimedia use is 72 ppi; this is also known as *screen resolution*. Do not confuse this with sending your prints over the Web to be printed. The resolution for these types of printers should be posted by your online photofinisher, but is typically 240 or 300 ppi.

If you try to use an image with insufficient resolution, there are not enough pixels to provide a sharp display and, as a consequence, pixelization occurs, also known as "the jaggies."

Figure 8.1a shows an image at the correct resolution, and Figure 8.1b shows an image suffering from the jaggies.

For the technically minded, you can estimate how large an image will print. Use the following formula:

$$\text{Image size in pixels} \times \text{Target resolution} \times \text{Output size in inches}$$

For example, if an image is 500 pixels wide, and we want to output at 300 ppi, then $500 \times 300 \times 1.667$, so the maximum size we can output this image at 300 ppi will be 1.667 inches. The same image would be 6.9 inches at 72 ppi ($500 \times 72 \times 6.9$). Both sizes contain exactly the same number of pixels because the image itself has not been altered. No pixels have been added in or taken out. Only the targeted size

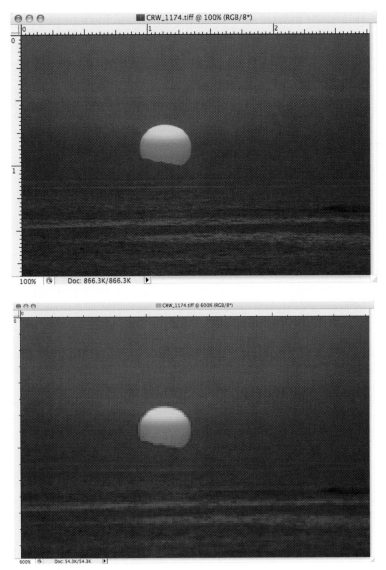

FIGURES 8.1A/B   Having insufficient pixels causes jaggies.

of the existing pixels has been changed. When we change only the target resolution, the process is called resizing. When you change the dimensions and the resolution, you will be resampling (interpolating).

Anytime you change the number of pixels in an image, you will lose some quality. Sometimes it is noticeable, and sometimes not. This is called *resampling*. Resampling is when you alter all the pixels in an image. When you change the physical size of a document, pixels have to be added or discarded and the image re-rendered. If you increase the size of an image without adding in more pixels, the photo doesn't have the pixels to fill the new size, so pixelization may occur. To solve this problem, we add in more pixels (upsampling). When you are reducing the size of an image, all the pixels are mashed together, and Photoshop has to throw away some pixels (downsampling).

A 6-megapixel camera will (roughly) yield a 7" × 10" print at 300 ppi. If you want to make a bigger print, you will need to upsample (add in pixels). If you want to make a smaller print, you will downsample (throw out pixels).

Image Interpolation

By now, you may be thinking what is the point in resizing an image if you are going to lose quality? Well, the loss of quality when printing is nothing new. As photographers, we have been experiencing this since the first enlarger was invented. Every time we enlarged a negative to make a print, we experienced a loss of quality. The loss of quality was there, we just didn't notice it. It is the same situation with digital files and resizing. Think of your digital file as a negative from your old film camera. When you made 3 1/2" × 5" or 4" × 6" prints, they looked perfect. If you made an 8" × 12" it still looked great. Now take that same negative and try to enlarge it to a 32" × 48" print. There would be an obvious loss of quality.

Digital images behave in the same way. Almost any current digital camera will produce great 8" × 10" prints, even though to get there, the image must be resized. Most can even produce fine 11" × 14" prints. It is usually above this size that the point-and-shoot style cameras will start to reveal artifacts or a loss of quality from the upsizing process. This of course is a general statement, and some cameras in this class can and do produce fine prints at this size and larger. At this point, it becomes more a matter of the viewers' tastes and their ability to recognize quality loss. Beginning photographers are less likely to be able to spot imperfections in their final prints, while a 20-year veteran will be more finicky about the results. Suffice it to say that if you are making 8" × 10" to 11" × 14" prints from your digital camera, you need not have any fear of upsampling your image!

The studious team of engineers at Adobe realized that you may want to change the size of your images at some point, so they incorporated a technology into Photoshop called *image interpolation*. Interpolation is a popular term in the scanning world. Chances are that your digital camera also has a form of interpolation—definitely if it uses digital zoom (a feature that should be avoided most of the time). Digital zoom analyzes a picture and, based on the pixel information, interpolates, or calculates, what pixels should be created to fill in all the gaps. The camera's interpolation engine will then kick in and draw the missing pixels just like magic. In theory, this works well, but you are better off not using the digital zoom. Instead, shoot using only the optical zoom (the zoom provided by your lens), and then crop and upsize using the tools provided by Photoshop.

The advantage to resampling in Photoshop is that you have a choice of interpolation methods (Adobe calls these *resizing algorithms*). The interpolation method you choose will depend on the size and type of image you are resizing. There used to be only three methods, but two new methods were introduced in Photoshop CS (Bicubic Smoother and Bicubic Sharper). In Photoshop CS and CS2, these algorithms were a bit of a mystery. To figure out which method was best for what kind of image, I developed a test chart that you can print out with your image. This chart shows both text and line art. You can find this image (`ch_8_Interpolation-chart.tif`) on the CD-ROM. Include this with a photo and try the different interpolations out. Figure 8.2 shows an image with the chart overlayed.

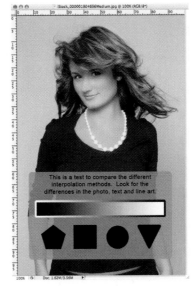

FIGURE 8.2   An image with the test chart overlayed.

Figure 8.3 shows the interpolation drop-down menu that was provided in Photoshop CS and CS2, but it's not much help. The folks at Adobe helped us out with the new drop-down menu in CS3. Figure 8.4 shows that we are now assisted in our decision making.

Here is a breakdown of the interpolation methods and their uses:

Nearest Neighbor: This method bases decisions on the adjacent pixels and is the lowest quality setting. It is best for line art type images.

Bilinear: This is a medium quality setting, good for solid color and text. It looks at the four pixels on the two sides, the top, and the bottom of each existing pixel.

Bicubic: This is high quality; it uses the eight surrounding pixels and is the default setting for most images. It's a good "Jack of all trades."

Bicubic Smoother: This is the best setting for upsampling images.

Bicubic Sharper: This is the best setting for downsampling images, according to the Adobe engineers. Be careful, though, because it can sometimes add unwanted sharpening to your images. Try it first to see if it is appropriate for your image.

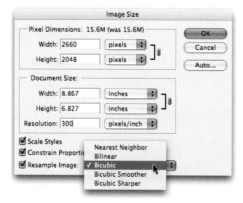

FIGURE 8.3   The old interpolation drop-down menu.

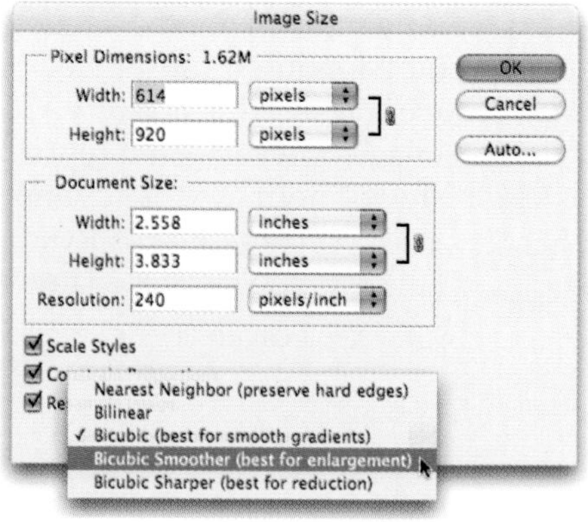

FIGURE 8.4   The new (more helpful) drop-down menu.

At first appearances, the only time you have access to different interpolation modes is when you open the Image Resize dialog box. However, whenever you use the Free Transform tool, interpolation is applied to the transformation. The Transform tool uses the settings in Preferences. You can set the method in the Preferences panel, shown in Figure 8.5. The default is Bicubic, which is a good general-purpose setting. This preference will be applied to all transformations and scaling.

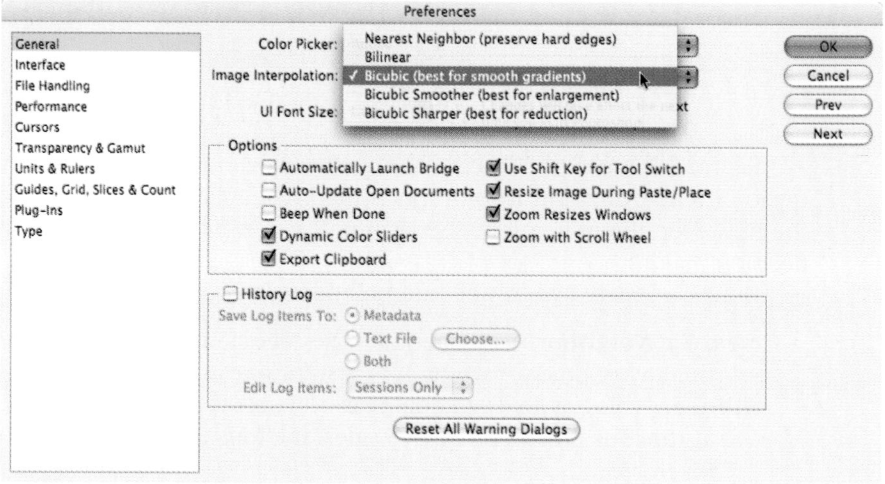

FIGURE 8.5   Setting default interpolation in Preferences.

When you change the resampling method setting in Preferences, the new setting is applied right away, and you don't have to restart Photoshop as with some of the other settings.

Sizing an Image for Print

You have taken the plunge; now you are going to resize your image to make a print. We will first explore the easiest and most direct way of doing this. Then we will explore the subtleties of the process.

1. From the menu bar, select Image > Image Size.
2. You will now see the dialog box shown in Figure 8.6, which displays the current image size and resolution of your picture.

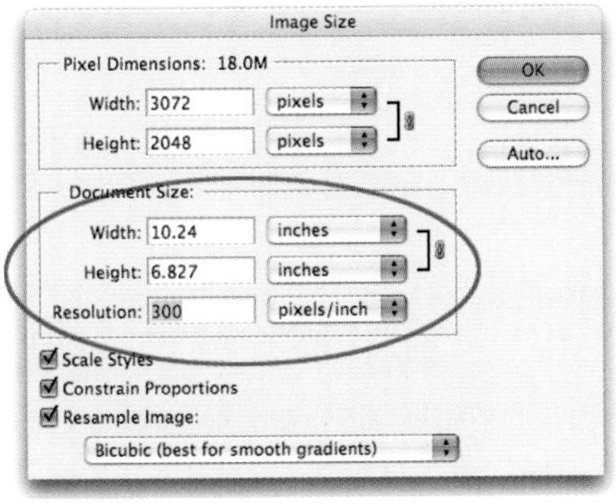

FIGURE 8.6   The Image Size dialog box.

3. The photograph that this box reflects is 6.8" × 10.24" high at a resolution of 300 ppi.
4. If you wanted to make a print that was 8" × 12", you would simply click inside the Width box and type in 12. The Height box would automatically change to read 8 as shown in Figure 8.7.

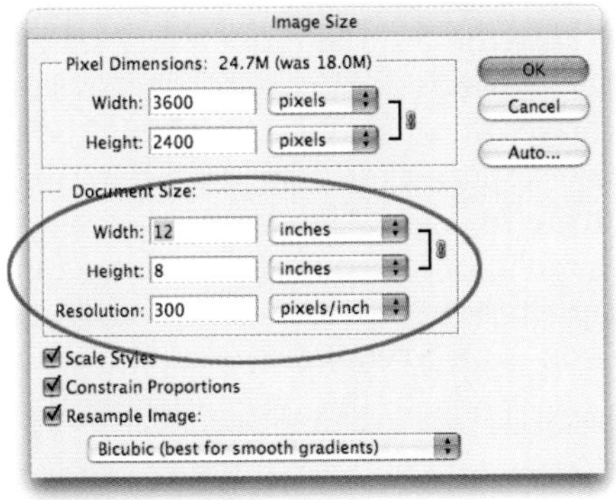

FIGURE 8.7   Setting the Width automatically changes the Height.

5. Click in the Resolution box, and type in a resolution of 300.

6. Click OK. That's it. You have just resampled your image! Wasn't that easy?

Okay, so that is the fast and easy way to size your image so that it will print out at the correct size and resolution. Let's explore what else is going on inside the Image Size box (see Figure 8.8).

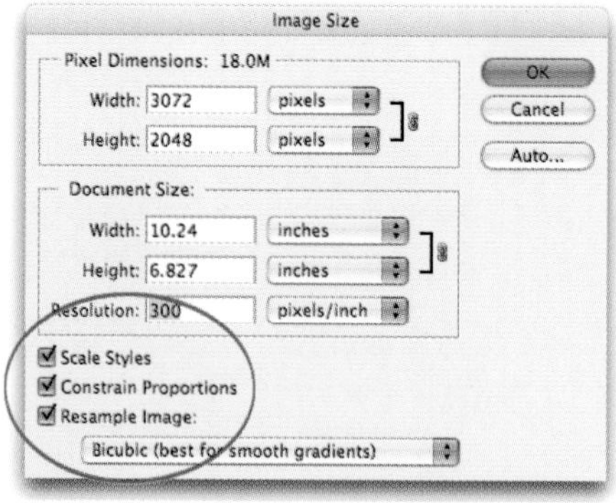

FIGURE 8.8 Options inside the Image Size dialog box.

7. When you first opened the Image Size dialog box, some boxes were checked by default.

Scale Styles: Keeping this box checked ensures that any styles that you have applied to layers will stay the same size as the corresponding layer. Without this button, any layer styles will look like a child wearing his parent's clothes, or an adult wearing a kid's clothes. We will use some layer styles in Chapter 9, "Special Effects." Usually, you just keep this checked.

Constrain Proportions: This is the box that allowed you to just type in 12. Because the proportions are constrained, the other dimension has to be 8. When this box is checked, it keeps you from stretching and morphing your image out of shape. This should be checked most of the time, unless you have a specific creative interest in turning your image into taffy.

Resample Image: Keeping this box checked gives Photoshop the permission to add in or take out pixels. This is typically what you want to do when you enter into this box, so keep this checked. There may be times, however, when you want to change the resolution of the image without adding in or taking out pixels. In this case, uncheck the Resample Image box.

Now for the resolution. As mentioned earlier, if you are printing to an Epson printer, type in a resolution of 360 ppi. If you are printing to any other home printer or you are taking your file to a lab, type in a resolution of 300 ppi.

Another place to look for information is at the top of the box. Here you will find the *Pixel Dimensions* (see Figure 8.9).

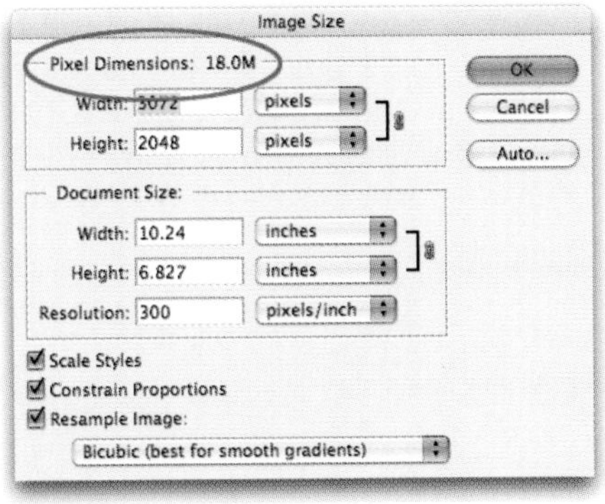

FIGURE 8.9   The Pixel Dimensions.

Think of this as your overall file size. It reflects all three channels of your image. Like film, digital files have three layers (channels) consisting of Red, Green, and Blue. The combination of these layers creates all the colors that are visible in your image. This image comes from a 6-megapixel camera, so if you were looking down on the file, you would see a rectangle made up of roughly 6 million pixels. But if you were to look at the cross section, you would see three layers of 6 million pixels each. Three layers of 6 million equals 18 million (roughly) pixels. So the pixel dimensions can be thought of as the total depth of your file. In this case, we have an 18 MB (megabyte) file. So when we resample an image, the pixel dimension changes to show how big the file will become. In this example (see Figure 8.10), when we upsample our image to 8" × 12" at 300 ppi, Photoshop tells us that the image was 18 MB but will be 24.7 MB after the upsample.

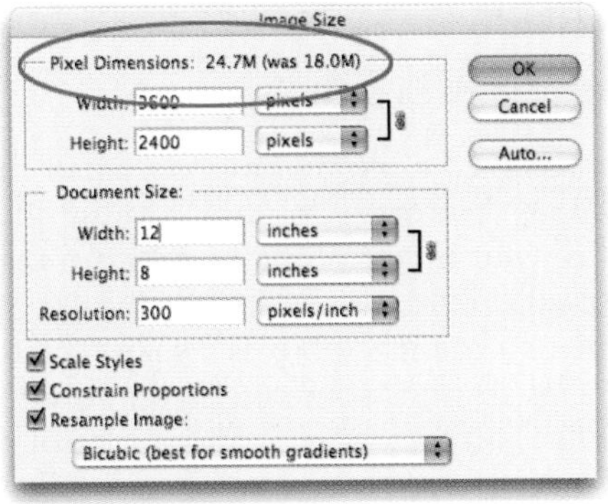

FIGURE 8.10   The Pixel Dimensions changes when you resample.

The Pixel Dimensions (circled in Figure 8.10) help you see whether Photoshop is going to upsample or downsample an image when you type in a new resolution and dimensions. Sometimes when you first open the Image Size dialog box, your resolution may show 72 ppi. The image could look like the one in Figure 8.11, which is 42.6" × 28.4" at 72 ppi. Is this image larger or smaller than our previous image of 10.24" × 6.8" at 300 ppi (see Figure 8.12)? They are the same size. A quick look up to the Pixel Dimensions shows that they are both 18 MB files.

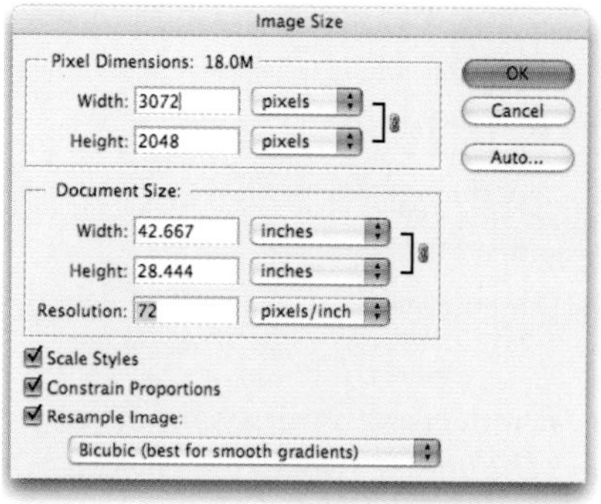

FIGURE 8.11   Image with a resolution of 72 ppi.

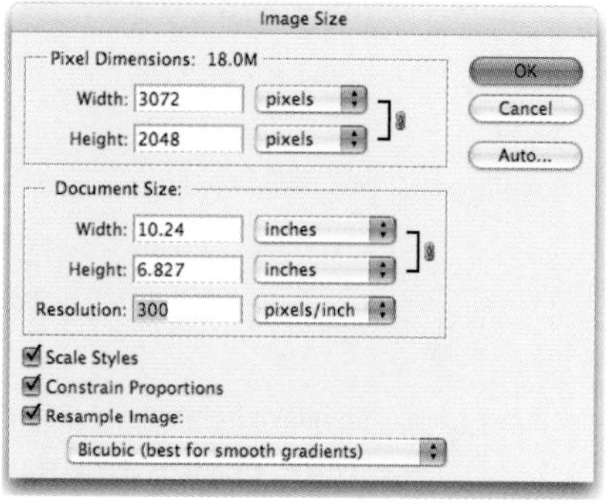

FIGURE 8.12   Same size image with a resolution of 300 ppi.

The last thing we need to focus on in this dialog box is the Interpolation method. Earlier in the chapter, we discussed the different methods and their uses. For photographers, our choices are pretty easy. When we upsample, we use Bicubic Smoother, and when we downsample, we use Bicubic Sharper. There are some exceptions to this rule that we will discuss shortly. So after typing in your Width, Height, and Resolution values, look up to the Pixel Dimensions. If your image is getting bigger, choose Bicubic Smoother. If the image is getting smaller, use Bicubic Sharper.

Sizing Your Print for the Web or Email

Have you ever received a photograph via email that appears to be 10 times bigger than your monitor? You have to scroll around just to see the entire image! If you learn how to size your image properly, you can teach your friends how to do it and save some aggravation. Sizing your image for use over the Web, whether it will land in your Web site or a friend's inbox is a snap. The first thing to realize is that the target for this type of sizing is someone's computer screen. Computer screens have a resolution just like printers. Some common resolutions are 800 × 600, 1024 × 768, or 1280 × 960. The newer LCD monitors are even bigger. These resolutions are the height and width measured in pixels. So if someone sends you an image that is 3072 pixels long by 2048 pixels wide, and you try to view it on your 1024 × 768 monitor, you will only be able to see a small section of it. The problem is that they didn't shrink their image to fit on your screen! Figure 8.13 demonstrates the theory.

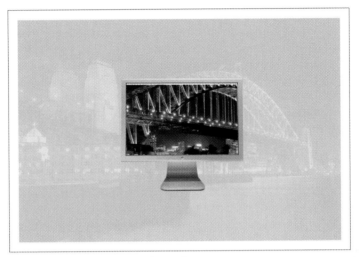

FIGURE 8.13   Email image too big to fit on your screen.

Most monitors these days are about 1024 × 768 or larger. This means that if we resize an image to be no taller than 600 or wider than 600, anyone will be able to view it. Sizing for email is similar to sizing for print.

1. From the menu bar, select Image > Image Size.
2. This time around, we are only concerned with the top of the Image Size dialog box (see Figure 8.14).
3. Find the longest dimension, in this case, the height, and type in 600. Figure 8.15 shows the resulting size of your image, 600 pixels wide by 400 pixels high. Small enough to fit on screen but large enough for the viewer to enjoy it. You can also see that the overall size of the file has dropped from 18 MB to 703 KB. This is rather small, but it will become even smaller in the next step!

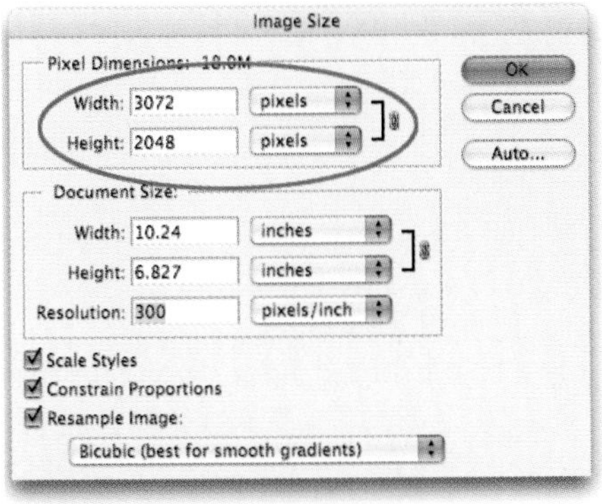

FIGURE 8.14   The Image dialog box.

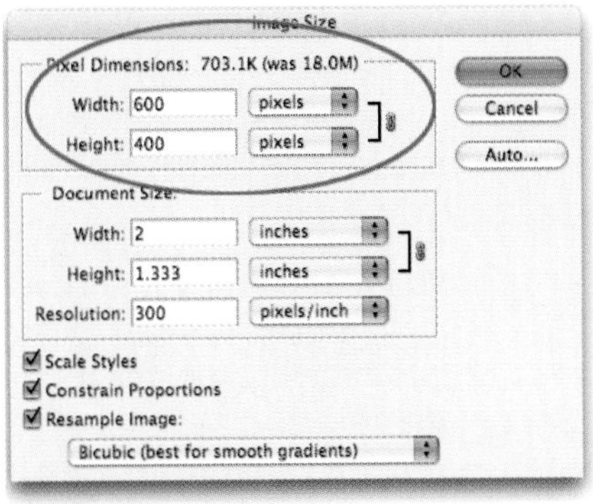

FIGURE 8.15   The resulting size of the file.

4. Choose File > Save As.
5. When you get to the Save As dialog box, choose to save your file as a JPEG. Give it a name, and save it to a folder that you will remember. Click Save.
6. Next the JPEG Options dialog box appears as shown in Figure 8.16. For the highest quality image, choose Quality 12, or move the slider all the way to Large File. Even at this setting, your image is now only 190 KB! You could email 10 images of this size with an email program that has a 2 MB attachment limit.
7. If you really need to get the size down, move the slider to the left to decrease the file size. You can watch your image and look for the first signs of image degradation. You can also check the Preview box on and off to monitor the amount of degradation. (We chose Save As rather than Save for Web because Save for Web in CS3 defaults to the sRGB colorspace, which is best for Web. Because you are emailing the picture, Adobe RGB is better because it will maintain your color settings.)
8. Click OK.

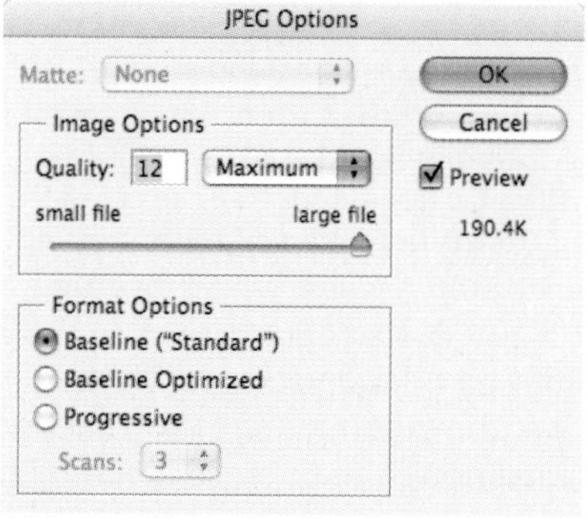

FIGURE 8.16   The JPEG Options dialog box.

That's it, and it couldn't be easier. But you may be thinking, "That's fine for 1 image, but I have 30 images that I want to email. Is there a way I can do it faster?" You bet.

Batch Sizing Images for Email

If you have a lot of images that need to be resized to the same dimensions, take a visit to the Bridge and check out the Image Processor. This tool will allow you to create multiple files and file types from a folder full of images.

Put all of the images that you want to size in one folder. Navigate the Bridge to this folder.

After your images are in the content pane of the Bridge, choose Edit > Select All from the menu.

Go up to the menu again and choose Tools > Photoshop > Image Processor. You will see the same box as in Figure 8.17.

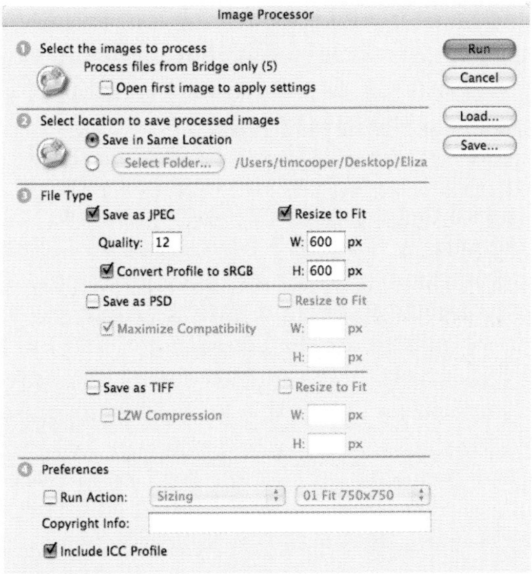

FIGURE 8.17   The Image Processor dialog box.

Step 1 of the dialog box is for Raw files. It allows you to open the first image and apply Raw settings, and then this processor will apply those Raw settings to the rest of the batch. You should adjust your images individually first and then leave this box unchecked.

By default, step 2 of the dialog box will have the Save in Same Location option selected. This is as good a place as any. It will create a new folder within this existing folder. But if you want them to be easily accessible, you can click the Select Folder button and select any folder that you want to store them in.

In step 3 of the dialog box, all the magic happens. Check the Save as JPEG box, and type in a Quality of 12. Next check the Resize to Fit box, and type in 600 in both the W and H boxes. Doing this will fit all of your images into a 600-pixel square box. No need to worry about whether the image is horizontal or vertical.

Check the Convert Profile to sRGB check box (this will keep your colors looking good if you're going to the Web). Uncheck the Save as PSD and Save as TIFF boxes (unless you want to make extra copies of these images).

Click Run. Photoshop will take over and open up each one of your files, resize them, and save them as JPEGs while you go and get a cup of coffee!

Do some experimenting with the sizing of your images to determine what size works best for you and those who receive them. For some, 600 pixels in the longest dimension might be too small, and for others too big. To try out some different sizes, follow the earlier sizing directions for a single image. Create some at 400 pixels, 600 pixels, and 800 pixels. Open them in Photoshop, and view them at Actual Pixels; from the menu, choose View > Actual Pixels. You could do the same thing by double-clicking on the magnifying glass. This will show you the approximate size of the image as it will appear on the Web or on your friend's monitor. Because all monitors are different, you can never be sure, but this definitely gets you in the ball park.

Increasing the Image Size Beyond 200%

Earlier in the chapter, we mentioned some guidelines for upsampling your images. Theory once said that if you go beyond double the original file size, your image will lose too much quality. There are ways, however, to break this rule.

As a rule of thumb, Photoshop does a good job of downsizing your image. With upsampling, you need to be more careful. There are a couple of ways of doing this.

The first is simply to use the Bicubic Smoother interpolation method. The earlier theoretical limits were based on the old Bicubic Interpolation method. We have made some large prints (24" × 30") using Bicubic Smoother and found the results to be very agreeable.

The second is called *Stair Step Interpolation*. This technique is credited to photographer Fred Miranda. The idea is that when enlarging to more than twice the original file size (say an 18-MB file to a 40-MB file), it's best to help Photoshop by choosing a size that is easy to calculate. If you size in increments of one-tenth (10%), you will find that the overall quality is better. This makes it possible for Photoshop to add or remove pixels in an even way.

ON THE CD

It can take a while to keep enlarging an image many times, so this is a great time to create an action. We have included a simple action on the CD-ROM, under the filename `PSDP_Colin_Smith.atn`. There are two actions in this set. The first is a 110% enlargement in a single step. The second is the same enlargement five times, which will save a bit of time.

To load an action:

ON THE CD

1. Open the Actions Palette (choose Window > Actions).
2. Choose the drop-down menu at the top right of the palette.
3. Choose Load Actions.
4. Navigate to the action on the CD-ROM.
5. Click OK.

You are now ready to run the action.

Click on the action itself (upsample by 10%), not the action set labeled PSDP. To run the action, click the right-facing arrow in the bottom of the Actions Palette. When you are running an action, you will no longer be viewing the Image Size dialog box. How will you know when you have reached your target size? Click on the arrow on the bottom left of the Document window (the status bar). Choose Document Dimensions for the preferences.

Third-party products are also available for resizing images, including the following:

- Alienskin Blow up at *http://alienskin.com/blowup/index.html*.
- Extensis™ pxl Smart Scale at www.extensis.com. (Extensis claims that an image can be enlarged to 1600% with no visible loss of quality.)
- Genuine Fractals™ at *www.ononesoftware.com/*.
- Fred Miranda's Stair Interpolation Action at *www.fredmiranda.com*.

PRINTING PROPORTIONS

Have you ever noticed that images never seem to quite match up with standard print sizes? We want an 8" × 10" print, but the lab tells us that they will either need to crop the image or make it smaller. This can be frustrating, especially in very carefully composed images. This mismatch has its roots in early photography when cameras had proportions of either 8" × 10" or 5" × 7". Photographic paper companies would manufacture paper to match these negative sizes. This is where we get the common paper sizes of 5" × 7", 8" × 10", and 11" × 14"—none of which match up with our current negative or digital file proportions of 1" × 1 1/2".

Figure 8.18 shows a typical 35 mm proportion. Figure 8.19 shows the image as it would be cropped to fit on 5" × 7" paper. Figure 8.20 shows how it would appear on 8" × 10" paper. As you can see, the forced cropping really affects the impact of the image. To keep the visual balance in this image, we would only want it to appear as a 1" × 1 1/2" proportion. The other crops just don't work as well.

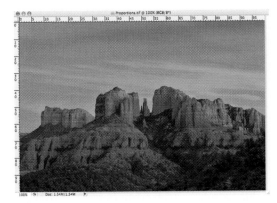

FIGURE 8.18 The original size file.

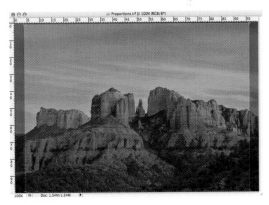

FIGURE 8.19 The image cropped to a 5" × 7".

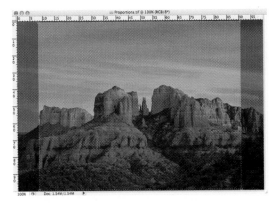

FIGURE 8.20 The image cropped to an 8" x 10".

If you try to print one of your 35 mm files to a print size of 5" × 7", it won't work because the proportions are wrong. It could either be 5" × 7.5" or 4.6" × 7". The only proportions that will work without cropping are 2" × 3", 4" × 6", 8" × 12", and so on. Any other proportion, such as 8" × 10", 8 1/2" × 11", 11" × 14", and so on, requires cropping. Return to the Crop tool, and type your desired dimensions into the option bar. See Chapter 3, "Cropping and Perspective," for more information on cropping.

PRINTING YOUR PHOTOGRAPHS

Photoshop has a few interesting features when it comes to printing. The most important thing to note as mentioned earlier in this chapter is the printing resolution.

As a reminder, 360 ppi is the native resolution of an Epson printer. You can also choose 240 ppi or 180 ppi if you want a smaller file size that will print faster. You may experience a slight drop in quality. For a Canon or HP printer, choose 300 ppi. Likewise, 150 ppi will work for smaller file sizes or contact sheets. Please also note that these printers will interpolate the images to match their native resolution. There is no advantage in trying to print at a higher resolution because the prints will still be downsized. Don't be fooled into thinking that because the printer has a higher dpi rating, a higher pixel resolution will produce a higher quality print.

Color Management

When you are printing your photos, the most frustrating thing is when the colors don't match what you see onscreen, but it is possible to get very accurate prints for your system.

The first thing you need to do is calibrate and profile your monitor. You need a sensor to read the colors on your screen. Monico OPTIX-XR, Pantone Huey, and the ColorVision™ Spyder2 all market affordable solutions. These devices are placed on the screen and read the colors as the included software calibrates your screen. When you use these devices, make sure that your room's lighting is set to your typical working conditions. You then install the included software and follow the onscreen instructions. This is very easy to do. For more information on color and color management see Chapter 5, "Color Correction and Enhancement."

After your monitor is calibrated, recalibrate every week or so to ensure that it's accurate. Warm up the monitor before running a calibration because the colors will change as the tube warms up. This is not so much an issue with LCDs, which are good enough for accurate color work. In the past, LCD technology lagged a little, and photographers didn't trust those monitors for high-end color work. Just be sure that you are using a display as high quality as your budget allows.

When working on an image, be sure to use the color profiles in Photoshop. We recommend the setting Adobe RGB (1998); this is the most popular setting in the industry. If you are working with an image that is unprofiled, assign this Adobe RGB from the Edit > Assign Profile menu. If you are shooting Raw images, choose the Adobe RBG option before opening the image into Photoshop. These color profiles will ensure that the colors are consistent between different systems and devices. You can choose Adobe RGB (1998) as the default from the Edit > Color Settings menu.

Printing Colors as Accurate as You See Onscreen

Photoshop CS3 allows for a very accurate preview of what your image will look like when it prints. This "preview" is called *Soft Proofing*. This technique will change the appearance of your file on the monitor to match the results you will see on paper.

Soft proofing is done with profiles. The better or more accurate the profile, the closer your monitor will look to your final print. Profiles are individual. One profile matches one type of printer with certain ink and one type of paper. During the initial loading of your printer driver (when you first install your printer), you are actually loading up profiles as well. The profile for a matte paper is a separate profile from glossy, which is a separate profile from semigloss. If you print on 10 different kinds of papers, you will need 10 different profiles.

The latest printer from Epson, the 2400, actually takes you to the Epson Web site to load up the latest profiles directly from them! Make sure you have an active Internet connection when installing this software. After installing the print driver, click on the Color Management Solutions, and then click on Premium ICC Color Profiles. This will take you to the Epson Web site to download the latest profiles. Three different sets are currently available on the Web site: Glossy Papers, Matte Papers, and Fine Art Papers Matte. We recommend downloading all three (each one is a separate download). Click on either Mac (Apple) or Win (Windows) to start the download.

If you are using a PC, the downloading will start an automatic install. If you are using an Apple, the download will place an icon on your desktop, which you then need to double-click to start the installation of your profiles.

In case you need to know where these profiles are going:

- On a Windows XP machine, the profiles are stored in the Color folder inside your C drive. Find it by opening C:\Windows\System 32\Spool\Drivers\Color.
- On an Apple machine, the profiles are stored in a Profile folder. Find it by opening up your hard drive, and choosing Library\ColorSync\Profiles.

Setting Up the Soft Proof

Start by creating the image you want. Adjust contrast, color, and anything else that needs taking care of. Now, in theory, the print that comes out of the printer should look like your screen, right? Well, sometimes. We can ensure a more accurate print by using a soft proof. This will actually change the image on the screen to look more like the print coming out of the printer. To do this with your image open, follow these steps:

1. Go up to View > Proof Setup > Custom. You will see the dialog box in Figure 8.21.

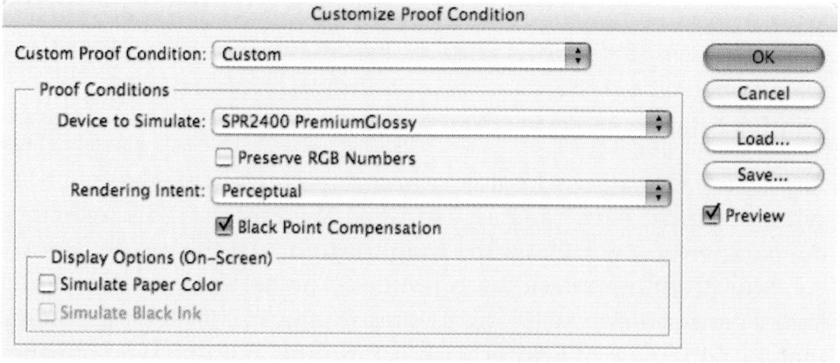

FIGURE 8.21   The Customize Proof Condition dialog box.

2. In the Device to Simulate drop-down list, choose the printer *and* paper that you want to print with. Both of these items create one profile. In this example, we have chosen to print with the Epson 2400 with Premium Glossy Paper.

3. Under Rendering Intent, choose the option that looks the closest to your original. Perceptual, Saturation, Relative Colorimetric, and Absolute Colorimetric are your choices. Go through the options, and click on and off the Preview check box to ascertain the closest match. *Remember* the setting you choose here because you will need this later. All other boxes should be set as they appear here.

4. Click OK, and your image will now be a better match to your print! Depending on the printer, paper, and profile, you may or may not see any change to your print.

5. Press Ctrl+Y (Cmd+Y for Mac) to toggle the proof on and off. If you see no change, you are in the money. If you do see a change, now is your chance to fix the problem before it goes to print. Adjust as necessary.

6. When you are happy with the way your print looks onscreen, it is time to navigate Photoshop's new Print dialog box. (see Figure 8.22).

CS3 has upgraded the old Print with Preview dialog box and consolidated a lot of options. It is now much more user friendly to open the Print dialog box, choose File > Print. It is a good idea to get to get in the habit of checking each option in this box. Following is a list of the options and some suggested uses.

1. Start at the top and work your way down. In the Printer box, choose the printer you will be using.

2. Click on the Page Setup button to set your paper size and orientation.

3. If you uncheck the Center Image check box, you can move the print around on the page.

4. You should probably ignore the Scaled Print Size box. We hope you have already sized your image to fit on the page using techniques discussed earlier in this chapter, which provide more controllable results.

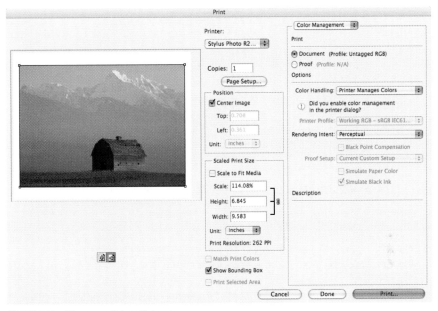

FIGURE 8.22   The new Print dialog box.

5. Checking the Show Bounding Box check box will also allow you to resize your image. Drag the corner handles to change its size.

6. Moving up to the upper-right side of the dialog box, you see the Color Management menu. You can click here to change the lower display to Output, although most of these options are for graphic designers. Return this to Color Management to proceed.

7. In the Print section, leave the Document option selected rather than the Proof option. This will take the document that is on your screen to the next step.

8. By default, Color Handling reads Printer Manages Colors. Because we are working with Profiles, we want Photoshop to Manage Colors. Choose this option as shown in Figure 8.23.

9. Choose the printer profile that you used to soft proof your image. Here we are printing to an Epson 7800 Printer using UltraSmooth Fine Art Paper with matte black ink. That is what USFAP_MK stands for in this profile.

10. The last step before clicking Print is to choose the Rendering Intent. Use the one that you thought looked most like your original image back in the soft proof stage. Perceptual is a good choice if you forgot to soft proof.

11. Click Print.

The next step is the printer's dialog box. Every printer manufacturer will have different options. You may even see differences from one model to the next within a certain line of printers! Following is a list of the things that should be checked to ensure high print quality:

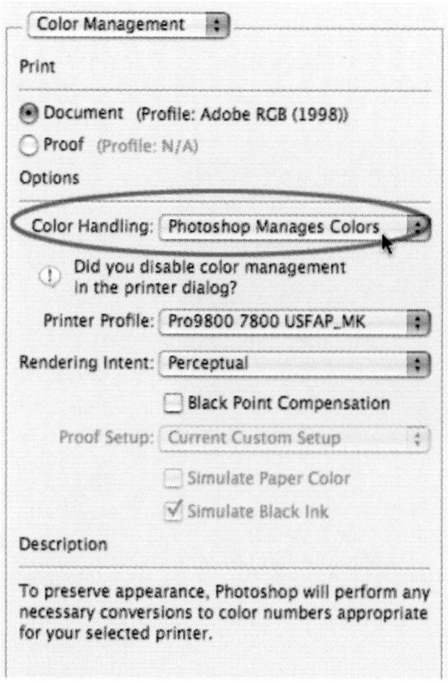

FIGURE 8.23 Setting the Color Handling.

12. Choose the type of paper or type of media you will use.
13. Set the highest print quality for best results. If you are working on an Epson, only choose the highest (2880) option when you have a lot of very smooth gradients in the image. For the most part, 1440 is fine.
14. Uncheck High Speed Printing if that is an option: This setting allows the print head to lay down ink when it travels both back and forth, which can lower the print quality.
15. Turn off the printer's color management so that the image is not twice color managed, or you will get some weird results.

On a Mac, choose Print Settings and the correct paper and highest quality settings. Click on Printer Color Management to reveal the No Color Adjustment button, as shown in Figures 8.24a/b.

In Windows, choose high-quality printing and avoid all the color enhancement features. Choose the ICM Color Management radio button, and then select No Color Adjustment. Figures 8.25a/b show screen shots from a PC printing with an Epson Stylus 2400.

If you followed these directions, your print should now be very close to what you see onscreen. If not, make sure you have the correct paper and ink installed. If you still have trouble, consult your printer manufacturer.

Creating a Test Print

It's a good idea to print a small portion of the image to see how it will look before committing the time, ink, and the expensive sheet of paper that it takes to print a full page.

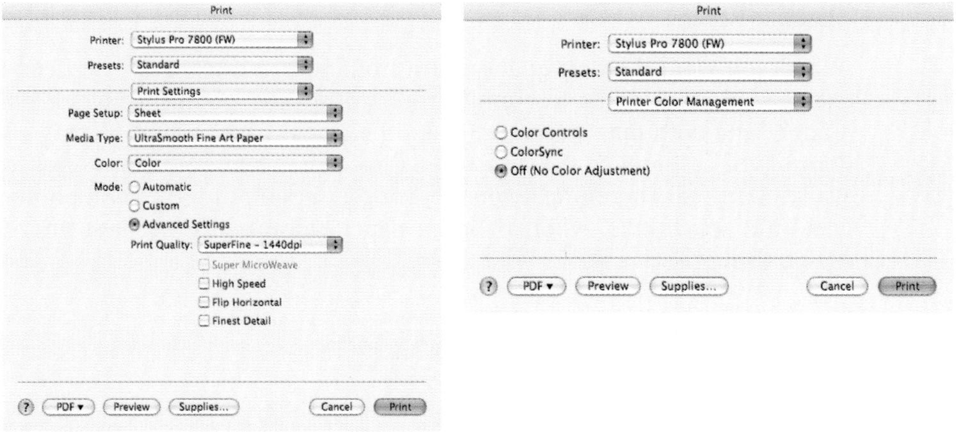

FIGURE 8.24A/B   Setting options in the printer's dialog box for a Mac.

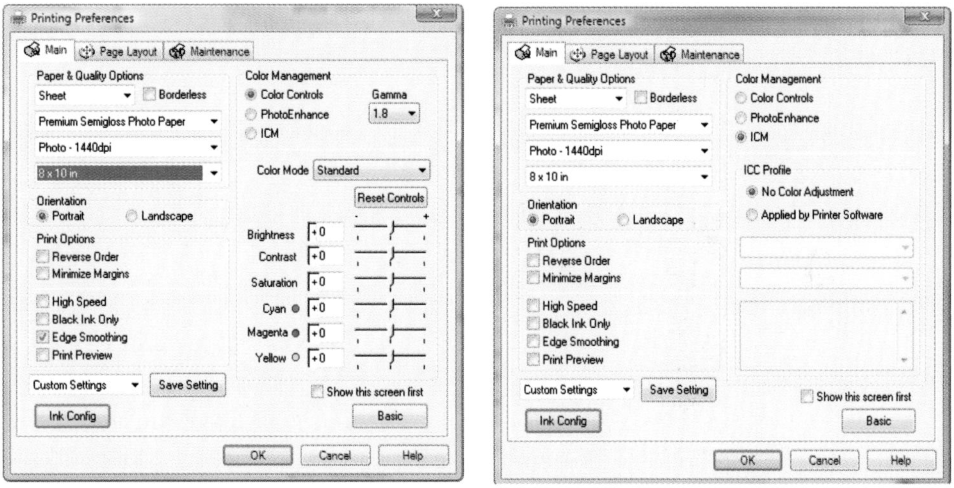

FIGURE 8.25A/B   Setting options in the printer's dialog box for a PC.

To do this, take a smaller portion of the image, print it, and then check it for color and tone accuracy. You could also take a few sheets of photo paper and cut them into smaller pieces to print on, thus reducing waste. Here is a strategy for creating a test print:

1. Open the image you want to print.
2. Choose the Rectangular Marquee tool, and make a selection around the portion of the image you want to print.
3. Choose Edit > Print with Preview.
4. Check the Print Selected Area box. The selected area will be printed in the center of the page.

Choosing Paper

When you want the best quality print from your printer, you will need to use the best paper. The two main manufacturers of quality photo printers are Epson and Canon, and both manufacturers make their own paper. These papers are specially formulated to produce the best results from the chemical composition of the specialty inks used. Therefore, if you are using a Canon printer, Canon photo paper will yield the best results, whereas Epson paper will produce the best images from an Epson printer.

SUMMARY

This wraps up this chapter on resizing and printing. You learned a lot about resolution and resizing images. We covered some pretty technical stuff, such as interpolation methods, but also had the opportunity to find some easy ways to get the job done. You also discovered how to make your print match the monitor by printing with profiles. Ensure that you follow the steps exactly to get great quality prints. It is very easy to miss one step!

III

EFFECTS

9

IMAGE RETOUCHING

In This Chapter

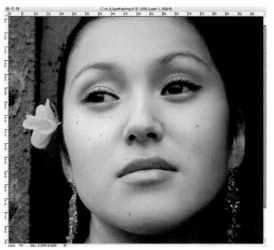

Image from iStockphoto.com.

In this chapter, we will follow the workflow that many professional retouchers use. You will learn how to make photos of people look better. After the images are captured and long after the models have retired to their cozy dwellings, it's time to do a little work. This is where we will make people look younger, more alive, and glamorous, and remove blemishes. If only this were possible in the real world, we would make a fortune!

There is the ethical question, of course. How much is too much? The answer is up to you and your client. Even supermodels are retouched for the covers of magazines, and all imperfections are smoothed out. You can use these techniques to fix minor problems or turn someone into a completely different person. Figure 9.1 shows an image that was retouched using the techniques shown in this chapter. The techniques are subtle and do not change the character of the model. The secret to good retouching is to make the photo not look retouched.

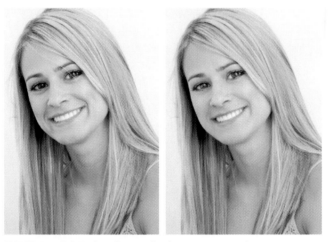

FIGURE 9.1   Original and retouched. Image from iStockphoto.com

TUTORIAL 9.1   REMOVING MOLES AND OBVIOUS BLEMISHES

This technique will quickly and painlessly remove moles. The same technique works just as well on pimples, warts, boils, and other unwanted growths. This is the first step in retouching. Fix the obvious first, and then move on to the subtle.

ON THE CD

Open ch_9_Mole.jpg from the CD-ROM, or use your own image. In Figure 9.2, we have a picture of a pretty face with a mole. Always check with your client before removing moles because these can be desired distinguishing marks in some cases, such as with Cindy Crawford.

1. Choose the Healing Brush (from the Tools Palette). Click and hold on the Spot Healing Brush icon as shown in Figure 9.3. From the resulting flyout menu choose the Healing Brush tool. This tool is almost magical. When you

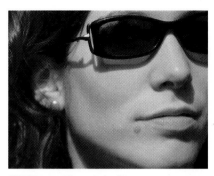

FIGURE 9.2   The original image. Image from iStockphoto.com.

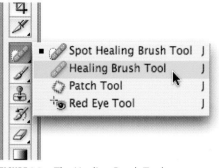

FIGURE 9.3   The Healing Brush Tool.

"clone" with the Healing Brush, it matches the texture and color tone of the part of the image that you pick up (sample) and attempts to blend that with the surface in and around the blemish.

2. Choose a portion of the skin similar to the portion with the mole. Press the Alt key (Option key for Mac), and click over this area to capture a sample.
3. Release the click, and move your mouse over the blemish, as shown in Figure 9.4.
4. Click and release the mouse, and the sample will blend into the existing image.

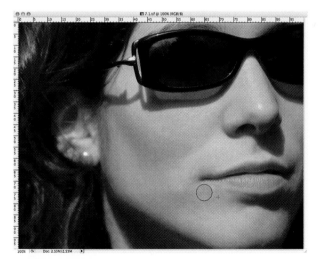

FIGURE 9.4   Removing the mole.

Just like magic, the mole is gone. Figure 9.5 shows the same image after just a few seconds of work. Use this technique to remove any obvious blemishes from the image.

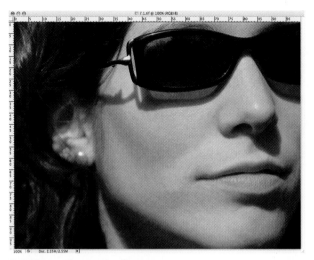

FIGURE 9.5   The repaired image.

THE SPOT HEALING BRUSH

Sometimes you may have many tiny blemishes such as acne and stray freckles (in this case, more moles) to clean up. The quickest method is to use the Spot Healing Brush. No need to take a sample first. Just make the brush size a bit larger than the mark you want to replace and simply click on top of the blemish. Figure 9.6 shows some minor spots that we will remove.

ON THE CD

Open ch_9_SpotHealing.jpg from the CD-ROM, or use your own image.

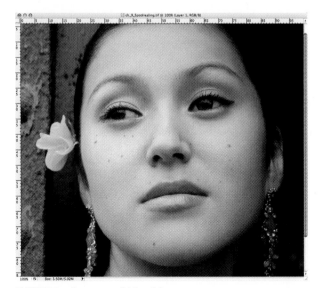

FIGURE 9.6   Some small blemishes.

1. Click and hold on the Healing Brush icon. From the resulting flyout menu, choose the Spot Healing Brush Tool.
2. Choose a small brush size somewhat larger than the blemish itself.
3. Click once on the affected area. The blemish will disappear. This technique is called *dabbing*. Dabbing away the blemishes is a good way to fix tiny spots without disturbing the surrounding skin.

Figure 9.7 shows the same image after a few seconds with the Spot Healing Brush. The same technique will also work with larger and more widespread spots.

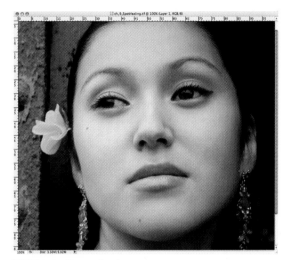

FIGURE 9.7   Retouched.

WRINKLE REDUCTION

While we wait for the invention of the miracle wrinkle cream, Photoshop can quickly remove a few years off our faces. In this tutorial, we will once again be using the Healing Brush. This time we will use it to reduce the signs of aging by reducing wrinkles. We don't want to completely remove all wrinkles or the face can tend to look like it's made out of plastic, which is hardly a convincing retouch.

TUTORIAL 9.2	REDUCING WRINKLES

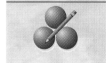

Open the image ch_9_wrinkles.jpg from the CD-ROM, or begin with one of your own. The woman in this image (see Figure 9.8) is about to drop several years from her appearance.

ON THE CD

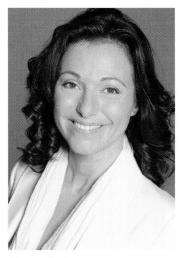

FIGURE 9.8   The beginning image. Image from iStockphoto.com.

A good practice to get into is creating a new layer and naming it Retouched (see Figure 9.9). Do this by going up the menu item Layer and choosing New > Layer. This will leave the original layer intact. You can also adjust the opacity of this layer later to lessen the effect of the digital plastic surgery and produce a much more realistic result.

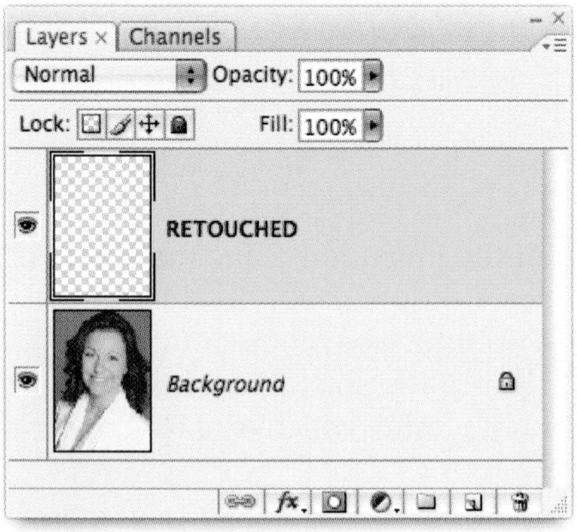

FIGURE 9.9   A new layer.

1. Select the Healing Brush tool.
2. Choose the Current & Below option from the Sample drop-down list in the Options bar (see Figure 9.10). This enables you to work on a blank layer. If you do not turn on this option, nothing will happen when you work on the Retouched layer.

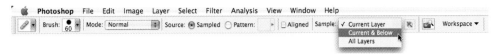

FIGURE 9.10   Choosing Current & Below from the Sample drop-down list.

3. Press Alt+click (Option+click for Mac) to sample.
4. Click to paint over the target area of the image. Rather than dragging the mouse with the Healing Brush, it's better to "dab" the effect. Click, move the mouse a little, and click again, slowly building up your effect. This technique produces a more subtle effect and blends much better. Sometimes, such as when you are working on a larger, more contrasted area, you may need to drag a little, but this is the exception rather than the norm.
5. Release your mouse button, and Photoshop does the blending.

Adjust the brush size for the area you are working on. Make frequent samples for a more accurate match.

6. Take a sample from below the eye, as shown in Figure 9.11.
7. Dab away the wrinkles around the eyes, as shown in Figure 9.12.

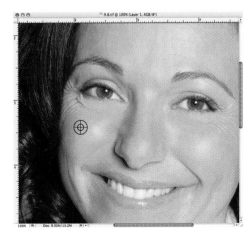

FIGURE 9.11   Sampling.

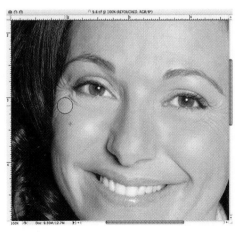

FIGURE 9.12   Dabbing with the Healing Brush.

Figure 9.13 shows the area of the eye being smoothed out and all wrinkles removed.

8. Keep working on the image until all the wrinkles are removed from around the eyes; you can also remove the smile lines.
9. Repeat the same process around the mouth to remove the wrinkle marks.

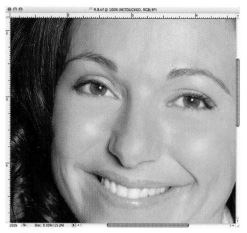

FIGURE 9.13 The wrinkles are smoothed away.

You may find dark marks appearing on the working areas. This is because either the brush is too soft or the sample is wandering into shadowed areas of the image. To fix this, reduce the size of the brush and make the edge hard rather than soft. You can do this from the Brush option on the Options bar.

10. Finish retouching all the wrinkles on the image (see Figure 9.14). Don't worry if it looks a bit plastic and unnatural, you will fix that next.

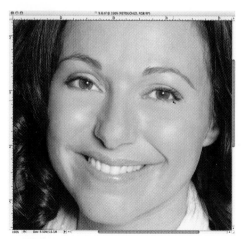

FIGURE 9.14 The mouth has been retouched as well as the eyes.

11. Reduce the opacity on the Retouched layer as shown in Figure 9.15. This fades the retouch and lets a hint of the wrinkles show through. By doing this, you retain the character of the person, without all the adverse effects of the wrinkles. This produces a younger-looking natural face.

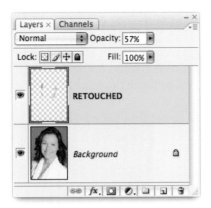

FIGURE 9.15   Reducing the Retouched layer's opacity.

Figures 9.16a and 9.16b show the image before and after the retouch.

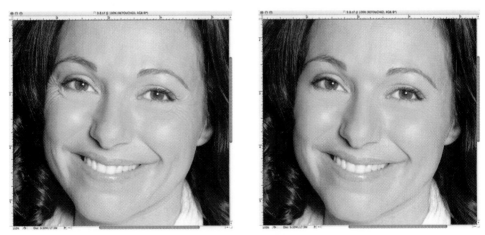

FIGURE 9.16A/B   Before and after a realistic looking retouch.

ENHANCING THE EYES

One of the most important parts of facial retouching is the eyes, and they deserve extra attention. The eyes will always capture the viewer's attention. When you look at any photo of a face, the first thing you look at is the eyes. It's in our nature to look at eyes; it's how we communicate and read people. We will walk through a few techniques to add some extra zing and life to the eyes.

TUTORIAL 9.3	**ENHANCING EYES**

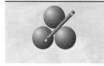

For this section of the chapter, open `ch_9_Eyes.jpg` from the CD-ROM (see Figure 9.17), or choose an image that you have taken showing some eyes. You probably have plenty in your collection.

ON THE CD

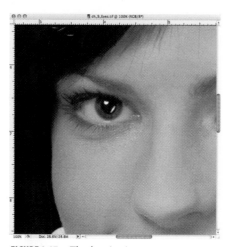

FIGURE 9.17   The beginning eye. Image from iStockphoto.com.

Removing the Red from the Whites

To remove the red, follow these steps:

1. Using the Magnetic Lasso tool or CS3's new Quick Select tool, carefully draw around the whites of the eyes as shown in Figure 9.18. (Actually, you

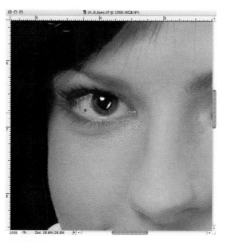

FIGURE 9.18   Making a selection.

can use any tool you prefer, including the Magic Wand.) Figure 9.19 shows the eye with the white selected. We will need to soften the edges of the selection so that the effect looks natural. Hard lines are a sure giveaway because they rarely exist in nature.

2. Choose the Refine Edge command from the Option bar. Click the Overlay Mode, and then set the Radius to 1.0, set the Feather to 4, and set the Expand to +12 (see Figure 9.20).

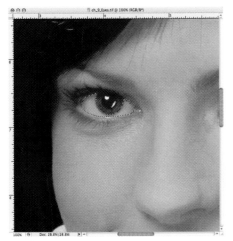

FIGURE 9.19   The white of the eye selected.

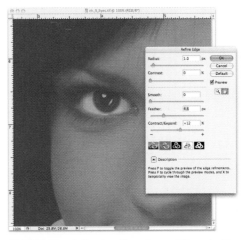

FIGURE 9.20   Softening the edges of the selection.

3. With the selection active, choose a Hue/Saturation adjustment layer. Click the Adjustment Layer icon at the bottom of the Layers Palette, and select Hue/Saturation.

4. Lower the saturation until just about all the yellow is gone as shown in Figure 9.21. You can also raise the Lightness if you want to brighten up the whites as well. Use caution here, however, because a little goes a long way. (You will use this same technique for instant dentistry later in this chapter: yellow to white teeth in a few clicks.)

Figure 9.22 shows the Layers Palette with the adjustment layer. Remember that a mask is automatically created from the selected area. This mask ensures that only the eye will be affected, and the rest of the image is protected from the correction. See Chapter 6, "Local Enhancements: Selections and Masks" for more on selections and masks.

Enhancing the Iris

To enhance the iris, follow these steps:

1. Choose the elliptical Marquee tool, and make a selection of the iris as shown in Figure 9.23. It can be tricky to get the selection in the correct position.

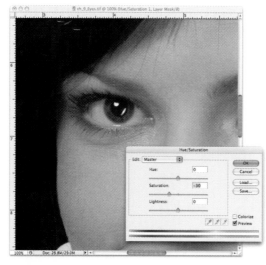

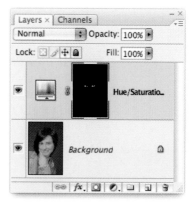

FIGURE 9.22   Adjustment layer.

FIGURE 9.21   Removing some of the natural red and yellow from the eye.

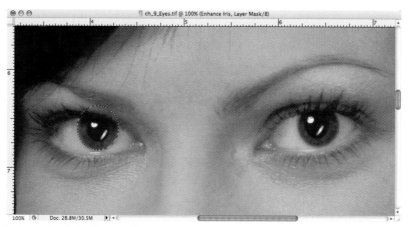

FIGURE 9.23   Selecting the iris.

Hold down the spacebar as you are making the selection. When the spacebar is depressed, you can reposition the selection.

2. With this selection active, create a Curves adjustment layer. Ctrl+click (Cmd+click for Mac) in the iris where you want to lighten the color. Use either your up- and left-arrow keys on your keyboard or the mouse to raise this point up and to the left. Increase the brightness until the iris looks good (see Figure 9.24). An added benefit of this method is that it increases the eye color as well as brightening it.

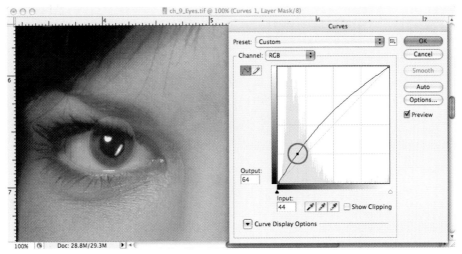

FIGURE 9.24   Lightening the iris with Curves.

3. This technique will usually leave the pupil looking a little too light, so click on the shadow point in the curve and move it to the right until your pupil becomes an agreeable depth of black (see Figure 9.25).

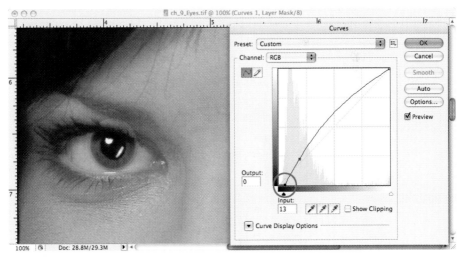

FIGURE 9.25   Darkening down the pupil with curves.

4. The effect of the curve has spilled out over the iris, due to the initial selection, so let's take care of that. Grab the paintbrush, and choose black as your foreground color. Paint away areas that should not be affected (see Figure 9.26). Press the X key to flip your foreground color to white, and paint in the adjustment on the other eye.

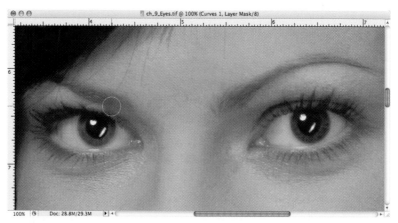

FIGURE 9.26   Painting out the overspill.

5. Once both eyes are painted in, you will have a much better idea of how the Curves adjustment looks. You may want to reduce the size of your image onscreen so that you can see the eyes in relation to more of the face. This will help in judging whether the effect was too heavy handed or not enough. If the effect is too much, you can simply reduce the opacity of this adjustment layer as shown in Figure 9.27.

6. If the effect is not enough, double-click on the Curves icon to reopen the Curves dialog box. Click on the middle point, and raise it further up and to the left, until you reach the desired effect.

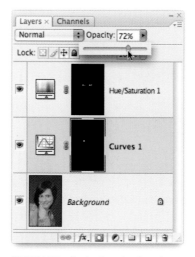

FIGURE 9.27   Reducing the Opacity of the adjustment layer.

Figures 9.28 and 9.29 show the before and after shots of the eye enhancement. You can now see how crisp the eye is looking without being too obvious. The reason the eyes appear much more alive is because the pupil is lighter and more colorful, and the whites of the eye have become less yellow and lighter. Again, be careful not to overdo these techniques, retouching should not really be noticeable until you compare it to the original.

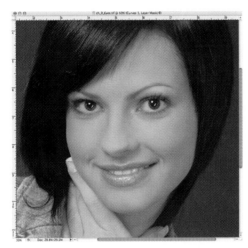 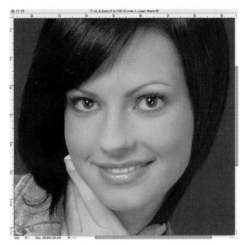

FIGURE 9.28   Before . . .   **FIGURE 9.29**   . . . and after.

TUTORIAL 9.4   WHITENING TEETH

ON THE CD

After you have worked on the skin and eyes, the next step is to make sure that those pearly whites are indeed white. It's amazing what a difference these Photoshop "whitening strips" can make. In Figure 9.30, we have a picture of a nice smile that can be made even nicer. Open ch_9_Whiten Teeth.jpg from the CD-ROM (see Figure 9.30).

1. Create a selection of the teeth using the Magic Wand as shown in Figure 9.31. Keep the Tolerance to around 25. If you don't get it all on the first click, choose the Add to Selection button, or press the Shift key and continue to click inside of the unselected teeth.
2. Choose a Hue/Saturation adjustment layer by clicking on the Adjustment Layer icon in the Layers Palette and choosing Hue/Saturation.
3. When the dialog box pops up, slide the Saturation slider to the left until the yellow in the teeth has disappeared. If the teeth are also too dark, you can lighten them up with the Lighten slider in the Hue/Saturation box. A word of caution, brightening them too much can look quite unnatural, so use a soft hand here (see Figure 9.32).

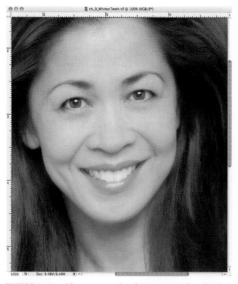

FIGURE 9.30 The untouched image with a little yellow on the teeth. Image from iStockphoto.com.

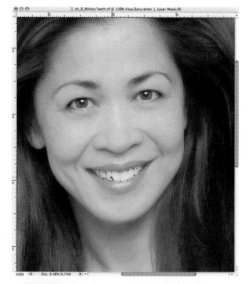

FIGURE 9.31 Creating a selection with the Magic Wand.

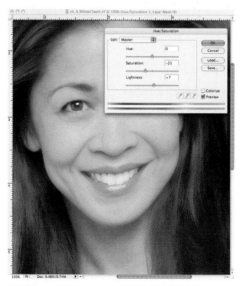

FIGURE 9.32 Desaturating the teeth.

4. In some cases, you may find at this stage that your selection is not perfect. An easy way to be sure of this is to overdo your desaturation or lightness adjustment to reveal any spill over. Take the time to go in with a paintbrush and fine-tune the mask. Remember that the rule of retouching is to make things look natural not to make it perfect. Figures 9.33 and 9.34 show the before and after.

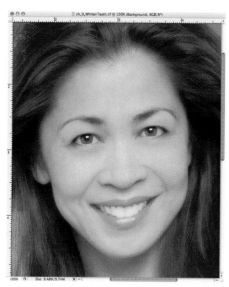

FIGURE 9.33   Before . . .

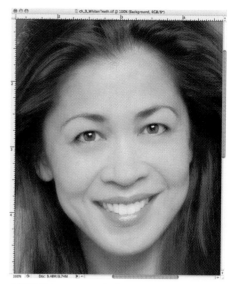

FIGURE 9.34   . . . and after.

So far, we have dealt with retouching subtle things in the image. You will take these steps with just about every image. From this point, we will look at some of the more extreme and specialty type fixes, starting with skin softening.

SOFT FOCUS FILTER

It is not uncommon for folks to want their skin smoothed out somewhat. Harsh sun and studio lights have a way of bringing out the imperfections in our imperfect skin. In the days of film, photographers would use a Soft Focus Filter. Today we can shoot without the filter and apply the same technique in a much more controlled and accurate manner. In keeping with our idea that retouching should be subtle, we will work on a separate layer to provide more control over the final result of this effect. Figure 9.35 shows the original image.

ON THE CD

1. Open the image ch_9_SoftFocus.jpg from the CD-ROM (see Figure 9.35).
2. Duplicate the background layer by choosing Layer > Duplicate Layer.
3. From the menu, choose Filter > Blur > Gaussian Blur.
4. Choose a Radius that makes your subject glow without throwing them too out of focus as shown in Figure 9.36. Don't worry about losing some of their finer detail; you will get that back later. Click OK.
5. Now create a mask so that you can control where and how much of this blur will be visible on the final image. From the menu, choose Layer > Layer Mask > Reveal All (see Figure 9.37).

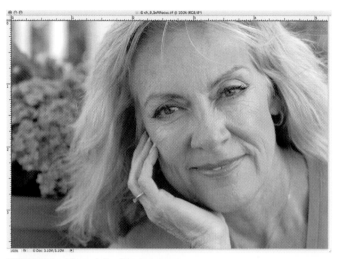

FIGURE 9.35 The original image. Image from iStockphoto.com.

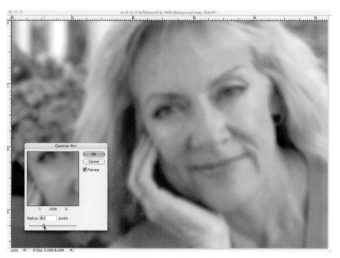

FIGURE 9.36 Blurring the Background copy layer.

6. At this point, you may want to lower your Opacity somewhat to get a better feel for the image as shown in Figure 9.38.
7. Now you need to paint away some of the blur. Paint at a lower opacity with a black paintbrush to make the effect look more believable. Completely removing the blur by painting at 100% sometimes looks unnatural. Choose the paintbrush, and make black your foreground color. In the Option bar, type 30% into the Opacity box (or press the numeral 3 key).
8. Paint over the eyes to reveal some of the sharper image beneath.

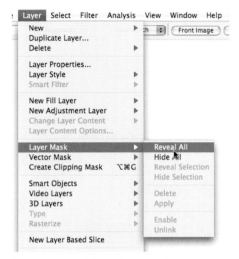

FIGURE 9.37   Adding a layer mask.

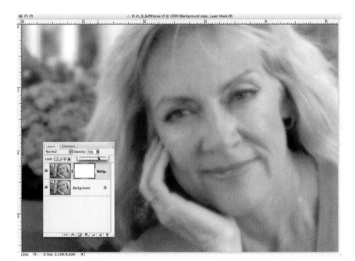

FIGURE 9.38   Lowering the Opacity.

9. Lower your brush Opacity to around 20% (or press the numeral 2 key), and paint over the nostrils and mouth. Painting at a lower opacity lets even less of the sharpness through.

10. At this point, you may want to tweak your Layer Opacity for the blurred layer. It is always easier to make the final call after the mask has been made. Figure 9.39 shows the final image.

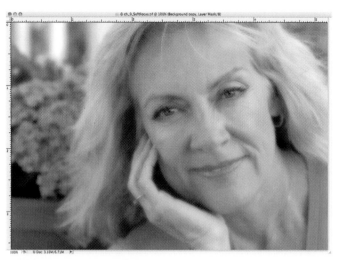

FIGURE 9.39   The final image.

Voila! Instant soft focus filter with that added advantage that we can blur more of the image while still keeping the eyes, mouth, and nose somewhat sharp! Also try experimenting with the other filters in the Blur menu. Both Box Blur and Surface Blur can create some nice results.

REMOVING RED EYE

Red eye is a common problem caused by using a flash that is too close to the lens. We are all familiar with it and can reduce this effect by shooting without flash, defusing the flash, or using an off-camera flash. Many digital cameras have a red eye reduction mode. This prefires the flash, causing the iris to contract, and then fires another flash to take the image. This option works in some cases but not others. The good news is that red eye can be fixed easier than ever using the Red Eye tool.

To remove red eye, follow these steps:

ON THE CD

1. Open `ch_9_redeye.jpg` from the CD-ROM (see Figure 9.40), or choose an image of your own that suffers from this common problem.
2. Choose the Red Eye Tool, which resides in the flyout menu with the Healing Brush Tool and Patch Tool (see Figure 9.41).
3. This tool is very intuitive and easy to use. Simply click once centering over the pupil to remove the red-eye effect.
4. Repeat for the other eye.

The red eye has been eliminated just like that! Figure 9.42 shows the corrected image.

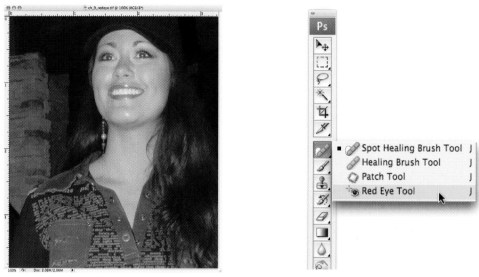

FIGURE 9.40   A little too much red eye.

FIGURE 9.41   The Red Eye Tool.

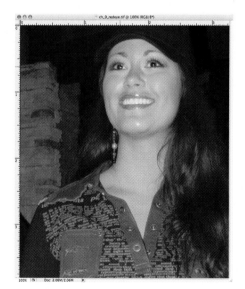

FIGURE 9.42   The corrected image.

REMOVING TATTOOS AND BIRTHMARKS

This tutorial will show you how to retouch larger portions of the image. We are going to use the Patch tool. This is similar to the Healing Brush but can affect much larger areas quickly.

TUTORIAL 9.5	**USING THE PATCH TOOL**

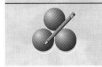

ON THE CD

Begin with the image `ch_9_Tatoo.jpg` from the CD-ROM (see Figure 9.43), or use your own.

1. Choose the Patch tool; click and hold your mouse on the Healing Brush, and the Patch Tool will appear from the flyout menu, as shown in Figure 9.44.

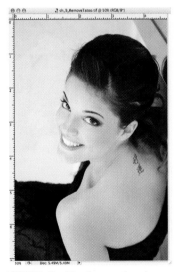

FIGURE 9.43 The image showing the tattoo. Image from iStockphoto.com.

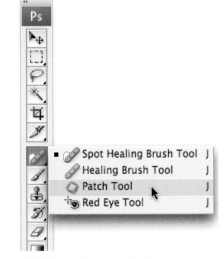

FIGURE 9.44 The Patch Tool.

2. Choose Source from the Options bar as shown in Figure 9.45.

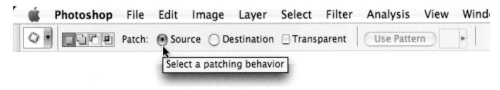

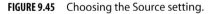

FIGURE 9.45 Choosing the Source setting.

3. Make a selection around the area that you want to replace using the Patch tool (see Figure 9.46). Click and drag as you would if using the Lasso tool.
4. Click anywhere inside the selection, and drag with the Patch tool. You will see the destination area previewed in the selected area as you move your mouse (see Figure 9.47).

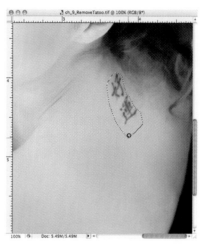

FIGURE 9.46   Making a selection.

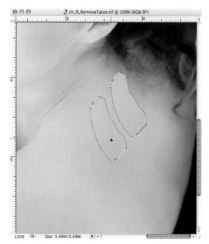

FIGURE 9.47   Choosing the replacement area.

5. Move the mouse until you have a smooth-looking match.
6. Release your mouse, and the Patch tool will smooth the edges of the selection. Choose Select > Deselect from the menu or press Ctrl+D (Cmd+D for Mac) to deselect the patch area.

As you can see in Figure 9.48, the area looks pretty good. Sometimes however, you may have some small areas of color around the replaced area that need to be touched up. If so, choose the Healing Brush, and clean up the edges.

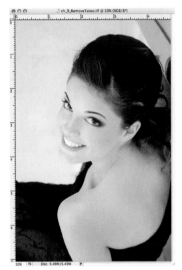

FIGURE 9.48 After a little fine-tuning with the Healing Brush, you would never know that a tattoo used to sit right there on her back. This technique is also great for birthmarks and other areas that require larger fixes.

REDUCING NOSES

The guy in Figure 9.49 doesn't really have an oversized sniffer. He just got a bit too close to a wide-angle lens and suffers from a case of lens distortion. By now, I'm sure you have discovered that some interesting perspectives can appear when you shoot really close. Never fear, you can reduce that nose in a jiffy.

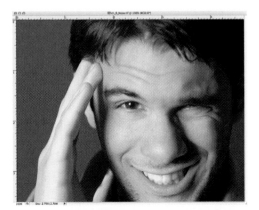

FIGURE 9.49 He got a bit close to the lens. Image from iStockphoto.com.

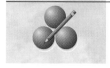

TUTORIAL 9.6   SHRINKING NOSES

ON THE CD

To shrink the nose, follow these steps:

1. Open `ch_9_nose.jpg` from the CD-ROM.
2. Choose Filter > Liquefy to launch the Liquefy tool.
3. Choose the Freeze Mask tool, as shown in Figure 9.50. Freeze Mask protects portions of the image from the results of liquefying.

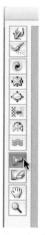

FIGURE 9.50   Choosing the Freeze Mask tool.

4. Paint around the nose to protect the eyes, lips, and cheeks. The mask will not hurt your image (see Figure 9.51).

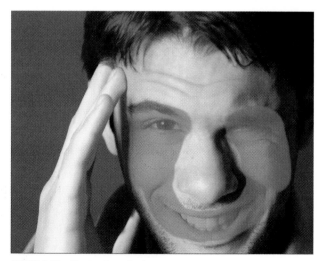

FIGURE 9.51   Protecting the image.

5. Grab the Pucker tool from the list of tools on the left of the interface. Figure 9.52 shows the Pucker tool selected.

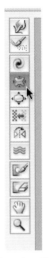

FIGURE 9.52   Choosing the Pucker tool.

6. Carefully click with the Pucker tool to reduce the nose a little (see Figure 9.53). This trick is very easy to perform but be delicate with it. There is a menu in the upper right where you can change the density of the brush (how much it will liquefy). The preview here might be somewhat deceiving. It usually looks a little sharper in the final image. Click OK to commit to the liquefy.

7. Immediately after clicking OK, go up to the menu and choose Edit > Fade. This will give you the chance to reduce your liquefy effect if you so desire.

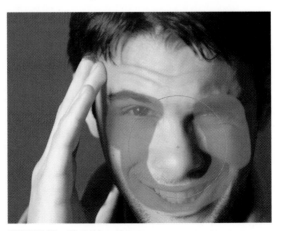

FIGURE 9.53   Shrinking the nose.

Figure 9.54 shows the original image, and Figure 9.55 shows the image after a little nose surgery. Notice that it looks natural because we didn't overdo it.

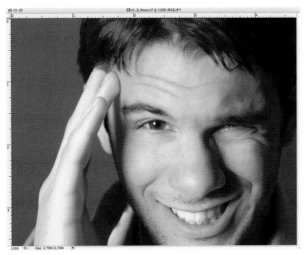

FIGURE 9.54   Before . . .

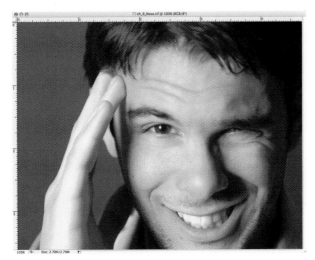

FIGURE 9.55   . . . and after.

EYES WIDE OPEN

Many things cause a person to squint, such as bright lights, smog, smiling, and even age. Even when the eyes are perfectly fine, they are enlarged by many professionals for cover shots and such uses because doing so causes the eyes to attract more attention, and slightly enlarging them will make a big difference in the image. We will examine two methods to open and enlarge the eyes. The first method is the traditional way. The second is with the Liquefy tool. Be very wary of the second method because it's easy to change the shape of the eyes, unless that is the result you are looking for.

TUTORIAL 9.7	**RESHAPING EYES**

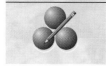

ON THE CD

For both methods, first open ch_9_WidenEyes.jpg from the CD-ROM (see Figure 9.56), or begin with an image of your own.

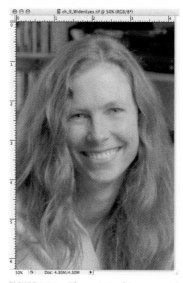

FIGURE 9.56   The original image with squinting eyes.

Method 1

To use the traditional method, follow these steps:

1. Choose the Lasso tool.
2. Make a selection around the eye area as shown in Figure 9.57. Try to keep a little distance between the selection and the eyes and eyebrows.
3. Click the Refine Edge button to soften the selection (or choose Select > Modify > Feather). Set the Feather to about 6 and the Expand to around 40 (see Figure 9.58). These figures will change according to the resolution of the image. The higher the resolution, the higher the settings. If you think about 10 pixels in a 72-ppi image, that can cover a reasonably large area. In a 600-ppi image, 10 pixels would be a much smaller area. Experiment with this setting if you are not getting the desired result.

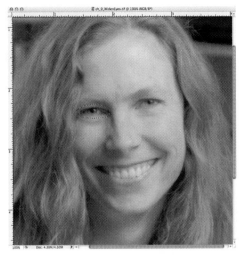

FIGURE 9.57   Making a selection.

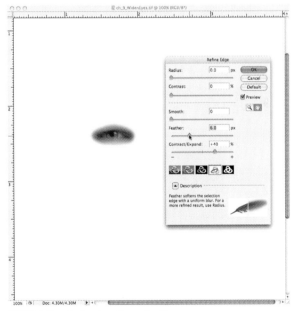

FIGURE 9.58   Softening the selection.

4. Select Layer > New > Layer Via Copy or press Ctrl+J (Cmd+J for Mac) to copy the eye to a new layer.

5. Repeat this process for the other eye. (Make sure you choose the background with the pixels on it again before trying to copy to a new layer. It's easy to forget.)

Your Layers Palette should now look like Figure 9.59, with the original image and each eye on its own layer.

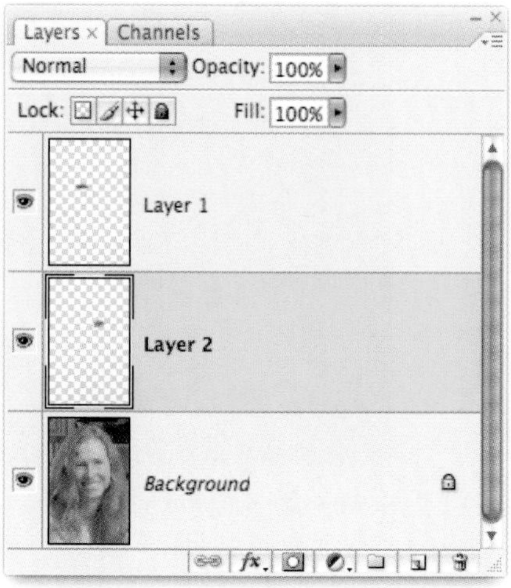

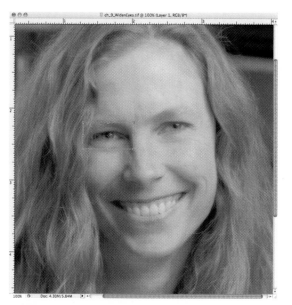

FIGURE 9.59 Copying the eyes to new layers.

6. Choose Edit > Free Transform, or press Ctrl+T (Cmd+T for Mac).
7. Click and drag on the resizing handles to open and enlarge the eye. Be careful not to overdo it (see Figure 9.60). You could also type into the Height box in the Option bar. In this case, we typed 107% in the Height box.

FIGURE 9.60 Transforming.

8. You may have to reposition the eyes after transforming as the center may have shifted slightly.

The image now has the eyes opened and enlarged (see Figure 9.61). See how much more eye-catching it is? This is a very flattering technique for the subject if it's performed with care. Repeat this for the other eye.

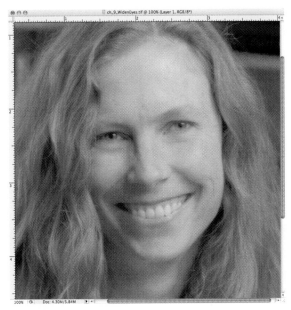

FIGURE 9.61   Opened eyes.

Method 2

You can really get carried away with this technique if you are not careful. You can also have a lot of fun with this tool.

1. Choose Filter > Liquefy. You will see the Liquefy tool open.
2. Choose the Forward Warp tool as shown in Figure 9.62.
3. Make the brush larger than the eye, and position the crosshairs outside the actual eye as shown in Figure 9.63. This is so that you don't warp the iris and make "cats eyes" by accident.
4. Click and drag carefully. Pull the edge of the eye to open it up. Be careful to be subtle with this technique, or it will look bad. Repeat the same technique, and open the tops of the eyes as well.

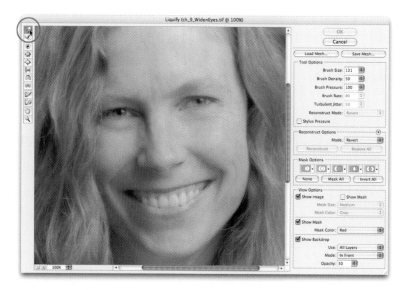

FIGURE 9.62 The Forward Warp tool.

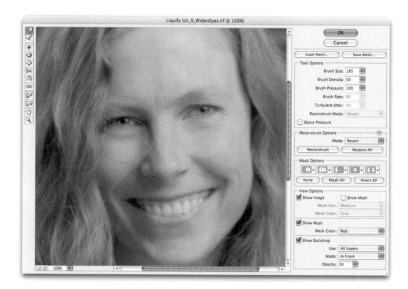

FIGURE 9.63 Liquefying the eyes.

Figure 9.64 shows the eyes after liquefying. This technique is more useful if you are working with an anonymous model rather than with a portrait for someone because when you change the shape of the eyes, you can really transform the appearance of a person.

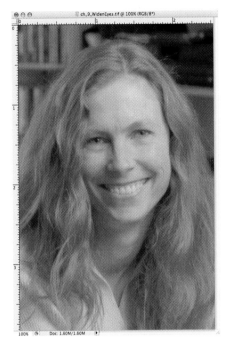

FIGURE 9.64   The finished image.

SUMMARY

You just finished the chapter on photo retouching. First, we followed a retouching workflow employed by the pros, and then we honed in on a few specific issues. You discovered amazing things that can be done with tools such as the Healing Brush. You will have a lot of fun retouching your images and making people look better than ever. Just remember, easy does it!

FRAME AND COLOR EFFECTS

In This Chapter

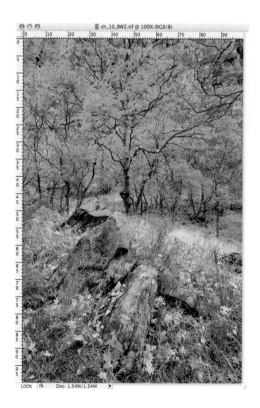

FRAME EFFECTS

In this chapter, we will look at two types of effects: frames and color.

Frame effects are a lot of fun and can help present your images in a new way. The mood of the photo can really be enhanced or altered by choosing different types of frames. The correct presentation can strengthen the feel you were looking for while taking the picture. Beware, however, the overuse of these effects or choosing the wrong type of frame for your image can make it look cheap.

TUTORIAL 10.1	**CREATING A VIGNETTE**

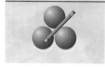

ON THE CD

One of the simplest and most classic edge effects is the vignette. This is when we take a picture and soften the edges as we fade it out. In this case, we will be fading to white to help achieve a High Key effect. There are several methods for creating this effect. The following method will not damage the original image, and it will allow flexibility later on.

Open the image ch_10_vignette.jpg from the CD-ROM (see Figure 10.1), and begin with the image open in Photoshop.

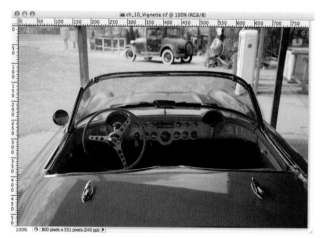

FIGURE 10.1   The original image.

1. Choose the elliptical Marquee tool from the toolbar.
2. Make a selection around the portion of the image that you want to add the edge to (see Figure 10.2).

If you hold down the spacebar while drawing the selection, it will enable you to reposition the selection while drawing. Holding down the Alt key (Option key for Mac) will draw the selection out from the center.

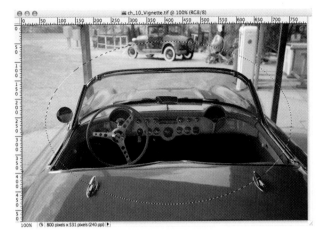

FIGURE 10.2   Making a selection.

3. Choose Select > Modify > Feather from the main menu.
4. Enter a setting in pixels. This will determine the softness of the selection (see Figure 10.3).

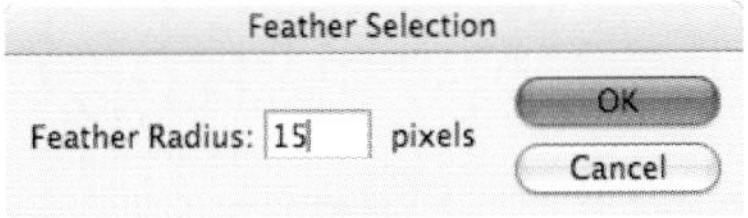

FIGURE 10.3   Entering a Feather Radius.

5. The main part of the image is currently selected, but we want to just select the portions that we want to fill with white.
6. Choose Select > Inverse to swap the selection.
7. Create a new layer by choosing Layer > New > Layer.
8. Fill with white via Edit > Fill. Choose White in the Use box. Figure 10.4 shows an example of what your Layers box should look like at this point.
9. Deselect by choosing Select > Deselect. Creating the new layer protects the original image, and all the effects will be performed on a separate layer. This is a good way to work whenever possible.

Another advantage of creating the effect on a new layer is the ability to make modifications. For example, guessing the initial amount to feather the selection can be difficult, but this step is not crucial. We can make the feather even softer by applying a Gaussian blur as we did in Figure 10.5. To blur the layer, ensure that you are highlighted on the layer (or else you will blur your photograph), and then select Filter > Blur > Gaussian Blur.

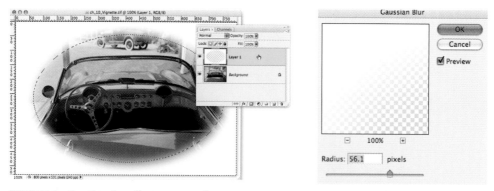

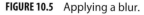

FIGURE 10.4 Creating the effect on a new layer.

FIGURE 10.5 Applying a blur.

Figure 10.6 shows the final image with the vignette effect. Try the same technique except fill with black in step 8 to create a darker vignette to draw the viewer's eye into the center of the photo. Reduce the opacity of the black to 10 to 20% for a classic lens vignette effect.

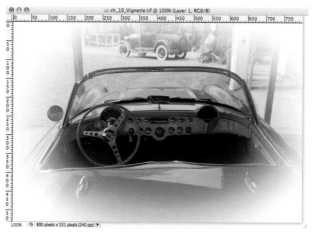

FIGURE 10.6 The final effect.

Using Quick Mask to Create an Edge Effect

This next edge effect is a bit more edgy (pardon the pun). You have likely seen different types of effects like this on brochures, posters, and commercials. They are the rough-cut type frames.

ON THE CD

1. Open ch_10_edge.jpg from the CD-ROM (see Figure 10.7), or use one of your own images.

2. Begin by making a selection. You could use the rectangular Marquee tool, but in this case, we will use the Lasso tool because it allows a more organic/random type selection (see Figure 10.8). We are not looking for perfectly straight edges for this effect; we want something a bit more daring.

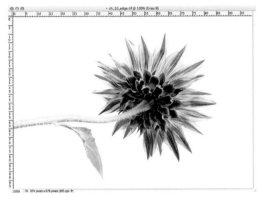

FIGURE 10.7   The original image.

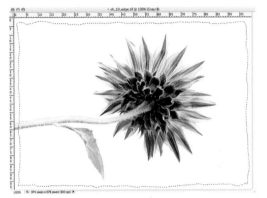

FIGURE 10.8   Making a selection.

3. Press the Q key on the keyboard to invoke Quick Mask. You will see a reddish color replacing the unselected portion of the image. The Quick Mask will replace a selection with a workable mask. (Actually, it creates a temporary alpha channel.) The advantage of Quick Mask is that we can apply filters to the mask that would be impossible to apply to the selection on its own (see Figure 10.9).

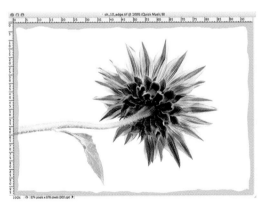

FIGURE 10.9   Quick Mask is on.

4. Let's apply some filters to the masked selection. Choose Filter > Artistic > Rough Pastels.

5. You will now see a large dialog box. Many of the filters are grouped into what is known as the Filter Gallery. The Filter Gallery allows you to combine a number of filters and change their settings, while previewing the result on the image without applying the filters. Make the adjustments to the Rough Pastels as shown in Figure 10.10.

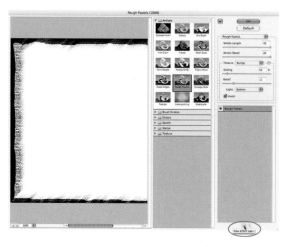

FIGURE 10.10 The Filter Gallery and Rough Pastels settings.

6. To continue creating adjustments to the mask with different filter effects, click on the New Effect Layer icon at the bottom of the Filter box as shown in Figure 10.10. This automatically sets this filter on the top of the stack. You sometimes might find it easier when building on effects to move this effect layer to the bottom of the stack as shown in Figure 10.11.

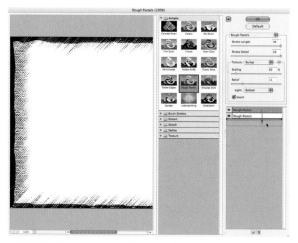

FIGURE 10.11 Moving the filter stack.

7. Click on any other filter now, and this layer will change to reflect that filter. Here Smudge Stick is used to smooth out the hard lines of the Rough Pastels. Make your adjustments as shown in Figure 10.12.
8. When you are satisfied with the result, you can apply them all at once. The result is an image that holds more of its integrity because it hasn't been filtered many times.
9. Click OK to apply the filter. Your image should now look like Figure 10.13. Notice that the filter has been applied to the Quick Mask.

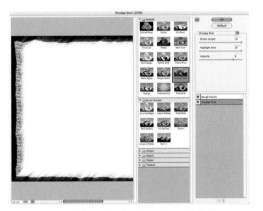

FIGURE 10.12   Adjusting the Smudge Stick filter.

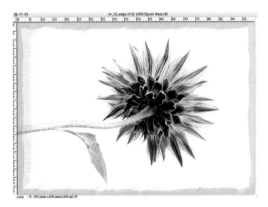

FIGURE 10.13   Quick Mask filtered.

10. Press the Q key once again to convert the Quick Mask to a selection again. This time the selection reflects our filters.
11. Invert the selection by choosing Select > Inverse. Remember that it's good to preserve the original image as much as possible. The same thing applies here, so create a new layer.
12. Fill the selection with your desired color. In Figure 10.14, it is filled with black. Finish by deselecting.

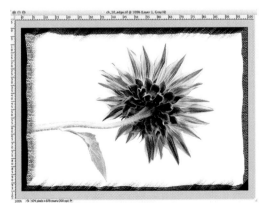

FIGURE 10.14   The final effect.

There are infinite effects you can create using the Quick Mask method. Experiment with different filters to see what kind of effects you can come up with on your own.

Adding a Three-Dimensional Wooden Border

A third type of frame effect mimics reality. We are going to make a traditional wooden frame to add a bit of color and contrast to this old image.

ON THE CD

1. Open `ch_10_WoodBorder.jpg` from the CD-ROM, or choose one of your own pictures.
2. Using the rectangular Marquee tool, make a selection inside the image (see Figure 10.15). This selection should be the desired thickness of the frame. Invert the selection so that only the border is selected.
3. Create a new layer.
4. Fill the selection with white as shown in Figure 10.16. Do not turn off the selection.

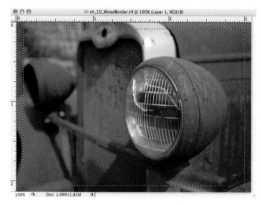
FIGURE 10.15 The image with a selection.

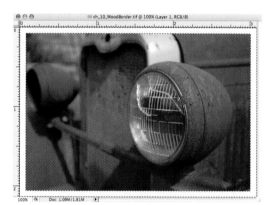
FIGURE 10.16 A white border.

5. We are going to use an alpha channel to create the wood texture. The reason to use alpha channels instead of layers for this effect is to control the depth into the wood grain. This will produce a more aged wood effect.
6. Choose the Channels Palette.
7. Click the Create Alpha Channel button. You should see a black screen with the white frame on the edges, as shown in Figure 10.17. Highlight the Alpha channel by clicking on it.
8. To create the wood texture, choose Filter > Noise > Add Noise. Use the Gaussian option for a more random noise pattern (see Figure 10.18).
9. Choose Filter > Blur > Motion Blur. Apply the blur at zero degrees of angle and make the distance about 8–15 pixels as shown in Figure 10.19. We need just enough to make the blurred streaks that will simulate wood grain. If

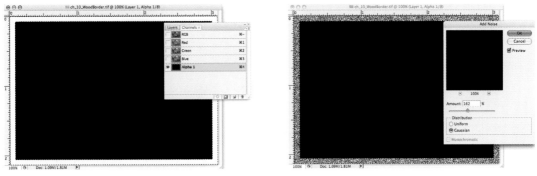

FIGURE 10.17   The Alpha channel.   **FIGURE 10.18**   Adding some noise.

you use a setting that is too high, it will reduce the opacity on the edges. We want to avoid that scenario, so keep the setting as low as possible while achieving a nice streak.

10. Switch back to the Layers Palette (see Figure 10.20), and choose the top layer where the border resides. The selection should still be active. We are now ready to apply the texture.

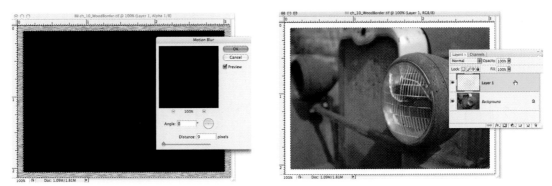

FIGURE 10.19   Adding motion blur.   **FIGURE 10.20**   Back to the Layers Palette.

11. Choose Filter > Render > Lighting Effects. If this option is grayed out, you will need to convert to RGB mode.
12. Enter similar settings to those shown in Figure 10.21. Be sure to choose a brown-colored light by double-clicking in the color square.
13. Choose Alpha 1 from the Texture channel, and the grain will be loaded into the Lighting effects.
14. Click OK to apply the texture to the border (see Figure 10.22). Look at how much depth is in the wood grain! The only problem is that the border itself looks a bit flat. No problem, read on.

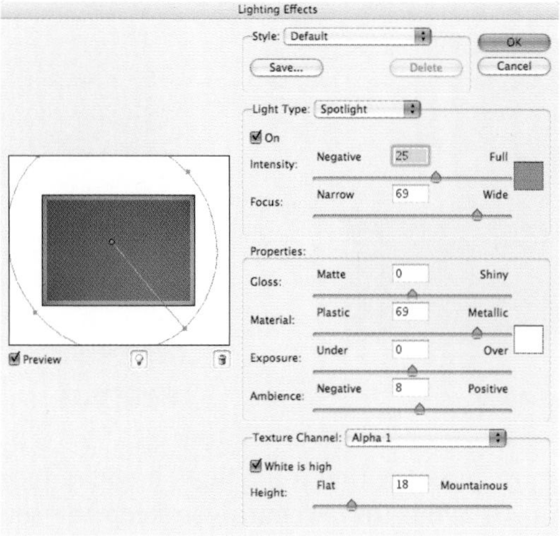

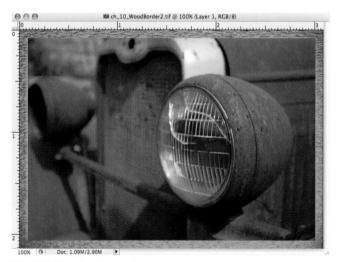

FIGURE 10.21   Lighting effects.

FIGURE 10.22   Wood grain frame.

15. To bevel the edges of the border, you use Layer Styles. Choose the small letter *f* at the bottom of the Layers Palette, and choose Bevel and Emboss.
16. Use the settings shown in Figure 10.23, and click the Drop Shadow box to apply a default drop shadow.
17. Click OK to apply the layer style.

We now have a pretty convincing wooden frame for our picture, as shown in Figure 10.24.

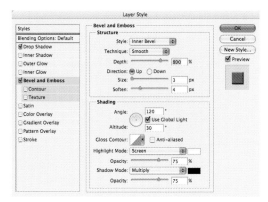

FIGURE 10.23   Layer Styles added for depth.

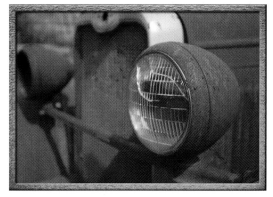

FIGURE 10.24   The image with a wooden frame.

Creating a Double Matte Effect

When framing and mounting a photo, it's common to use a matte or even a double matte for nicer presentation. Here is a way to fake the matte effect. This technique can be used for printing your image in a catalog, displaying on a Web page, emailing, or printing just for fun.

ON THE CD

Begin by opening `ch_10_matte.jpg` from the CD-ROM, or use your own image. The first step is to enlarge the page size—we don't want to lose any of our image, so we will resist the temptation to just matte inside the existing image.

1. Duplicate the background layer. This will leave you a full size image to work with.
2. Choose Image > Canvas Size. This is where you will resize the page "canvas."
3. Click on Relative; you don't have to do any math now. The setting you enter will be added to the overall size.
4. Let's make the matte 20% wider than the width. Click on the Inches box and change this to read Pixels. This shows that the image is 1,000 pixels wide. So enter 200 for both height and width, as shown in Figure 10.25. Use a relative size for the size of the image you are working on.
5. Make sure the background color is set to white, and click OK.
6. Let's add a texture to the matte. Choose the background. (We have copied a layer of the image, so we can just texturize the whole background.)
7. Choose Filters > Texture > Texturizer.
8. Select Canvas as the texture. Use the settings shown in Figure 10.26, or lower the relief for a more subtle effect. Click OK to apply the texture.
9. Let's make a selection the same size as the original image. With the background still selected, press the Ctrl key (Cmd for Mac), and click on the Background copy thumbnail in the Layers Palette. You will now see the marching ants as shown in Figure 10.27.

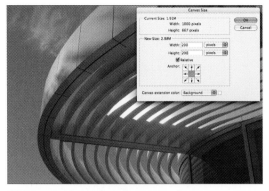

FIGURE 10.25 Extending the canvas size.

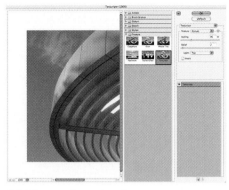

FIGURE 10.26 Texturing the matte.

10. Right now, just the image size is selected, so select the outside and ignore the center. Choose Select > Inverse.
11. Press Ctrl+J (Cmd+J for Mac) to make a new layer from the selected portion of the background.
12. Name the new layer *Matte* as shown in Figure 10.28.

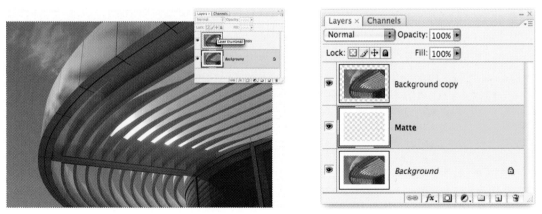

FIGURE 10.27 Making a selection.

FIGURE 10.28 Creating the new matte layer.

13. Drag the Matte layer to the top layer of the Layers Palette; you can now see a textured matte around the image. It's very flat looking but not for long.
14. Choose Drop Shadow from Layer Style in the Layers Palette.
15. Use similar settings to those shown in Figure 10.29. If you are using a higher resolution image, you will need to increase the settings until you have a natural result.

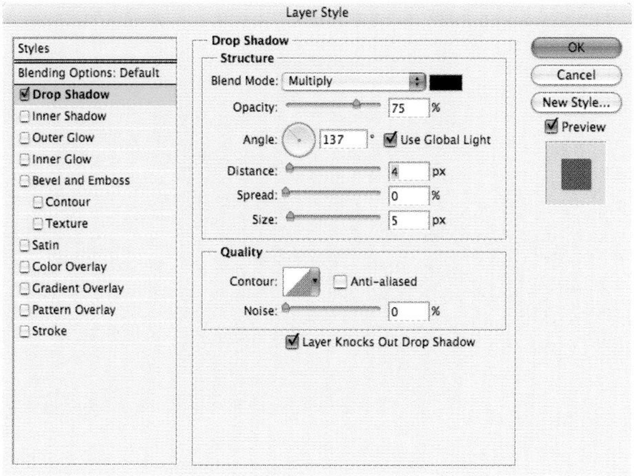

FIGURE 10.29   Drop Shadow.

16. We are now going to solve two problems in one move. We will add the depth of the matte and change the lighting angle, which will also affect the drop shadow.

17. Choose Bevel and Emboss from the Layer Style dialog box. Click on the words *Bevel and Emboss* to access the options for that style.

18. Choose Chisel Hard from the Technique drop-down menu. Choose a small bevel as shown in Figure 10.30 to determine the thickness of the matte.

19. Change the angle as indicated in Figure 10.30. Changing this angle will affect all the styles. Position the light more on top of the matte; this will produce a more pleasing result.

20. Click OK to apply the style. You should now see a realistic looking matte on your image (see Figure 10.31).

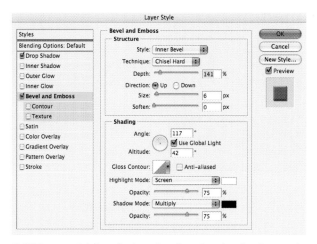

FIGURE 10.30   Adding the bevel and setting the shading angle.

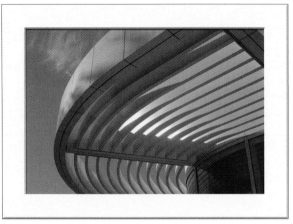

FIGURE 10.31 The matte applied.

21. Two is always better than one, so we will now make a double matte. The good news is that we don't have to do all the steps again.
22. Duplicate the Matte layer, and click on the lower Matte layer in the Layers Palette.
23. Press Ctrl+T (Cmd+T for Mac) to access the Free Transform tool.
24. Click on one of the side handles, and drag it toward the center of the page. By holding down the Alt/Option key, you can move both sides in at the same time. If you click on a corner handle, you can control the top and bottom as well as side-to-side transformation all in one go as shown in Figure 10.32.

We have now completed our matte effect, as shown in Figure 10.33.

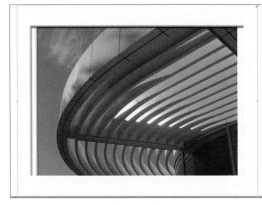

FIGURE 10.32 Resizing the inside matte.

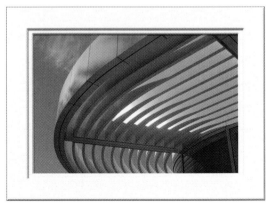

FIGURE 10.33 Final image with the double matte.

COLORIZING EFFECTS

Black-and-white images have always had a timeless effect. With most digital cameras shooting in color, we need some techniques that can retrieve that black-and-white look. Some digital cameras can shoot in a black-and-white mode, however, I recommend keeping the image in color and doing your conversion back in Photoshop. This provides two advantages. First, you have more control over how the final image will look. Second, you preserve the color values in case you decide to print it differently. A lot of mood or drama can also be added to an image by adding or tweaking the color. The following collection of effects are all related to color.

Color to Grayscale

Converting a color image to grayscale (the technical name for black and white) can be quite simple. You can use several methods to achieve this result. The quickest (not necessarily the best) way is to convert the image to Grayscale mode. All the color information will be discarded, and you will be left with only the gray tones. Another method is to desaturate an image. Although this removes all of the color from the image, it does not always create a pleasing black-and-white image. The problem with these methods is that you have no control over the conversion, and a lot of contrast will be lost when the tones are merged. Using a Channel Mixer adjustment layer or the new Black and White adjustment layer is a much more refined method of changing a color image to black and white. These processes will improve control over the conversion and allow you to create a pleasing tonal contrast. Figure 10.34 shows you an image that has been converted using the methods of desaturate, changing it to grayscale, and using the Black and White adjustment.

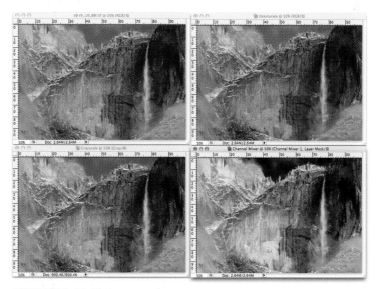

FIGURE 10.34   Multiple conversions.

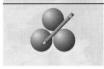

TUTORIAL 10.2   TURNING COLOR TO GRAYSCALE

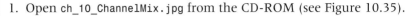

1. Open ch_10_ChannelMix.jpg from the CD-ROM (see Figure 10.35).

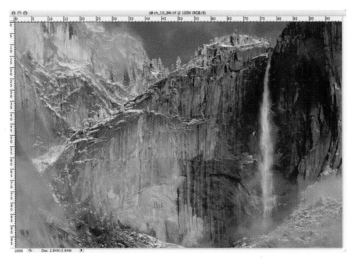

FIGURE 10.35   The original image.

2. Click into the Channels Palette. Note when you enter the Channels Palette that all of the eyeballs are on. This means all channels are visible. Examine each channel one at time by clicking in the channel as shown in Figure 10.36. The image looks best in the red and green channels, and blue doesn't contribute too much. So, you need the red channel with a bit of the green. Start by putting all of the eyeballs back on and then clicking on the top RGB composite layer.

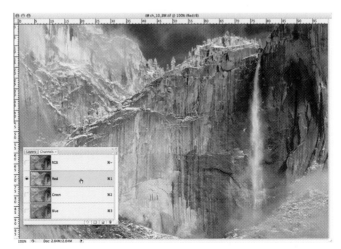

FIGURE 10.36   Viewing the channels.

3. Return to the Layers Palette. Click on the New Adjustment Layer icon in the Layers Palette, and choose Channel Mixer. This adjustment allows you to create a composite based on the amount of each channel you choose.
4. Click Monochrome, which will convert the preview to grayscale.
5. By default, the Channel Mixer will turn to 40 Red, 40 Green, and 20 Blue (this is the same setting you would get if you changed your image to grayscale via the Image > Mode > Grayscale option) as shown in Figure 10.37.
6. Remember that you saw more detail and contrast in the Red and Green channels? Here is your chance to tweak the mix of channels. Increase the red and green and lower the blue until you are satisfied with the result as shown in Figure 10.38. Depending on the image, different settings would be used. This method is fairly simple to use and produces much better results than simply converting to grayscale.

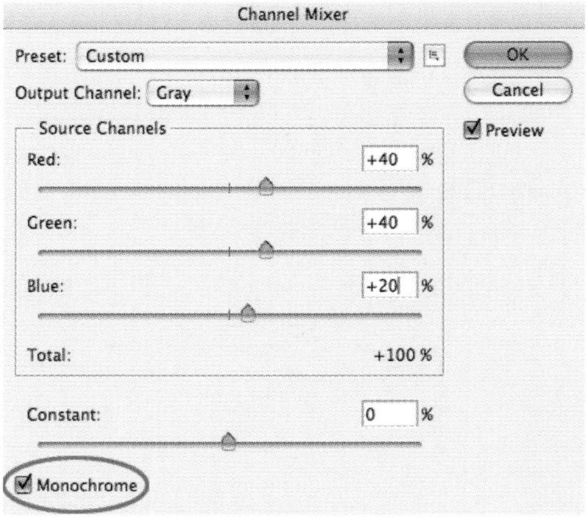

FIGURE 10.37   Channel Mixer dialog box.

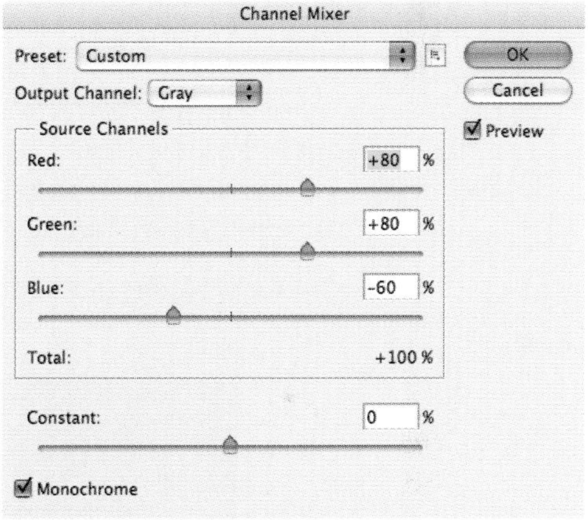

FIGURE 10.38   Adjusting the Channel Mixer.

Figure 10.39 is the result of a conversion using the Channel Mixer. Another advantage of this method is that because you used an adjustment layer, the original layer is still intact, and you can make changes whenever you want simply by double-clicking on the Channel Mixer Adjustment Layer icon.

A new update to the Channel Mixer box is the addition of the Total indicator as shown in Figure 10.40. This number represents the total amount of the channels being mixed together. To stay on the safe side, this number should read 100%. If you are below 100%, you run the risk of losing shadow detail. More than 100% and you can lose highlight detail as shown in Figure10.40. When your total is more than 100%, the Channel Mixer box displays a Caution symbol. The Constant slider can be used to lower or raise the overall brightness if your desired mix of channels goes above or below 100%.

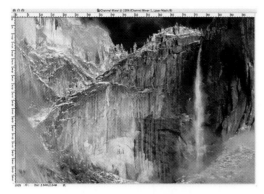

FIGURE 10.39 Conversion using the Channel Mixer.

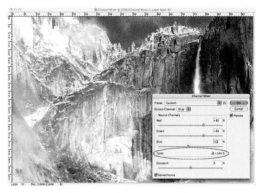

FIGURE 10.40 The new Total warning feature.

Converting to Sepia Tone

You have probably seen sepia tone images before. They are very popular in today's image culture because the retro look has made a big comeback. The effect is a single-colored tint over the entire image.

We will now describe the process of producing this result. We will add a cool twist at the end that will really make your image leap out at the viewer.

ON THE CD

1. Open `ch_10_Sepia.jpg` from the CD-ROM (see Figure 10.41).

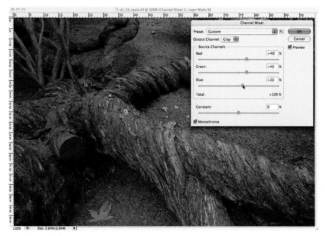

FIGURE 10.41 Original image.

Convert the image to grayscale using Channel Mixer as demonstrated in the previous tutorial. If you already have a grayscale image, then continue with the following steps.

2. Choose the Hue/Saturation adjustment layer from the bottom of the Layers Palette.

3. Choose the Colorize box in the bottom right of the dialog box. By default, the box will show a Hue of 0 and a Saturation of 25 as shown in Figure 10.42. You can change both of these settings to suit your tastes.
4. Choose your desired tint from the Hue slider as shown in Figure 10.43.

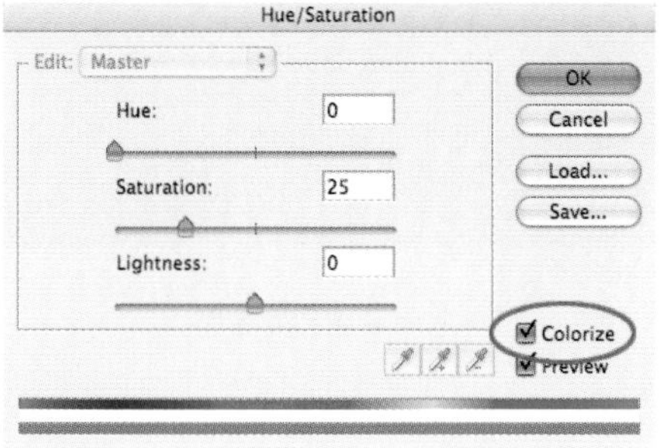

FIGURE 10.42   Hue/Saturation adjustment layer box.

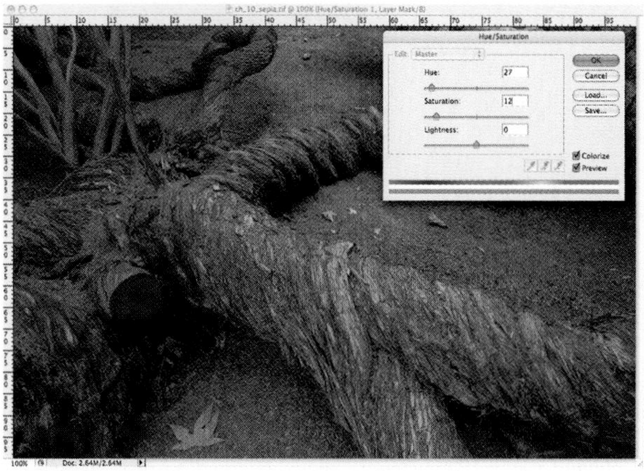

FIGURE 10.43   Changing Hue and Saturation.

5. Lower the Saturation so there is just a hint of color.
6. Click OK to apply the adjustment.
7. To only affect the color and leave the luminosity alone, change the Layer Blending mode to Color as shown in Figure 10.44.

Figure 10.45 shows the original and the final sepia tone image.

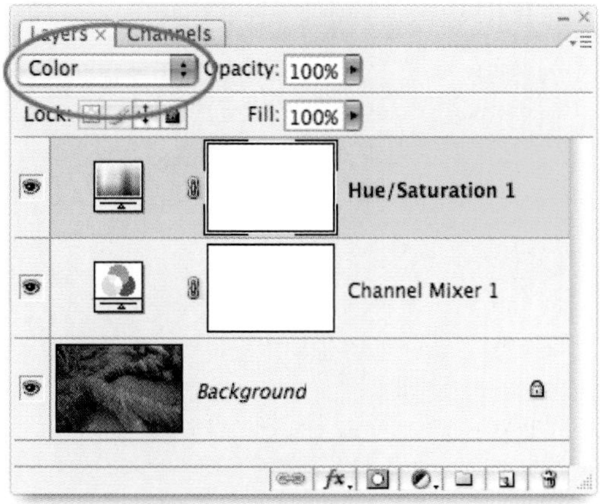

FIGURE 10.44   Changing the blending mode.

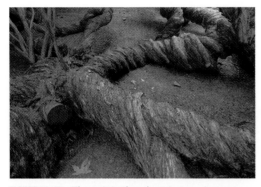 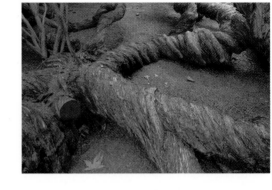

FIGURE 10.45   The original and sepia tone images.

Using the New Black and White Adjustment

The Black and White adjustment is a great alternative to the Channel Mixer. This tool creates a black-and-white image by changing the brightness of several different colors within the image. When a color is brightened, it becomes a lighter shade of gray in the final image. Decreasing the brightness of a color will create a darker shade of gray. In the following example, we will take an image that looks fairly flat with the default B&W settings and create a more interesting final image.

ON THE CD

1. Open ch_10_BW.jpg from the CD-ROM (see Figure 10.46).

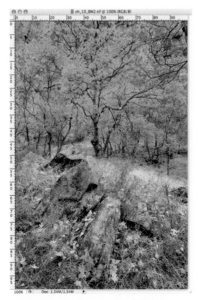

FIGURE 10.46   The original image.

2. Choose B&W adjustment layer from the bottom of the Layers Palette. The adjustment will appear with default settings as shown in Figure 10.47.
3. Adjust the color sliders to lighten or darken tones within the images. Here we will decrease the Green, Cyan, and Blue sliders to darken the grass as shown in Figure 10.48.

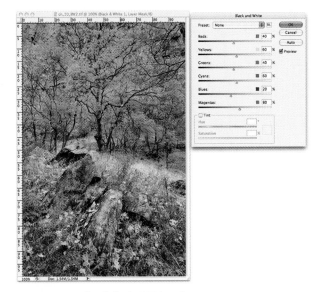

FIGURE 10.47   The default B&W settings.

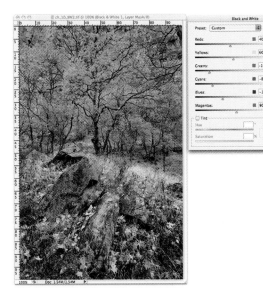

FIGURE 10.48   Decreasing the green, cyan, and blue.

4. Next increase the Red and Yellow sliders as shown in Figure 10.49. In this example, the magenta has also been decreased to darken the background.

5. When finished adjusting the sliders, click OK to apply the adjustment.

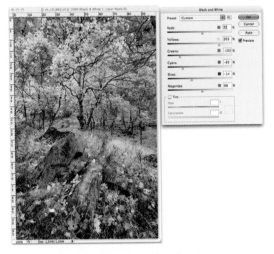

FIGURE 10.49   Increasing the red and yellow.

As you can see from the previous examples, the B&W adjustment has the ability to separate many different colors within an image. This tool gives you more possibilities and a new level of control over converting your color images to black and white. Caution should be exercised, however, when pushing the sliders too far in any one direction. Increasing or decreasing the slider too much can result in a choppy or unrealistic look to the image. Keep an eye on the image as you push the sliders back and forth. Viewing the image at Actual Pixels (100% magnification) will help you spot these irregularities. To view your image at 100% while the B&W adjustment is open, click your mouse while pressing the Ctrl+Spacebar (Cmd+Spacebar for Mac) simultaneously. Look to your title bar to see your current magnification. You can also adjust any of the tones by clicking on the image and dragging to the left or right. Notice that the targeted tones adjust without moving the sliders. Photoshop knows which slider to move!

Creating a Dramatic Effect

We are now going to add some drama to the image by pushing the contrast and mixing a "slide sandwich" effect. However, the control offered by the digital medium will provide control that the slide sandwich effect could never accomplish.

The first thing we need is a copy of the image on a layer with the blending mode applied. We could flatten the image and then copy the layer, but this will not allow flexibility later. Instead, we will copy the contents from all the layers and place them onto a new layer without flattening the layers. This is called a *composite layer*, and it's easy.

1. Create a new layer at the top of the Layers Palette, and choose it.
2. Press Ctrl+Alt+Shift+E (Cmd+Option+Shift+E for Mac) to merge all the contents onto the new layer as shown in Figure 10.50.

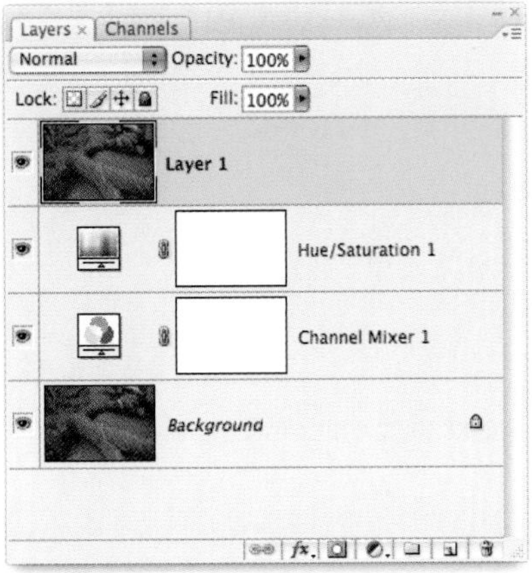

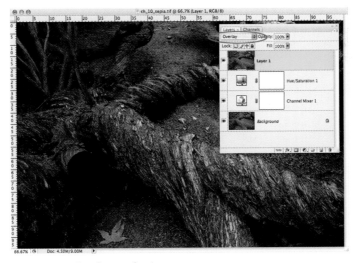

FIGURE 10.50   Creating a composite layer.

3. Change the Layer Blending mode to Overlay. Notice the high-contrast look with rich color as shown in Figure 10.51.

FIGURE 10.51   Overlay mode.

4. Choose Filter > Blur > Gaussian Blur.
5. Adjust the radius until you have a nice soft blended effect as shown in Figure 10.52. You could stop here if you desire or continue for a final step.

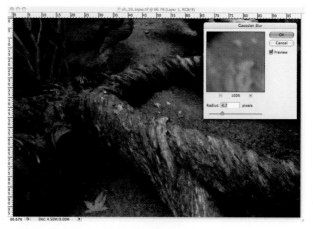

FIGURE 10.52   Blurring the top layer.

6. Lower the opacity on the top layer to create an appealing blend between the layers (see Figure 10.53).

The result, as shown in Figure 10.54, is far more interesting and appealing than the original photo.

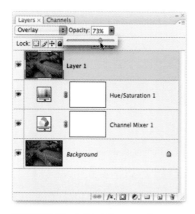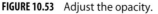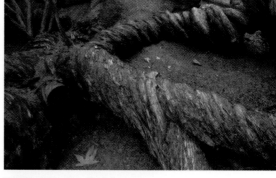

FIGURE 10.53   Adjust the opacity.   **FIGURE 10.54**   The final image.

TUTORIAL 10.3   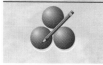   **CHANGING THE COLOR OF AN OBJECT PAINLESSLY**

Perhaps you want to change the color of someone's shirt in an image. Instead of retaking the picture, use this method to change the color of an object in an image without affecting the rest of the image. Most clients will not be able to tell that you changed the color.

1. Open `ch_10_ChangeColor.jpg` from the CD-ROM, or use your own image. Figure 10.55 shows the original. We are going to do the unthinkable; we will change the color of this New York cab from its familiar yellow to a shade of red.

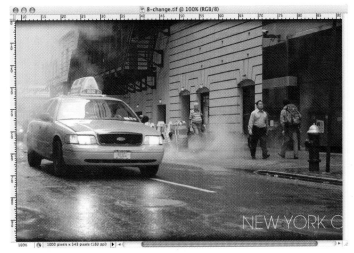

FIGURE 10.55   Original image.

2. Choose Hue/Saturation from the Adjustment Layers icon at the bottom of the Layers Palette.
3. Change the Edit drop-down menu to Yellow (the color doesn't really matter, this just moves you into sampling mode).
4. When you move the pointer over the image, you will see an Eyedropper tool. Click on the color that you want to change, in this case, the yellow cab (see Figure 10.56).

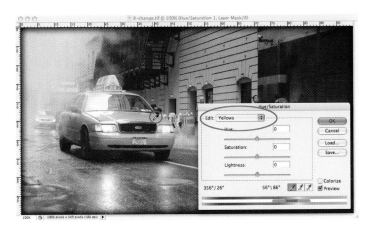

FIGURE 10.56   Sampling a color.

5. Slide the Hue slider until you see your image change color. Notice that your sampled color now changes to a different color as shown in Figure 10.57.

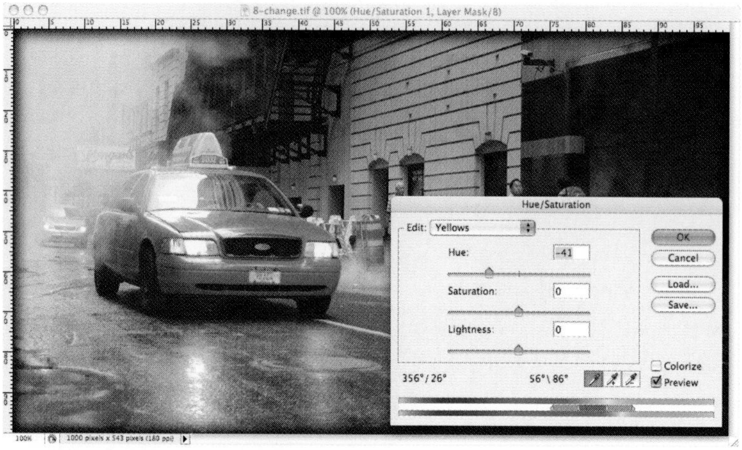

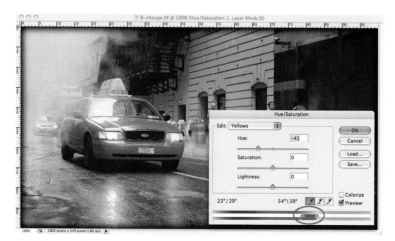

FIGURE 10.57 Shifting the color.

6. Frequently, this is all that's required, but sometimes, you may need to do a little fine-tuning. Perhaps all the color wasn't picked up or alternatively more colors than you wanted have been affected.
7. When you took the color sample, sliders were added to the gradient ramp at the bottom of the Hue/Saturation Palette as indicated in Figure 10.58. Move the outside sliders inward to keep those near colors from being affected by the hue change. Try to keep them from touching the inner sliders. If they become too close or they touch, your colors can end up posterizing.

FIGURE 10.58 Fine-tuning.

8. Most of the fine-tuning should have been accomplished by adjusting the gradient sliders; however, other objects in the image with a similar color have also been changed. Click OK to apply the adjustment.
9. All adjustment layers come with a layer mask. Click on the mask to activate it.
10. Choose black as the foreground color and a soft brush.
11. Paint in the image window, concentrating only on those areas where you want to restore the color. Figure 10.59 shows painting out the mask to allow the original yellow to show through on the reflection on the pavement.

Figure 10.60 shows the image with the color on only the cab changed. This is a convincing effect, and the whole process only takes a couple of minutes to accomplish. Don't tell your clients or coworkers how easy this was! 🎨

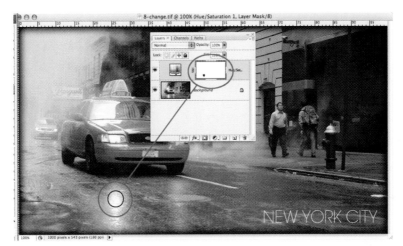

FIGURE 10.59   Touching up.

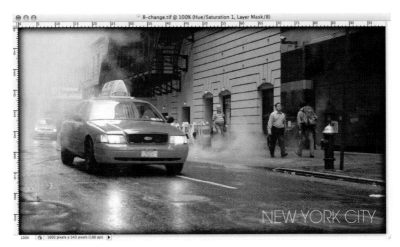

FIGURE 10.60   Final image.

SUMMARY

In this chapter, you learned how to create different frame effects and transform the appearance of your images. Among other things, you discovered how to add some interesting color effects. These effects can totally change the feel of an image and add some excellent visual interest. Freely experiment with these techniques and try combining them, or doing something different with these effects. They are meant to be a springboard, propelling you to new heights of creativity.

ADVANCED CONCEPTS

11

SPECIAL EFFECTS

In This Chapter

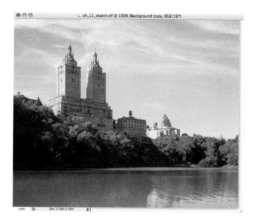

DEPTH OF FIELD EFFECTS

You can use two methods to simulate a depth of field effect that will keep the foreground objects sharp while blurring the objects in the distance. Both methods use a feature in Photoshop called Lens Blur. The first method is very quick and easy and produces a good result. The second method is more in-depth and will be indispensable for producing detailed results that will even fool the experts.

Depth of Field with a Layer Mask

This method produces pretty good results and works best on images that have smooth flat surfaces.

TUTORIAL 11.1	ADDING DEPTH OF FIELD

Open the image ch_11_lens.jpg from the CD-ROM in Photoshop. You can see we have a tall building, just begging to look taller by adding some depth of field (see Figure 11.1).

ON THE CD

You are now going to use Lens Blur to simulate the depth of field. This filter works off a gradient map that you create in an alpha channel. The tones will control where the blurring will occur. The next tutorial describes Lens Blur in more depth. For now, let's just get started.

1. Open the Channels Palette. If the Channel Palette is not visible, choose Window > Channel.
2. Create a new channel by clicking the New Channel icon in the Channels Palette.
3. Choose the Gradient tool, and set it for Foreground to Background, Linear (see Figure 11.2).

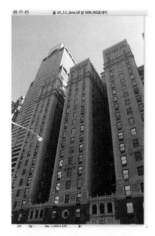

FIGURE 11.1 The original image.

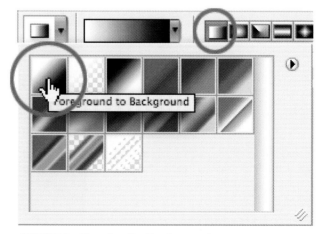

FIGURE 11.2 Choosing the Gradient tool.

4. Press the D key to reset the foreground and background colors.
5. Drag the gradient from top to bottom in the image window. You should now see something like that shown in Figure 11.3.

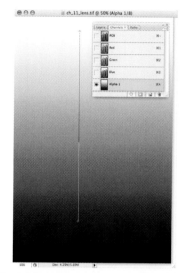

FIGURE 11.3   Adding the gradient onto the alpha channel.

6. Click on RGB to view all the channels.
7. Click on the Layers Palette, and choose Filter > Blur > Lens Blur.
8. For source, choose Alpha1 from the drop-down menu.
9. Choose an amount of blur, and see the instant depth of field effect as shown in Figure 11.4.
10. To change the portion of the image that is in focus, slide the Blur Focal Distance slider; this is just like focusing a lens. Figure 11.5 shows the opposite part of the building in focus.
11. Click OK to apply the effect.

You can have a lot of fun with this filter. Experiment with different types of gradients; circular ones work really well too. Now let's move on and create a complex effect with the same filter.

Depth of Field Using Lens Blur and Depth Map

The Lens Blur filter simulates the effect of an aperture and focal length on a camera lens. To really get the best out of this filter, you need to create a depth map. The filter uses a map to blur the image selectively. You can assign areas with different levels of grayscale and then have the filter focus on the tones and apply a varying blur according to how dark or light the map is in the chosen areas.

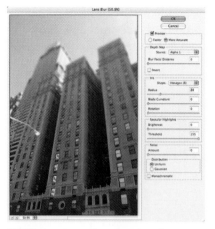

FIGURE 11.4   Lens Blur, showing the top blurred.

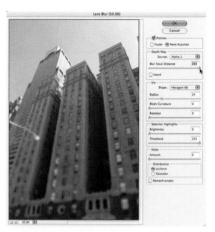

FIGURE 11.5   Lens Blur, showing the bottom blurred.

TUTORIAL 11.2   ADDING DEPTH OF FIELD USING LENS BLUR AND DEPTH MAP

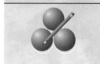

ON THE CD

Open `ch_11_Fishing_blur.psd` from the CD-ROM (see Figure 11.6).

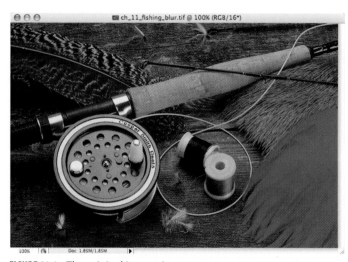

FIGURE 11.6   The original image. (Royalty Free Image from Hemera™.)

1. Duplicate the background to preserve the original image in case you change your mind later.
2. Create a new layer, and name it "Mask" (see Figure 11.7). This is where we begin creating the depth map. A map has been created on the sample image if you don't want to create one yourself. If this is the case, skip to step 15.

3. Choose a white brush, and paint the area of the image that should appear in focus. Usually this will be the highest point of the image. Use the Marquee tools to help with the painting if desired, as shown in Figure 11.8. (Remember to deselect when finished!)

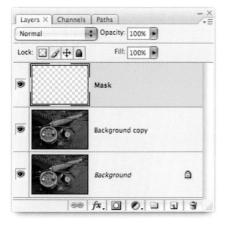

FIGURE 11.7   Creating the mask layer.

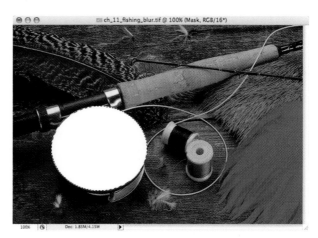

FIGURE 11.8   Assigning the highest points, which will be the sharpest.

4. Create a new layer, and move it beneath the mask layer. Name the new layer "Mid Mask" (see Figure 11.9). This is where you will define the areas that should be half in focus.
5. Use a soft brush set to 50% gray, and paint over the portions of the image that are higher than the background but not as high as the main focused portion of the image, as shown in Figure 11.10.

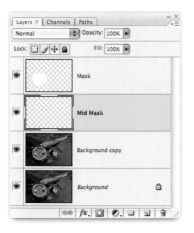

FIGURE 11.9   Creating a layer for the middle levels.

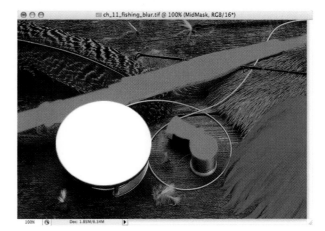

FIGURE 11.10   Paint the middle grounds in 50% gray.

6. Add a Gaussian blur to the midtones. The blur is added to soften the edges of the mask. If the blurs drop off softly, they will appear more natural. Choose Filter > Blur > Gaussian Blur, as shown in Figure 11.11.

7. Create one more layer and name it "Low Mask," as shown in Figure 11.12.

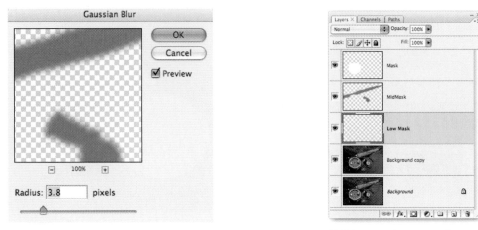

FIGURE 11.11   Blur the map to soften the edges.

FIGURE 11.12   Create another layer for the lows.

8. Choose a dark gray; about 75% will work. Define the low points of the image, but leave the very lowest portions alone. These portions will be mostly blurred but will retain a slight amount of sharpness (see Figure 11.13).

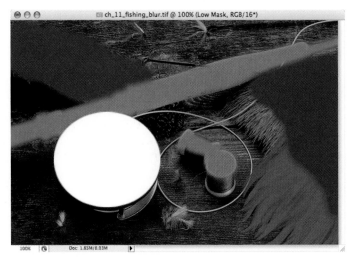

FIGURE 11.13   Paint with a dark gray.

9. Hide the background layers so that only the masks are visible. Now that you can see the mask more clearly, clean it up a bit with the brush tools, and fill in any spots that may have been missed, as shown in Figure 11.14.

10. Merge the three mask layers. Choose Merge Visible from the flyout menu on the top right of the Layers Palette. Make your Background and Background Copy layers visible again. Your Layers Palette should now look like that in Figure 11.15.

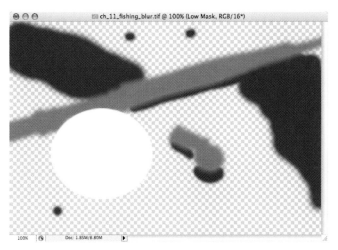

FIGURE 11.14   The map on its own.

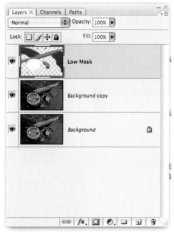

FIGURE 11.15   Merging the mask layers.

11. You have created the depth map. Now you will transfer it to a channel and prepare to filter the image.

12. Select the entire mask layer by pressing Ctrl+A (Cmd+A for Mac) on the Mask layer.

13. Choose Edit > Copy.

14. Open the Channels Palette.

15. Add a new alpha channel by clicking the Create New Channel icon at the bottom of the palette.

16. Choose Edit > Paste, and then deselect. The alpha channel should now look like Figure 11.16. (You will notice that the sample image already has a map created for your use if you have had trouble creating one yourself: the Alpha channel Blur-Map.)

17. Click on RGB in the Channels Palette. Choose the Layers Palette, show the image layer, and hide the mask layer as shown in Figure 11.17.

18. Everything is now set up; it's time to apply the filter.

19. Choose Filter > Blur > Lens Blur (see Figure 11.18).

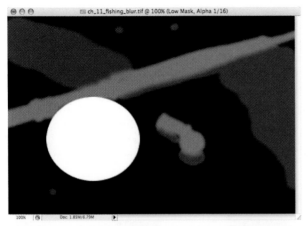

FIGURE 11.16   Copying the depth map into an alpha channel.

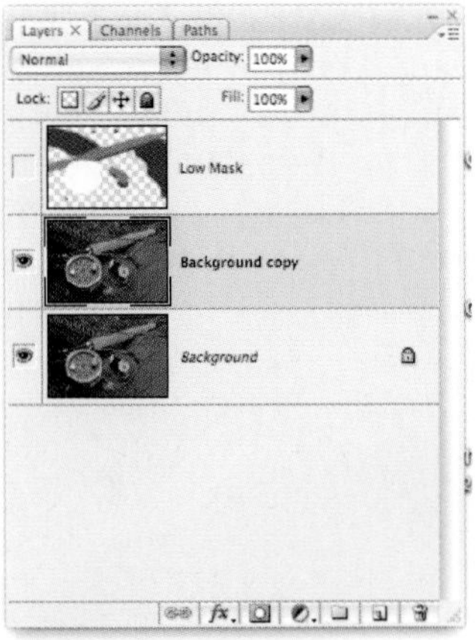

FIGURE 11.17   Choose the top layer and hide the mask.

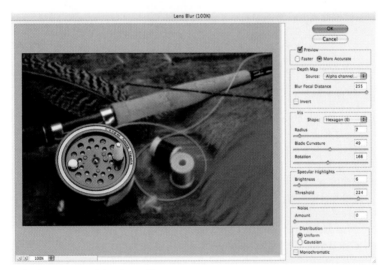

FIGURE 11.18   Applying Lens Blur.

20. Choose Alpha 1 for the source (Channel Blur Mask if you used the included map).
21. When you slide Blur Focal Distance, you will see the focus change in the preview as it interacts with the depth map. Move it to 255 (this represents the 256 shades of gray in an alpha channel).
22. Adjust Radius to change the amount of blur. You can play with the other iris settings if you wish. The shape, curvature, and rotation all simulate the blades of a camera's iris.

23. Adjust Specular Highlights to cause bright parts of the image to become specular highlights. The brightness can be adjusted; Threshold determines the cutoff point at which tones will be turned into highlights.
24. The noise is available for images with grain. As you know, when a blur is applied to an image, the grain is lost. These settings allow you to simulate the grain back to the blurred portions of the image and make the effect more realistic. No grain is present in the example image, so leave the settings at 0. If you were applying grain, you would choose between Gaussian and Uniform under the Distribution section. The Gaussian setting is more random, but you would make the choice that best matches the existing grain of the image.
25. Click OK to apply the effect.

Figure 11.19 shows the image with the depth of field applied to it. Notice how portions of the image appear more in focus than others. This is a great filter that produces stunning results.

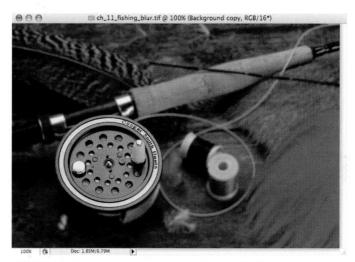

FIGURE 11.19   The result, with a realistic depth of field.

NATURAL MEDIA

This section discusses the techniques used to turn photographs into images that mimic fine art. After you have finished this section, feel free to experiment, using what you have learned as a springboard into your own discovery.

From Photo to Sketch

This technique will show you how to turn a photo into something that resembles a pencil sketch.

TUTORIAL 11.3	**TURNING A PHOTO INTO A SKETCH**

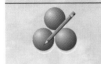

Open `ch_11_sketch.jpg` from the CD-ROM (see Figure 11.20), or open your own image.

1. To preserve your original image, duplicate the original layer; we will work on the duplicate.
2. Choose Image > Adjustments > Desaturate to remove the color as shown in Figure 11.21. The image should now appear in grayscale.

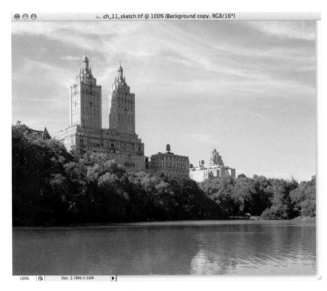

FIGURE 11.20   The original image.

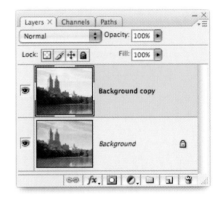

FIGURE 11.21   Duplicated, desaturated layer.

3. Duplicate the Grayscale layer.
4. Invert the duplicated layer, as shown in Figure 11.22. Press Ctrl+I (Cmd+I for Mac) to invert.
5. Switch the Layer Blending mode to Color Dodge, as shown in Figure 11.23. The image should now appear almost white.
6. Now set the outline of the sketch. Choose Filter > Blur > Gaussian Blur, as shown in Figure 11.24. Be careful not to overdo the blur, or the result will re-semble a photocopy more than a sketch (unless that is the effect you want).

You will now see something that resembles a pencil sketch (see Figure 11.25). Creating two layers, one inverted over the other, and choosing the blending mode causes the layers to cancel each other out. When the blur is added, it will cause the blurred area to be visible because those portions have changes from the cancelled portions.

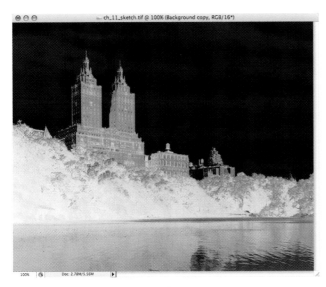

FIGURE 11.22   The inverted layer.

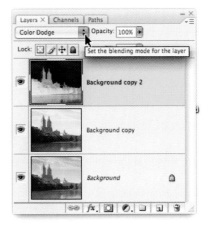

FIGURE 11.23   Changing the Blending mode to Color Dodge.

FIGURE 11.24   Setting the blur.

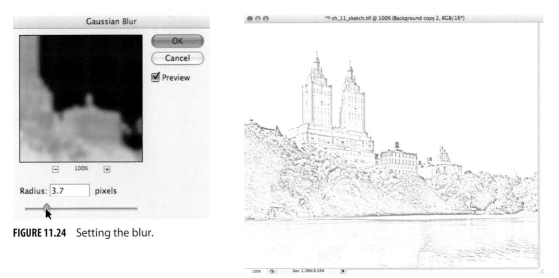

FIGURE 11.25   A pencil sketch.

A variation would be to change the Blending mode to Hard Mix. This will produce an etched effect, as shown in Figure 11.26.

From Photo to Watercolor Painting

This effect will show you how to turn a photo into a watercolor-type painting.

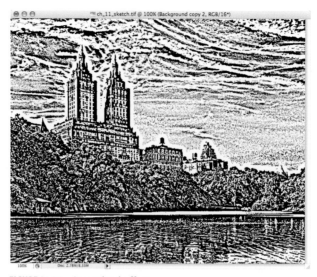

FIGURE 11.26 An etched effect.

TUTORIAL 11.4 TURNING A PHOTO INTO A WATERCOLOR PAINTING

ON THE CD

Open ch_11_WaterColor.jpg from the CD-ROM (see Figure 11.27), or begin with an image of your own. Go to Image > Mode, and ensure that your image is in 8-bit depth by checking 8-bits/channel.

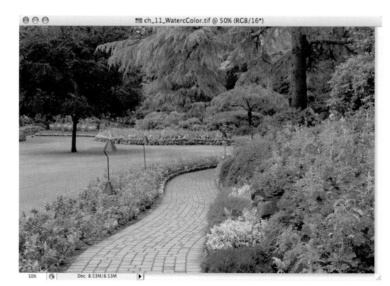

FIGURE 11.27 The original image.

1. Duplicate the background image twice. You should now have three identical layers.
2. Choose the top layer.
3. Select Filter > Stylize > Find Edges. The image will take on the appearance of an outline.
4. The midtones need to be reduced so that mainly the outline is showing. Choose Image > Adjustments > Levels. Slide the Midtone slider to the left as shown in Figure 11.28. This will clean up the stray detail. Click OK in the Levels box.
5. Hide the top layer by clicking on the eyeball to the left of the layer (see Figure 11.29), and click on the middle layer to activate it.

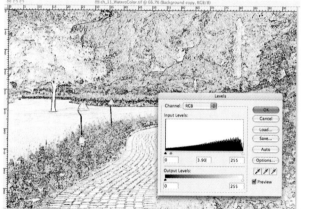

FIGURE 11.28   Adjusting the filtered layer.

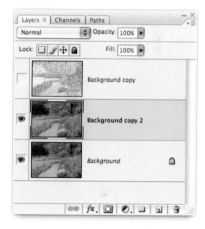

FIGURE 11.29   The Layers Palette.

6. The Filter Gallery will be used to create the effect of a painting.
7. Choose Filters > Artistic > Paint Daubs.
8. Apply a setting that will produce a result similar to that in Figure 11.30. The desired result is enough of an effect that the image appears painted but not so much that all definition is lost.
9. Click the New Layer icon in the Filter Gallery to choose a second effect.
10. Select the Underpainting icon in the Artistic section of Filter box. You are going to use this filter to add some texture to the image.
11. Choose settings similar to those shown in Figure 11.31.
12. So far, the image should resemble Figure 11.32. The image reminds us of a watercolor, but it lacks the fine brush detail.
13. The top layer will provide the fine-brushed detail. Turn the top layer's visibility on as shown in Figure 11.33. Change to Multiply mode, and experiment with the Opacity. Try numbers from 10–35%.
14. To further fine-tune your image, you can adjust the opacity of the second layer. In this example, the opacity is 77%.

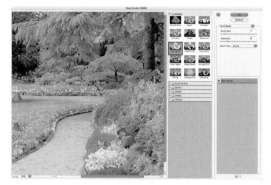

FIGURE 11.30 The Paint Daubs filter.

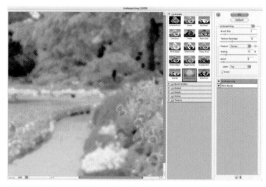

FIGURE 11.31 Adding the Underpainting filter for some texture.

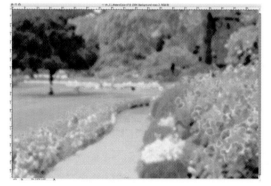

FIGURE 11.32 The filtered image.

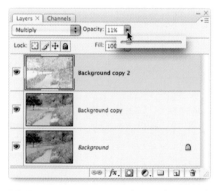

FIGURE 11.33 Turning on the top layer and adjusting Opacity.

As you can see in Figure 11.34, the final image resembles a hand painting.

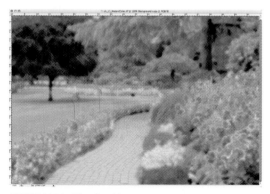

FIGURE 11.34 The final image.

TRENDY EFFECTS

The next two effects use repeating patterns in different ways to produce results that are very popular in the advertising industry. These effects can add some real visual punch to your images.

Pop Dots

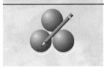

Pop dots are very popular with the youth and sports culture. If you turn on MTV, you won't have to wait long to see this effect in action. To make it easier to focus on the effect, an image has already been extracted and prepared for you on the CD-ROM. The process for extracting an image is covered in this book so that you can apply the same effects to your own stock of images.

TUTORIAL 11.5   **ADDING BACKGROUND POP DOTS**

Open ch_11_motocross.jpg from the CD-ROM (see Figure 11.35). On opening the image, you will notice that there is a hidden layer called Cutout. You will be using that layer soon.

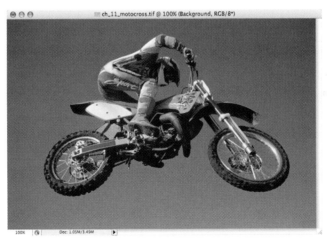

FIGURE 11.35   The original image. (Royalty Free Image from Hemera™)

1. Duplicate the background layer by choosing Layer > Duplicate Layer, or just drag the thumbnail into the New Layer icon in the Layers Palette.
2. Fill the background with white or whatever the preferred color is that will show through on the final image. Adding this extra layer gives you the flexibility to change the background color at any time. The Layers Palette should look like Figure 11.36.
3. Choose the middle layer as in Figure 11.36.

4. Click on the Quick Mask button to activate Quick Mask, as shown in Figure 11.37. When you paint in Quick Mask mode, you are creating a mask that will be converted to a selection when Normal mode is resumed. Pressing the Q key will also invoke Quick Mask.

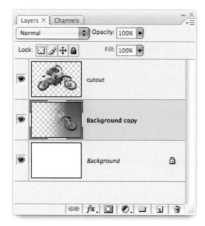

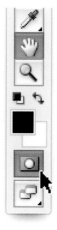

FIGURE 11.36   The background is a solid color.

FIGURE 11.37   Quick Mask.

5. Choose the Linear Gradient tool. Press D to reset the Color Palettes to black and white. Select the Foreground to Background option from the Options bar.
6. Drag the gradient from right to left so that the image resembles Figure 11.38.
7. The advantage of using Quick Mask is that filters can be applied to the gradient before it is toggled back to a selection.
8. Select Filter > Sketch > Halftone Pattern.
9. Choose Dot as the pattern type, and select settings similar to those in Figure 11.39.

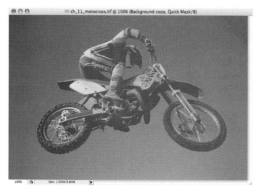

FIGURE 11.38   Adding a gradient.

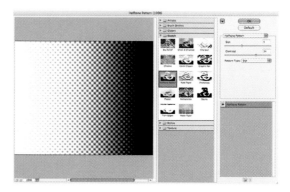

FIGURE 11.39   Adding the Halftone Pattern filter.

10. Click OK to apply the filter. Your image should now resemble Figure 11.40. See how the pattern has affected the gradient? This is exactly the result we are looking for.
11. Press the Q key to toggle back to Normal mode. The mask will be turned into a selection as in Figure 11.41.

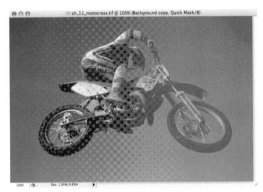

FIGURE 11.40   The filtered gradient in Quick Mask mode.

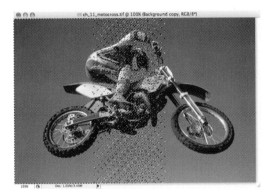

FIGURE 11.41   Selection active.

Be very careful that the Background Copy, and not the Background, is active or this won't work.

12. Press the Delete key to remove all the selected pixels.
13. Press the D key to turn off the selection. You should now see something like Figure 11.42. This is the basis of the effect. To wrap things up, you will dress things up a little.
14. Turn on the visibility for the Cutout layer.

This completes the effect. Figure 11.43 shows the result.

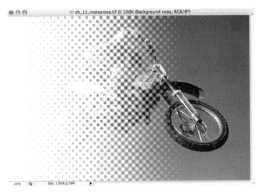

FIGURE 11.42   Pop dots.

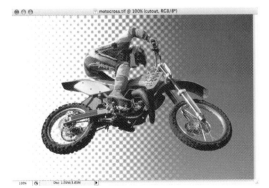

FIGURE 11.43   The final image.

An optional step that adds some visual interest is to add a drop shadow to the Cutout layer. Notice in Figure 11.44 how this makes the image appear to float above the background. The drop shadow is easily added with the layer effects.

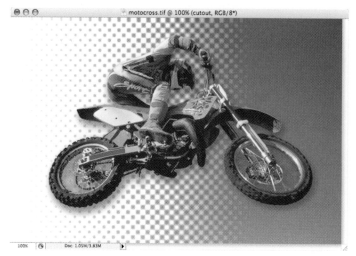

FIGURE 11.44   Pop dots with a drop shadow.

Scan Lines

The scan-line effect reproduces the interlacing effect that is seen on a TV screen. To accomplish this, a custom pattern will be created. This effect is included in the book because it is extremely useful to know how to create and use patterns.

TUTORIAL 11.6   CREATING SCAN LINES

Begin with any image open in Photoshop, such as Figure 11.45, titled `ch_11_ScanLines.jpg` on the CD-ROM.

ON THE CD

1. We will now create the pattern that will be used for the effect.
2. Create a new document (File > New), and make it 4 pixels × 4 pixels in RGB mode with a white background and 72 ppi. At the end of this tutorial, you will see why we chose a white background rather than a black one (it has to do with flexibility).
3. Zoom in to 1600% so that you can see what you are doing.
4. Use the Pencil tool, which is nested with the Paintbrush tool. Make the settings a single pixel and black in color. Fill in half the image with black as shown in Figure 11.46.

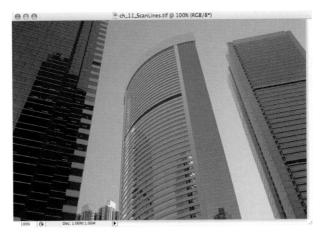

FIGURE 11.45   The original image. (Royalty Free Image from Hemera™)

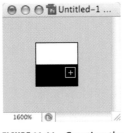

FIGURE 11.46   Creating the pattern.

5. We will now turn this image into a reusable, repeating pattern.
6. Press Ctrl+A (Cmd+A for Mac) to select the entire document.
7. Choose Edit > Define Pattern to add the selection to the Pattern Library.
8. A dialog box (see Figure 11.47) will open with a preview, offering the opportunity to assign a name to the pattern. Enter scanline, and click OK. The pattern is now added to the Pattern Library. The document that the pattern was created on is no longer needed and can be discarded.

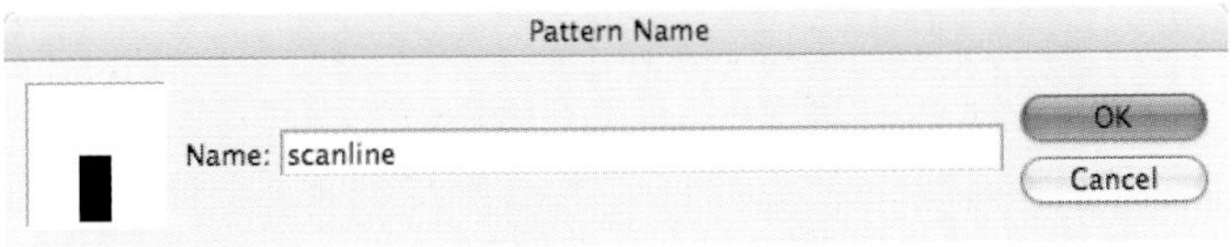

FIGURE 11.47   Defining a pattern to the library.

9. Choose the image that will have the scan-line effect applied to it.
10. Create a new blank layer.

11. Choose Edit > Fill from the menu. A dialog box like that shown in Figure 11.48 will open.
12. Select Use > Pattern. Click on the thumbnail, and select the scanline pattern from the library.
13. Click OK to apply the pattern to the top layer. The pattern will now fill the entire screen, hiding the image underneath as in Figure 11.49.

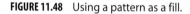
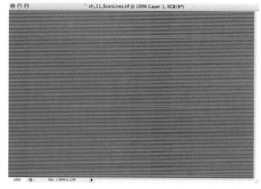

FIGURE 11.48   Using a pattern as a fill.   **FIGURE 11.49**   The scanline pattern.

14. Change the Layer Blending mode to Screen, and lower the Opacity to about 30% to blend the scanline into the image. Figure 11.50 shows the result of the scanline. Tweak the Opacity to produce the desired result.

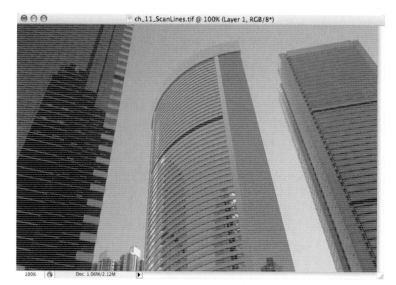

FIGURE 11.50   The final image with scan lines.

Another alternative is to use Multiply mode to produce darker scan lines. This is the reason we created a black-and-white pattern and not a transparent pattern for the scanline. We can make the pattern darker or lighter than the base image.

Adding Color

Another trendy effect is to add color to images to make them more dramatic. This simple technique offers lots of room for experimentation.

1. Begin with any image open in Photoshop, such as Figure 11.51.
2. Create a new layer.
3. Choose Edit > Fill from the menu. From the Use box, choose Color.
4. The Color Box opens to allow you to choose a color. This example uses a deep blue, as shown in Figure 11.52. At this point, your image will be the solid color you have chosen.

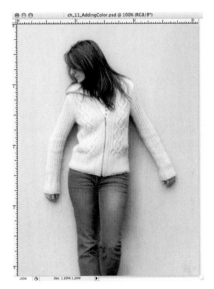

FIGURE 11.51   The original image.

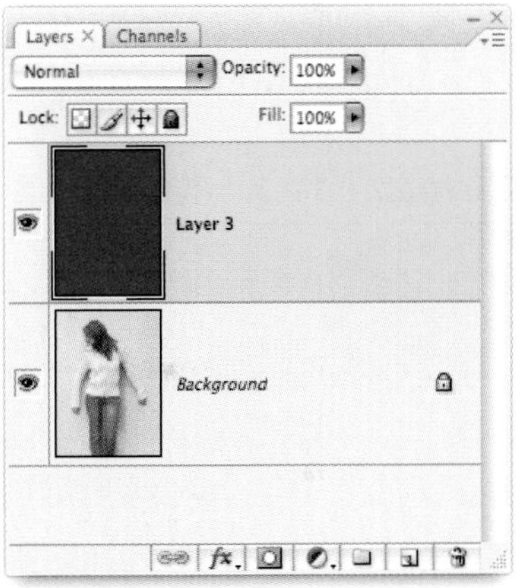

FIGURE 11.52   A new layer added and filled with blue.

5. Now for the fun. Experiment with changing the blending mode of this layer. Each blending mode will provide a unique effect. Not all will look good, and some will only look good when you lower the opacity of the layer. Try each blending mode, and vary the opacity each time to create different effects. Experiment with changing the contrast after you have decided upon a blending mode and layer opacity (see Figures 11.53, 11.54, and 11.55).

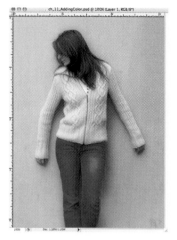

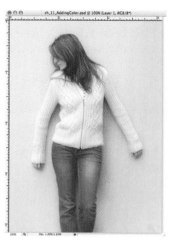

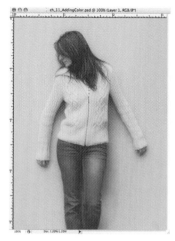

FIGURE 11.53 Blending mode of Soft Light with a Layer Opacity of 70%.

FIGURE 11.54 Blending mode of Linear Dodge with a Layer Opacity of 50%. Curves were applied to lighten up the midtones.

FIGURE 11.55 Blending mode of Exclusion with a Layer Opacity of 50%.

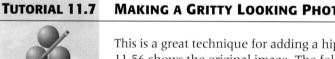

TUTORIAL 11.7   MAKING A GRITTY LOOKING PHOTO

This is a great technique for adding a hip style to your photographs. Figure 11.56 shows the original image. The following steps will show you how to create grain in any type of photograph.

1. Create a new blank layer. Choose Edit > Fill. Choose 50% Gray from Contents.
2. Change the blending mode to Overlay as shown in Figure 11.57.

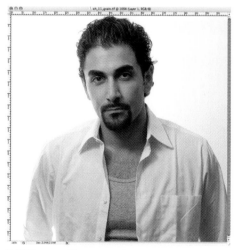

FIGURE 11.56 The original image.

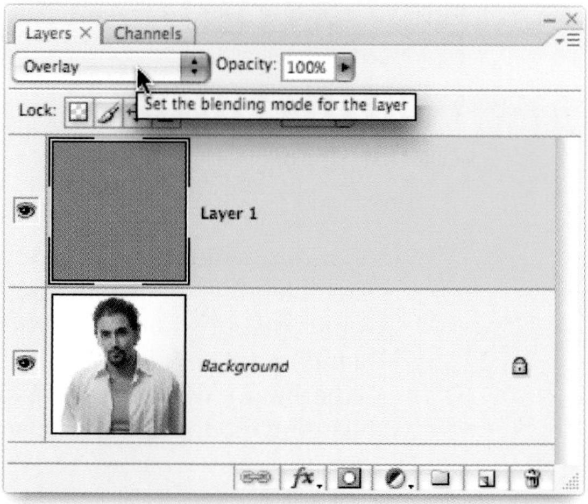

FIGURE 11.57 Changing the blending mode.

3. Add some noise to the image by choosing Filter > Noise > Add Noise. Click Gaussian and Monochromatic. As you watch your image, move the Amount slider until the desired amount of grain is introduced (see Figure 11.58).

4. Create a new Hue/Saturation adjustment layer, and then lower the saturation. For this example, the saturation is –40. The Opacity of the Grain layer is also lowered to 75%. The final effect is shown in Figure 11.59.

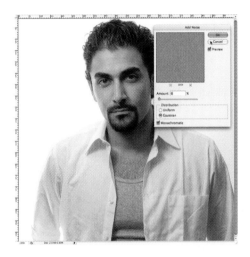

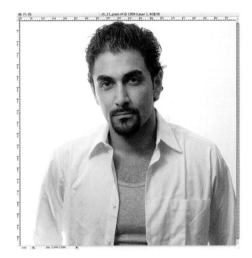

FIGURE 11.58   Adding noise.

FIGURE 11.59   The final image.

Looking for something with an edge? To expand on this technique, try the following steps:

5. Duplicate the Background layer. Desaturate this layer by pressing Ctrl+Shift+U (Cmd+Shift+U for Mac). The Layers Palette is shown in Figure 11.60.

6. Now duplicate this layer, and Invert the duplicate (Image > Adjustments > Invert). Your image and Layers Palette should now look like Figure 11.61.

7. Change the blending mode of this layer to Color Dodge. Your image will appear totally white. Choose Filter > Blur > Gaussian Blur. Increase the radius to obtain the effect shown in Figure 11.62. This is an interesting look in itself and could be the final image. To add the color back into the image, continue with the tutorial.

8. With the upper (blurred) image layer active, choose Merge Down from the Layers menu as shown in Figure 11.63. This will merge the duplicate layers together without affecting the other layers in the image.

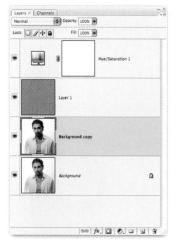

FIGURE 11.60 Duplicate the layer and desaturate.

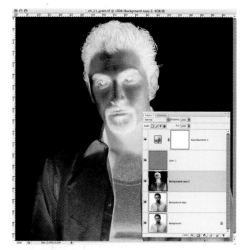

FIGURE 11.61 Inverting the duplicate layer.

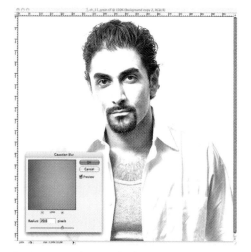

FIGURE 11.62 Blurring the layer.

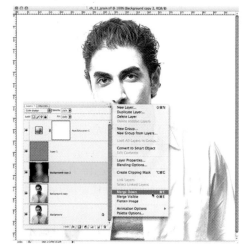

FIGURE 11.63 Merging the duplicate layers.

9. Change the blending mode to Overlay. Figure 11.64 shows the final image. This technique offers a lot of room for experimentation and can be applied to many types of images.

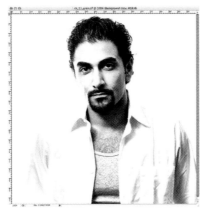

FIGURE 11.64   The final image.

TUTORIAL 11.8	**CREATING AN IMAGE WITH HIGH COLOR AND TONAL CONTRAST**

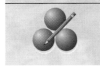

This technique can be applied to all types of images but seems to work well with portraits that are somewhat flat in color and contrast. It is a trendy effect, but the principles behind it will be useful in many situations.

ON THE CD

1. Open ch_11_ColorContrast.jpg from the CD-ROM, or use your own image (see Figure 11.65).

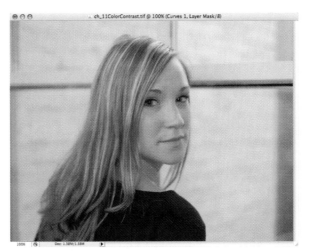

FIGURE 11.65   The original portrait.

2. Create a Levels adjustment layer, and ensure that the image is producing a deep black by moving the Shadow slider to the left edge of the histogram.
3. To brighten up the midtones and highlights, create another Curves layer (see Figure 11.66), and choose a color from the Channel drop-down menu. In

this case, I have chosen the blue channel to work with. Through the Color Channels in Curves, you can add both blue into the shadows and yellow into the highlights or vice versa. The same could be accomplished with the Green/Magenta with the Green Channel or Red/Cyan with the Red Channel.

4. Put a point in the center of the curve to lock it down. Pulling down the upper part of the curve will push the highlights toward yellow. Lifting up the lower part of the curve will add blue into the darker areas of the image as shown in Figure 11.67.

Figure 11.68 shows the final image after adding tonal contrast via Curves and Levels and color contrast via the Blue Channel in Curves.

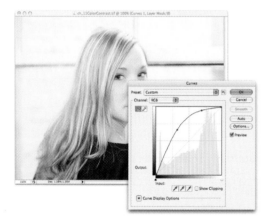

FIGURE 11.66 Curves to brighten the highlights and midtones.

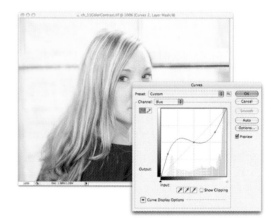

FIGURE 11.67 Adding yellow to the highlights and blues to the shadows via the Blue Channel in Curves. Your curve may not look the same as this one. Experiment to see what looks best for your photo.

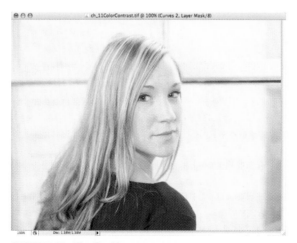

FIGURE 11.68 The final image.

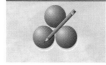

TUTORIAL 11.9   CREATING DRAMATIC SKIES WITH SPLIT NEUTRAL DENSITY EFFECT

This effect is most useful for landscape photographers. Usually the sky is brighter than the objects on the landscape. Because a camera doesn't have the dynamic range of the human eye, you cannot properly expose for both the sky and the ground. You can either expose for the sky and the ground will become very dark, as we have done in Figure 11.69, or expose for the ground and the dramatic clouds in the sky get lost. To combat this problem, photographers have for many years used a split neutral density filter. This graduated filter sits in front of the lens and darkens the sky. This allows a correct exposure for the entire scene. The effect you are about to use will simulate this effect but with more control. To use this effect, you must have an image that has a properly exposed sky and darker foreground. Once the highlights are overexposed, you cannot bring them back!

ON THE CD

1. Open ch_11_Split.jpg (see Figure 11.69) from the CD-ROM, or use your own image.

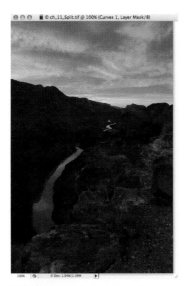

FIGURE 11.69   The original photo.

2. This next step can be done a few ways. The best way is to begin by shooting two images, the first exposed for the sky and the second for the landscape (bracketed). Alternatively, if you are using Raw, you can open two copies, each adjusted for the sky and landscape. Place each of these images on its own layer within the same document and then skip to step 5.
3. If you only have a single image (as in the images from the CD-ROM), you will be all right, just follow along.
4. Choose a Curves adjustment layer, and adjust the foreground, as shown in Figure 11.70. Don't worry about the loss in the sky yet.

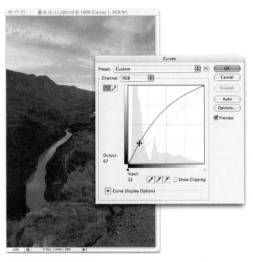

FIGURE 11.70 Making a curves adjustment.

5. Select the mask on the adjustment layer. (Create a mask on the top layer if you are using two images instead of an adjustment.)
6. Select the Gradient tool. Choose a linear black to white gradient.
7. Drag the gradient through the horizon. Try about an inch above and drag to an inch below. If the effect is too abrupt, increase the distance of the gradient. Figure 11.71 shows the Layers Palette with the gradient mask.

This final image (see Figure 11.72) shows the picture with the foreground brightened up without losing any of the drama in the sky.

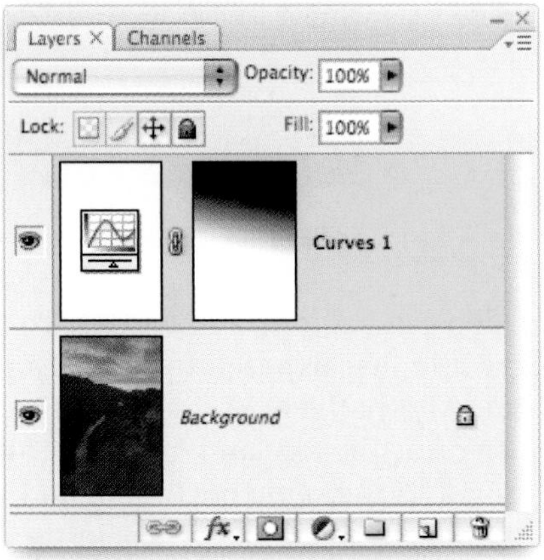

FIGURE 11.71 Creating a gradient mask.

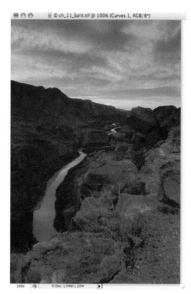

FIGURE 11.72   The final image.

TUTORIAL 11.10   **CREATING A VANISHING POINT**

Vanishing Point is an astonishing new tool that allows you to define a plane in surface. After the plane has been defined, you can then clone, paint, select, copy, and paste—all in 3D space. That's right, all the tools in Vanishing Point respect the perspective of the image. The tools even work around corners on different planes. Let's take a tour of Vanishing Point.

ON THE CD

1. Open ch_11_Vanishing.jpg from the CD-ROM.
2. Choose Filter > Vanishing Point. You will now see the interface as shown in Figure 11.73.
3. The first task is to define a plane.

Do not press the Escape key while using this tool or the Vanishing Point window will close and all your work will be lost.

4. Choose the Create Plane tool as indicated in Figure 11.74.
5. Click on the first corner, then click on the next corner, and you will notice a line. When you click on the third corner, the indicator will change to a box. Position your pointer over the fourth corner and click. You will now see a grid, and the tool will automatically revert to the Edit Plane tool as shown in Figure 11.74.

Press Z to temporarily zoom in while working in Vanishing Point.

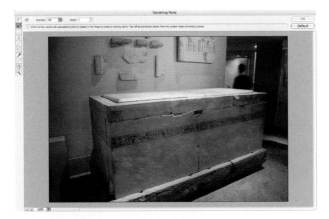

FIGURE 11.73 Vanishing Point.

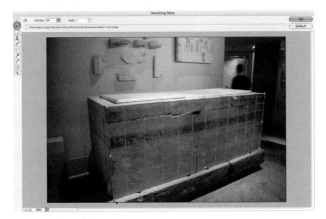

FIGURE 11.74 Defining a plane.

6. Now create another plane on the side of the box. You don't have to create an entirely new plane. Choose the Create Plane tool, and click on the middle handle of the previous plane. Click and drag. Notice that you are now creating a new plane that is perpendicular to the previous one, as shown in Figure 11.75.

7. Make sure the Edit Plane tool (the top one) is selected, and use it to drag a corner to fine-tune the plane as shown Figure 11.76. This will take a bit of practice.

8. Continue to drag perpendicular planes until you have covered four surfaces as shown in Figure 11.77.

9. After the planes have been defined, you can begin working on the image.

10. Choose the Stamp tool. Its operation is very similar to that of the Clone Stamp in Photoshop, but this one works in perspective!

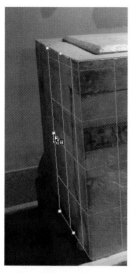

FIGURE 11.75   Creating an adjacent plane.

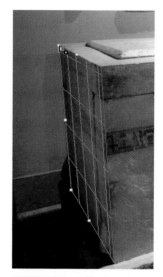

FIGURE 11.76   Adjusting the corner.

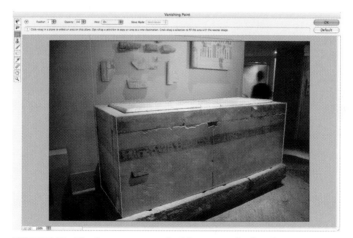

FIGURE 11.77   The image mapped with perpendicular planes.

11. Clean up the crack in the front of the box. Press the Alt/Option key and click. This will pick up a sample of that area (and keep it visible). Hover your mouse over the area that you want to cover and click. You can also drag and paint with the tool. To reposition the sample, press Alt/Option and click again. Turn on Healing from the Vanishing Point Options bar for some spectacular results. Figure 11.78 shows this tool in action. As you can see from Figure 11.79, this tool does a great job of cloning in perspective as you drag!

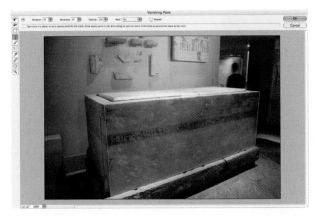

FIGURE 11.78 Using the Stamp tool.

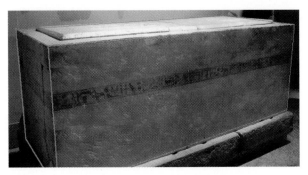

FIGURE 11.79 After a little cloning, the cracks are gone.

12. Now for the grand finale of the Stamp tool, press the Alt/Option key and click to make a sample of the front pattern. Click on the side of the box. The tool can actually work around a corner!

13. Another way to clone is to use the Rectangular Marquee tool. Choose the Marquee tool, and make a selection around an object on the wall (see Figure 11.80). You will notice that this tool also works in perspective.

14. Switch on the Heal option for this tool from the Vanishing Point Options bar.

15. Hold down the Alt key (Option key for Mac), and click inside the selection. Then drag a copy of the selection to the front of the box (sarcophagus). Release your mouse button, and the object will blend into its environment (see Figure 11.81).

16. Without deselecting, hold down the Alt/Option key, but this time add the Shift key. The Shift key will constrain your movements to the perspective of the plane. Begin to copy multiple instances of the shape, as shown in Figure 11.82.

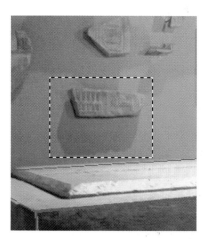

FIGURE 11.80   Selecting an object.

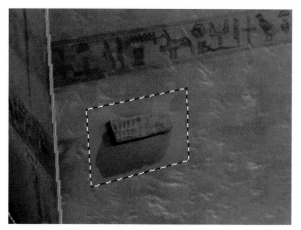

FIGURE 11.81   Copying the object to another surface.

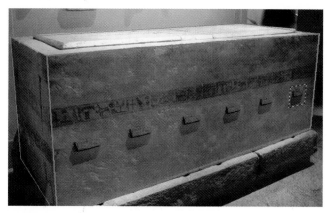

FIGURE 11.82   Making multiple copies.

17. Experiment a little to see what else Vanishing Point can do. Make a selection on the front of the box. Copy the selection to the back wall, as shown in Figure 11.83. Notice what a nice job Healing does to the color and texture.
18. When you are satisfied, click OK to apply. Figure 11.84 shows the results of your work.

Following are some useful tips when working with Vanishing Point:

- Create a new blank layer before working with Vanishing Point. This tool works very well on a layer, and this will give you more control later.
- To add your own texture or logo, copy the image to your clipboard. Once you are in Vanishing Point, you can paste your clipboard's contents.

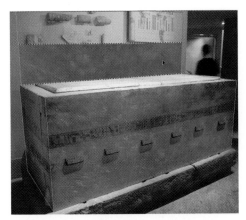

FIGURE 11.83   Moving surfaces onto the wall.

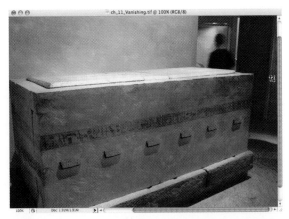

FIGURE 11.84   Compare the final image with the original in Figure 11.73.

USING THE IMAGE WARP TOOL

The Image Warp tool was introduced in Photoshop CS2. This tool allows you to mold and shape your images to fit any surface. It is different from Liquify, because it's easier to work with, is reversible, and comes with preset warps. In fact, this tool works the same as the Text Warp tool except that you are now working with images. We will use two images that I snapped to give you an idea of what this tool is capable of.

ON THE CD

1. Open `ch_11_ImageWarp.jpg` from the CD-ROM.
2. You will see the image with two layers; select the top layer. You are going to make the gauges follow the contours of the car.
3. Choose Edit > Transform > Warp as shown in Figure 11.85. A quicker way is to apply this shortcut: Press Ctrl+T (Cmd+T for Mac), right-click (Crtl+click for Mac), and choose Warp.
4. Drag each of the corners into position, so that they follow the edges of the object as shown in Figure 11.86. This is a good "anchor" start.
5. Click and drag the handles (lines with dots on the end that are sticking out from the corners). Use the handles to make the curves the same shape as the front of the car.
6. Click and drag the edges of the grid to mold the shape of the layer to fit the curves on the car. This may take a little practice, but it will come quickly. Figure 11.87 shows the layer shaped to fit the car.

Finally, to finish things off a bit, I changed the Layer mode to Screen and reduced the opacity. Then I used a layer mask to hide the edges of the layer. The final image is shown in Figure 11.88. Masks and modes are covered in Chapter 6, "Local Enhancements: Selections and Masks."

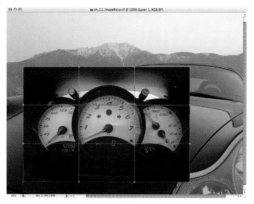

FIGURE 11.85   Choosing the Warp tool on the starting image.

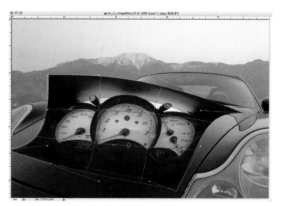

FIGURE 11.86   Positioning the corners.

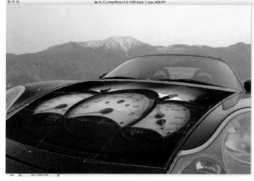

FIGURE 11.87   Warping the top layer to match the contours of the car.

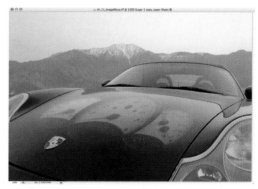

FIGURE 11.88   The final image using the Warp tool.

The great thing about these techniques is that everything is nondestructive. You can go back to the original shape any time by choosing None from the drop-down menu in the Options bar that currently says Custom.

TUTORIAL 11.11   **DOUBLE EXPOSURE BLUR**

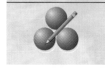

A favorite technique among photographers shooting film was the double exposure blur. Setting the camera to shoot two exposures on one frame of film, we would shoot the first exposure sharp and the second one out of focus. This would have the final effect of a sharp image with blurry romantic feel.

ON THE CD

1. Open `ch_11_DblBlur.jpg` from the CD-ROM as shown in Figure 11.89.
2. Duplicate the background layer.

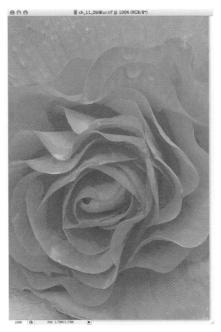

FIGURE 11.89 The original image.

3. Press Ctrl+T (Cmd+T for Mac) to transform this layer. Type 100.5% in the Height and Width boxes in the Option bar (see Figure 11.90). This will make the top layer slightly bigger than the lower layer, emulating the enlargement that occurs when you defocus a lens. Click the check mark in the Options bar to commit to the transformation.

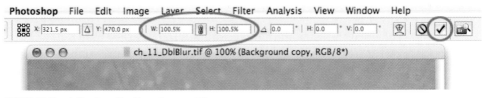

FIGURE 11.90 Adjusting the Transform settings.

4. Choose Filter > Blur > Gaussian Blur.
5. Set the Radius to an amount that you feel may be a bit too much. You can lower the Opacity layer to suit your tastes. Click OK.
6. Lower the Opacity of the top layer to achieve the desired effect. Figure 11.91 shows the final image.

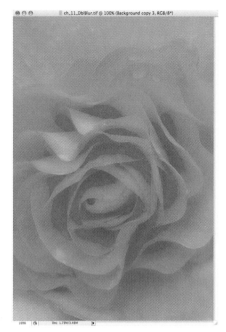

FIGURE 11.91   The final image.

SMART FILTERS

Smart Filters, a new addition in CS3, are Adobe's latest invention for nondestructive editing. A Smart Filter is any filter that is applied to a Smart Object. For a photographer's purpose, a Smart Object is an image that stands in for the actual image. Although you are seeing the image and working with it normally, no edits (adjustment layers, and so on) are applied until you flatten it. Additionally, when you open a Raw image as a Smart Object, you retain the ability to re-edit the image in the Camera Raw Converter at any time by simply double- clicking on the layer.

When you apply a filter to a Smart Object, it becomes a Smart Filter. The advantage of a Smart Filter is that you can adjust, hide, mask, or remove the Smart Filter at any time before flattening. This is a huge advantage over applying a filter in the past.

Most of the filters in the Filter menu can operate as a Smart Filter, including the Shadow/Highlight and Variations Adjustments under the Image > Adjustments menu. Filters that cannot be applied as Smart Filters are Extract, Liquify, Pattern Maker, and Vanishing Point.

Many of the techniques in this chapter can benefit from the use of Smart Objects and Smart Filters. To create a Smart Filter:

1. Right-click on your layer, and choose Convert to Smart Object. You will see a little black-and-white square in the bottom right to indicate that this is a Smart Object.
2. Select the Smart Object layer in your Layers Palette.
3. Choose the desired filter, and set the options. You will see the filter appear in the Layers Palette below the Smart Object (see Figure 11.92).

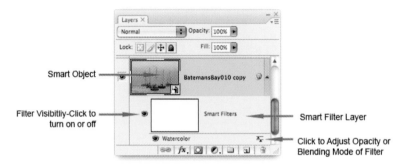

FIGURE 11.92 A Smart Filter applied to a Smart Object.

4. Toggle the effect of the filter on and off by clicking on the upper Visibility Eyeball next to the mask.
5. Double-click the name of the Smart Filter in the Layers Palette to make adjustments to the filter.
6. Right-click the name of the filter or the icon on the Smart Filter in the Layers Palette, and choose Edit Smart Filter Blending Options to change the Blending Mode or adjust the Opacity of the Filter layer as shown in Figure 11.93.

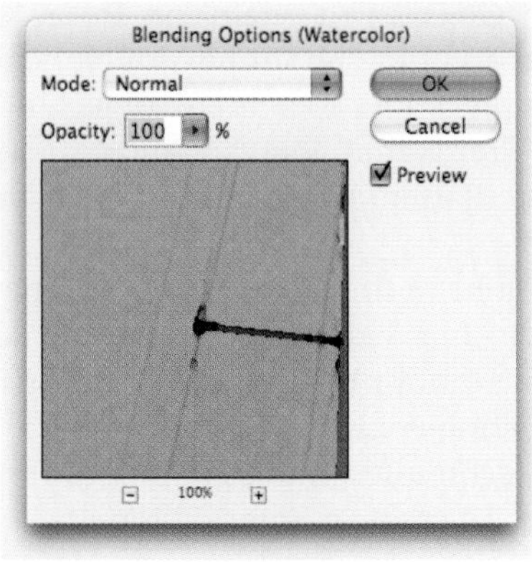

FIGURE 11.93 The filter Blending Options box.

7. Add other filter effects by clicking on the Smart Object and choosing another filter. The new filter layer will appear below the current Smart Filter as shown in Figure 11.94.

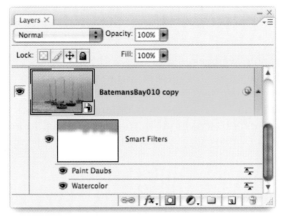

FIGURE 11.94   Multiple Smart Filters.

8. Paint on the mask if you want to remove the filter from part of the image. Figure 11.95 shows gray painted on the mask to partially block the effects of the filter. This works exactly like a regular layer mask and is covered in Chapter. Chapter 6, "Local Enhancements: Selections and Masks."

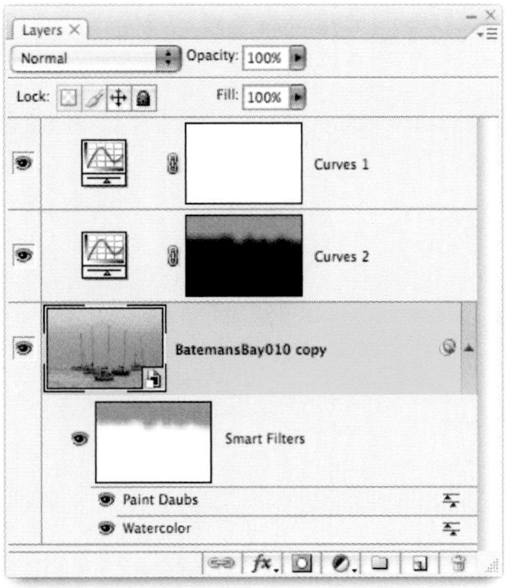

FIGURE 11.95   Multiple Smart Filters and adjustment layers.

9. Figure 11.95 shows the Layers Palette with multiple Smart Filters applied in addition to adjustment layers applied in the normal fashion. When multiple filters are applied, use the individual eyeballs to toggle on or off the effect of that filter. The upper eyeball will now turn off all the filters at once.

SUMMARY

In this chapter, we peeked into the world of special effects, but we just skimmed the surface. These effects are a lot of fun to experiment with. The only limit to the special effects that can be created is your imagination. The key to producing interesting effects is an understanding of how different filters work together. Remember the importance of experimentation! If you have special interest in these types of effects, check out the videos at *www.photoshopCD.com* by the author of this book.

COMBINING IMAGES FOR CREATIVE RESULTS

In This Chapter

In this chapter, you will work with multiple images. We will begin with extracting an image from its background and the technicalities involved in achieving a believable placement into a new environment.

The next part of this chapter will deal with some of the more creative expressions of collaging and compositing images.

REMOVING AN OBJECT FROM ITS BACKGROUND

At the very core of compositing is the challenge of removing an object from its background. The long method is to use the Pen tool or the Lasso tool. These tools are covered in some depth in the user's manual and online help. We will look at two quicker approaches in this section.

Using Color Range

The first method works best for an image that is on a somewhat uniform background color. Most people reach for the Magic Wand tool. Although this is a viable method, Color Range provides extra control over the fine-tuning of the selection. A fine-tuned selection will have cleaner edges.

TUTORIAL 12.1	**USING COLOR RANGE TO REMOVE AN OBJECT FROM ITS BACKGROUND**

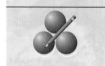

ON THE CD

1. Open ch_12_Motocross.jpg from the CD-ROM. You can see the image in Figure 12.1.

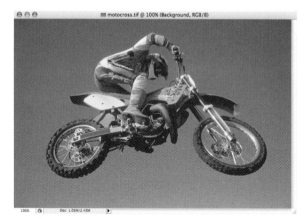

FIGURE 12.1 The original image. (Royalty Free Image from Hemera™)

2. Choose Select > Color Range. You will see the Color Range dialog box, as shown in Figure 12.2.

3. Choose Selection from the options to see a grayscale preview of the selected area. It will be much easier to select all the blue areas instead of the intricacies of the subject itself. Move the cursor into the image area, and you will notice that the cursor turns into an eyedropper.

4. Click the blue area, as shown in Figure 12.3. Notice that the selected color turns white in the preview.

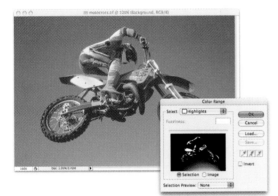

FIGURE 12.2   Color Range dialog box.

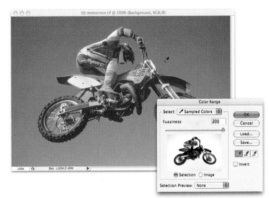

FIGURE 12.3   Clicking a color to sample.

5. Choose the Eyedropper tool with the plus sign (+) next to it in the Color Range dialog box. The tool will now add any selected colors to the existing selection.

6. Click on the darker blue to add it to the selection. Keep clicking on the different blues until the background shows as a solid white, as shown in Figure 12.4.

7. Move the Fuzziness slider to fine-tune the selection. We are looking for the background to remain white while the object turns black as shown in Figure 12.5. This is defining the selection area. You cannot perform this fine-tuning step with the Magic Wand, which is why we used this method.

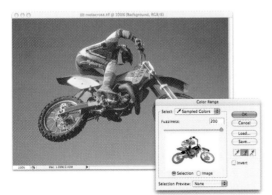

FIGURE 12.4   Adding colors to the sample.

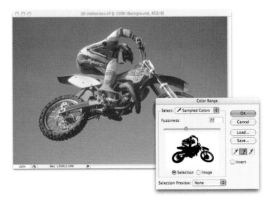

FIGURE 12.5   Adjust Fuzziness.

8. To temporarily toggle between the Selection view and the image, press and hold the Ctrl key (Cmd key for Mac), as shown in Figure 12.6. This can help to refine the selection.

9. Click OK to apply Color Range. A selection will now appear around the areas that were white in the Preview window, as shown in Figure 12.7. The blue areas are all selected now.

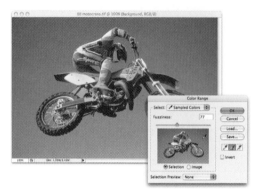

FIGURE 12.6 Pressing Ctrl/Cmd for a temporary preview of the image.

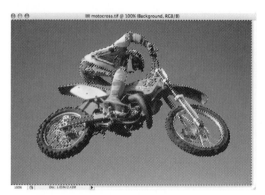

FIGURE 12.7 The blue is selected.

10. Because some of the object is blue, the selection has also selected unwanted portions of the image. Let's clean these up the easiest way possible. Press the Q key on the keyboard, or click the Quick Mask button at the bottom of the Layers Palette to enter Quick Mask mode as shown in Figure 12.8. The selection will now be painted in a mask. Another method is to extract the image and use the History brush to paint back the missing areas. The Quick Mask method enables you to get a clean selection right away. This is useful if you want to save the selection as an alpha channel.

11. Choose a hard-edged brush and black for the foreground.

12. Paint over the unmasked areas of the image until the entire object is painted a Rubylith color, as shown in Figure 12.9.

13. Press the Q key again, or select Standard Mode from the bottom of the Layers Palette to turn the mask into a selection again. The selection will now be visible, as shown in Figure 12.10. Now to fine-tune the edge. Whenever a selection tool is active, you'll see a button on the Options bar called Refine Edge. This tool will allow you to make the edges nice and crisp. We have covered this feature in depth in Chapter 6, "Local Enhancements: Selections and Masks." The Refine Edge tool will get a nice crisp edge before cutting out the object from its background.

14. Choose Select > Inverse to change the selection from the background to the object.

15. Press Ctrl+J (Cmd+J for Mac) to copy the selected object to a new layer and hide the background to reveal the extracted image, as shown in Figure

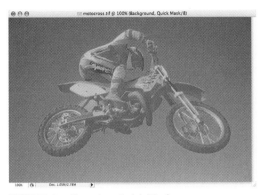

FIGURE 12.8   Choosing Quick Mask.

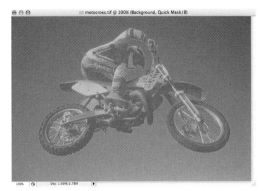

FIGURE 12.9   All the gaps are filled.

12.11. You could have just deleted the background instead for step 14, but it's a good practice to preserve the original image whenever possible.

Figure 12.12 shows the extracted object placed onto another picture. To do this, simply open another image and drag and drop the extracted layer to the new document. The object will become a new floating layer.

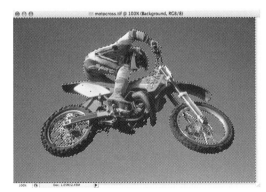

FIGURE 12.10   Fine-tuned selection.

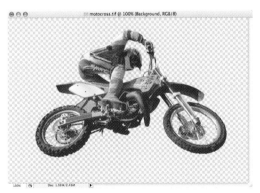

FIGURE 12.11   The image has been removed from the background.

Extracting Images Using the Extract Tool

This method is the best for objects that are on multicolored and complex backgrounds. The Extract tool also works well for complex soft edges, such as hair and fur by defining an edge. You tell Photoshop what you want to keep by filling a defined area. Everything inside the area is preserved, and everything outside the area is discarded. Where the magic happens is on the line that is drawn around the edges. The Extract tool will separate what should be kept and what should be discarded based on the color on either side of the edge. There are also a couple of touch-up tools available to further refine the edges of extracted images.

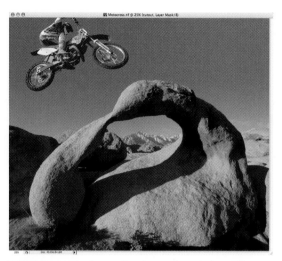

FIGURE 12.12 The image has been placed on a different background.

TUTORIAL 12.2 EXTRACTING IMAGES WITH THE EXTRACT TOOL

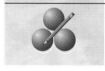

1. Open ch_12_couple-sailing.jpg from the CD-ROM. The task is to cut out the people and the wheel from the background. Figure 12.13 shows the original image.

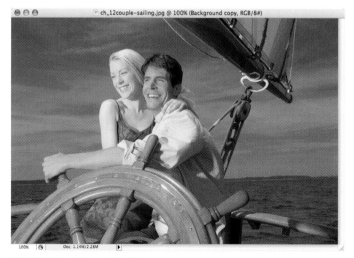

FIGURE 12.13 The original image. (Royalty Free Image from Hemera™.)

Make a duplicate layer and work from the duplicate, hiding the background. This is done purely for preserving the original image. The reason to do this rather than just save a copy is that by duplicating the layer and hiding it, it will always be there and travel with the image. For instance, if you want to work on this image in a year from now, the original will be embedded in the PSD file, and you won't have to hunt for another document. This workflow is preferred and recommended but not necessary; you should use a workflow you are comfortable with.

2. Using the Edge Highlighter tool, draw along the hard edges of the object. It is important for the pen to be in the middle of the desired edge, with half the stroke in the foreground and half covering the background. This is how the Keep and Discard colors are flagged. Choose the Smart Highlighting box for the hard edges. This will attempt to detect the edges and snap the tool to the recognized edges, thus making it easier to draw around the perimeter of the object, as shown in Figure 12.14.

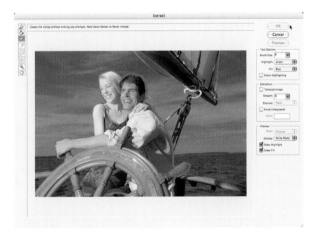

FIGURE 12.14   The Extract tool.

3. Switch off Smart Highlighting, and choose a larger brush size for soft areas such as hair. Cover all the hairs that you want to keep, as shown in Figure 12.15.
4. Be sure to define areas where holes are present, as shown in Figure 12.16.
5. Make sure that there are no gaps present in the defined edge. The edge of the screen is included in the edge, so there is no need to draw around the edges of the screen.
6. When the edges are defined, choose the Fill tool, and fill the area that you want to keep by clicking inside it, as shown in Figure 12.17. This tells Photoshop what area should be discarded.

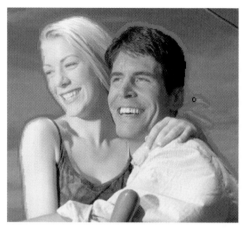

FIGURE 12.15 Defining the edges.

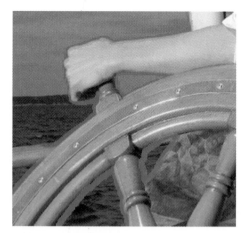

FIGURE 12.16 Filling in the gaps.

7. Choose the Preview button (see Figure 12.18). Extract will now remove all the areas outside the filled selection and calculate what should be kept and what should be discarded from the edges.

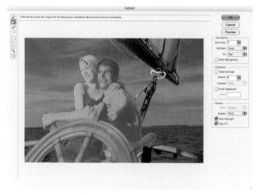

FIGURE 12.17 Filling the area to keep.

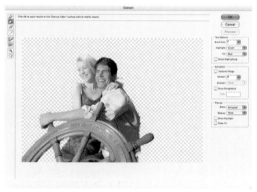

FIGURE 12.18 Preview.

8. To see what is going on better, choose a solid color from the Display window. The white matte chosen in Figure 12.19 is for display purposes only and will not affect the image. You can see there are some areas that need to be cleaned up.
9. Use the Edge Touch Up tool to clean up any stray pixels on the edges, as shown in Figure 12.20. Use the 0–9 keys to adjust the pressure.
10. Finally, use the Clean Up tool to fix areas manually. As you paint with the Clean Up tool, it will erase pixels. To paint back pixels that were erased accidentally, hold down the Alt/Option key as shown in Figure 12.21, where we

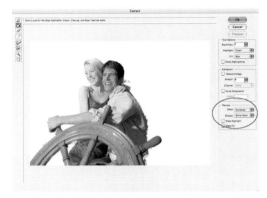

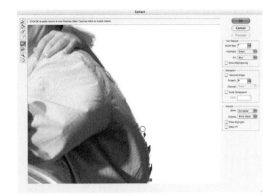

FIGURE 12.19   Choosing a white matte.

FIGURE 12.20   Cleaning up the edges.

are painting back a portion of the shoulder that was removed by an overzealous extraction.

11. When you are satisfied with the preview, click OK to apply the extraction to the image. It should now look like Figure 12.22.

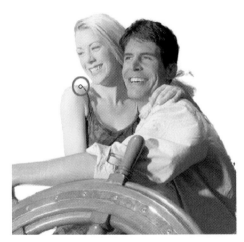

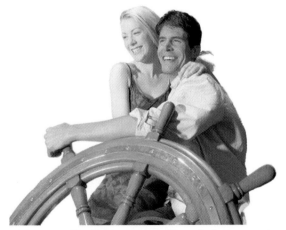

FIGURE 12.21   Fixing the selection.

FIGURE 12.22   The image separated from its background.

12. You can now drop this image onto another background for a fantasy effect as shown in Figure 12.23.

13. Open the image `ch_12_Stars.jpg` from the CD-ROM (Royalty Free Image from Hemera™). Both images should now be open.

14. Return to the *Sailing Couple* image. The bottom layer should not be visible. Click off the eyeball on this layer. You will now see your extracted image surrounded by gray and white squares. Click on the top (extracted) layer and drag it onto the other image. It is always better to drag from one image to the other.

ON THE CD

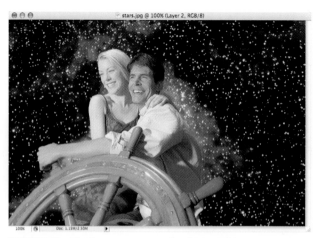

FIGURE 12.23   The image on a new background.

If you copy and paste, you use the clipboard and use up more RAM. This results in a longer copy and paste, and a greater chance of a computer crash.

15. Click on the Move tool to move them into the desired position.
16. The color scheme of the two different images may not be an exact match, so bring them a little closer together. Create a new blank layer above the Sailors.
17. Choose the Eyedropper tool, and click in the red color of the image as shown in Figure 12.23a to change your foreground color to this red. You will apply this color to the sailors. With your blank layer active, choose Edit > Fill, and use Foreground Color from the Use box. Your image will be completely filled with this color.
18. Set the Blending mode to Color Burn and Reduce the Opacity of the layer. The Opacity is 22% in this example. This blending mode will take the color of the layer and influence the brighter tones of the image. Figure 12.23b shows how the shadows in the shirt remain blue, but their faces and lighter portions of the face begin to pick up the red color. ✄

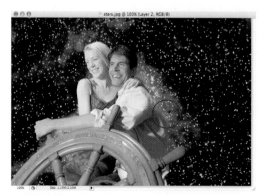

FIGURE 12.23A   Choosing a new foreground color.

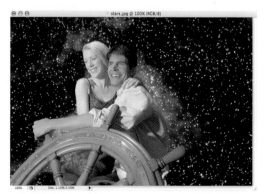

FIGURE 12.23B   The new image with a closer color match.

RULES FOR COMPOSITING TWO IMAGES

When taking a selected portion of one photo and dropping it into another photo, there are a few things to watch out for. If these rules are ignored, the image will appear fake.

Figure 12.24a shows a correct composition. We will look at some bad compositions and discuss what rules are being ignored.

Color/Hue Match: In Figure 12.24b, the girl has a redder tint than the background, making it obvious that she was added after the fact. The solution is to color correct the girl using one of the methods discussed in Chapter 5, "Color Correction and Enhancement."

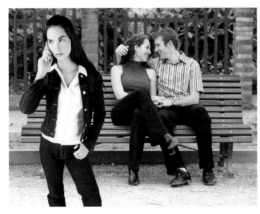

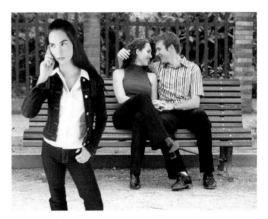

FIGURE 12.24A   A correctly composited image.
(Royalty Free Image from Hemera™.)

FIGURE 12.24B   Color mismatch.

Brightness: In Figure 12.24c, the girl is brighter than the rest of the image. This is a real giveaway and sometimes can be seen in green screen situations in movies when poor correction techniques are applied. The solution is to use the techniques in Chapter 4: "Tonal Correction and Enhancement," to either darken the girl or brighten the rest of the image so that they match.

Saturation: Saturation is the amount of color. In Figure 12.24d, the girl is more saturated than the rest of the image. In this case, it is exaggerated. Saturation is easy to miss and will cause the image to appear mismatched. The solution is to use the Hue/Saturation or Curves tools discussed in Chapter 5 to reduce the saturation of the color in the girl.

Film Grain: Different ISO settings and lighting conditions can cause inconsistent grain in the images. In Figure 12.24e, our girl is grainier than the rest of the image. The solution is to either reduce the grain in the girl using techniques discussed in Chapter 7, "Sharpening and Noise Reduction," or add grain to the rest of the image using Filter > Noise > Add Noise or Filter > Artistic > Film Grain.

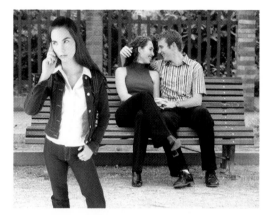

FIGURE 12.24C   Brightness mismatch.

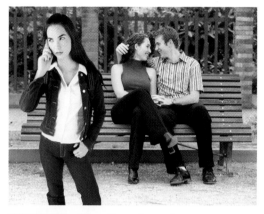

FIGURE 12.24D   Saturation mismatch.

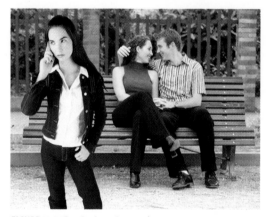

FIGURE 12.24E   Grain mismatch.

There are some other things to watch for, too:

Proportion: Make sure that objects are scaled to the correct size to fit in with the perspective of the target image.

Shadows/Light Source: Make sure that the light source matches the images. If they are lit from opposite sides, it will look very artificial. Use of the Dodge and Burn tools can help with this, but it's best to choose your images carefully before compositing.

Wind: This problem is rare, but it's good to keep an eye on. If wind is present in the image, be sure it is blowing in the same direction.

COMBINING IMAGES TO CREATE AN ADVERTISEMENT

Using what you have learned so far, you will create an advertisement for a fictitious timetable Web site of someone who has missed his train.

TUTORIAL 12.3   COMBINING IMAGES

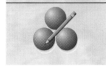

ON THE CD

1. Open `ch_12_Trainstation.jpg` and `ch_12_TeenagerPose.jpg` from the CD-ROM, or choose a couple of your own images. Figure 12.25 shows the original image.

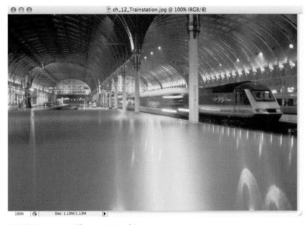

FIGURE 12.25   The original image. (Royalty Free Image from Hemera™.)

2. The image of the teenager is part of the Hemera Photo-objects series and comes with an alpha channel already included. To remove it from the background, click on the Channels Palette and then Ctrl-click (Cmd-click for Mac) on the alpha channel thumbnail (named "Cutout") to load the selection. Return to the Layers Palette, and then choose the Move tool. Drag the object into another image as shown in Figure 12.26. If you are using another image, use the techniques demonstrated at the beginning of the chapter to remove the object from its background.

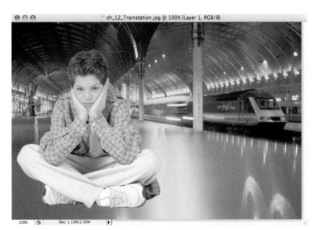

FIGURE 12.26   Drop the object onto the background.

3. Sometimes there can be a tiny fringe visible around the object. This can be removed by choosing Layer > Matting > Defringe and choosing a small setting, as shown in Figure 12.27.

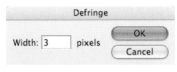

FIGURE 12.27   Defringing.

4. Notice in Figure 12.28 how the image looks much cleaner around the head now.
5. The boy looks a little large in comparison to the rest of the picture so lets downsize him a bit.
6. Choose Edit > Transform > Scale. Grab one of the corner handles of the transform box and drag it inward while pressing the Alt/Option key to keep the proportion the same, as shown in Figure 12.29. Click the check mark in the Options bar to commit to the transform.

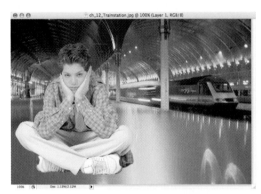

FIGURE 12.28   Cleaning up the halo on the head.

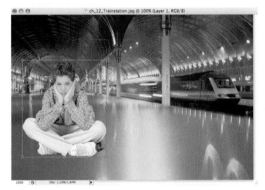

FIGURE 12.29   Scaling the boy down.

7. It also looks like the boy is floating in the air. We need to make him interact with the background. The floor is very reflective, so adding a reflection to the floor will cause the image to interact with the environment.
8. Duplicate the Teenager layer.
9. Choose Edit > Transform > Flip Vertical.
10. Move the transformed layer beneath the Teenager layer.
11. Reposition the flipped layer, as shown in Figure 12.30.
12. Notice that other reflections in the floor appear streaky. We will need to do the same with the flipped layer to make the image believable.
13. Choose Filter > Blur > Motion Blur.
14. Choose an angle of 90° and a distance of 8 pixels, as shown in Figure 12.31.

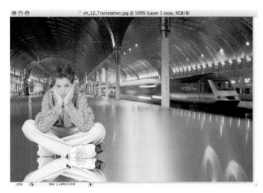

FIGURE 12.30   Dragging into position for a reflection.

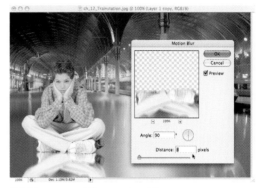

FIGURE 12.31   Adding motion blur.

15. To complete the effect, reduce the Opacity of the layer to 68%. It now appears that the teenage boy is sitting firmly on the floor while his train is speeding away. Figure 12.32 shows the finished reflection.

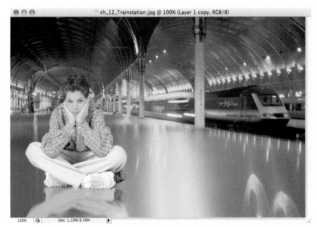

FIGURE 12.32   The finished reflection.

16. Again we may want to draw this image (and its reflection) closer in color to the background. Start by clicking on the uppermost layer and choosing Merge Down from the Layers menu. This will merge the upper layer with the lower layer.

17. Grab the Eyedropper tool, and click in a section of blue.

18. Now we will create an adjustment layer that will only apply to the layer just below it rather than the whole image. Choose Layer > New Adjustment Layer > Photo Filter. From the New Layer box, click in the Use Previous Layer to Create Clipping Mask box as shown in Figure 12.33. This will keep the adjustment from affecting the entire image.

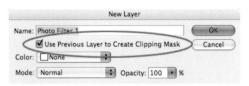

FIGURE 12.33 Creating a clipping mask.

19. Click on the color square in the Photo Filter box, and then click on the foreground color in your toolbar. This will load up the previously picked blue color into the color square. Click OK in the Select Filter Color box. Raise or Lower the Density slider to add or subtract the blue color from the boy. Figure 12.34 shows the final image. In the final image, I have also added a Curves layer to the image to darken the boy. Create the Curves layer in the same way you did the Photo Filter by using the clipping mask.

To wrap up the advertisement, add some text as shown in Figure 12.35.

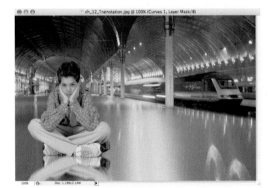

FIGURE 12.34 The final image.

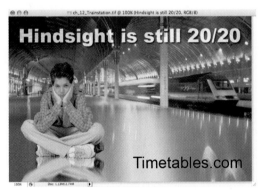

FIGURE 12.35 Adding text for an ad.

Adding a Cast Shadow

Another way to add realism is to reproduce the effects of light hitting an object at an angle and producing a cast shadow. This is a fairly easy effect to reproduce.

TUTORIAL 12.4   CREATING A CAST SHADOW

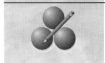

ON THE CD

1. Open ch_12_phone_man.psd from the CD-ROM. Figure 12.36 shows the image.
2. Duplicate the layer with the man on it.
3. Select the bottom man layer as shown in Figure 12.37.
4. Ctrl-click (Cmd-click for Mac) on this Layer to create a selection of the man. Fill with black.

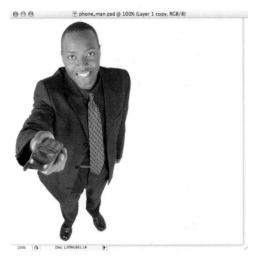

FIGURE 12.36   The original image. (Royalty free image from Hemera™.)

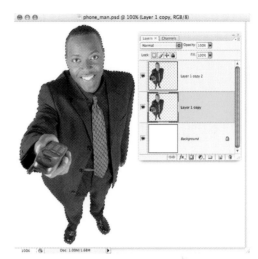

FIGURE 12.37   Duplicate the layer, and select it.

5. Choose Free Transform by pressing Ctrl+T (Cmd+T for Mac).
6. Right-click (Ctrl-click for Mac), and choose Skew.
7. Drag the top-center handle to the right, as shown in Figure 12.38. The light is hitting the man on the left of the forehead, so the shadow should fall in the opposite direction. Commit to the transformation, and deselect.
8. To soften the shadow, choose Filter > Blur > Gaussian Blur. Enter a setting of 2.5 (see Figure 12.39).

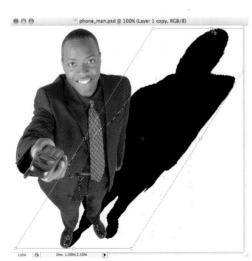

FIGURE 12.38   Creating the cast shadow.

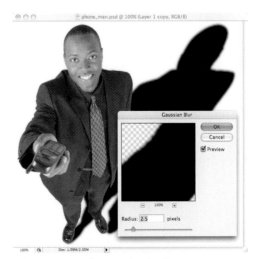

FIGURE 12.39   Softening the shadow.

9. As a shadow gets further away from the object, it tends to soften. You will create the softer shadow and then blend the two shadows together to create a gradual falling-away effect.
10. Duplicate the Shadow layer. Hide the top shadow, and select the bottom one, as shown in Figure 12.40.
11. Make this one softer with a 9.5-pixel Gaussian blur, as shown in Figure 12.41.

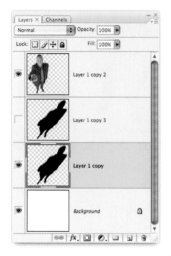

FIGURE 12.40   Duplicating the shadow.

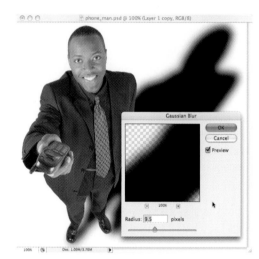

FIGURE 12.41   Softening the shadow.

12. Drop the Opacity of this layer to 36% (see Figure 12.42).
13. Show the top shadow, and make the Opacity 38%. Figure 12.43 shows both shadows.

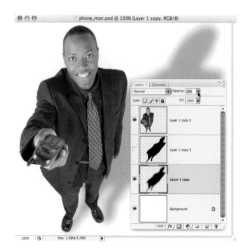

FIGURE 12.42   Lowering the Opacity.

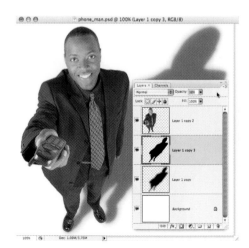

FIGURE 12.43   Showing both shadows.

14. You will now blend the shadows together.
15. Create a layer mask on the top shadow.
16. Choose the Linear Gradient tool. With white as the background, black as the foreground, and the Gradient option set to Foreground to Background, drag the gradient from top to bottom in the layer mask, as shown in Figure 12.44. The shadow should soften at the top.
17. The image can be easily added to another background for an interesting effect. Shadows are key to making an image fit within a new background and look like it was shot that way. Figure 12.45 shows the final image.

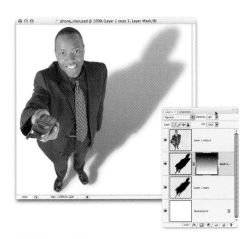

FIGURE 12.44   Blending the shadows.

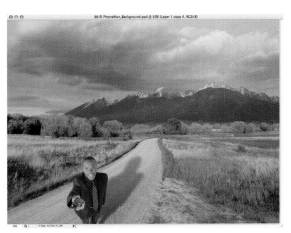

FIGURE 12.45   The final composite.

CREATING A PANORAMIC IMAGE

When it comes to landscape and scenic photos, there is seldom anything as breathtaking as a sweeping panoramic image. With Photoshop CS3, this is within the grasp of any photographer. All you need is a camera, some scenery to shoot, and Photoshop. Of course, a tripod will help a lot.

Take three (or more) images of the scenery. Take a picture to the left, one in the middle, and another to the right of the scene.

- While taking the shot, be sure that the camera is held level, and slightly overlap each image by about 30%. Try to avoid too much more overlap as well as not overlapping enough.
- Avoid shooting with auto exposure, because it's better if each image has the same exposure settings, which will maintain uniform brightness. Set your camera into Manual Exposure mode, find the medium exposure for the three images, dial that into the camera, and use it for all three shots.
- Avoid using a polarizer. This can create an uneven sky.

- It also helps to use normal lenses rather than wide-angle lenses. Wide-angle lens tend to distort the images at the edges, making it harder for Photoshop to do its job.

After you have taken your pictures, it's time to work on this tutorial, which "will show you how to splice them together using one of the features in Photoshop: Photomerge™.

 If you don't have your own images ready, use the three images provided on the CD-ROM called ch_12_Pano_1.jpg, ch_12_Pano_2.jpg, and ch_12_Pano_3.jpg (see Figure 12.46).

ON THE CD

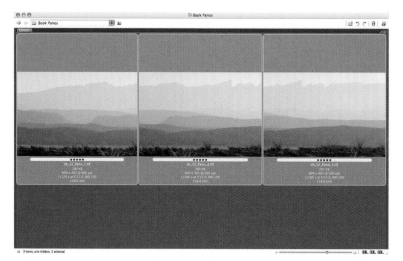

FIGURE 12.46   The three images selected in the Bridge.

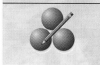

TUTORIAL 12.5   CREATING A SEAMLESS PANORAMA

1. Open the Bridge and navigate to the folder that contains your images. Select all of the images that you want to be part of the panorama. If they are Raw or JPEG images, you can open them all into Raw Converter to make any changes.
2. Once opened into the Raw Converter, be sure to click Select All. This will ensure that all the images receive the same treatment. When finished, click Done, and return to the Bridge.
3. All of your images should still be selected; if not, reselect them. Choose Tools > Photoshop > Photomerge. You will see a dialog box with the open images displayed. In this box, you have the Layout options of Auto, Perspective Cylindrical, Reposition Only, and Interactive Layout as shown in Figure 12.47. Look to the end of this tutorial for the examples of the different Layout options.

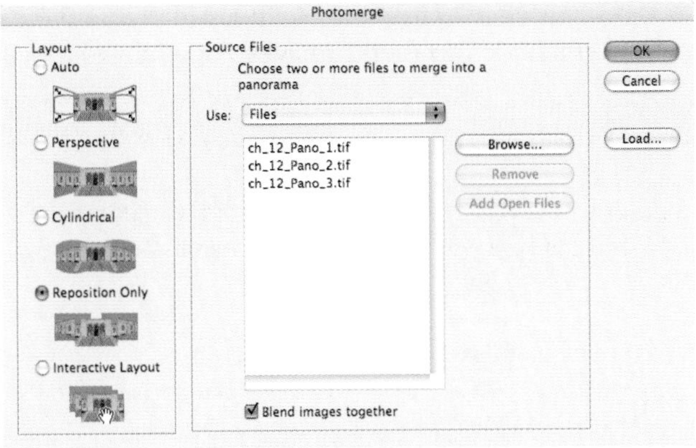

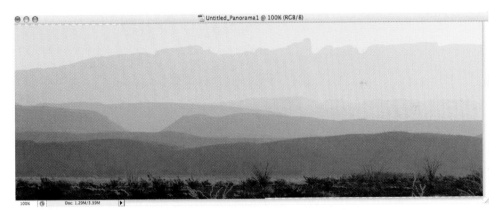

FIGURE 12.47   The Photomerge dialog box.

4. To keep the perspective looking the way you saw it, choose Reposition Only and click OK. Photoshop combines the images and blends them together for you! Figure 12.48 shows the merged images.

FIGURE 12.48   The three images blended together.

5. The Photomerge command in CS3 has been greatly improved, but even so, it is a good idea to enlarge your image to Actual Pixels and scan the entire image for areas that do not match. Photoshop does not always blend the image perfectly!

6. If your image has spots where the blend isn't quite right, it's time to switch to manual! We will have Photoshop merge the images together for us, but we will do the blending.

 Make a copy of your original images and then downsize them. Use these as your test subjects. If you like the results, repeat the process with your full-size images.

7. Close out your image and begin again. When you arrive at the Photomerge box, uncheck the Blend Images Together box (see Figure 12.49). This will leave your images as layers in the final composite as shown in Figure 12.50.

8. Click on each layer, and apply a layer mask, as shown in Figure 12.51.

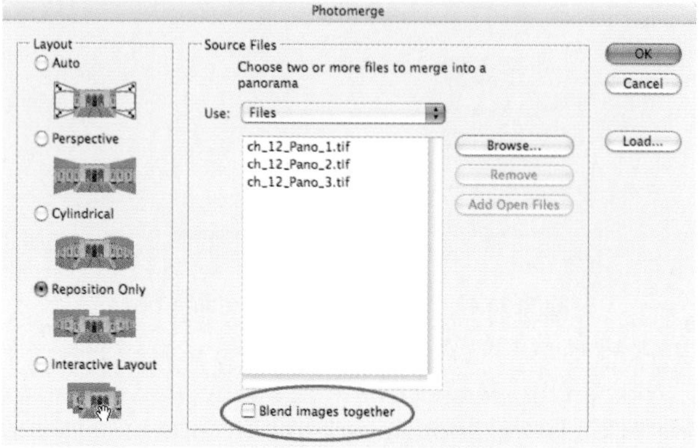

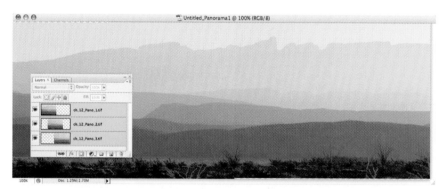

FIGURE 12.49 Uncheck the Blend Images Together box.

FIGURE 12.50 The final merge with the overlapping lines visible.

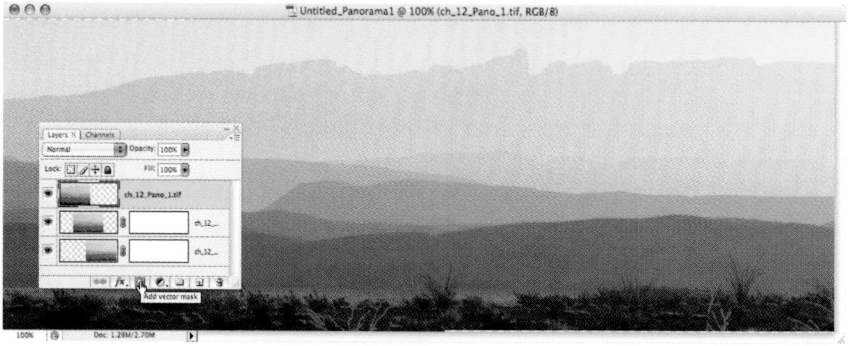

FIGURE 12.51 Adding Layer Masks to the layers.

9. The next step is to paint on the mask over the edge of the image line. Click on and off the eyeballs to target the mask you want to paint on. Use a soft brush and paint with black to manually blend the images together as shown in Figure 12.52.

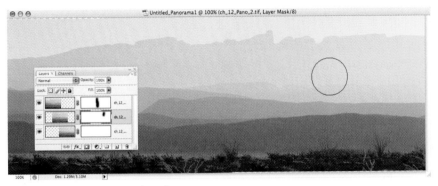

FIGURE 12.52 Painting over the edges.

10. Finally, crop the image to remove any background transparency that may be present (the gray and white squares). Figure 12.53 shows the final merged, blended, and cropped image.

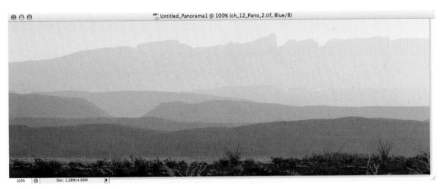

FIGURE 12.53 The final image.

In the beginning of this tutorial, you saw the several Layout options from which to choose. Figures 12.54a through 12.54e show the results of using the different Layout options to create your panoramic image. Figures 12.54d and 12.54e match most closely what I saw through my lens.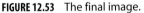

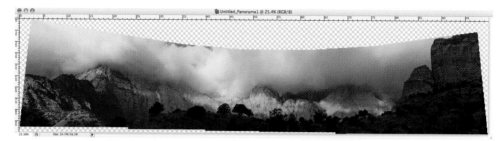

FIGURE 12.54A Auto.

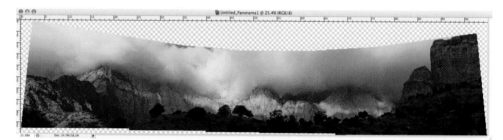

FIGURE 12.54B Perspective.

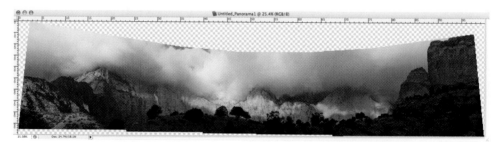

FIGURE 12.54C Cylindrical.

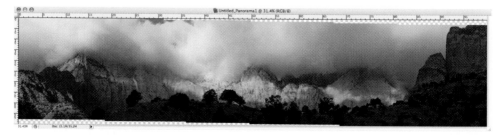

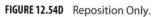

FIGURE 12.54D Reposition Only.

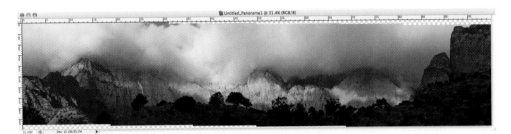

FIGURE 12.54E Interactive Layout.

MERGE TO HDR

The Merge to HDR feature was introduced to Photoshop back in CS2, but the latest version has undergone some powerful upgrades! Although the HDR command looks the same, the images it produces are much better. HDR stands for High Dynamic Range. So often in photography, we find that the overall contrast in a scene is more than our digital sensors or film can handle. By shooting multiple exposures of the same scene, we can bring them into Photoshop and let Merge to HDR blend them together for us. The key to blending images together is having the right images to begin with. You need images that contain both highlight detail and shadow detail. Most times, this can only be achieved by shooting many exposures. Any of the following methods can be successfully employed with anywhere from two to eight images. Most likely even more images can be used if you have the patience to create a series of images:

- Ensure that your range of exposures contain one image that contains enough shadow detail, one that contains enough highlight detail, and enough in between to produce a smooth blend. Figure 12.55 shows the exposures that contain both highlight and shadow detail.

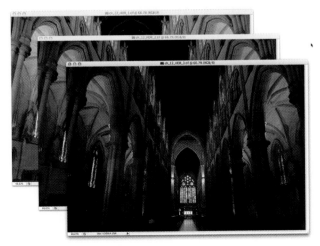

FIGURE 12.55 A range of exposures.

- Shoot the first shot so that your highlights are exposed correctly. This will undoubtedly result in pure black shadows and midtones. Keep opening up on your subsequent exposures until you get detail in your shadows.
- Bracket exposures in 1 stop increments.
- Bracket using your shutter to avoid Shape and Depth of Field change in your images that you would get by changing the aperture setting.

Using the Merge to HDR Command

1. Open the Bridge, and select all of the images that you want to merge, or open them in Photoshop.
2. Choose Tools > Photoshop > Merge to HDR, or if your images are open in Photoshop, choose Automate > Merge to HDR. The images will tile while Photoshop creates an initial view.
3. The first box that appears allows you to set the value of your brightest point. First change the Bit Depth to 16 Bit/Channel as shown in Figure 12.56. Changing the image to 16 Bit/Channel rather than leaving it in 32 Bit/Channel will give you more control in the following steps.

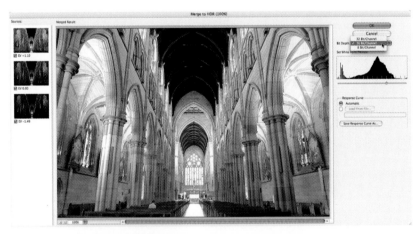

FIGURE 12.56   Changing the Bit Depth to 16.

4. While watching the Preview, move the slider to the right until all the desired highlight detail is revealed as shown in Figure 12.57. Caution should be used here not to over darken the highlights. This can result in a somewhat fake-looking image. Remember that highlights should be bright, just not completely blown out. Click OK.
5. The next box that appears allows you to use different conversion methods. Your choices, as shown in Figure 12.58, are Exposure and Gamma, Highlight Compression, Equalize Histogram, and Local Adaptation. Choose Local Adaptation (the only method that will allow you to manipulate the Curves dialog box).

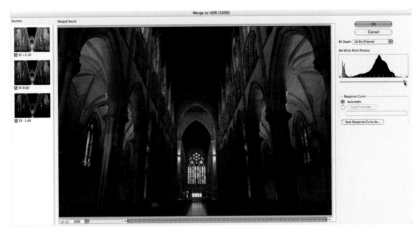

FIGURE 12.57   Setting the white point.

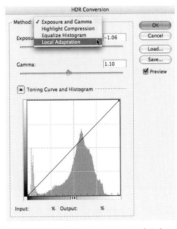

FIGURE 12.58   Choosing Local Adaptation.

6. The initial preview may be shocking as shown in Figure 12.59. Not to worry. You will fix this in the following steps. By manipulating the curve, you can achieve a high degree of both artistic expression and/or realism. Start with the shadow area.

7. Click on the arrow next to Toning Curve to reveal the Curves box. Move the shadow point on the curve to the right until your image shows a deep black. An image without a pure black may look fake. Remember to release your mouse to see the effect as you set this point. Unlike in other aspects of Photoshop, you can ignore the Histogram here. Make your decision by watching the image on the screen as you adjust the curve. Figure 12.60 shows the effect of moving the shadow point. Sometimes, this is all the image may need. Other times, you are going to have to continue to tweak the curve.

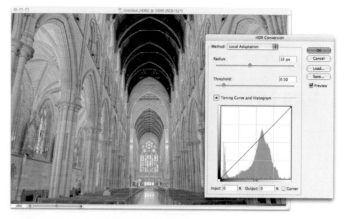

FIGURE 12.59   The initial Local Adaptation preview.

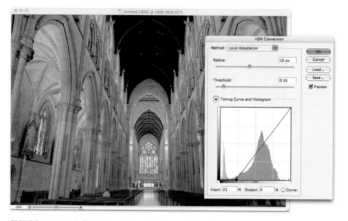

FIGURE 12.60   Adjusting the shadow point.

8. If your highlights seem too dark, grab the very top-right corner of the curve and move it to the left. This will brighten up the highlights as shown in Figure 12.61.

9. Finish up this image by adding more midtone contrast by creating an S-curve as shown in Figure 12.62.

10. Click OK to finish the procedure. Your final image will now be created. Remember that the image is still in 16-bit mode, so it can still tolerate a lot more tweaking if need be. It is not uncommon for an image to need a little more midtone contrast at this point. Create a Curves adjustment layer to fine-tune. Figure 12.63 shows the final HDR image.

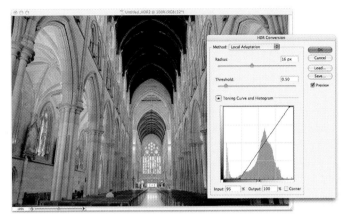

FIGURE 12.61   Adjusting the highlight point.

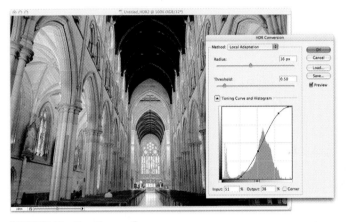

FIGURE 12.62   Creating an S-curve.

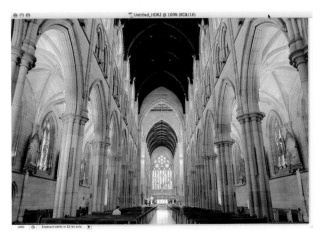

FIGURE 12.63   The final image.

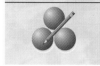

TUTORIAL 12.6   **AUTO ALIGN AND AUTO BLEND**

The Auto Blend and Auto Align commands make up a fascinating new technology that is used within the Photomerge and HDR processing functions. They can, however, be used to create much more than just panoramas or high dynamic range images. Although I recommend using a tripod to create images that will be blended together, these new commands can align images that were taken handheld. The possibilities are endless with this technology. In the following example, I have taken three photographs at different times of day of the same subject. Each image highlights a desired part of the scene. The HDR feature wouldn't allow for the full effect of each section. The Auto Blend and Auto Align features are perfect for the job. Figures 12.64 through 12.66 show the three images.

If you don't have your own images, use the three images provided on the CD-ROM called `ch_12_Pool_lights.jpg`, `ch_12_RedMtn.jpg`, and `ch_12_shadows.jpg`.

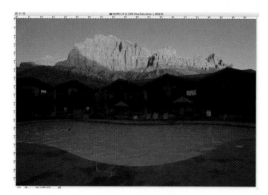

FIGURE 12.64   Warm light on the mountain.

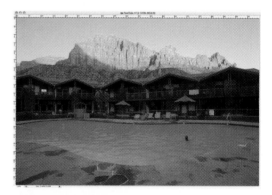

FIGURE 12.65   Detail in the shadows of the building.

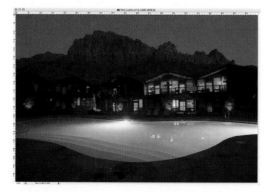

FIGURE 12.66   Lights on in the pool and building.

The goal is to have the final image show the orange glow of sunset on the mountain, the glow of the pool and indoor lights, and the detail in the shadows of the building. Begin by opening the three images into Photoshop and then follow these steps:

1. Drag two of the images into the third image. Adjust the stack of images so that the orange mountain is on the top as shown in Figure 12.67.
2. Select all of the layers at once by highlighting the bottom layer and then Shift+clicking on the top layer. Choose Edit > Auto-Align Layers. Your image will look like Figure 12.68.

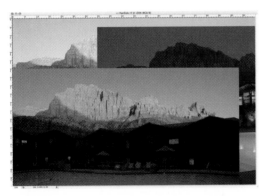

FIGURE 12.67   Three images layered into one document.

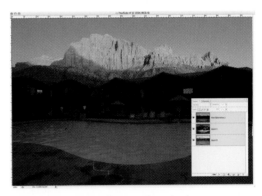

FIGURE 12.68   Auto-Align to align the layers.

3. Add a mask to the top two layers by highlighting each layer and choosing Layer > Layer Mask > Reveal All. The Layers Palette will now look like Figure 12.69.
4. Paint on the masks with a black brush to reveal the image below. You can also create selections and fill them with black. Figure 12.70 shows the bottom of the building painted out to show the lighter pool underneath.

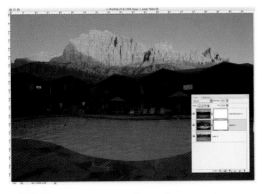

FIGURE 12.69   Creating masks on the upper layers.

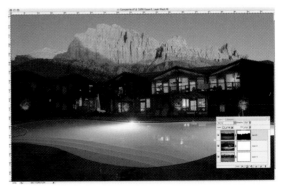

FIGURE 12.70   Painting to reveal the lower layer.

5. This looks pretty good already, but we could fix it up a bit. The shadow areas of the building are still pretty dark. Change the blending mode of the middle layer to Lighten. This blending mode will allow the lighter pixels below the current layer to show through. You can see that in Figure 12.71 the windows that are bright stay the same, but the darker areas of this layer (shadows) have been replaced with the lighter pixels from the layer below. This is a lot faster than painting in all of the shadow areas to show the layer below.

6. For the most part, the Lighten blending mode works quite well. The only problem is in the pool. Part of the pool from the bottom layer is showing through because it is brighter.

7. Click on the mask of the lowest layer, and with a black paintbrush, paint on the mask in the pool area. This will remove the pool from being visible on that layer, which will allow the entire pool from the second layer to show through as shown in Figure 12.72.

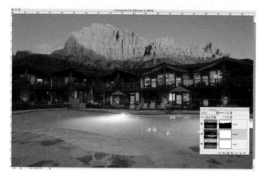

FIGURE 12.71 Changing the blending mode to Lighten.

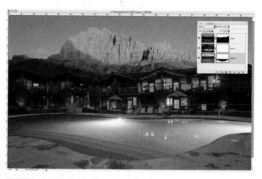

FIGURE 12.72 Painting the pool.

8. For a final realistic touch, darken down the bright foreground poolside. Make a simple selection around the poolside as shown in Figure 12.73. Create a Curves adjustment layer to darken down this section. Figure 12.74 shows the final image.

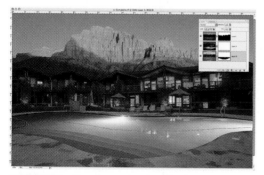

FIGURE 12.73 Creating a simple selection.

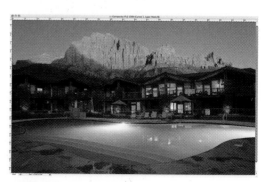

FIGURE 12.74 The final image.

TUTORIAL 12.7   **AUTO ALIGN: EXAMPLE TWO**

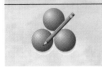

In this example, I was trying to take a picture of a local courthouse through constant traffic without a tripod. Each image is slightly crooked due to handholding my camera. Through the use of the Auto Align command and the Stacks blending modes, we can create an image free of cars! Figures 12.75, 12.76, and 12.77 show the three initial images.

ON THE CD

1. On the CD-ROM, open the image called `ch_12_Auto_Align.psd`. The image has the three layers already stacked into one document. If you are following

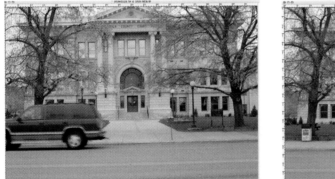
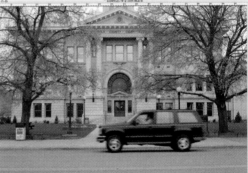

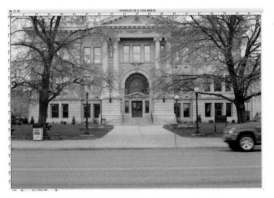

FIGURES 12.75–12.77   The three images showing different car placement within the frame.

along with your own images, drag the other open documents all into one image. Pressing the Shift key while dragging will center the new layer over the other layers. Figure 12.78 shows the image with three stacked layers.

2. Select the three layers by clicking one and then Ctrl-clicking (Cmd-clicking for Mac) on the others as shown in Figure 12.79.

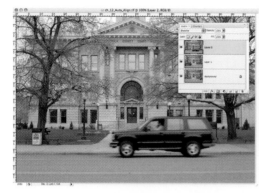

FIGURE 12.78 The starting image with three stacked layers.

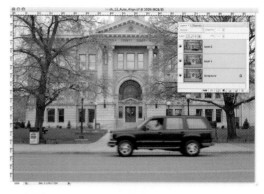

FIGURE 12.79 Selecting the three layers.

3. Choose Edit > Auto-Align Layers. The progress bar will appear indicating the layers are being aligned. The larger the images the longer this process will take.
4. When the layers are aligned, choose Convert to Smart Object from the Layers menu as shown in Figure 12.80. Your three layers will turn into one Smart Object.

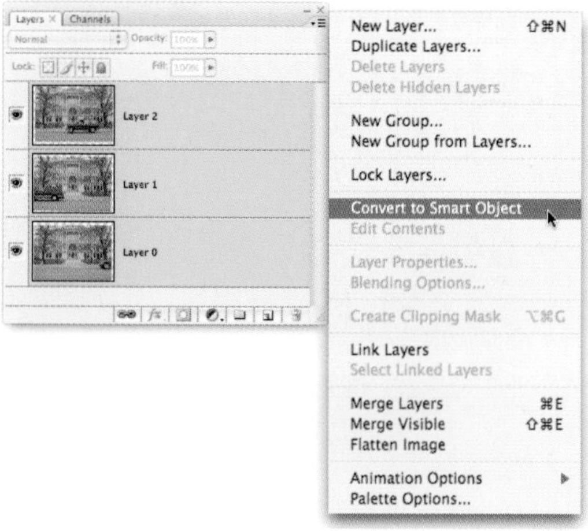

FIGURE 12.80 Converting to a Smart Object.

5. Choose Layer > Smart Objects > Stack Mode > Median as shown in Figure 12.81. This Stack Mode will replace anything that does not appear at least 50% of the time. Figure 12.82 shows the final image after cropping.
6. This technique will work wonders with CS3 Extended version (it is a great noise reduction technique!). If you have the standard version of CS3, the same results can be achieved with the manual application of masks to the

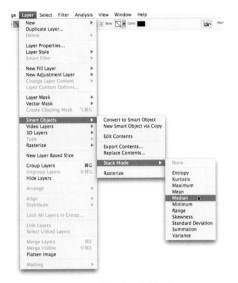

FIGURE 12.81 Apply a Stack Mode.

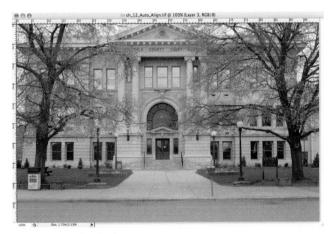

FIGURE 12.82 The final image.

individual layers and painting out the objects on the appropriate layers. Follow steps 1 to 4 in this tutorial and then create masks and paint as you did in the previous example of the pool.

TUTORIAL 12.8   ADDING A NEW SKY

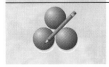

How often do you have the good composition, but the sky is either too bright or lacks any interest at all? No problem. Just use a better sky from a different image! The technique is surprisingly simple. Once again, the trick is to use the right images. If your composition was created with a wide-angle lens, then the sky that you drop in should be a wide-angle shot as well. Putting a sunset sky into an image that was shot in the middle of the day will not look very convincing. If your foreground was created on an overcast day, you will have more luck using a sky that is very light, rather than a dark blue. In this example, we will use two wide-angle photographs.

1. Open the images ch_12_whitesky.jpg and ch_12_clouds.jpg provided on the CD-ROM (see Figures 12.83 and 12.84).

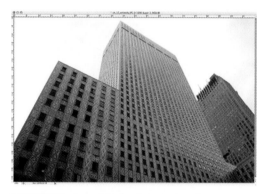

FIGURE 12.83   In need of an interesting sky.

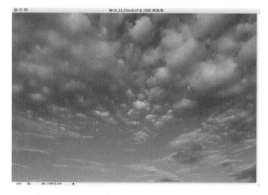

FIGURE 12.84   An interesting sky.

2. Activate the White Sky image, and using the Magic Wand, select the sky. Check the Contiguous option for the Magic Wand to keep it from wandering outside the sky and into the buildings. If the first click does not select the whole sky, add to the selection by pressing the Shift key and clicking again. Figure 12.85 shows the sky selected. When working on images of your own, you may find that the Color Range tool creates good selections of the sky.

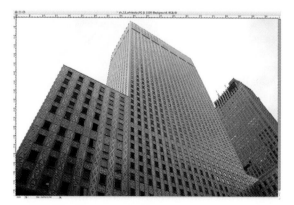

FIGURE 12.85   The sky selected.

3. Choose the Clouds image, and choose Edit > Select All. Then Choose Edit > Copy.

4. Return to the White Sky image, and choose Edit > Paste Into. Voila! You have a new and interesting sky as shown in Figure 12.86. The Paste Into command is convenient because it automatically unlinks the mask from the layer as show in Figure 12.87. This means you can use the Move tool to move the sky around in the background. Go ahead and try it.

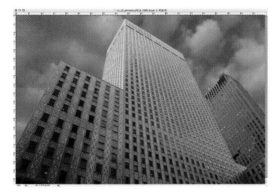

FIGURE 12.86   The final image.

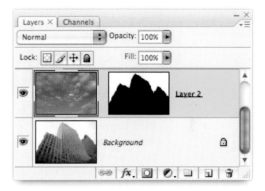

FIGURE 12.87   The unlinked mask.

5. This is a dramatic improvement, but we are not finished yet. A sky should look believable when placed into another image. This one seems dark compared to the buildings. Choose Layer > New Adjustment Layer > Curves. In the New Layer box, click the Use Previous Layer to Create Clipping Mask box. Adjust the curve to lighten the sky as shown in Figure 12.88.

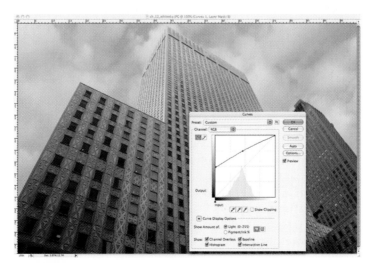

FIGURE 12.88   Lightening the sky with Curves.

6. Sometimes, the sky is too large or too small to fit properly within the scene. This can be changed with the Transform tool. First downsize the image so that you can see the Transform handles. While holding down the Alt/Option+ Spacebar keys (to turn your cursor into the minus Magnifying glass), click a couple of times within your image. This shrinks the screen view for the next step.

7. Activate the Clouds layer by clicking on it. Choose Edit > Transform > Scale. You will see a bounding box surrounding your Clouds layer as shown in Figure 12.89. Adjust the size of your image by pulling in or out on the corner handles. Pressing the Alt/Option and Shift keys simultaneously will constrain the proportions as you resize the image. Click inside the box to move the Cloud layer into position. Click the check mark in the Option bar to commit to your transformation.

8. Now to refine our mask. The building to the right suffers from a mask with an edge problem. In this case, the mask is not quite large enough. This permits some of the edge of the building and some white sky to show through. The trick is to enlarge the mask. You should only do it in this area, however, because the rest of the mask looks good. Start by selecting the area of the mask that needs enlarging. In Figure 12.90, I used the Lasso tool to create the selection.

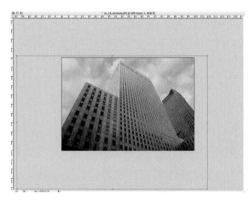

FIGURE 12.89   Transforming the sky.

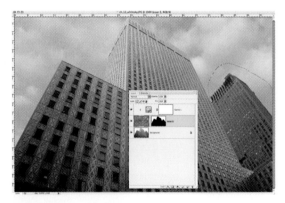

FIGURE 12.90   Selecting the problem area of the mask.

9. Click on the mask (not the cloud icon) to activate it. Choose Filter > Other > Maximum. This command enlarges the mask only within the selected area as shown in Figure 12.91. For images that need this treatment globally, skip the selection step. For images whose masks need to be shrunk, use Filter > Other > Minimum.

10. Increase the Radius slider, and watch how the mask grows. By enlarging the mask, more of the Clouds image becomes visible around the edges of the building giving a better blend!

11. In many cases, this may be enough. If the edge now seems too sharp, apply a blur to the mask. First, feather the selection using the Edge Refine button. Click any selection tool, and then click the Refine Edge button.
12. Increase the Feather Radius until the selection is blurred as in Figure 12.92. Click OK.

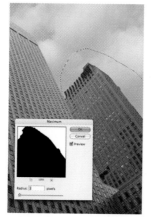

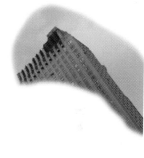

FIGURE 12.91   Enlarging the mask with the Minimum command.

FIGURE 12.92   Feathering the selection.

13. Choose Filter > Blur > Gaussian Blur to blur the mask inside the selection. Figure 12.93 shows that a small Radius of .4 was all that was needed. Figure 12.94 shows the final image.

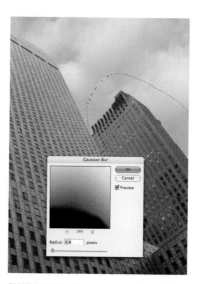

FIGURE 12.93   Blurring a section of the mask.

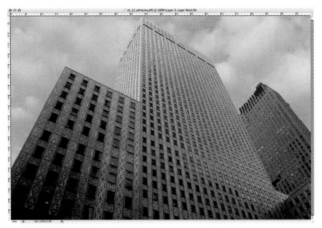

FIGURE 12.94   The final image.

COLLAGING TECHNIQUES AND BLENDING MODES

So far, we have been combining images into a single document. We are now going to take those principles a bit further and use features such as layer masks and blending modes to produce some artistic collages.

A Blended Collage Using Layer Masks

First a little review from Chapter 6. A layer mask can be applied to a layer. By default, the mask is filled with white, which has no effect on the host layer. When the mask is filled with black, it causes the host layer to be rendered invisible. Different levels of grayscale affect the host layer as levels of transparency. For example, if the mask were filled with 50% gray, the layer would render at 50% transparent. You might ask, "Why use a mask and not just adjust the opacity of the layer?" You can paint onto a mask with a paintbrush or gradient, thus changing the transparency of any part of the layer you choose. Because of this, you can have different levels of transparency on a single layer.

TUTORIAL 12.9 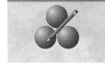 ON THE CD	**BLENDING BETWEEN IMAGES**

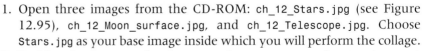

1. Open three images from the CD-ROM: ch_12_Stars.jpg (see Figure 12.95), ch_12_Moon_surface.jpg, and ch_12_Telescope.jpg. Choose Stars.jpg as your base image inside which you will perform the collage.
2. Position the moon surface image so that you can see the stars image at the same time.

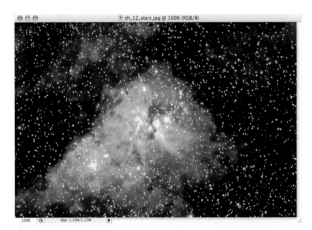

FIGURE 12.95   The star field image. (Royalty Free Image from Hemera™.)

3. Choose the Move tool, and click your mouse inside the moon image, hold down the mouse button, and drag the moon image into the stars image. The moon image will now become a new layer in the stars image as shown in Figure 12.96. (If you hold down the Shift key as you move the image, the layer will be perfectly centered in the new document.)

4. Click the New Layer Mask icon in the Layers Palette. We will now blend the two images together smoothly.

5. Choose the Gradient tool. Press the D key to reset the colors. Select the Linear option and Foreground to Background from the Options bar.

6. Click from the top of the moon image, and drag most of the way to the bottom of the page. You should now see a smooth blend as shown in Figure 12.97. If you don't, try dragging the gradient in the opposite direction.

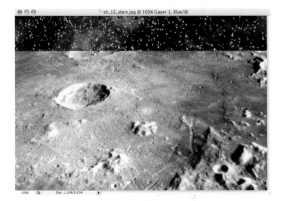

FIGURE 12.96   Adding a photograph to an existing image. (Royalty Free Image from Hemera™.)

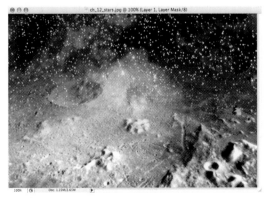

FIGURE 12.97   Blending the image.

7. Drag the telescope image into the working document and make sure it's on the top of the layer stack (see Figure 12.98). To move a layer up or down the stack, just click and drag the thumbnail in the Layers Palette. Think of the top of the Layers Palette as the front of the image stack and the bottom of the layer as the back. The higher on the Layers Palette a layer appears, the more to the front of the document the layer will appear.

8. Add a layer mask to the telescope, and create a horizontal gradient to blend it in as shown in Figure 12.99.

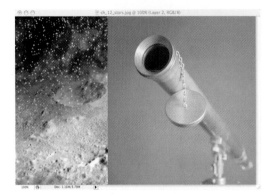

FIGURE 12.98 Inserting the telescope. (Royalty Free Image from Hemera™.)

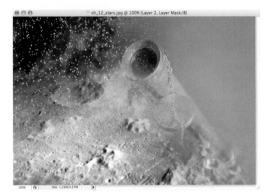

FIGURE 12.99 Blending a mask.

Figure 12.100 shows the completed collage after some slight touch up on the edges of the mask with a soft black brush. We can take it a bit further if we want.

A variation of the collage is the use of color to pull everything together. When an adjustment layer is added, it will affect everything underneath it.

9. Choose the New Adjustment Layer button in the Layers Palette. Choose the Hue/Saturation option.

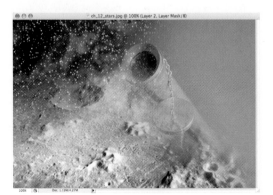

FIGURE 12.100 The finished collage.

10. Click the Colorize option, and adjust the hue as shown in Figure 12.101.

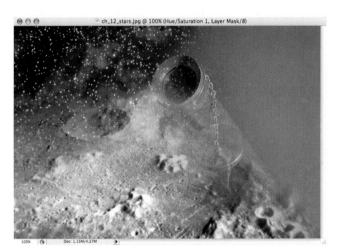

FIGURE 12.101   Hue/Saturation with Colorize checked.

Figure 12.102 shows the result of the Hue/Saturation adjustment layer.

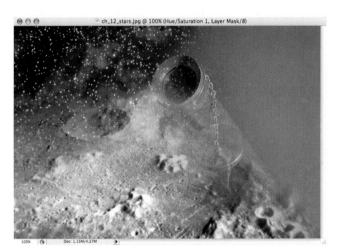

FIGURE 12.102   Colorized effect.

 Whenever an adjustment layer is created, it comes with a built-in layer mask.

11. Click on the adjustment layer's mask. Choose a black brush and paint inside the image. Notice that the black hides the effects of the adjustment layer.

In Figure 12.103, the telescope's color is painted back using the adjustment layers mask. This provides one more creative option for collaging. 🕸

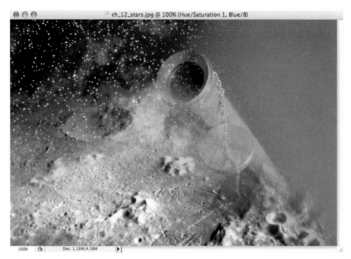

FIGURE 12.103   The hue mask painted.

USING BLENDING MODES FOR COLLAGING

More great tools for mixing images are the 25 layer blending modes. These blending modes affect the way that layers interact with one another. Some modes lighten, some darken, and some work on the grayscale portions of the image. For a full description of each, refer to the online help in Photoshop. The best advice for the modes is experimentation. Try several different blending modes to see which one produces the most desirable results. The following concept was shown to me by a former student, Alfred D'Sa. I thought the technique was so cool that I had to share it with you!

TUTORIAL 12.10   COLLAGING WITH BLENDING MODES

ON THE CD

1. Open ch_12_BlendingModes.jpg and ch_12_BlenidngModes_2.jpg from the CD-ROM (see Figures 12.104 and 12.105).
2. Drag the Fountain image into the woman image as shown in 12.106. The image doesn't look like much yet...
3. Begin to experiment with the blending modes. You can also change the opacity of the upper layer as well to vary the effect. Figure 12.107 shows the blending mode set to Pin Light at 100% Opacity.
4. The Darkening Blending modes such as Darken, Multiply, Color Burn, Linear Burn, and Darker Color will not affect the background because it is darker. To counter the darkening effect, create a Curves adjustment layer

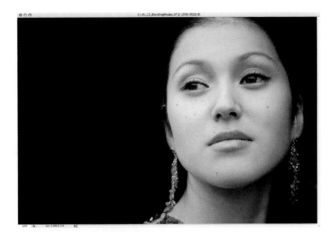

FIGURE 12.104   The base image. (iStock.com.)

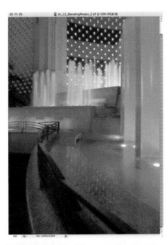

FIGURE 12.105   The overlay image.

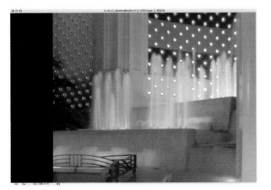

FIGURE 12.106   The overlay image over the base image.

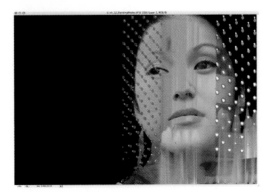

FIGURE 12.107   The upper layer set to Pin Light.

below the top layer to lighten the bottom layer. Figure 12.108 shows the image with the top layer's blending mode set to Darker Color at an opacity of 60% and a curve to lighten below.

5. Let's add more flexibility to the technique by masking out the woman's face. Turn off the top layer. Use the Magic Wand to select the black background as shown in Figure 12.109.

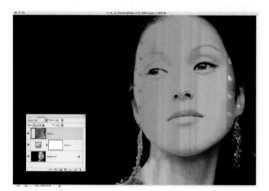

FIGURE 12.108   The upper layer set to Darker Color.

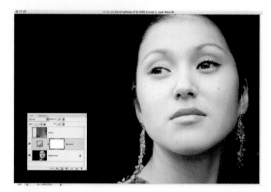

FIGURE 12.109   Selecting the background with the Magic Wand.

6. Inverse the selection by choosing Select > Inverse.
7. Turn the top layer back on, and apply a layer mask. Now the top layer will only affect the face. Unclick the chain in between the layer and the mask. This will allow you to move the upper layer around while keeping the mask in place. For added creativity, transform the upper layer to alter the look. Figure 12.110 shows the image with a blending mode of Linear Light and Curves layer below to lighten the base image. I have also painted with black brush at 50% Opacity to show some of the base layer.

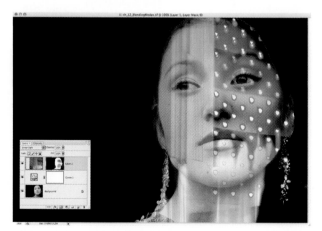

FIGURE 12.110   Linear Light blending mode and Opacity at 100%.

As you can see, blending modes offer an endless range of creative options. For further experimentation, open up a very bright image and drop a darker one on top. Toggle through the lighter blending modes to see what kind of magic you can create!

ADVANCED BLENDING

You are now ready to jump into advanced blending. This is a lot easier than it sounds. You choose a range and adjust a threshold level, and this level measures the color of the top layer versus the layer underneath and assigns transparency to the top layer.

TUTORIAL 12.11	**ADVANCED BLENDING**

1. Open `ch_12_advanced-blending.psd` from the CD-ROM. Figures 12.111 and 12.112 show the two images layered together.
2. Select the top layer, and click on the Layer Styles button in the Layers Palette.
3. Choose the blending options (see Figure 12.113).

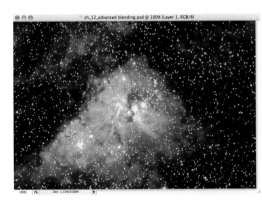

FIGURE 12.111   Background. (Royalty Free Image from Hemera™.)

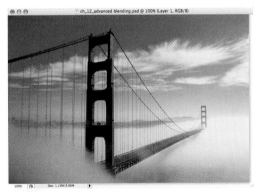

FIGURE 12.112   The top layer. (Royalty Free Image from Hemera™.)

You will now see the Advanced Blending options. The only area that concerns us is the bottom Blend If section.

4. Choose Blue as the Blend If color to replace the blue from the sky with the nebula in the top image.
5. Hold the Alt key (Option key for Mac), and drag the top right slider toward the left as shown in Figure 12.114. Pressing the Alt/Option key will cause the slider to split, providing a smoother transition.

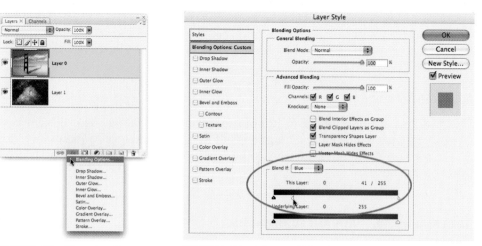

FIGURE 12.113 Choosing the blending options.

FIGURE 12.114 Advanced blending.

6. Slide the slider until the sky is replaced with the field of stars and the bridge is still visible (see Figure 12.115).
7. Choose Image > Adjustments > Levels.
8. Slide the Midtones and White Point sliders to fine-tune the blend, as shown in Figure 12.116. As you slide, you will notice that the transition between the layers changes.

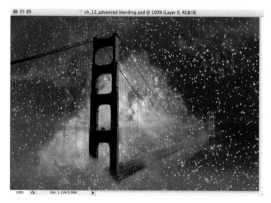

FIGURE 12.115 The image being blended.

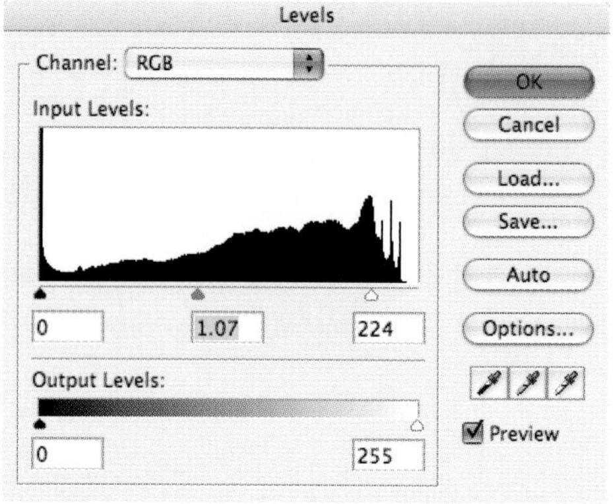

FIGURE 12.116 Fine-tuning with levels.

As shown in Figure 12.117, the blended layers provide a nice fantasy sky to the Golden Gate Bridge, making it look like it is in space, without the need for any selections or extracting.

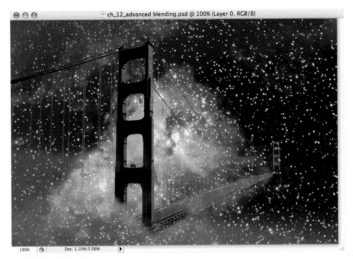

FIGURE 12.117   The finished blend.

PRODUCING ANIMATION

You may have seen this effect on a Web page. A normal image sits and gently smiles at you, much like any image on the Web page. All of a sudden, the image changes into another image. You just witnessed an animated Graphics Interchange Format (GIF). Of course, with the advent of Adobe® Flash™, and other technologies such as AJAX and DHTML, a lot is possible in the area of animation. What we are talking about, though, is an image that can be placed onto an ordinary Web page, without the need for Flash or any programming. This image will be treated like any other image and can be handled in exactly the same way. What will make it different is the fact that there are actually several images hidden inside the one image. Over time, the images will cycle, changing and adding interest to your Web page. This effect is accomplished by using ImageReady, an application that ships with Photoshop and is installed on your computer right now.

Let's walk through the process of creating an animated GIF.

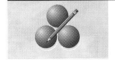

| TUTORIAL 12.12 | **MAKING AN ANIMATION** |

ON THE CD

Open the `ch_12_Advanced_Blending.psd` image that you used in the last example, as shown in Figure 12.118 from the CD-ROM, or create a new document with two images, each on its own layer.

You will need to resize the image for online viewing. The smaller the image, the faster it will load. In this case, you will size it to 450 pixels for the sake of learning. In reality, though, you wouldn't really want it much larger than 150 pixels because it would take a long time to download over the Internet. When you are shrinking an image, remember to use Bicubic Sharper at the bottom of the Image Size dialog box, as shown in Figure 12.119.

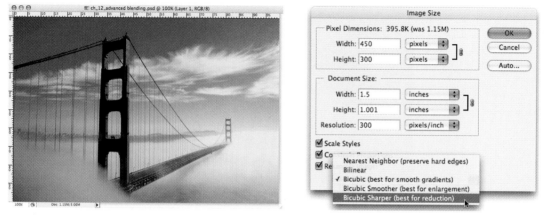

FIGURE 12.118 Opening the image.

FIGURE 12.119 Resizing.

1. Choose Window > Animation to open the Animation Palette as seen in Figure 12.120. This is where you will do most of the work for this task. If you have Photoshop CS3 Extended and the Animation Palette tab reads Animation (Timeline), click the button on the bottom right. The tab should now read Animation (Frames). If you don't have Extended, then ignore this step.

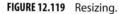

FIGURE 12.120 The Animation Palette.

2. Click the New icon in the Animation Palette. This looks just like the New Layer icon in the Layers Palette, except this creates a new frame, as shown in Figure 12.121. The animations are based on frames. Photoshop will cycle through each frame, quickly producing the effect of movement in the same way that animations are produced for movies.

3. Currently both frames are identical, so nothing will happen. We want to change from the image of the bridge to the image of the stars.

4. With frame 2 selected, hide the top layer, as shown in Figure 12.122.

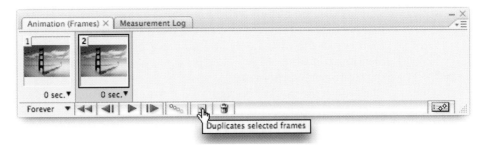

FIGURE 12.121   Adding a frame.

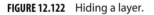

FIGURE 12.122   Hiding a layer.

5. The frame will now update to show the stars (see Figure 12.123). Notice that frame 1 is still showing the bridge.

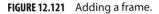

FIGURE 12.123   The changed frame.

6. You could use that as your animation if you wanted. The images would change. There are two problems, though. The animation would run so fast that the images would just flicker, and the transitions are very abrupt.

7. You will fix the abrupt transition first. You need the frames to fade slowly into each other. You could create some frames between frame 1 and 2 and then adjust the opacity of the top image on each frame to produce a slow blending transition. That's exactly what you are going to do, but you can let Photoshop do all the work!
8. Click the arrow at the top right of the Animation Palette, and you will see a drop-down menu. Choose Tween from the options. Figure 12.124 shows the Tween Palette. This tool creates the between frames. Choose 4 for the number of frames to add.

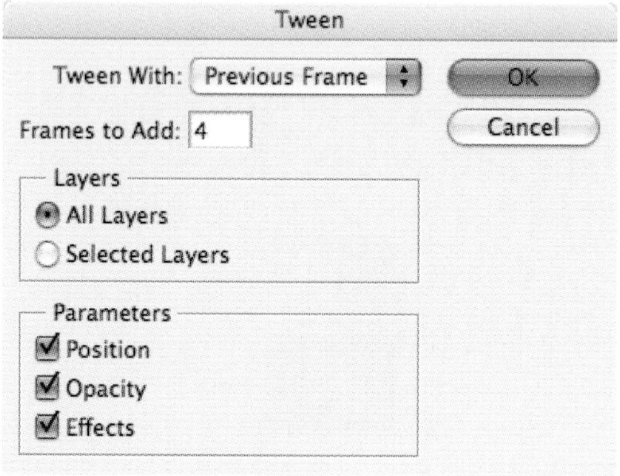

FIGURE 12.124   Tweening.

9. Click OK. All the frames will now be added to the Animation Palette.
10. To test the animation, click the Play button, as shown in Figure 12.125. To stop, click the same button again.

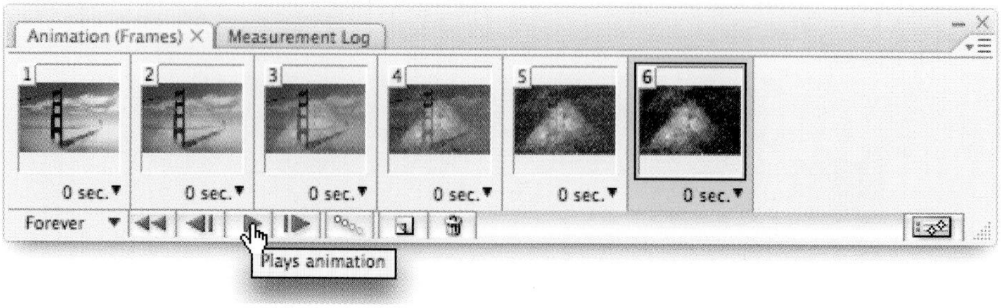

FIGURE 12.125   Previewing the animation.

11. The animation should now work, and the second problem will become evident. The animation is running much too quickly. You can fix it easily enough by assigning a delay time to the frames.

12. Choose frame 1. Hold the Shift key, and click on the last frame. All the frames should now be highlighted.
13. Click on the words "0 Sec" at the bottom of one of the thumbnails, and you will see a pop-up menu with delay times attached.
14. Choose 0.2 seconds (see Figure 12.126). Because all the frames were selected, the delay will be added to all the frames.

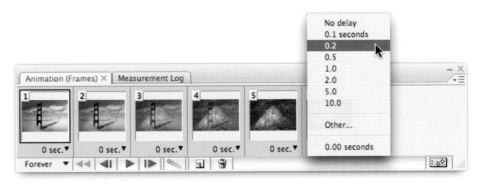

FIGURE 12.126   Setting the overall delay.

15. The transition will run a bit slower now and look smoother because we want the images to be displayed longer so they can be viewed and enjoyed. To achieve this, you need to assign a separate delay time to the first and last frames.
16. Click on the last frame's thumbnail. This will deselect all the frames, leaving only the last frame selected.
17. As shown in Figure 12.127, change the Delay time to 2 seconds in the same manner as you set the delay just a moment ago.

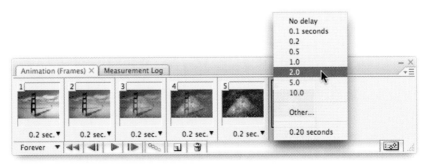

FIGURE 12.127   Setting Delay for frames.

18. Add a 2-second delay to the first frame, also.
19. Test the animation again by clicking the Play button.

It looks much better, however, the fade works only one way. When the image changes back from the stars to the bridge, it is abrupt again. You need to add another fade effect. Let's look at a quick way to create a smooth looping animation.

20. Select all the frames as shown in Figure 12.128.

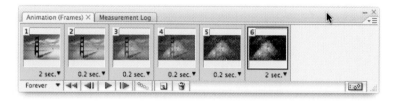

FIGURE 12.128   Selecting all the frames.

21. Click the upper-right arrow, and choose Copy Frames from the drop-down menu.
22. Click again, and choose Paste Frames.
23. You will see the dialog box in Figure 12.129. Choose Paste After Selection to paste the frames at the end of the animation.

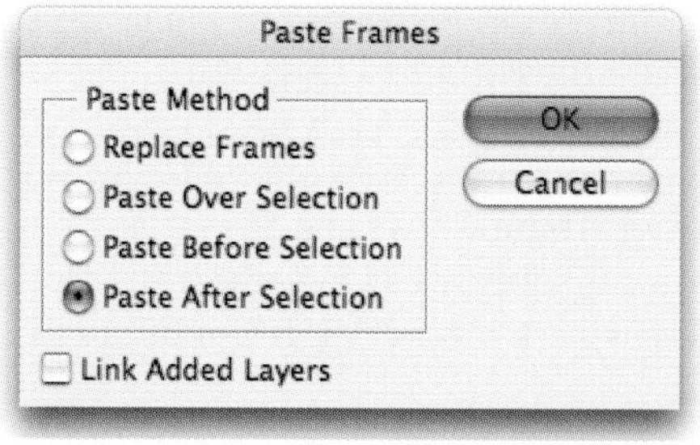

FIGURE 12.129   Copying and pasting frames.

24. You will see the frames repeated at the end of the Animation Palette as shown in Figure 12.130. Do not deselect them yet because you need to reverse their direction.

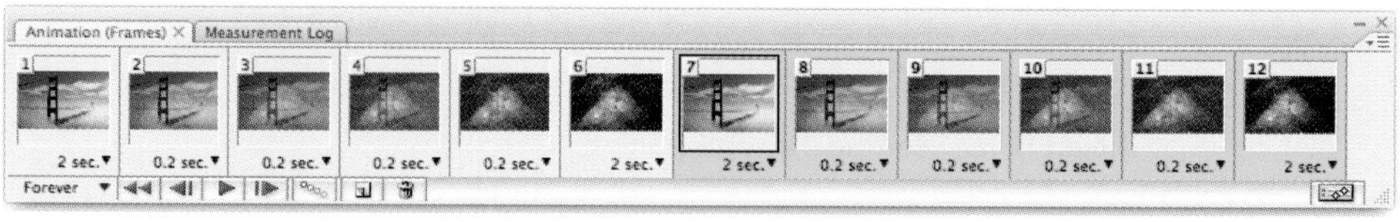

FIGURE 12.130   The pasted frames.

25. Click on the top-right arrow again, and choose Reverse Frames. They will now be rearranged in the reverse order (see Figure 12.131).

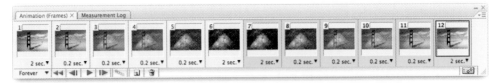

FIGURE 12.131   Reversed frames.

ON THE CD

26. Click on the Play button to test the animation again. It should now run smoothly. You can view the finished animation from the CD-ROM (see Figure 12.132). It's named `Animation-large.gif`, and it will run from any Web browser.

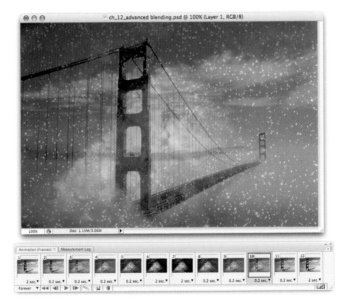

FIGURE 12.132   The finished animation.

Now it's time to get the image ready to display on the Web. Choose File > Save for Web and Devices. If you click on the Optimized tab at the top of the window, you will see a preview of how the image will look after it is exported, as shown in Figure 12.133. We will now optimize the image to make the file size smaller for uploading to the Web.

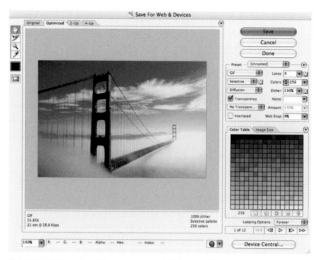

FIGURE 12.133   The File > Savefor Web and Devices box.

OPTIMIZATION

Optimization is a word used for image compression. We can force an image's file size to be reduced by lowering the quality of the image. The reason we may want to do this is to reduce the time a viewer has to wait for the image to load on the screen. With an animated GIF, you are dealing with several images at a time, so optimization has a big impact. The difficult part is balancing between acceptable image quality and acceptable file size. You cannot increase one without sacrificing the other. Go with the minimum quality image that you can possibly get by with for your needs and thus reduce the waiting time as much as possible. Generally, when you are adding animated GIFs to a Web page, you will want to keep them as small as possible in physical size. Shrinking the image will reduce the file size dramatically. After you have reduced the image's actual size, you can use the optimization features in Save For Web to further reduce the file size.

1. Look at the top right of the Save For Web Palette. GIF should be the selected option because it is the only image format that will support animation.
2. Click the tab for the Color Table option. The palette will now show all the colors in the image.
3. Click on the Colors box. This is how you optimize a GIF file. By reducing the number of colors, you will reduce the file size. The default is 256, which is the maximum number of colors supported by GIF (see Figure 12.134).
4. Choose 128, and test the animation to see how it looks. (Click the Play button under the color table.) These are the transport controls for the animation. Try 64 colors and test again. Every image is different. What you are looking for is the lowest number of colors that looks acceptable to you. Be

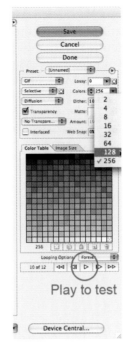

FIGURE 12.134   Optimizing the image for faster download.

sure you preview in the Optimized window because the Original window will not reflect the optimization settings.

5. When you have found a satisfactory setting, choose Save and choose a location and name. When you see the save options, choose Images Only.

You are now ready to add animations to your Web pages to attract some attention. Be warned, though, that too many animations will not impress your visitors. In fact, they can be annoying. Imagine trying to read this book with little things spinning all over the page The image can be embedded into a Web page in the same way that you would attach a normal image.

The key is moderation and good taste.

SUMMARY AND CONCLUSION

In this chapter, you learned some creative uses of multiple images and the use of animation.

We hope that you have enjoyed reading this book and learned some new techniques that will help you to create new and exciting things with your photographs or perform some old tasks more efficiently. No one expects you to remember everything you have read on these pages. That's why it's a good idea to keep this book handy for future reference. Nor do we think that this book has exhaustively covered everything there is to know about Photoshop and photography. You have a good start, though, and are pointed in the right direction. The next step is up to you. Experiment and unleash your creativity. The best way to improve is through practice, and the more you perform the tasks you have learned, the faster and better you will become at them. Visit Colin's Web site at *www.photoshopcafe.com* for many more Photoshop resources, including tutorials and forums, that will help you improve in your skills. Drop by the forums and tell us you have purchased this book.

A

ABOUT THE CD-ROM

There is some great bonus material on the CD-ROM. We have enclosed most of the images used in the book projects and some of the techniques on video.

Image Files: You will find all of the image files used for the tutorials. The names of the images are listed in the tutorials. Each image is organized under the chapter number. Look in the `SourceImages` folder

Videos: Enjoy an hour's worth of bonus video training from Colin Smith. Nine video clips are included from the collection at *www.photoshopcd.com*. Easily view the clips right off the CD-ROM using an advanced interface. Choose the `Videos` folder and then launch the videos by double-clicking the start-win.exe icon (start-mac on Mac).

Photoshop Plug-ins: Find Demos of some of the most popular plug-ins for Photoshop.

Nik Software (niksoftware.com):

- Color Efex Pro (Mac/Win)
- DFine (Mac/Win)
- Sharpener Pro (Mac/Win)

Alien Skin software (http://www.alienskin.com/)

- Blowup (Mac/Win)
- Exposure (Mac/Win)
- Snap Art (Mac/Win)
- Xenofex (Mac/Win)

AutoFX software (http://www.autofx.com/)

- DreamSuite (Mac/Win)
- Photo Graphic Edges 6 (Win)
- Mystical Lighting (Mac)

MINIMUM SYSTEM REQUIREMENTS

Windows

- Intel® Pentium® III or 4 processor
- Microsoft® Windows® 2000 with Service Pack 3 or Windows XP/Vista
- 256 MB of RAM (512 MB or higher recommended)
- 280 MB of available hard-disk space
- Color monitor with 16-bit color or greater video card
- 800 × 600 or greater monitor resolution
- CD-ROM drive
- Internet or phone connection required for product activation

Macintosh

- PowerPC® G3, G4, or G5 processor
- Mac OS X v.10.2 through v.10.3
- 256 MB of RAM (512 MB or higher recommended)
- 320 MB of available hard-disk space
- Color monitor with 16-bit color or greater video card
- 800 × 600 or greater monitor resolution
- CD-ROM drive
- Internet or phone connection required for product activation

INDEX